D1327129

# VIVES: ON EDUCATION

Juan Luis Vives

(1492–1540)

# VIVES: ON EDUCATION

A TRANSLATION OF THE

*DE TRADENDIS DISCIPLINIS*

OF JUAN LUIS VIVES

WITH AN INTRODUCTION BY

FOSTER WATSON, D.Lit.

AND A FOREWORD BY

FRANCESCO CORDASCO



ROWMAN AND LITTLEFIELD

TOTOWA, N. J.

1971

Original edition, 1913

Reprinted, 1971 by
Rowman and Littlefield

ISBN 0-87471-009-X

Printed in the United States of America

# FOREWORD

## JUAN LUIS VIVES: EL GRAN VALENCIANO INTERNATIONAL EDUCATOR AND PHILOSOPHER

by
Francesco Cordasco

### I

Juan Luis Vives was born in Valencia, on the eastern coast of Spain in 1492, the year that Erasmus became a priest.[1] Of his early teachers he most mentions Antonio de Librija, who brought Italian humanism to Spain in 1507 and whom he calls "the restorer of the Greek and Latin languages among the Spaniards." Librija was less a grammarian and stylist than a critic, philosopher, cosmographer, and historian, and he was not unacquainted with law, medicine, and theology. This broad interest and versatility he seems to have imparted to Vives, who shows a wide knowledge with the literature of many fields of learning.

In 1509 Vives went to the University of Paris, and most of the remainder of his life was spent outside Spain in the Low Countries, England, or at Paris. To some extent his life is a parallel of that of Erasmus. In 1512 he came to Bruges, and here he wrote a number of religious works which he sent to Spanish noblemen. Interestingly, one of these early works, the *Christi Triumphus,* is in the form of a Platonic dialogue. For a time he taught Aristotelianism at the University of Louvain, and wrote treatises on the philosophy of history and against the pseudo-dialecticians (e.g. *Liber in Pseudodialecticos,* 1519).[2] At the same time, he engaged in purely literary exercises, writing, for example, an introduction to the *Georgics* of Virgil and a whole series of declamations on themes in the *litterae humaniores* such as Sulla, Cicero, etc. In 1521-22 he wrote a commentary on Augustine's *Civitas Dei* which he dedicated to Henry VIII. In the preface he wrote a glowing account of his friendship for Erasmus, one of the most sincere and emphatic tributes of admiration for Erasmus's scholarship.[3] At this point, he was invited to England by Wolsey. If Wolsey induced him to come to England, it must largely have been the aim of Catharine of Aragon, of King Henry VIII himself, and Sir Thomas More.[4] Once in England he became the tutor of young Mary Tudor, for whom he wrote the *De Institutione Christianae*

*Feminae* (1523) and a textbook, the *Satellitium* (1524). He returned to Bruges in 1524 to get married. He wife was Margaret Valdaura who was related to him on his mother's side. He returned to England and taught at Corpus Christi College, Oxford, where he seems to have been appointed to a university lectureship in Rhetoric in succession to Thomas Lupset who had also been lodged in Corpus Christi College. He would be happy here entering into the spirit of Bishop Fox, the new master, for the college was to be "a bee-garden, wherein scholars like ingenious bees are by day and night to make wax to the honour of God, and honey-dropping sweetness, to the profit of themselves and all Christians."[5] At Corpus Christi Vives received the doctorate in Civil Law. When Henry VIII's divorce action arose, Vives sided with his country-woman and patroness, Catharine of Aragon. He was imprisoned for eight weeks, and released by the king only on condition that he quit England. He withdrew to Bruges, and later on, to Paris in 1536. He returned to Bruges in 1538 where he died in 1540, not yet fifty years old. The amount of reading and writing he accomplished within that short span is remarkable.

## II

An attempt has been made to show that Vives met Erasmus as early as 1514, but this is disputed.[6] It is certain, however, that the two met at Louvain to which Erasmus had gone from Basle in 1517. Here Erasmus stayed for three years in connection with the College des Trois Langues, recently established by Jerome Busleiden to further the new Renascence reading and study of the old authors, a task completely congenial to Erasmus, at any rate, in its aim. The College des Trois Langues was opened in September, 1518, and Erasmus undertook to act for the executors of Busleiden's will as the "promotor" of the college which sought affiliation with the University (founded in 1426). By 1518 Vives was a student of Erasmus at Louvain, and in 1519 was a lecturer at the University. In the mornings he expounded Pliny's *Natural History,* and in the afternoons, in his private house in the rue de Diest, he lectured on the *Georgics* of Virgil. In 1522 he set himself to deliver a third lecture each day on Pomponius Mea, the geographer. He is also said to have given public courses on Cicero's *De Legibus, De Senectute,* and on the fourth book of the *Rhetorica ad Herennium;* on the *Convivia of Philelphus,* and on his own *Christi Triumphus.* Among his students were Honorato Juan, Pedro Maluenda, Diego Gracian de Alderete, Antonio de Berges, and Jeronimo Ruffald (Jerome Ruffault). There is an extant letter of an English student, one Nicholas Daryngton, which mentions attendance at Vives' lectures on Cosmography.[7] Surprisingly, time remained to write books. At Louvain Vives wrote his *Meditationes in Septem Poenitentiae,* dedicated to the youthful Guillaume de Croy, Cardinal and Archbishop Designate of Toledo, Vives' pupil and patron; the *Liber in Pseudo-dialectos,* which made him a central figure in the conflict with the dialecticians; the *Pompeius Fugiens;* and the *De Initiis,*

*Sectis, et Laudibus Philosophiae,* perhaps the first modern history of philosophy.[8] All of these publications underscore the great fight between Medievalism and the Renascence. The question was the preeminence of either grammar and rhetoric on one side, or the dialectic and logic on the other. The terms, grammar and rhetoric, stood for the critical reading and study of authors. In the *Pseudo-dialecticos,* Vives struck a death-blow to the obscurities and barbarisms of the logicians. The new scholar is described by Vives when he speaks of Guillaume Budé, Erasmus's friend of long standing: "This man's sharpness of wit, quickness of judgment, fulness of diligence and greatness of learning, no Frenchman ever paralleled, nor in these times any Italian. There is nothing known in Greek or Latin but he hath read it over and discussed it thoroughly. In both these tongues he is alike, and excellently perfect. He speaks them both as familiarly as he doth French, his natural tongue."[9] Budé established himself as the greatest Greek scholar of his age by the publication of the *Commentarii Linguae Graecae* in 1529.

## III

In April of 1523, Vives finished the *De Institutione Feminae Christianae.* This work has been commissioned by Queen Catharine, and it was published in Antwerp. So impressed with the book was Catharine that she asked Sir Thomas More to translate it into English but More's duties as Chancellor left him little time. The work was translated into English by Richard Hyrde and appeared in 1540.[10] It became the leading theoretical manual on woman's education of the sixteenth century, and its precepts must have been those which Vives inculcated in his tutorship of young Mary Tudor. It is a rather full compendium whose significance lies in its parting from the ways of Medieval conventual precedents in woman's education to the modern humanism. The new humanism is hardly mistakable. He requires the teacher to teach the child in the vernacular instead of Latin, and enjoins young women to say their prayers in the vernacular. A novel idea, to be propounded years later in Roger Ascham's *Schoolmaster* (1570), was to induce pupils to keep paper-books which were, in substance, the student's own grammar textbook with collected, systematized examples of Classical usage. There is, too, in the work a startling stress on obedience, and utter revulsion for women's reading of romances. The *Amadis de Gaul,* as with Cervantes a century later, is particularly scorned. But much in the compendium is not philosophy. Much of it is simple, matter-of-fact instruction in the most utilitarian arts. For example, the maiden is to be thoroughly trained in needlework, embroidery, weaving, cloth-making, and in all housecraft, as well as cooking. And as a continuation of the Medieval tradition, women are to be most skilled in the medical and surgical arts: e.g., the preparation of drugs, the use of herbs, the management of dislocations, and the treatment of wounds.[11]

A great deal in the *Institutione* is mere negation. Women should not love apparel too much; they should shun personal decoration (cosmetic) ; they should not frequent public places; they should avoid dancing and dicing. But in all this Vives is merely summarizing the best social and religious outlook of his time, and that of the entire Tudor period. The cardinal principle was aptly expressed; *maxima debetur puero reverentia.* Two excerpts will illustrate the deep, almost mystical piety on one hand, and the utterly mundane practicality on the other. If there is a unifying thread, that thread is the *ardor intellectualis* of the classical literature.

> When a maid may for household business, be alone and pray, first let her give herself wholly to God, let her worship Christ, and ask pardon and peace of Him, and then consider herself to be a Christian virgin, Christ's spouse, and the follower of Mary, and that the Virginity of the body is nought worth except the mind be pure withal, and if that be, nothing to be more clean, nothing more pleasant to God, and herself to be the follower of the most holy Mother of our Lord.[12]

Contrast this mystical exhortation with the following:

> And who, I pray you, will count them to be fair, that he knoweth to be slubbered with painting, and not rather the fouler? They lose all the honour of beauty, when they be painted. For all the beauty that there is, is counted to be in the painting. And also the tender skin will ryvill the more soon, and all the favour of the face waxeth old and the breath stinketh, and the teeth rust, and an evil air all the body over, both by the reason of the ceruse and quicksilver, and specially by reason of the soaps, wherewith they prepare the body as it were a table, against the painting on the next day. Wherefore Ovid called these doings venomous ,and not without a cause. Also Juvenal asketh a question properly: She that is with so many ointments slubberd and starched, is it to be called a face or a sore?"[13]

In 1524 Vives wrote a characteristic little book for the Princess Mary called *Satellitium* or *Symbola,* a book of maxims to serve as a body guard for the child's mind. He addresses it to the Princess, saying that he has often been requested by the Queen, "an illustrious and most holy person," to place a guard about the child's soul. The book contains 239 symbola, each being a maxim or motto, and he tells the Princess Mary she will be protected by these 239 guards, if "she refuses to depart a finger's breadth from them." He concludes with the motto *Sine Querela* (i.e., without fault), and he tells the child it is his own motto.[14]

The importance of the Renascence concern with the education of women is particularly underscored in the fact that in all the Middle Ages only seven books actually appeared in England which dealt with this problem, and two of these were in Latin.[15] Both the *Institutione* and the *Satellitium* have received high praise. A French scholar calls them the "epitome of the new modernism."[16] and Foster Watson is lavish in his praise:

> Starting from his early familiar surroundings, as he admittedly does, Vives reaches forth into the universal. Not even modern writers have realized more vividly than he that the object of education is to help the formation of character, and that this aim extends over the whole range of life. He thought, like the ancient Greek philosophers, that virtue can be taught, and perhaps the reader may resent with impatience his stress on the presentation of precepts, though accompanied by fitting examples. But Vives kept clearly in mind that all life is an education, and since he lived in an age which owed its intellectual expansion chiefly to the discovery of the old literatures of Greece and Rome, it was but natural that he should believe in the vitalizing influence of the written word, even for morality.[17]

Conjointly with, and forming a kind of introduction to, the *Institutione* and the *Satellitium* is the *De Ratione Studii Puerilis* which appeared in 1523, and which was written at the behest of Queen Catharine to serve as a brief plan of study for Mary Tudor.[18] This is actually a detailed prospectus and syllabus of authors through whose recommendation Vives teaches pronunciation, parts of speech, writing, memory, vocabulary, and Latin conversation. At random a few of the names, contemporary and classical, are listed: Erasmus Linacre, Antonious Mancinellus, Melanchthon, Aulus Gellius, Cato, Livy, Seneca, Valerious Maximus, Thomas More, Plutarch. The brief advices on "Latin Conversation" are of particular interest, for, it must be kept in mind, they are intended for a little girl of seven years.[19]

> Let the princess speak with her tutor and fellow-pupils in Latin. Of fellow-pupils let her have three or four; for it is not good to be taught alone. But do not let them be many, and let the few be most carefully chosen, and most piously and liberally educated, from whom she will not hear or learn anything which would injure her morals; for conduct *(mores)* ought to be the first care. Let her be stimulated now by small rewards, now by emulation. Let her herself be praised, and let others be praised in her presence. Let her attempt to express in Latin what she has been reading in her authors, and in the same manner let her listen to others speaking of what they have been reading. To those whom she thinks to be learned, let her give most close attention, and so let her herself speak; for this is *imitation*—a method of no small usefulness, especially in a tender age which takes to nothing more willingly or to better purpose than imitation. But not only should she imitate the words, but also the pronunciation, so as not to err in correct accent.[20]

A careful reading of the *De Ratione* will make clear that Vives regards grammar as subordinate entirely to the reading of authors. The rules of grammar are established by the student's observation of authors. Grammar becomes merely an epitome of the grammatical facts and constructions which the student finds in the authors. Vives was far ahead of his time. The writing of Latin was, for him, an active, not a passive, exercise. Throughout, Vives keeps his mind intent on the pupil's point of view and the exercise of the pupil's activity. Or to use Professor Watson's felicitous phrase, "Vives was a heuristic Latinist in his pedagogy."[21]

## IV

The *De Tradendis Disciplinis* was first published in Antwerp in 1531. This was Vive's capolavoro. An American scholar[22] has ranked it with Bacon's *Novum Organon*. Certainly, it is as ambitious as the *Organon*. Vives succinctly states its purpose: "This then is the fruit of all studies; this is the goal. Having acquired our knowledge, we must turn it to usefulness, and employ it for the common good."[23] The work is divided into twenty books. Seven books are on the Corruption of the Arts (*De Corruptis Artibus*); and five are on the Transmission of the Arts (*De Tradendis Disciplinis*); the remaining eight books consist of treatises on the arts: *De Prima Philosophia; De Explanatione Cuisque Essentiae; De Censura Veri; De Instrumento Probabilitatis; De Disputatione*. The *Prima Philosophia* is divided into three books and the *De Censura Veri* into two books. Excepting the *De Tradendis Disciplinis,* which Professor Watson translated into English in 1913, the work remains in Latin.[24]

The seven books of the *De Corruptibus Artibus* deal with the negative side of the education problem. The question is posed: why has knowledge as a whole degenerated from its active, vital search for truth, especially after the times of the great thinkers of antiquity.[25] Watson calls it "the best contemporaneous account of the aims and methods of the teaching of the times, critically considered by a writer who wished above all things to free himself from illusions as to the golden age of past scholarship, or even as to any finality in the current Renascence standards."[26] It is strange that to the best of my knowledge, this has never been translated out of Latin into English.[27] It contains a scathing attack on the dialecticians whom Vives must have known at the University of Paris. Their methods are minutely described: the choosing of short passages, or short texts, from recognized scholars or theologians; the reproduction of seas of commentaries and glosses regarding the chosen texts; the involvement of teachers and students in *realitates, formalitates, entitates, de modo significandi vocum*. The dialectic had borrowed from Metaphysics and clouded the minds of all kinds of students. Professor Watson has translated a passage which is worth quoting, for it gives ample testimony of its temperament:

> When a boy has been brought to the school, at once he is required to dispute, on the very first day, immediately he is

> taught to wrangle, though as yet unable to talk. The same practice is pursued in Grammar, in the Poets, in History, as in Dialectic and Rhetoric, and in absolutely every subject. Someone may wonder how the most apparent, simple rudimentary matters can be susceptible of argument? But nothing is so clear that some little questions cannot be raised about it, and even as by a wind, stirred into action. These beginners are accustomed never to be silent, to asseverate confidently whatever is in their mouths, lest at any time they should seem to have ceased speaking. Nor does one disputation a day suffice, or two, as with eating. At breakfast they wrangle, after lunch they wrangle, after supper they wrangle. In the house they wrangle, out of doors they wrangle. At meals, at the bath, in the swating room, in the temple, in the city, in the country, in public, in private, in every place, at every time, they are wrangling.[28]

Not a pretty picture, and the five later books of the *De Tradendis Disciplinis* were intended to correct it. Their purpose was to provide "a constructive system of Christian education on a critical, reasoned basis, which should show the aims, methods, and resources of education as Vives found it, for the purpose of the development, by educational processes, of scholars thoroughly trained, physically, intellectually, morally; not only capable, but also eagerly desirous, of taking their part whole-heartedly in the affairs of life, and of devoting themselves in whatever career they chose, to making their profession an effective instrument of the public good."[29] An ambitious undertaking, but one that Vives seems to have realized. The five books, which Professor Watson has called and translated as the *Transmission of Knowledge* are entitled: (1) Educational Origins; (2) Schools; (3) Language Teaching; (4) Higher Studies; (5) Studies and Life. Each of these is a detailed presentation, and to cite but one example, in Book III, there is presented a detailed argument for a universal language.[30]

It is fitting to close this brief paper with a summary from Professor Watson, who gave so much time to the study of Vives:

> Who was Vives? . . . He was the central figure in the conflict with the dialecticians. In the extended use of the scientific method of induction, coupled with the concentrative employment of observation and experiment, he is the precursor of Bacon. He is the first writer to urge an organized system of poor-relief as a civic and national duty. He is an apostle of universal peace, a position by no means as popular in the days of 16th century Tudor absolutism and imperial ambition as it is in the present day. In this hatred of war, of course, his efforts were linked with those of Erasmus. Lastly, of all the humanists, it was Vives who gave the closest attention to the

study of education; and the after history of education, in its main principles and many of its details, is to be found foreshadowed in his *De Disciplinis*.[31]

## NOTES

1. Most of the material for the life of Vives is to be found in Bonilla y San Martin, *Vives y la fiosofia del Renacimiento* (2nd ed., 3 v., Madrid 1929) whose material is drawn from primary sources. The best account in English is Foster Watson, *Luis Vives* (Oxford, 1922), who draws most of his information from Bonilla's work. Strangely, Vives is not mentioned by Ticknor, the historian of Spanish literature, or in the Spanish translation of that work. For an interesting account of German interest in Vives, see Foster Watson, *Vives on Education* (Cambridge, 1913), pp. xix-xx. Beyond Bonilla y San Martin, the fullest work is by Fermín de Urmeneta, *La Doctrina Psicológica y Pedagógica de Luis Vives* (Barcelona: Consejo Superior de Investigaciones Científicas, 1949) which includes a bibliographical appendix (pp. 545-605) listing some 394 studies by 246 different authors. See also, Marian Leona Tobriner, ed., *Vives' "Introduction to Wisdom": A Renaissance Textbook* (New York: Teachers College Press, Columbia University, 1968).
2. Although the *Pseudo-dialecticos* was a stinging attack on the dialecticians, still it was favorably received. See Bonilla, *op. cit.*, I, p. 321.
3. The book was for a short time on the "Index of Prohibited Books," *dunc corrigatur.* The irony was complete, for no more attached son of the Church could be found than Vives, though no church could constrain the strength and freedom of his thought. See Watson (*Vives on Education*, p. lxxii) for a restrained Victorian estimate.
4. Bonilla, *op. cit.*, I, pp. 231-237.
5. Quoted in Watson, *Vives on Education*, p. lxxvii.
6. *Ibid.*, p. lxix; see also Bonilla, *op. cit.*, I, 321-22.
7. Quoted by Watson, *Vives on Education*, p. xii. Daryngton says Louvain is a pleasant place, and he is less disturbed in studies than he had been at Cambridge.
8. Recognized as such as early as 1767 by J. J. Brucker, *Historia Critica Philosophiae.* See Watson, *Vives on Education*, p. c, and Bonilla, *p. cit.*, III, p. 27.
9. Quoted in Watson, *Vives on Education*, p. xxi.
10. The translation was reprinted by Watson in *Vives and the Renascence Education of Women* (London, 1912). Richard Hyrde acknowledges in his preface assistance given him by Sir Thomas More in the translation. See *ed. cit.*, p. 31.
11. Vives mentions Thomas Linacre's translations from the Greek into Latin of Galen's *De Sanitate Tuenda* and *Methodus Medendi.* These were translated in 1517 and 1519.
12. Watson, *ed. cit.*, p. 87.
13. *Ibid.*, p. 72.
14. This is also translated by Watson and included in the *ed. cit.* Watson's book is a treasurehouse, for it includes, in addition to the above mentioned, Vives's *De Ratione Studii Puerilis* (see *infra*); *The School of Sir Thomas More*; Sir Thomas Elyot's *Defence of Good Women*; and a selection from Vives's *De Officio Mariti.*
15. See Watson, *ed. cit.*, p. 3.
16. J. Parmentier, "Vives: de ses theories sur l'education et de leur influence sur les pedagogues anglais," *Revue Internationale de l'enseignement*, vol. XXV (1893), pp. 421-55.
17. Watson, *ed. cit.*, pp. 27-28.
18. Watson, *ed. cit.*, pp. 137-149. Watson first translated this into English for *Educational Times*, October, 1907. See also Miguel Bertrán Quera, "Resumen y Comentario al Documento Pedagógico de Juan Luis Vives: *De Ratione Studii Puerilis*," *Revista Española de Pedagogía*, vol. 26 (1968), pp. 191-209.

19. Mary Tudor was born in 1516. An accomplished Latin and Greek scholar, she translated Erasmus's *Paraphrase on St. John's Gospel* when the English translation of the whole work edited by Nicholas Udall appeared in 1547.
20. Watson, *ed. cit.*, p. 145. There is a companion piece to the *De Ratione* for boys which Vives wrote in the same year for Charles Mountjoy. There are some interesting differences. See text in Watson, *Vives and the Renascence Education of Women*, pp. 241-250.
21. *Op. cit.*, p. 138.
22. Lynn Thorndike, "John Louis Vives: His Attitude to Learning and to Life" in *Essays in Intellectual History* (New York, 1929), pp. 327-342. This *festschrift* essay is somewhat disappointing. See also, William Sinz, "The Elaboration of Vives' Treatises on the Arts," *Renaissance Studies*, vol. 10 (1963), pp. 68-90.
23. Watson, *Vives on Education*, p. 283.
24. Watson, *Vives on Education* (Cambridge, 1913) is actually the first English translation of the five books of the *De Tradendis Disciplinis*.
25. The *De Corruptibus Artium* is not in English translation. It is most easily accessible to the modern student in the 1782 edition of Vives's works published by Gregorious Majansius in Valencia in eight volumes, of which it forms volume six.
26. Watson, *Vives on Education*, pp. xcii-xciv.
27. At best it is a formidable undertaking. It numbers some 600 pages in the edition cited in fn. 25. See also G. Marañon *Luis Vives, Un Espagñol fuera de España* (Madrid, 1942).
28. Watson, *op. cit.*, pp. ix-x.
29. *Ibid.*, p. xciv. See also, Walter A. Daly, *The Educational Psychology of Juan Luis Vives* (Washington: Catholic University of America Press, 1924), and Emilio Redondo, "La Integración del Concepto de Sabiduría en la Pedagogía de Luis Vives," *Revista Española de Pedagogía*, vol. 24 (1966), pp. 99-111; and in a broader framework, see Eugene F. Rice, *The Renaissance Idea of Wisdom* (Cambridge, Mass.: Harvard University Press, 1958).
30. Book III, chap. I; in Watson's translation, p. 91 f.
31. Watson, *op. cit.*, pp. xcviii-xcix.

*A Further Bibliographical Note*

The fourth centenary of the death of Vives was the occasion for the publication of important catalogues and notices of expositions. See Felipe Mateu y Llopis, *Catalogo de la Exposición bibliographica Celebrado con Motivo del IV Centenario de la Muerte de Luis Vives* (Barcelona: Casa Provincial de Caridad: Imprenta-Escuela, 1940), with *Supplements* in *Anales del Centro de Cultura Valenciana*, II, #2 (1941); III, #3 (1942); IV #7 (1943); V, #10 (1944); Juan Estelrich, Vives: *Esposition Organisée a la Bibliothéque Nationale* (Paris, Janvier-Mars, 1941, Dijon: Imprimerie Darantiere, 1942).

Montclair State College

# VIVES: ON EDUCATION

# PREFACE

WAS Vives a greater thinker on educational matters than Erasmus? The answer which most people would give to this question probably would be: "We never heard of Vives, and we are perfectly familiar with the outstanding importance of the work of Erasmus, therefore we are provisionally prepared to stand by the premier position of Erasmus. If we err, we err in good company, for have not the intervening centuries placed Erasmus as the leader of the progressive forces of the Renascence?"

Nevertheless, even in a matter of such a widely spread tradition as that of Erasmus' leadership in education, at least if the term is understood in the sense of insight into educational principles and a comprehensive treatment of its problems, it is clear that the student of the history of education should preserve an open mind. Moreover, he will realise that he cannot form an opinion on the subject until he has read at least as much of the works on education written by Vives, as he has read of Erasmus.

Hitherto there has been no translation of Vives' main educational work, the *de Tradendis Disciplinis*, into English, so that however willing to present the open mind to Vives and to form an opinion as to his relative position as an educational thinker, no one has been able to do so without wading through the Latin text of Vives, unless, indeed, within recent years, he has read the translations into German of Heine, Wychgram or Kayser. So that to form a judgment about Vives has hitherto involved much labour, and this translation will at least make available to the English reader important material for estimating the value of Vives' contribution to the subject of education. In answer to the consideration, suggested above, that Vives has been held in lower esteem than Erasmus throughout the intervening centuries, it has seemed necessary, or at least desirable, to trace in the Introduction the influence which Vives has exercised on the development of educational theory, and to point out that if his name has not always been *en évidence*, yet clearly his views, if not present to the mind of certain later writers, at least have been so nearly reproduced in their statement and exposition as to suggest irresistibly that whether such later writers consciously borrowed from Vives or not, any claim to originality attributed to them, might *à fortiori*, attach to the earlier advocate of the same educational truths.

The object in making this translation into English, and of writing the Introduction is not to settle the exact position to be accorded to Vives in the history of education, but to provide the student of education with the material for his own judgment as to the significance of Vives.

Yet, perhaps, the most decisive way of attacking the problem of Vives' position is, without prejudice, to ask boldly the question: Was Vives, judging from the extant works of both, a more fruitful thinker on educational questions than

Erasmus? There is no loss of reverence for Erasmus involved in raising the question. Vives had been his pupil, and was always proud of his master. It is not too much to say that the younger man in attaining any educational influence would have experienced at least as much satisfaction in the credit going to his master for his wise training, as in any personal glory achieved by independence of opinion; though he would have cared more for the truth of what he asserted than for the glory either of his master or of himself.

Nor need we hesitate to institute a comparison between Vives and Erasmus on a specific point. Erasmus has himself set an example of a similar kind. He wrote in the *Ciceronianus* that Jodocus Badius, the printer, had ability as a writer of Ciceronian style, whilst Guillaume Budé, the greatest living Greek scholar of the age, had it not. The Budaeans raged because he had compared Badius favourably with Budé. But Erasmus answered that he had only made the comparison on one point, not in all respects, and that on that one point, Budé would not wish to claim pre-eminence for himself. So in the present volume it is suggested that there is a *prima facie* case for inquiry, whether Vives in his desire for the social good, and all questions bearing upon that standpoint, has not treated the subject of education so fruitfully as to be emphatically the greatest European educational leader of the first half of the sixteenth century, in spite of the fact that Erasmus, without inquiry, is often placed in that position.

At any rate, Vives' book on the *Transmission of Knowledge* affords an interesting insight into the transition stage from Mediaevalism to the Renascence and modern times, and is stimulative and suggestive in the spirit of high educative endeavour even for the present day.

The portrait of Vives, the frontispiece of this volume, is taken from Theodore de Bry's engraving in J. J. Broissard's *Icones Virorum Illustrium* [1597–8]. The date in the left-hand bottom corner [1541] is wrong, Vives died in 1540.

The marginal descriptive insets and the reference notes are chiefly translated from the only edition [in Latin], probably printed in Leyden, of an English editor, Henry Jackson[1], in 1612, Fellow of Corpus Christi College, Oxford, the College in which Vives lived when he lectured in Oxford.

The reader may find the subject-matter of Vives' treatise closer to modern educational interests if studied, on the first reading, in the following order: Dedicatory Address, Vives' Preface, the Appendix, and then, Books V, IV, II, III, I.

[1] See note, p. cvii *infra*.

FOSTER WATSON.

CALEDFRYN,
ABERYSTWYTH.
*March* 13, 1913.

# CONTENTS

## THE TRANSMISSION OF KNOWLEDGE

# BIBLIOGRAPHY OF THE LATIN TEXTS OF *DE DISCIPLINIS*

**1531** Antwerp: Michael Hillenius in Rapo, 1531, mense Julio Cum Privilegio Caesareo. Fol.

Contains twenty books. De corruptis artibus, libri VII. De Tradendis Disciplinis, libri V. De Artibus: de prima philosophia (three books); de explanatione cuiusque essentiae; de censura veri (two books); de instrumento probabilitatis; de disputatione.

**1532** Cologne: Joannes Gymnicus 1532 (mense Januario). 8°.

**1536** Cologne: Joannes Gymnicus. 8°.

**1551** Lyons: Apud Joannem Fellonium. 8°.

All the above contain twenty books.

**1612** [Leyden ?] *De Disciplinis. Hi de Corruptis Artibus Doctissimi viri notis, illi de tradendis Disciplinis cuiusdam Studiosi Oxoniensis annotationibus illustrati. Cum indice copioso. Impressum* 1612. 8°.

The British Museum catalogue suggests Leyden as the place of publication.

**1636** Leyden. Ex officina Joan. Maire 1636. 12°.

**1764** Naples. Ex Typographia Simoniana, Superiorum permissu.

# CHRONOLOGICAL TABLE OF THE LIFE OF JUAN LUIS VIVES

**1492** (Apparently March 6) Vives was born at Valencia. Baptised in the Church of St Andrew.

**1508** At the Academy or University of Valencia.

**1509–14** In Paris. At the College of Beauvais.

**1514** Stayed several weeks in Bruges, in the house of Bernard Valdaura.

Nov. 14 and Dec. 2, Vives' name occurs in two legal documents at Bruges (Archives de la Prévôté de Saint-Donatian).

**1518** Guillaume de Croy, Cardinal and Archbishop designate of Toledo, becomes the pupil of Vives.

At Louvain. Writes his *Meditationes in septem psalmos poenitentiae.*

Gives lessons to Jerome Ruffault, who afterwards became Abbot of St Peter at Ghent.

**1519** At Louvain. February 13, finishes his *Liber in Pseudo-dialecticos*—and in April, his *Pompeius fugiens.*

Middle of the year, visits Paris for several months and becomes acquainted with Guillaume Budé.

Taught at Louvain.

**1520** (towards the end of) Vives began his Commentaries on St Augustine's *Civitas Dei.*

**1521** (January 10). Death of his former pupil Cardinal de Croy (aged 23 years).

Vives falls ill, and is taken to Bruges, where he can have better medical treatment in the Spanish colony there. He is received in the house of his compatriot, Pedro de Aguirra, a rich merchant.

July 10. Vives writes to More, stating his hopes of royal favour and monetary help from Wolsey's prospective visit.

Vives was present at fêtes given in honour of Cardinal Wolsey, who was then at Bruges.

Published *De Initiis, sectis, et laudibus Philosophiae* (written in 1518; published in 1521, on the advice of Pâquier or Pascal de Bierset (Berzelius), Benedictine monk of the St-Laurent-lez-Liége Monastery).

In November. Returned to Louvain.

**1522** At Bruges, to take leave of compatriots who were joining the Emperor in his journey to Spain. Death of Pedro de Aguirra.

Stayed in the Lange Winckel at Bruges—the quarter of Spanish merchants.

Finished Commentaries on St Augustine's *Civitas Dei*, which he dedicated to King Henry VIII.

The Duke of Alva sent a proposal to Vives to become tutor to his son, offering 200 golden ducats for salary. A Dominican monk failed to deliver the document conveying the offer.

First visit of Vives to England, where he failed to secure any post or patronage.

**1523** April. Vives finished the *de Institutione Feminae Christianae*. At the request of Wolsey, Vives came to England, and had the direction of the Princess Mary placed in his hands, for whom he wrote the *de Ratione Studii Puerilis* (completed October 1523).

October 10, incorporated as LL.D. in Oxford University. Stayed in Corpus Christi College, Oxford.

Wrote his *de Consultatione* for Louis de Flandre, seigneur de Präet.

Translated an Oration of Isocrates for Wolsey, Dec. 15, 1523.

**1524** April. Returned from Oxford to Bruges, and there married Margaret Valdaura (age 20) on May 26, daughter of Bernard Valdaura, whose wife was Clara Cervent.

November. In London and Oxford.

**1526–27** Divided between Bruges and England, the summer in England; the winter in Bruges.

**1526** Louis de Flandre, seigneur de Präet, who had met Vives in England induced him to write *De Subventione Pauperum*, which was finished 6 January 1526–7. The Collège des Echevins of Bruges presented Vives with a silver cup and the book was translated into Dutch at the charges of the magistracy of Bruges.

**1528** Took the part of Catharine of Aragon in the divorce project of Henry VIII. Examined by Wolsey as to his interviews with Catharine. Placed *in libera custodia* for six weeks, then sent from the Court and the country to Bruges, and the King's pension withdrawn.

November. Margaret of Savoy sent Vives a safe-conduct to England to defend Queen Catharine, but on the failure of Vives to appear as Catharine's advocate, the Queen's pension like the King's was withdrawn. (*Cal. State Papers.*)

Vives published the *de Officio Mariti.*

**1529** The sweating-sickness, on which John Caius wrote, appeared in Bruges. Vives was asked by the authorities of St Donatian at Bruges to write an office: *Sacrum diurnum de sudore Jesu Christi: Concio de nostro et Christi sudore.*

Vives wrote the *de Concordia et Discordia in Humano Genere.*

**1531** (July). The *de Disciplinis* was published at Antwerp.

**1535** At Antwerp, whence he dates the preface to *Exercitationes animi in Deum.*

**1536** Vives was for six months in Paris.

**1537–38** At Breda, tutor to Mencia de Mendoza, the Marchioness del Canete.

**1538** (September). Vives published (at Basle) the *de Anima et Vita*, the first modern work on psychology. In this year was published at Breda his *Linguae Latinae Exercitatio* (i.e. School Dialogues).

**1540** Vives died at Bruges 6 May—at the age of 48 years. Buried in the Chapel of St Joseph, in the Church of St Donatian at Bruges.

**1543** Vives' theological work published by John Oporinus at Basle: *de Veritate Fidei Christianae (contra Ethnicos, Judaeos, Agarenos, sive Mahometanos, ac perverse Christianos) libri quinque.*

**1552** (October 1). Margaret Vives, his widow, died.

"We (scholars) must transfer our solicitude (from princes) to the people."

J. L. Vives, *Transmission of Knowledge*, p. 278 *infra.*

"This then is the fruit of all studies ; this is the goal. Having acquired our knowledge, we must turn it to usefulness, and employ it for the common good."

*Ibid.*, p. 283 *infra.*

# INTRODUCTION

## CHAPTER I

### VIVES: KNOWN AND UNKNOWN

It has been pointed out[1] that Vives is not mentioned by Ticknor, the best historian of Spanish literature. The omission was not remedied even by the translators[2] of that work into Spanish. But Spain has shown much literary activity since that time, more than sixty years ago, and the name of Vives now is honoured as a discovery of a great man of letters with a satisfaction not altogether dissimilar to that experienced in the time of the Revival of Learning, when the works of an ancient Latin or Greek author came to the light of day. No one can now write about Vives without reference to the work of research by Señor D. Adolfo Bonilla y San Martín[3], a veritable storehouse of knowledge with regard to Vives; his life, his works, and his relation to his times, from the point of view of Spain, and also of Europe at large.

1 See L. Massebieau: *Les Colloques Scolaires du XVIe Siècle* (Paris, 1878).

2 Viz. Pascual de Gayangos and E. de Vedia, Madrid, 1851.

3 Entitled: *Luis Vives y la Filosofía del Renacimiento. Memoria premiada por la Real Academia de Ciencias Morales y Politicas*, Madrid, 1903.

This great work must now occupy the highest position for its comprehensive account of Vives, a position which students of all nations will as gladly recognise as fittingly falling to Spain, as Spanish students will rejoice that it was Señor Bonilla who undertook the onerous but congenial task—yet there were forerunners in the re-discovery of the importance of Vives, whose labours made possible a thorough study of the facts of Vives' life and works.

The pioneer writer in collecting the facts concerning Vives was Gregorius Majansius, a Spaniard, who wrote the life of Vives which accompanies his edition of Vives' works in eight volumes published in 1782, at Valencia[1], the birthplace of Vives. This magnificent edition was published at the expense of the Archbishop of Valencia, Francisco Fabian et Fuero. It reminds the reader of the lordly publishing enterprise of the Renascence Cardinal Jimenez at the Spanish University of Alcála, in the early years of the 16th century.

The men to whom we owe the deepest debts, after Majansius, in the way of direct research, are A. J. Namèche[2], Professor of Rhetoric in the Collège de la Haute-Colline in the University of Louvain, in 1841; Emile Vanden Bussche[3],

[1] The title of the complete works of Vives in this Valencian edition is: *Joannis Ludovici Vivis Valentini Opera Omnia, distributa et ordinata in Argumentorum Classes praecipuas a Gregorio Majansio...Item Vita Vivis Scripta ab eodem Majansio... Valentiae Edetanorum.* This eight-volumed edition of 1782 constitutes the real basis of all later enquiries into the life and works of Vives. References in this Introduction to *Vivis Opera* are to this edition.

[2] *Mémoire sur la Vie et les Écrits de Jean-Louis Vivès.* In *Mémoires couronnés par l'Académie royale des Sciences et Belles-Lettres de Bruxelles.* Tome XV. Première Partie 1840–41. Bruxelles: M. Hayez, 1841.

[3] *Luiz Vives. Notes biographiques. Un Mot.* In *La Flandre, Revue des Monuments d'Histoire et d'Antiquités.* Bruges: Daveluy, 1876. Vanden Bussche brings together every fact ascertainable from the thorough investigation of civic documents at Bruges, with regard to the residence there of Vives, who was a citizen of public spirit, as we shall see, of whom the city is justly proud.

archiviste de l'État at Bruges in 1876, and for expository criticism of Vives' works, A. Lange[1], author of the *History of Materialism*, in 1887. In these writers we have representative scholars: Belgian, Flemish, and German, with one Spaniard beginning and another at the end of the series. Many others have written longer or shorter accounts of Vives, or of his works[2], and have made selections of the educational portions, but Namèche, Vanden Bussche and Lange went to the original sources of knowledge, and came back with the richest harvests.

Attention was drawn in the 19th century to the significant pedagogical aspects of the Spanish scholar's works by Karl von Raumer[3], who was the first to make Vives generally known as an educationist in Germany.

[1] Lange's monograph on Vives appeared as an article in the *Encyklopädie des gesammten Erziehungs- und Unterrichtswesens*, herausgegeben von Dr K. A. Schmid und Dr W. Schrader (1887), Band ix. Abteilung III. pp. 776–851. Leipzig: Fues's Verlag.

[2] The following editions of Selected Works of Vives include translations into German of the Latin text of the *de Tradendis Disciplinis*.

1881. Dr Rudolf Heine. *Joh. Ludwig Vives. Ausgewählte Pädagogische Schriften* [with comprehensive notes]. Leipzig: Siegismund und Volkening. Band XVI. Pädagogische Bibliothek, herausgegeben von Karl Richter.

1883. Dr Jacob Wychgram: *Johann Ludwig Vives' Ausgewählte Schriften.* Wien and Leipzig: R. Pichler's Witwe und Sohn.

1896. Dr Friedrich Kayser: *Johannes Ludovicus Vives' Pädagogische Schriften.* In the *Bibliothek der Katholischen Pädagogik.* Herausgegeben von F. X. Kunz, Band VIII. Freiburg im Breisgau: Herdersche Verlagshandlung. I gratefully acknowledge help from these editions at different points of my text. I have also found very useful the excellent treatise by Franz Kuypers: *Vives in Seiner Pädagogik.* Leipzig: Teubner, 1897. Apparently, Vives' *de Tradendis Disciplinis* has not been translated into any language except German, not yet even into Spanish.

[3] *Geschichte der Pädagogik, von Wiederaufblühen klassischer Studien bis auf unsere Zeit.* Vol. I. appeared in 1842 and the second in 1843. This work is still of considerable value for the student though the latest edition was issued in 1879.

The re-discovery of Vives affords an interesting example of the service which the study of the history of education has rendered to the history of general literature. It is true that Namèche published his account of Vives in 1841, a year before Raumer's *History of Pedagogy* appeared. But it was Raumer who first made clear to the 19th century the influence exercised by Vives on Francis Bacon, and many later educationists. Henry Barnard in the United States of America translated into English to American educationists Raumer's high opinion of Vives, and Karl Schmidt developed Raumer's view for German readers, and lastly, Lange elaborately did full justice to the subject. The study of the history of education is only beginning to justify itself in the general history of literature. One outstanding instance is the position now conceded to Vittorino da Feltre, won for the great humanist, in the modern perspective of historical accounts of the Renascence, by the devoted labours of Carlo de' Rosmini, Sabbadini, Paglia, Luzio, and our own Professor W. H. Woodward. In the case of Vittorino, as soon as the facts were known, it was felt that such a commanding personality in the field of education passed beyond the mere territory of sectional claims into the broader highway of human greatness, and although Vittorino wrote no "monument of literature," no historian of the development of Renascence culture is likely in the future to overlook the influence of the great educationist. So with Vives. Since Raumer introduced him to the historians of general literature and culture, he has won an entrance again to the attention of those interested in the steps by which modern letters and culture were developed. What his place will be as the 20th century perspective of the 16th century revival of letters comes to be more fully re-shaped, it is difficult to say. It is not improbable that he will rank in new re-constructions of learning and culture at the beginning of the 16th century, at least higher relatively to that century than even Vittorino to the 15th. For like Vittorino he is revealed by the facts with which laborious research has provided us, as a commanding and attractive personality, though with great differences in detail from that of Vittorino. Both of them have characteristics that admit them not only amongst the great educationists, but also amongst the large-minded humanists in both thought and life, who transcend the limits of their specialised occupation.

Vives, as a writer, has indeed been ranked high. A Spanish literary authority has regarded him in power of intellect as the equal of Descartes[1]. J. Andres[2] says that he regards the *de Disciplinis*, the chief work on education of Vives, as "a great marvel of learning, sound understanding and right judgment at the beginning of the 16th century *as the Organum of Bacon* was at the beginning of the 17th century." This suggests the question of the relation of Bacon to Vives, to which reference will be made in this Introduction. These suggestions of the equality of later with earlier thinkers must always have an unreality about them, since the accumulated national experience of a later century, together with differences of country and traditions and of training make the comparison extremely difficult[3]. I shall not attempt an answer to the problems of superiority thus raised, but content myself with the observation that it is sufficiently remarkable that Vives foreshadowed so much of what became the distinctive lines of later scientific progress.

[1] Señor Castelar, whose opinion is quoted by Massebieau, *Les Colloques*, p. 166.

[2] *Dell' Origine, progressi e stato attuale d'ogni Letteratura*, Parma 1785, Vol. I. p. 394.

[3] As a matter of speculation, it would perhaps bring out the problem of relativity more clearly if the suggestion had been: How would Bacon, or Descartes, compare with Vives, if we attempt to read away from their writings, all the intervening experience with which the former two started as an advantage over Vives. It is obviously unreasonable to expect that the earlier writer could by intuition acquire a forecast of the subject-matter of the scientific inquiries and accumulation of knowledge, which was entered into as a birthright by the later writers.

There is one question of less startling speculation, perhaps, than the comparison of Vives with Bacon or with Descartes, for it is one which happily can be solved with actual certainty—viz. What was the position of Vives, in his own century, in the opinion of his contemporaries themselves? This question is of far more significance than might appear, at the first glance, because later centuries have taken upon themselves to settle the relative positions of men of letters at the Revival of Learning quite differently from, and often without regard to, the intuitive judgments of the contemporary scholars. Later literary judgments may be, indeed ought to be, far weightier than those of earlier times. But this proposition will not hold for judgment in which personality is a large factor. The comparison of personalities at a date long removed from the time at which the men concerned were living, often foregoes none of the assertiveness which characterises the judgments on concrete achievements, either on canvas or on paper, which are handed down to posterity. Tradition quickly stereotypes the orthodox view, and reputations are established as fixed, when a judgment has once become current, whether the grounds on which it was based were completely determined, or not. Thus, when we hear that Vives was born in 1492 and died in 1540, we realise that he was living at the same time as Erasmus, who was born in 1466 and died in 1536. We congratulate ourselves on being able to place a mark on him by saying, "He lived, then, in the Age of Erasmus." Accordingly, Vives may simply get dismissed from remembrance because he lived in the Age of Erasmus. Erasmus is well known (as a name) and may easily absorb all the modern interest that can be spared for "his Age." If, however, free from prejudice, we ask: What did his contemporaries think of Vives? we can readily find answers. Sir Thomas More, himself one of those charming personalities, whose opinion on men and affairs of his times, appeals with more weight, perhaps, than that of any man of the Court of Henry VIII, wrote to Erasmus, in 1519, that a visitor from Louvain had shown him some works of Luis Vives "than which I have not seen for a long time anything so elegant and learned. How few you will find, nay rather, you will scarcely find one, anywhere at so green an age (for you state that he is still young[1]) who has mastered so completely the whole round of knowledge. Certainly, my Erasmus, I am ashamed of myself and of others with like advantages, who take credit to ourselves for this or that insignificant booklet, when I see a young man like Vives producing so many well digested works, in good style, and with such learning in the background. It is a great accomplishment to be polished in one of the classical languages. He proves himself a drilled scholar in both. But it is a greater and more fruitful achievement to be well versed, as he is, in the highest branches of knowledge. Who is there, in this one respect—who surpasses Vives in the number and quality of his studies? But what is most admirable of all is, that he should have acquired all this knowledge so that he may be able to communicate it to others, by way of instruction. And who instructs with more clearness, with more pleasure, or with more success than Vives?"

To this letter of More, Erasmus returns the answer: "As to the ability of Ludovicus Vives, I rejoice that my estimate of him agrees with yours. He is *one of the number of those who will overshadow the name of Erasmus*[2]. There is no one to whom I am better inclined, and I love you the more, since you are attracted to him so sincerely. He has a wonderfully philosophical mind. He despises courageously that goddess to whom all offer sacrifice though few propitiate her. Yet he is of such ability that fortune cannot neglect to reward such literature as his. No other man is more fitted to utterly overwhelm the battalions of the dialecticians in whose camps he served for a long time."

[1] Vives was, at the time, 27 years of age.

[2] *Erasmi Epistolae*, col. 642 C. (1642 ed.).

It is not too much to say that on the continent, the contemporary judgment of More and Erasmus on Vives was reinforced in the course of the 16th century by scholars of the highest rank. Andreas Schott[1], of Antwerp, the friend of Isaac Casaubon, a hundred years later, found and confirmed the rank of Vives as a member of the Triumvirate in the Republic of Letters of the beginning of the 16th century, of which the other members were, in his opinion, Erasmus and Budaeus. Schott's account is (and it apparently was the accepted judgment of the time) that of the Triumvirate thus acknowledged, Budaeus held the palm in mental ability, Erasmus in literary resource of expression, and Vives in the soundness of his judgment[2]. The high rank of Vives was thus emphasised in his own age, and maintained in the following century.

In the beginning of the 18th century we can refer to the literary judgment of D. G. Morhof, who says, on the subject of the training of good minds, that Vives produced his praiseworthy books—not only the *Transmission of Knowledge* (*de Tradendis Disciplinis*) but also the *Causes of the Corruptions of the Arts* (*de Causis Corruptarum Artium*). He adds that "these are distinctly golden books full of good fruit—and *they should be most diligently read by all learned men.*"

Towards the end of the 18th century (viz. between 1782 and 1790) came the splendidly produced edition, already mentioned, of the *Opera Omnia* of Vives[3]. We thus see that Vives was held in high recognition, contemporaneously by

[1] In the *De Bibliothecis et claris Hispaniae viris*, 1608.

[2] Not content with a critical statement as to the Triumvirate of Budaeus, Erasmus and Vives, Schott emphasises the juxta-position of the names by Latin verses to celebrate the literary powers of the Triumvirate. Majansius' Life of Vives, *Vivis Opera*, I. p. 41.

[3] This does not, however, include Vives' *Commentaries* on St Augustine's *De Civitate Dei*, nor, as had been originally intended, the translations of certain of his works into Castilian. The first collected edition of Vives' works was published in two folio volumes at Basle in 1555.

More and Erasmus; in the 17th century by Andreas Schott; in the 18th by Morhof, and the splendid devotion of Gregory Majans, in the re-issue in noble form of his works. These tributes to Vives must be regarded as typical; they could be supplemented by many notices from others, of shorter length, or from less important writers, or of less conspicuous praise[1].

Two facts call for notice in the history of opinions concerning Vives. First, in spite of the issue of the monumental eight-volumed edition of the *Opera Omnia* (1782–90), there was later a clearly-marked lull, if not almost to be called collapse[2], of interest in Vives, until the re-discovery of him by Namèche, Vanden Bussche, and Lange. The complete works of Vives in the 1555 edition had no doubt become scarce, but the 1782–90 edition might have been expected to create a greatly increased attention to Vives. This, however, was not the case. In the early part of the 19th century he almost dropped out of notice. The explanation probably is to be found in the educational influences connected with the French Revolution. The world entered into a new economic and educational order, not less than into a revolution of political ideas. Without doubt the old educational thinkers who had survived to the second half of the 18th century, let us say, John Milton or John Locke, in England; or Rabelais and Montaigne in France; were absolutely submerged in the whirlpool of change. The old serene aristocratic atmosphere which these writers breathed was alien to the new forces which irresistibly forced themselves to the front.

1 Bonilla y San Martín supplies the following names of authors who notice the works of Vives: Paul Jovius, Francis Swertius, Possevin, Schott, Barth, Valerius Andrés, Albert Mireus, G. J. Vossius, Königius, Lipenius, Paul Freher, Moréri, Pope-Blount, Dupin, Richard Simon, A. Teissier, Johann Fabricius, Cave, Baillet, J. G. Walch, Niceron, J. F. Foppens, Brucker, Paquot, Dugald Stewart, Schwartz, Von Raumer, etc. Of course even such a list is not really comprehensive. His list of Spanish writers who held Vives in honour is valuable, since the point might have been overlooked by non-Spanish students, had he not supplied it. See Bonilla, p. 739.

2 Except for a few publications in Spain, of secondary importance.

The new circumstances brought about a new national self-consciousness, new economic goals and starting-points. And again, in England, the inventions consequent on the discovery of the significance of steam-power, and throughout Europe the new ideas of Rousseau of "the sovereign power of the people," and of the State as "the expression of the general will of the people" necessarily turned the whole emphasis of educational thought to the democratic centre, to the problems of the education of the great mass of the people—i.e. to primary education. The advocates of political freedom had to transfer their attention not only to the release of negro-slaves, but also to the employment of factory children, who were the slaves of a combination difficult to combat, viz. that of parents joined with employers. The value of the educationist to society was to be determined by the practical answer he could give to the question: When the child is emancipated what is to be done with him? How can the educationist help the nation to redeem what might become an irresponsible mob into a well-disciplined army of recruits for the national industrial service. Educational necessity was the mother of educational invention. Rousseau supplied the French Revolution with its educational cry: "Return to Nature[1]." Pestalozzi, Fellenberg, Froebel, all set themselves to meet the new democratic conditions. Men like Lancaster, Bell, Robert Owen, in England, and like-minded men abroad, helped forward the arrangements and organisations to suit the new order. There was apparently no room or time for the old educational thinkers, who had prescribed for students with long years of linguistic preparation, an encyclopaedia of knowledge which had become impossible. Locke was the last of the encyclopaedists, and even he had had

[1] For instance, Rousseau begins his *Émile*: "Everything is good as it comes from the hands of the Author of Nature; but everything degenerates in the hands of man." It is interesting to note that Vives had said: "All things in this world as they were made by God are good and beautiful" (p. 33).

to modify his position by adopting a utilitarian standard as the test for each subject proposed to be taught. With the 19th century Locke himself had become exacting beyond the limits of patience. The educational systems which had prepared the training of gentlemen, as well as those which sought to produce scholars, were obsolete, or nearly obsolete. They went under along with the idea of the old aristocracy. The soul of educational activity and thought was concentrated on the quantitative aspect—How can one man teach a thousand children in the same room, at the same time? That was quite a different kind of problem from what had been considered by the writers of the 16th and 17th centuries. In the new era of democratic emergencies those educational writers, even the most conspicuous of them, were lost sight of—Vives amongst the rest. For the older writers kept their strained vision fixed on the qualitative aspect—How can the very highest educational results be achieved under the most favourable of conditions? The problem before the future is: How to unify the two aspects, the quantitative and the qualitative? The impartial study of the history of education will play a great part in disciplining thought on this problem.

The second fact which perhaps needs explanation in connexion with the history of opinion about Vives is the slight amount of notice he and his works have received in England, as compared with the rest of Europe. This is the more remarkable since between 1522 and 1528 Vives spent a portion of each year in England, either in Oxford or in London, returning to Bruges for the rest of the year. He came to England under the aegis of not only Sir Thomas More, but also of Mountjoy, who had been Erasmus' pupil, and the great Cardinal Wolsey. Moreover, he seems to have been in receipt of a pension from both King Henry VIII and from Queen Catharine. He was incorporated as Doctor of Laws in the University of Oxford in October, 1523, and lectured successfully in that University. He was called upon by the Queen,

Catharine of Aragon, his fellow-countrywoman, to sketch a course of study for her daughter Mary, afterwards Queen Mary I, a child in her eighth year. He was further asked along with Linacre to direct her education. He dedicated his work on the education of women[1] to Queen Catharine, and his *Satellitium Animi* to the Princess Mary. Vives was warmly attached to mother and daughter—too warmly attached to make his course easy, when the rupture between Henry VIII and Catharine took place. The events connecting Vives with the divorce-question have been carefully pieced together[2] by Mr P. S. Allen, who says: "As a Spaniard, Vives naturally took Catharine's part. In February, 1528, he was examined by Wolsey and forced to reveal the substance of his conversations with Catharine. After being kept under surveillance six weeks[3] he was dismissed from the Court, and returned to Bruges; and his stipend from the King and Queen cut off.

"It does not appear that Vives visited England again. In January, 1531, he wrote to Henry VIII from Bruges, complaining that he had received no pension from him for three years, but nevertheless withstanding him manfully about the Divorce, concerning which Henry was then consulting the Universities of Europe."

Let us now consider further events, and if we trace them in connexion with the neglect that befell Sir Thomas More and his *Utopia* we shall be prepared to find that Vives, who shared his views, and in addition was a Spaniard, *à fortiori* was in long continued disgrace and neglect.

In July of the year 1531, Henry abandoned Catharine and at once joined himself with Anne Boleyn. In 1534, the

[1] *De Institutione Feminae Christianae.* The dedication is dated April 5, 1523.

[2] In the *Pelican Record* (Corpus Christi College, Oxford), Dec. 1902, p. 156 *et seqq.* The account is founded upon the Calendar of State Papers (Domestic Series).

[3] See letter to Juan Vergara quoted p. lxxx *infra*.

Pope declared the marriage of Catharine valid, whereupon an Act of Parliament was passed, limiting the succession to the throne to the offspring of the marriage with Anne Boleyn, and making it high treason to oppose the tenour of the Act. Sir Thomas More refused to conform twice, and was committed to the Tower. Eventually the indictment was changed to that of his denial of the Act of Supremacy, and on July 6, 1535, he was put to death. Vives' attitude, there can be no doubt, was certainly sympathetic with the opposition of More to the Act of Succession, which repudiated Catharine, and to the Act of Supremacy, which repudiated the Pope. It stands on record that it was accounted treason to speak of More as a martyr[1]. During the whole of the 16th century, i.e. during the reigns of the Tudors (omitting of course that of Mary), it was dangerous to speak appreciatively of More, and when the despicable Frenchman Nicholas Bourbon reviled More's memory in his nasty Latin epigrams, Queen Elizabeth made herself the poet's special patroness[2]. It is true, in the Catholic revival of Mary's reign, More's English works were published[3]. But on the other hand, although, as the learned writer of *Philomorus* says, we find "Lives of Sir Thomas More in almost all the languages of Europe," none appeared in England till the reign of Charles I[4]. Similarly, More's *Utopia* was under a cloud. The English translation by Ralph Robinson[5] ran through two editions in 1551 and 1556. The third edition did not appear till 1597 and the fourth in 1624. The Latin editions apparently were all published abroad. Finally, it is not too much to say that no work with

[1] See *Philomorus*, 2nd ed. p. 255.

[2] *Ibid.* p. 261.

[3] In 1537 by Wm. Rastell, his nephew.

[4] This was the life by Wm. Roper, his son-in-law, published in 1627. Thomas Stapleton, the Jesuit, included the life of More in the *Tres Thomae* (i.e. Thomas the Apostle, St Thomas à Becket and Sir Thomas More) which was published in 1588, but abroad, at Douai.

[5] Robinson was, like Vives, associated with Corpus Christi College, Oxford.

anything like the originality and stimulus to thought of the *Utopia*, at home or abroad, written as early as 1516, counted for so little in England during the period of the great Elizabethan and Jacobean writers.

If the memory of More, with his *Utopia*—the most distinctively noble work on social philosophy of the century—was sacrificed to Tudor hostility, there is little cause for wonder that Vives suffered also in England. For Vives was a Spaniard, and Spain was above all dreaded as the foremost country in Europe and in South America, and came into collision with us on the high seas—of the Atlantic, as our chief competitor—in the race for adventure and for wealth. Spain was the foe, which at the time of the marriage of Philip and Mary seemed not unlikely to absorb us. Actual dread was removed by the defeat of the Spanish Armada, but fear was alchemised into a source of bitter enmity against the defeated foe, both on account of the methods of diplomacy employed and the standing feud of religion. Nor must it be forgotten that with the growth of a great national literature, the need of further reliance upon the old great republic of Latin letters was diminishing. Roger Ascham and Richard Mulcaster made bold to write on education in the English language. The claim was proudly made by the latter that no language "be it whatsoever, is better able to utter all arguments" than the English language.

The Tudor unrelenting triumph over the friends of Catharine of Aragon, and the evolution of hatred against Spain, together with the growth of English as a vehicle for educational writing, all helped to crowd out in absorbing counter-interests any attention to the Spanish Vives. Yet it would be a mistake to suppose that though there was but little open recognition of Vives, that his influence was therefore unfelt. Authors on subjects treated by Vives did not hesitate to read him, to profit by him, and to use his ideas, and oftentimes, his very words, but without disclosing the source of their inspiration.

One conspicuous example has recently been carefully elaborated, though not indeed intended to serve as an illustration of the influence of Vives, but simply as the statement of the result of an investigation into the sources of a prose work of one of the great Elizabethan dramatists—the curiously-named *Timber or Discoveries* of Ben Jonson. To M. Castelain is due the announcement in detail of Jonson's indebtedness to Vives[1]. Mr Percy Simpson, in England, independently has made the same discovery[2]. "All that I can now attempt," says Mr Simpson, "is to indicate, by reference rather than quotation —for I should not know where to stop—Jonson's debt to the great humanist, Johannes Ludovicus Vives." One of the sections noted by Mr Simpson as borrowed by Jonson from Vives is the following passage in which Jonson says:

"Wisdom without honesty is mere craft and cozenage. And therefore the reputation of honesty must first be gotten, which cannot be but by living well. A good life is a main argument."

This passage, characteristic of Vives' view of life, occurs amongst the pages of the text of Jonson's *Timber* (Schelling's edition pp. 5, 6) and the two pages are identified by both M. Castelain and Mr Simpson as a free translation of a part of one[3] of Vives' smaller works.

A further passage in the *Timber*, which begins a long section of Schelling's edition (pp. 59–66), is taken from

[1] M. Castelain has enquired into the origins of Ben Jonson's *Timber* with characteristic care and thoroughness. He prints Jonson's English passages side by side with the Latin prototypes in Vives. The parallels are close and sustained in long passages.

[2] In an article entitled: "Tanquam Explorator": Jonson's method in the *Discoveries*, in the *Modern Language Review*, Vol. II. (1907), pp. 201–10.

[3] The *de Consultatione* was composed by Vives at Oxford in 1523. It was written at the suggestion of, and dedicated to, Ludovicus à Flandria, dominus Pratensis. For the Latin of the whole section in Vives see *Vivis Opera* (Majansius' ed. II. pp. 244–8), or in M. Castelain, *Jonson's Discoveries*, pp. 7–9.

another of Vives' works. I only give the first few sentences:

"Speech is the only benefit man hath to express his excellency of mind above other creatures. It is the instrument of society. In all speech, words and sense are as the body and soul. The sense is as the life and soul of language without which all words are dead. Sense is wrought out of experience, the knowledge of human life and action, or of the liberal arts, which the Greeks call 'Εγκυκλοπαιδείαν. Words are the people's, yet there is a choice of them to be made; for *verborum delectus origo est eloquentiae.* They are to be chose[n] according to the persons we make speak, or the things we speak of[1]."

"*Natura non effoeta.* I cannot think Nature is so spent and decayed that she can bring forth nothing worth her former years. She is always the same, like herself; and when she collects her strength is abler still[2]. Men are decayed, and studies: she is not[3]."

"*Non nimium credendum antiquitati.* I know nothing can

[1] Vives, *de Ratione dicendi*, Majansius' ed. II. pp. 94–5. The Latin of Vives is as follows:

"Materia hujus artis est sermo, et haec utique mutuata, non propria: finis bene dicere; artificis autem explicare quae sentiat, aut persuadere quae velit, aut motum animi aliquem excitare, vel sedare. In sermone omni sunt verba et sensa tamquam corpus et animus. Sensa enim mens sunt, et quasi vita verborum; ideo etiam mens et sensus vulgo nominantur. Inanis ac mortua res sunt verba sensu amoto; verba autem sedes sunt sensorum, et veluti lumina in tantis nostrorum animorum involucris. Sed neque sensa tamen neque verba hujus sunt instituti, non magis quam sermo: quippe sensa ex singulis artium petuntur, aut ex prudentia et vita, nempe illa, quam Graeci ἐγκυκλοπαιδείαν appellant: verba sunt populi publica, nullius artis, aut privati juris. Aptatio tamen tum verborum, tum sensuum, quomodo cuique fini applicabuntur, hujus sunt propositi."

[2] Schelling's ed. p. 7. Mr A. C. Swinburne notes "as in the production of Shakespeare—if his good friend Ben had but known it." "How grand is this!" is the remark of Mr Swinburne on this passage, not realising that it is Vives he is praising!

[3] Mr Swinburne says of these words: "Jonson never wrote a finer verse than that [prose]!"

conduce more to letters than to examine the writings of the ancients, and not to rest in their sole authority, or take all upon trust from them, provided the plagues of judging and pronouncing against them be away; such as are envy, bitterness, precipitation, impudence and scurrile scoffing. For [in addition] to all the observations of the ancients, we have our own experience, which, if we will use and apply, we have better means to pronounce. It is true they opened the gates, and made the way that went before us, but as guides, not commanders: *Non domini nostri, sed duces fuere.* Truth lies open to all; it is no man's several. *Patet omnibus veritas; nondum est occupata. Multum ex illa, etiam futuris relictum est.*"

This noble passage in the *Timber* is taken direct from Vives' Preface to the *de Disciplinis*[1]. The fact that such

[1] See pp. 8–9 *infra*. But I cannot forbear the quotation here of Vives' Latin text (Majansius ed. VI. pp. 6–7):

"Porro de scriptis magnorum auctorum existimare multo est litteris conducibilius, quam auctoritate sola acquiescere, et fide semper aliena accipere omnia, absint modo judicandi et pronuntiandi pestes, livor, acerbitas, praecipitatio, impudentia, et dicacitas scurrilis; neque enim effoeta est jam vel exhausta natura, ut nihil prioribus annis simile pariat; eadem est semper sui similis, nec raro tamquam collectis viribus pollentior, ac potentior; qualem nunc esse credi par est robore adjutam et confirmatam, quod sensim per tot secula accrevit. Quantum enim ad disciplinas percipiendas omnes aditum nobis inventa superiorum seculorum aperiunt, et experientia tam diuturna? ut appareat posse nos, si modo applicaremus eodem animum, melius in universum pronuntiare de rebus vitae ac naturae, quam Aristotelem, Platonem, aut quemquam antiquorum, videlicet, post tam longam maximarum et abditarum rerum observationem, quae novae illis ac recentes admirationem magis pariebant sui, quàm cognitionem adferebant. Quid? Aristoteles ipse, annon superiorum omnium placita convellere est ausus? nobis examinare saltem ac censere nefas erit? praesertim quòd, ut Seneca sapienter dicit, *Qui ante nos ista moverunt, non domini nostri, sed duces sunt*: patet omnibus veritas, nondum est occupata: multum ex illa etiam futuris relictum est." The further passage (see p. 9 *infra*, beginning: "I do not profess myself the equal of the ancients...make your stand wherever you think she is") taken by Jonson in the *Timber* quite directly (with omissions) from Vives, receives the comment from Mr Swinburne

passages as those quoted have been regarded as highly suggestive and significant for Jonson[1] to have written, shows that the ideas of Vives, written a hundred years before, could be still regarded as original or as representative of the best progressive thought of a full century later. It might be doubted if anything more eloquent and more distinctive was written by Francis Bacon himself[2], on the hopefulness of the search for truth by the modern thinker, than the substance of the last quoted passage.

Mulcaster was the most original writer on education in the Elizabethan era. He had the courage to acknowledge Vives on one occasion. Mulcaster is speaking against over-haste in the education of boys. He says: "Among many, if onely Vives the learned Spaniard, were called to be witness, he would crave pardon for his own person, as not able to come for the gout, but he would substitute for his deputy his whole twenty books of disciplines, wherein he entreateth how they [pupils] came to spoil [i.e. to be spoiled], and how they may be recovered. Lack of time, not onely in his opinion, but also in whose not? brings lack of learning, which is a sore lack, where it ought not to be lacking[3]."

This one acknowledgment of Vives is to Mulcaster's credit. Yet there are other subjects with regard to which Mulcaster has received high commendation for originality which were already *en évidence* in Vives. First, the vigorous advocacy of the claims of the vernacular. This important factor in Vives' pedagogy I shall consider later[4]. Secondly, the suggestion of conferences of

that it would "be passed over by no eye but a mole's or a bat's." This criticism surely would have been as sound for Vives as for Jonson.

[1] Jonson died in 1637. The *Timber* was published posthumously in 1641. Schelling is of opinion that its composition belongs to the last years of the poet's life.

[2] On the subject of Vives as the pioneer of Bacon, see p. ciii *et seqq*.

[3] *Positions* (1581), Quick's Reprint, p. 259.

[4] See p. cxli *et seqq*.

the teachers of each school. Mulcaster, as Parmentier[1] has pointed out, developed Vives' idea, and suggested conferences between parents and neighbours, between teachers and neighbours, parents and teachers, and finally, conferences between teachers. But the source of this suggestion is apparently to be found in Vives[2]. "Four times a year let the masters meet in some place apart where they may discuss together the nature of their pupils and consult about them." Thirdly, Mulcaster suggests "our school places,...in the heart of towns might easily be chopt [changed] for some field situation, far from disturbance, and near to all necessaries[3]."

At least Mulcaster refers to Vives, but in the case of Roger Ascham it is probable his indebtedness to Vives in matters of education was as great as was that of Mulcaster, but, apparently, there is no more acknowledgment on the part of Ascham in the field of education, to Vives, than there is in the field of literary criticism on the part of Ben Jonson[4]. The parallels, it should be said, in Ascham's case, are not so much verbal as material, and it might therefore be that they are accidental. Still the case is one for inquiry. Vives argues[5] that the wits of boys should be tested before they are committed to learning. He says: "When a father has many sons, let him not destine for study any one he likes just as he would take an egg from a heap to boil or fry, but the one who in his opinion and in that of his friends is best suited for study and erudition. Some parents ..send to school those boys who are unfit for commerce or war, or other civil duties, and order them to be taught,...and

[1] Jacques Parmentier: *Histoire de l'éducation en Angleterre*, p. 14. For Mulcaster's opinions on conferences see *Positions*, Quick's ed. p. 281.

[2] See p. 62 *infra*.

[3] See pp. 53–55 *infra*. Milton makes very similar suggestions to those of Vives, for his Academy. See p. cli note[4] *infra*.

[4] Schelling, Saintsbury and A. C. Swinburne (in his elaborate appreciation of Jonson) seem to have overlooked Vives as a source of Jonson's views.

[5] See p. 83 *infra*.

they devote to God the most contemptible and useless of their offspring, and think that he who has not judgment and intellect for the smallest and most trifling matters has quite enough for such great duties." Ascham says, in the same strain: "For if a father have four sons, three fair and well formed both mind and body, the fourth wretched, lame and deformed, his choice shall be to put the worst to learning as one good enough to become a scholar." The whole subject of the "choice of wits" as developed by both Ascham and Mulcaster, is parallel to the treatment, at length, of the same topic in Vives.

The comparison of quick wits with slow wits, and the preference on the whole for the slow wit, and distrust for precocity is common to Vives and Ascham. The adaptation of the master's methods to the particular individuality of each pupil is emphasised both by Vives and by Ascham. The views on gentleness in teaching and deprecation of severity of punishment for which Ascham has received such deserved praise, are to be found in the spirit of Vives' methods of treating pupils and in his views on punishment[1]. They recommend, in common, the student to take due exercise in games and recreation; Vives adding the suggestion, that the deeper studies of, say, metaphysics, call for still more physical exercise than the simpler subjects of study. Both believe that the early training in good conduct is far more essential than the early acquisition of knowledge. Both reduce grammar study to a minimum in the learning of languages.

It is possible, of course, in these instances, and in many others which might be added to them, that each writer came quite independently to treat on these subjects, and to form his own opinion, and that it happened by chance to be the same in the two writers. Two further instances remain to be considered, in which the agreement is on matters much more specialised in their nature.

There is no method of learning Latin more characteristically

[1] See pp. 118–19 *infra*.

treated by Ascham than his system of Paper-books, two for translations, one to contain translations into English, the second to contain re-translations back to Latin, and the third to contain, under certain headings, the pupil's collections of instances of the use of words, phrases and expressions, and grammatical forms found in his reading of authors—properly classified; in fact, a self-made dictionary of words, phrases, syntax, and memorabilia. We, in our days, are, of course, accustomed to a system of note-books, and it may seem that this is another of the devices which might occur to educational thinkers independently. Yet Ascham has received high credit for the idea, and, in any case, the suggestion of the plan a full generation earlier involves even more credit to the earlier thinker. The old teaching methods of the Middle Ages were oral, and the change to writing methods is very critical in the history of education. The early suggestion of Paper-books was, therefore, more startling than we are apt to realise. Note-books became a recognised necessity only after the invention of printing, and as we know commonplace books developed into an institution with the scholars in the first half of the 16th century. Nevertheless it might readily have happened that Paper-books for pupils might have been delayed as a device for school purposes, had it not been for the suggestion of enthusiastic educationists. For written methods were revolutionary; and the memories of schoolmasters and boys were better trained than in modern times. Schoolmasters, parents and boys tended to conservative methods, and these countenanced the learning by heart of intricate grammars, such, for instance, as that of the authorised Lily, even in the time of Ascham, and, in prior generations, of those barbarous and effete works of which Erasmus so bitterly complains, and which he so scathingly satirises. Such methods required no use of note-books. The boldness of Ascham's suggestion[1]

[1] A further practical objection to the use of Paper-books was the cost of paper. Sir E. M. Thompson says paper was first used for College and

is apparent, when we realise that he dares to dispense with the time-honoured grammars, and merely asks for the "three concords learned" and the simple declension of nouns and conjugations of verbs before the reading of authors. Whatever may be in store for the twentieth century, it is perfectly certain that the nineteenth century did not attain to the attractive simplicity of this idea of Ascham of dispensing with grammar books and setting the pupil to collect the accidence and syntax himself, as he proceeds in his reading of authors and his own translation and re-translation, and of building up a grammar for himself in his Note-book. Such an idea, relatively to the cumbrous methods of the teaching of the Middle Ages, deserves to rank high as a discovery in language-teaching. And Ascham certainly deserves the acclamation of all teachers for its advocacy. It is not without significance for his adoption of a Note-book method that Ascham was a calligrapher. At any rate he emphasised written methods in the pupil's work as no one had done in England before him.

But all the more, if there was an earlier pioneer in this important method of teaching, we must be prepared, not to withdraw our admiration for Ascham, but to admit Ascham's predecessor to a similar recognition, and to that further consideration which priority of advocacy confers.

Vives, in his work *On the Transmission of Knowledge* (1531)[1], describes in more systematic and realistic detail than Ascham the Paper-book method, and delivers his soul on the whole art of language note-taking. But earlier still[2], in 1523, he had

Municipal Records in the 14th century. The first manufactory of paper in England was in the early part of the 16th century. Paper in schools had to be provided at the cost of the parent, as is seen in the Orders for St Albans School, 1590.

[1] See p. 108 *infra*, beginning l. 5, "Let them be convinced," to the end of the second paragraph on that page.

[2] In the *de Ratione Studii Puerilis*, dated London, 1523, dedicated to Charles Mountjoy, son of William Mountjoy, the pupil and friend of Erasmus.

suggested the method requiring the pupil actually to construct for himself the Paper-book in which he was further to enter his own grammatical collections. Vives gives full directions, and as this is appaently the first mention of any such system, the full details are of interest:

"Make a book of blank leaves of a proper size. Divide it into certain topics, so to say, into nests (nidos). In one, jot down the names of those subjects of daily converse, e.g. the mind, body, our occupations, games, clothes, divisions of time, dwellings, foods; in another, rare words, exquisitely fit words; in another, idioms, and *formulae dicendi*, which either few understand or which require often to be used; in another, *sententiae*; in another, joyous expressions; in another, witty sayings; in another, proverbs; in another, difficult passages in authors; in another, other matters which seem worthy of note to thy teacher or thyself. So that thou shalt have all these noted down and digested. Then will thy book alone know what must be read by thee, to be read, committed and fixed to the memory, so that thou mayest bear in thy breast the names thus handed down, which are in thy book and refer to them as often as is necessary. For it is little good to possess learned books if your mind is unfurnished for studying them."

And in 1524, Vives wrote on the same subject:

"Thou shalt have alwayes at hande a paper booke, wherein thou shalt wryte suche notable thynges as thou readest thy selfe, or hearest of other men worthi to be noted, be it other feate sentence or worde, meete for familiar speeche, that thou mayest have in a redynes, when tyme requyreth[1]."

These passages establish the position that Vives has priority

[1] *Introductio ad Sapientiam*, Antwerp, 1524. This was translated into English by Sir Richard Moryson, *c.* 1540, as *An Introduction to Wisdom*. The quotation above is given from his version in the section: "Of the Mynde." The *Introduction to Wisdom* is a small manual for the student at the beginning of his studies, consisting of wise and moral maxims to be kept in mind by all who devote themselves to letters.

over Ascham in the matter of Paper-books, and it is difficult to believe that the tutor of Queen Elizabeth was not aware of Vives' views. For Vives had been the tutor of the Princess Mary, the half-sister of Elizabeth, and, as we have just seen, Vives made known his views in three different works.

The other great feature of Ascham's method of teaching Latin was double translation—i.e. translation from a Latin author into English, followed, after an interval, by re-translation from the English back into Latin. Vives also recommended double translation[1] but in the reverse order. Passages in the vernacular were to be translated into Latin, and afterwards re-translated into the vernacular. Vives wished to secure that the teacher in the first place gave the pupil passages of good vernacular[2]. Good Latin was actually more accessible, e.g. in Cicero. Ascham wished the boy to be familiarised with Cicero, and risked the sort of English into which he would render Cicero, and from which he would re-translate. The fact is that each system requires supplementing by equal attention from the teacher, in providing good standards for both the Latin and the vernacular. But as with the Paper-book, so with Double Translation, Vives was also a protagonist before Ascham.

Finally, Ascham refers to mediaeval romances in terms of deprecation which readily recall Vives' attacks, many years earlier. Ascham introduces the subject of this "fayned chevalrie" both in the *Scholemaster* and in the *Toxophilus*. Both Vives and Ascham ascribe the pleasure felt by the readers of these romances as due to love of slaughter and of licentiousness. But Ascham improves the occasion, by ascribing the

[1] See pp. 113–14 *infra*. Samuel Johnson said that Ascham's *Scholemaster* contains "perhaps the best advice that was ever given for the study of languages." Yet Ascham's advice is mainly the same as that of Vives.

[2] There is no doubt lack of knowledge of the vernacular by schoolmasters themselves, in England, was a formidable difficulty in teaching good Latin in the early Tudor period. See p. cxliii *infra*.

composition of books such as the *Morte d'Arthur* to "idle monks and wanton canons, in our forefather's time when Papistry, as a standing pool, covered and overflowed all England." Vives, on the other hand, attributes their vogue to the fact that their readers have never tasted the delights of reading Cicero, Seneca or St Jerome.

It must be remembered that if Ascham in these cases did borrow (or as "the wise term it, 'conveyed'") from Vives, the doctrine of Imitation which he held, justified, or rather required, that changes should be made in the "conveyance." Imitation, according to Ascham[1] (and the humanists of his age) consists not only in similar treatment of dissimilar subject-matter, but also in the dissimilar treatment of similar subject-matter (*similis materiei dissimilis*). If Ascham had Vives in mind, as Erasmus clearly had when he dealt with amatory stories and songs[2], he carried out his own precepts in regard to Imitation, not by "conveying," in the exact words, but by the use of the similar subject-matter of Romances and their evil influence on sound living and sound learning, whilst he introduced the dissimilar treatment of ascribing the origin and development of the evil to Papistry and Abbeys and Monasteries, and also obtained in the subject-matter of Romances a background for his argument against the "books made in Italy."

It is perhaps possible, in this general way, without entering into further details, to indicate the possible grounds for the inclusion of Vives, as a member of the Triumvirate of letters in the early part of the 16th century, and to account for his decadence in estimation, in England, in the later part of the same century. He paid the price of loyalty to Catharine of Aragon, in his life-time and in his reputation after his death.

[1] The *Scholemaster* (Mayor's ed.) p. 139.

[2] In the *de Matrimonio Christiano*, 1526 (1650 ed. p. 430). For the passages on Romance-reading, by Vives, see Foster Watson, *Vives and the Renascence Education of Women*, pp. 58–9 and 196, and in the *de Causis Corruptarum Artium*, at the end of Bk II. Majansius ed. VI. p. 109.

However we explain such facts, it is clear that the advocacy of views by Vives in literary criticism and on education, which have brought fame and distinction to Ben Jonson and to Ascham (and I take those as typical examples), although the latter two had the advantage of browsing on the rich pasturage bequeathed by the whole of the first half of the 16th century, justifies the interest in asking and answering the question: Who was Vives?

# CHAPTER II

## JUAN LUIS VIVES

By birth, Juan Luis Vives was a Spaniard, of the city of Valencia. He received his school education at Valencia, and spent his college life in the University of Paris. His manhood was spent in Louvain and Bruges, chiefly the latter, with, between 1522 and 1528, portions of the year spent in residence in England. It will be convenient to deal with the formative influences in his development in connexion with those cities in which he lived.

### (1) *Vives at Valencia.*

Vives was born in the year of the discovery of America by Columbus, 1492; a few days after the Moorish Granada fell into the hands of Ferdinand and Isabella. His father's Christian name was also Luis. His mother's maiden name was Blanca March. He was baptised in the Church of St Agnes, a church which still remains in Valencia. The house in which he was born is described by Vives himself[1]. Vives' father was sprung from an old Spanish noble family tracing itself to the branch known as Vives del Vergel or Verger[2]. The arms of this family consisted of a square in the azure ground of which there rose a plant of golden-yellow

[1] In the School Dialogues (*Exercitatio Latinae Linguae*, 1539) one of the dialogues entitled *Leges Ludi*, with the sub-title "A varied dialogue on the city of Valencia," refers to the house.

[2] Majansius gives an elaborate genealogy of Vives, showing the nobility of his family. See *Opera*, vol. I. immediately before the beginning of the life.

colour[1] which the Spaniards call *Perpetuas* or *Siempre Vivas*, and the French *immortelles.* Vives' mother, Blanca March, was also of illustrious descent, and proudly claimed several well-known poets amongst her ancestry. Nevertheless the parents of Vives were only of moderate means. They were united by a strong tie of affection which is worthily recorded by their son[1]:

"My mother Blanche when she had been fifteen years married unto my father, I could never see her strive with my father. There were two sayings that she had ever in her mouth as proverbs. When she would say she believed well anything, then she used to say, even as though Luis Vives had spoken it. When she would say that she would [wished] anything, she used to say, even as though Luis Vives would it. I have heard my father say many times, but especially once, when one told him of a saying of Scipio Africanus the younger, or else of Pomponius Atticus, and I ween it were the saying of them both, that they never made agreement with their mothers, 'nor I with my wife said he, which is a greater thing.'" The son tells us that the "concord of Vives and Blanche" became a proverb in Valencia. But with the reserve characteristic of filial *pietas* he adds: "But it is not to be much talked of in a book made for another purpose, of my most holy mother, whom I doubt not now to have in heaven the fruit and reward of her pure and holy living." Yet Vives treasured up in his thoughts the idea of writing a "book of her acts and life[2]."

[1] In the *Institution of a Christian Woman* (Hyrde's translation), see Foster Watson, *Vives and the Renascence Education of Women*, p. 117.

[2] In Vives' Commentaries on St Augustine, *de Civitate Dei* (translated by John Healey, 2nd ed. 1620), p. 439, there is a dictum of his mother recorded: "My mother Blanche, a modest matron (or piety deceives me), had wont to tell me when I was a child that the sirens sung sweetly in a tempest and lamented in fair weather: hoping the latter in the first, and fearing the first in the later." For, Vives observes, happiness is far better after misery than misery after happiness.

It has indeed been said that in Vives is to be marked the first appearance in modern times of literary tribute by a scholar to the virtues of a mother, and it is probable that we should have to search far in the documents of the Middle Ages to find the record of such high delight in recalling a mother's influence. It is a new channel or at least a much deeper channel in which the humanist elemental joy in life found expression. Whether Vives was the first of the humanists to dwell on the theme or not, his words strike home in their sincerity.

The mother who took pains with the boy's training rather belonged to the old Roman, or even Spartan, type. She is thus described: "No mother loved her child better than mine did me, nor any child did ever less perceive himself loved of his mother than I. She never lightly laughed upon me, she never cockered me, and yet when I had been three or four days out of her house, she wist not where, she was almost sore sick; and when I was come home, I could not perceive that ever she longed for me. Therefore there was no body that I did more flee, or was more loath to come nigh, than my mother when I was a child. But after I came to young man's estate, there was nobody whom I delighted more to have in sight; whose memory now I have in reverence, and as oft as she cometh to my remembrance, I embrace her within my mind and thought, when I cannot with my body[1]."

With human graciousness, though without ecclesiastical sanction, Vives includes his mother amongst the saints, with Agnes, Catharine, Agatha, Margaret, Barbara, Monica, etc., "although," he says, "I do fear to be reproved that I do thus commend my mother, giving myself too much to love and pity, the which truly doth take much place in me, but—" he eagerly adds, "yet the truth much more[2]."

[1] *Vives and the Renascence Education of Women*, p. 131.

[2] In the *Office and Duties of an Husband* (Thomas Paynell's translation of Vives' *de Officio Mariti*, 1529). See Foster Watson, *Vives and the Renascence Education of Women*, p. 208.

Vives was to become the pioneer in the advocacy of the vernacular as the instrument of education, at least half a century before Mulcaster. How far the pleas which arose in the 16th century for the recognition and use of the vernacular were made by educationists who had the good fortune to be well-trained by their mothers, in the early years, would be an interesting inquiry. But we are left in no doubt as to the inspiring cause of Vives' interest in the mother-tongue, and his belief in the high part mothers could accomplish in this matter. "Let the mother," he says[1], "give her diligence, at leastwise because of her children, that she use no rude and blunt speech, lest that manner of speaking take such root in the tender minds of the children, and so grow and increase together with their age, that they cannot forget it. Children will learn no speech better, nor more plainly express, than they will their mother's. For they will counterfeit both the virtue and the vice, if there be any in it."

In connexion with his own Spanish language, Vives recognises the historical importance of having been born in Valencia. He notes that James the Conqueror, the king of Aragon, conquered Valencia in 1238, delivering it from the Moors, and introduced into it men from Aragon and Lérida, "So the children that came from them both, with all their posterity *kept their mother's language, which we speak there unto this day*[2]." Vives was writing in 1523, and thus for nearly three hundred years there had been a steady development of the mother-tongue in the city of Valencia, and self-defence against the Moors made it a matter of patriotism to take a pride in its use. Circumstances such as these must be taken into account in tracing to its origin Vives' interest in the vernacular and the advocacy of its use in early education, together with incidental passages showing a breadth of view in regard to the historical study of the vernacular, and its employment even in

[1] *Vives and the Renascence Education of Women*, p. 124.

[2] *Ibid.*, p. 124

composition, and as a field for style[1], altogether foreign to Erasmus and with few exceptions[2] to the other humanists of the early part of the 16th century.

It may be added that Vives owed his love of the Spanish language to his mother and his home, and not to the public school of Valencia to which he went.

This school (*gymnasium*) had been restored by Pope Alexander VI in 1500 and by Ferdinand the Catholic in 1502[3]. There is a description of the school itself in one of Vives' works[4]. It is always of value to consider the kind of teachers under whom an important man has studied at school.

1 See on the relation of Vives to the vernacular, pp. cxli–cxliv.

2 In Spain we shall see directly that Antonio de Lebrija favoured the vernacular; in Italy Bembo.

3 Comprehensive historical notes as to the school and the course of instruction in it are given in Majansius, p. 10 *et seqq.*, and in Bonilla y San Martín, chap. I.

4 *The Ovatio Virginis Mariae* (1st printed 1519) in Majansius' ed. VII. p. 127. The passage is spoken in the name of Siso, one of Vives' schoolmasters: "There is a place at the first entrance into the schools which becomes easily muddy with the crowd of scholars who have walked through the rain and the dust. When you have got over this a little you come upon a high flight of stairs, which lead to decorated bedrooms, and halls in which teaching is carried on. It is very well provided, as I hope, with the very best teachers who will come to the place. The forecourt is often somewhat dark, but the arcades are not unpleasant. There is a great cerulean stone under the stair-case, on which very often packmen, if they have anything new, flock together to sell their books, as if they were condemned to live on the stone. It was when Daniel reclined on that stone that Michael Ariguus and Parthenius Tovar the poet came to him, for the latter had only arrived a short time before, from Murviedro (Saguntum). I, at that time only a youth, used to follow Parthenius about. You know, Christophorus, and you, Vives, what a noble, serious and eloquent poet he was, not much inferior to that poet of the same name whom Tiberius Caesar suggested was worthy of imitation." The *Ovatio* contains the first reference in Vives' writings to Erasmus. On this point, of considerable interest in the history of the relations between the two, see Lange (in Schmid and Schrader's *Encyklopädie*, 2nd ed. 1887, Band IX., Abteilung 3, p. 780, and Bonilla y San Martín, pp. 37 and 67).

One of the teachers of Grammar at the Valencian school was Jerome Amiguet, who is described by Majansius[1] as notable in his barbarism (*insigniter barbarus*). He edited the *Sinonima* of Stephen Fliscus in 1500. Another teacher was Daniel Siso. He had written in 1490 a *Compendium* of grammar and Vives calls him a "good man and serious theologian[2]." Bonilla[3] conjectures that Vives may have learned Greek from Bernard Villanova ó Navarro. Reading between the lines it becomes evident that the school was still mediaeval in tone, continuing the traditions of Donatus, Priscian, Alexander de Villa Dei, and the other grammarians steeped in the intricacies of mystic grammar as a preparation to the didactic disputations which characterised the Universities. There is one incident of Vives' school-days which requires notice. Amiguet vigorously opposed the introduction of the new *Institutiones grammaticae* of Antonio Calà, Harana Del Ojo, better known as Antonius Nebrissensis (i.e. of the city of Lebrixa or Lebrija). Antony had returned from his studies continued for ten years at Bologna and other Italian Universities in 1473, and brought with him the knowledge of classical authors, which he wished to expound in Spain, and the new light on linguistic studies generally from the Italian Renascence. Hallam says[4] "Lebrixa became to Spain what Valla was to Italy, Erasmus to Germany or Budaeus to France....By the lectures which he read in the Universities of Seville, Salamanca and Alcalá, and by the institutes[5] which he published on Castilian, on Latin, Greek and Hebrew grammar, Lebrixa contributed in a wonderful

[1] *Vivis Opera*, vol. I. p. 10. Majansius gives the evidence for this characterisation of Amiguet's Latinity. It may be noted that Amiguet produced an edition in 1500 of an English author, viz. Thomas Bradwardine's *Arithmetic* and *Geometry*, the latter of which was recommended in Vives' account of Mathematics. See p. 207 *infra*.

[2] Majansius' *Life*, I. pp. 19, 20.

[3] *Luis Vives*, p. 38.

[4] Quoting from McCrie's *History of the Reformation in Spain*, p. 61.

[5] *Institutiones Grammaticae*, published at Seville in 1481.

degree to expel barbarism from the seats of education, and to diffuse a taste for elegant and useful studies among his countrymen." Lebrixa was the compiler of the first Spanish grammar and dictionary.

To innovations of this kind the older grammarians were determinedly opposed. It is related[1] that Amiguet gave the boy Vives exercises in the routine disputations of the school to prepare invectives against the revolutionary Lebrixa. The warmly loyal boy had no hesitation in espousing the cause which his master supported. For to the boy's imagination his master was sure to be right in his judgments. Accordingly in 1507 Vives, at the beginning of his sixteenth year, made orations in opposition to the foremost scholar[2] in Spain, who had set himself to bring into that country the new light of the Italian Renascence and to extirpate the barbarism which oppressed the teachers and scholars. The story runs that not content with spoken declamations, Vives took in hand his pen and wrote them out.

Vives, thus, is an excellent representative of the Renascence,

[1] Gaspar de Escolano, *Decada primera de la historia de Valencia* (1610), lib. v. cap. xx. pp. 1037, 1057. Quoted by F. Kayser: Vives' *Schriften*, p. 131.

[2] There were others worthy of high consideration who should perhaps be named, since they influenced Vives at a later stage. Arias Barbosa, who had also studied for years in Italy, under Politian and others, came in 1489 to Salamanca, where he taught for many years Greek and rhetoric. He later undertook the duties of tutor in the Portuguese Royal Family. Barbosa was the great Spanish scholar in the Greek language. The brothers John and Francis Vergara were professors at Alcalá. Vives refers to Juan Vergara as his pupil in the *Transmission of Knowledge* (p. 207 *infra*). There is also a letter from Vives to John Vergara (*Vivis Opera*, VII. p. 148). Nuñez de Guzman wrote the Latin version for the Complutensian Polyglot, and was many years professor at Salamanca and afterwards at Alcalá. There was also the learned Juan Martínez Poblacion, a native of Valencia, of whom Vives wrote: "I will avouch his theory in physic so exact, that either the ancient physicians never wrote of [a certain disease], or if they did, their books are lost and perished" (in *Commentaries on St Augustine's Civitas Dei*, Healey's translation, p. 845).

since he ran through in his own person the whole gamut of progress from the orthodox mediaeval scholar to that of one of the most advanced Renascence thinkers. In the course of his progress, he had the opportunity of reversing his earliest opinions regarding Lebrixa, and paying mature tribute to his scholarship and judgment[1].

The mediaeval routine grammar and disputational training he received at school was probably a small part of what he imbibed from his native Valencia. The training in his home was not confined to the influence of his father and mother and sister. His maternal grandfather, Henry March, was a jurisconsult, and had begun to train Vives in the subject of law, a study in which he was deeply interested, as can be seen in the *Transmission of Knowledge*[2].

It is not known how many years Vives spent at the Valencia gymnasium[3]. But he was born in 1492, and he left Valencia for Paris in 1509, and he was certainly at the gymnasium in 1507 and 1508. We shall not be far wrong, probably, if we conclude that though Vives did not owe a great deal, in his early training, to the school, yet in the early influences of his home[4] and home-surroundings there was much that served as the bed-rock of his character and intellect. For wherever he went, in his wanderings as a scholar, he carried with him, as has been said, the sound of the bells of Valencia's reputed three hundred churches.

He has himself described the attractiveness of his native city. When Everard de la Marck, bishop of Liège[5], was

[1] In 1531, when Vives published the *de Disciplinis*, he had altered his opinion regarding Antony de Lebrixa. See p. lvi n[2].

[2] See pp. 262–71 *infra*. Vives also wrote the *Ædes Legum*, *Vivis Opera*, v. pp. 483–93.

[3] This same institution is called a school, gymnasium, and a university, by different writers.

[4] Vives' father is supposed to have died about 1507 or 1508, and his mother a few years afterwards.

[5] A friend to humanistic studies, to whom Erasmus dedicated his *Paraphrases* on the Epistles of St Paul to the Corinthians.

appointed to the Archbishopric of Valencia in 1520, Vives, then at Louvain, was stirred to show good-will to a distinguished man, going to his own city, and dedicated to him one of his small works[1]. In this dedication, Vives *de plein cœur*, describes the *genius loci*: "Which shall I first congratulate, on your election as Archbishop of Valencia, reverend Father, and most illustrious Prince, yourself, or my fellow-citizens and myself? For both parties must be congratulated." Vives then praises the natural beauty of the district in and around Valencia, and the "humanity" of the nobles and gentry there, "with whom intimate intercourse will never pall." He concludes by saying the charms of Valencia are greater than can be compressed into a letter. "I speak of my country as of my possessions, somewhat modestly, lest my words should afford ground for the suspicion that I am boasting."

The natural features of Valencia burnt themselves into the consciousness of Vives as a youth. In the latest of his books which he wrote for boys, the School Dialogues[2], there are several passages, which hint at a joy in nature and an observation of the district, which show a love of Valencia, not dissimilar to that of the distinguished living Spanish novelist Blasco Ibañez, also a Valencian[3]. The same features are common to the older and the present Valencian,—the nightingale, the wonderful sky, the rich fruit, the scent of flowers, and so on. When Vives wrote the School Dialogues, at Breda in Brabant, surely we may trace what his boyhood had built up in him at Valencia from such a passage as the following:

"Let us go on the green walk, and not take it as if in

[1] Viz. *Joannis Ludovici Vivis Valentini Somnium, quae est Praefatio ad Somnium Scipionis Ciceroniani. Vivis Opera* II. p. 62.

[2] The *Exercitatio*, 1539 (translated in Foster Watson's *Tudor School-boy Life*. The passage quoted occurs pp. 88–90).

[3] Translations are given of nature-passages from Ibañez in A. F. Calvert's *Valencia and Murcia*, pp. 3–7.

a rush, but slowly and gently. Let us make the circuit of the city walls twice or three times and contemplate the splendid view the more peacefully and freely." Surely he was not thinking of the Netherlands but of Spanish Valencia when he goes on to describe spring.

[After contemplating the view] Joannius says:

"There is no sense which has not a lordly enjoyment! First the eyes! what varied colours, what clothing of the earth, and trees! what tapestry! what paintings are comparable with this view?...Not without truth has the Spanish poet, Juan de Mena, called May the painter of the earth. Then the ear. How delightful to hear the singing of birds, and especially the nightingale. Listen to her (as she sings in the thicket) from whom, as Pliny says, issues the modulated sound of the completed science of music....In very fact you have, as it were, the whole study and school of music in the nightingale. Her little ones ponder and listen to the notes, which they imitate. The tiny disciple listens with keen intentness (would that our teachers received like attention!) and gives back the sound. And then again they are silent. The correction by example and a certain criticism from the teacher-bird are closely observed[1]. But Nature leads them aright, whilst human beings exercise their wills wrongly. Add to this there is a sweet scent breathing in from every side, from the meadows, from the crops, and from the trees, even from the fallow land and the neglected fields! Whatsoever you lift to your mouth has its relish, as even from the very air itself, like the earliest and softest honey."

Vives thus reveals himself as an observer and lover of Nature, even in a book designed for Latin exercises. "After the last returns the first." The mature man in Brabant returned to the memories of his Valencian boyhood. The boy's unconscious and undirected training in sense observation

[1] This clearly anticipates the main principle of the interesting naturalist W. J. Long in his *School of the Woods*.

was the preparation for insight into the problems of Nature-study, and the advocacy of sense observation as a necessary part of early education. For it was Vives, and not Bacon, as is sometimes supposed, who first insisted on the significance of Nature-observation, and the necessity of sense training as a basis for intellectual education. And, as we saw in connexion with the advocacy of the vernacular in education, so in his attitude to Nature-study and to sense training, Vives is on the whole pressing forward far more distinctively than Erasmus on to the highroad of modern scientific and educational progress. It is clear that his early life at Valencia was a formative factor in bringing him to this realistic attitude.

In addition to the city of his birth we must also recognise that that nationality to which he belonged by birth was always near to his heart[1]. When Vives left Spain to go to Paris he went amongst Spanish friends. When, in after years, he describes his experiences in Paris, it is to his Spanish teachers he refers, as it was his school teachers at Valencia that he remembered affectionately, despite the fact that they belonged to the old order. When Vives came to England it was to the court of his compatriot, Catharine of Aragon. When he spent the last years at Bruges, he sought that city because there was a Spanish quarter there. Once, when ill at Louvain, he removed to Bruges to have a Spanish physician at hand and the comfort of Spanish nursing. He married a lady of Spanish descent, of a collateral branch of his own family, at Bruges. And, finally, he himself tells us, as the highest commendation that he can pass on Bruges, that it seems to him from its Spanish connexions to be a second Valencia.

In all this family, local, and national attraction, he is

[1] The effect of the Spanish influence on England in connexion with the education of women is traced in *Vives and the Renascence Education of Women* (Introduction). The Age of Ferdinand and Isabella, into the results of which Vives entered, were to Spain roughly what the Elizabethan Age was to England a century later.

far removed from Erasmus. Vives always carried his past with him, and built on it as the basis of his development and the evolution of his ideas, even when incorporating freely, gladly and critically from his environment, including in that term his reading of the ancients and the experience of the present. Erasmus was in revolt against his own past. He acknowledged no father-land. He formed no intimate local ties. He was a free-lance, an iconoclast. He towered above the world in his detachment. His lonely greatness in some degree hindered that sense of sympathy with the mass of men that is so essential to the inspiring educationist. He built up no system of educational thought. If he mercilessly attacked mediaeval Aristotelian dialectic, he offered no suggestions for a new logic. If he scathingly attacked the old grammars of Alexander de Villa Dei, or Eberhard, or the *Florista*, he himself devised no grammar on a new and approved model, though he revised that of Colet and Lily. As an educationist his strength was largely on the negative side. Vives it is true wrote on the *Corruptions of the Arts* and was thus far negative. But his real educational interest was constructive, as was shown in the *Transmission of Knowledge*.

Vives is more in line with the beginnings of modern educational developments because his early formative influences of attachment to home, city, nation, were more in accordance with what have become the essential conditions of later educational practice than were those of Erasmus.

## (2) *Vives at Paris.*

In 1509 Vives left the Valencian school or university and proceeded to Paris. He was now 17 years of age. He attended the courses of the Collège de Beauvais[1]. According to the organisation of the University of Paris from the 12th century

[1] Emile Vanden Bussche, *Luiz Vives: Un Mot.* In *La Flandre* (1876), p. 298.

students were divided into four Nations[1]. The "Nation" of the Gauls included Paris, Sens, Rheims, Tours and Bourges. It was to this last-named division that Italians and Spanish were attached[2]. All students were supposed to come already equipped with a knowledge of the elements of reading, writing, grammar, i.e. Latin grammar, and with a certain amount of training in disputation, and in fact with all the preparatory studies in the liberal arts[3] desirable for a prolonged dialectical course. All these studies served the purpose of training for theology, law, medicine, which were acquired by dialectical and disputational methods. The chief text-books[4] used in the University were the *Catholicon* of Johannes de Janua, the *Vocabularium* of Hugotio or of Papias, the *Mammetractus* or *Mammotrectus* of Giovanni Marchesini, the *Floretus* or *Cornutus* of Johannes de Garlandia, the *Doctrinale* of Alexander de Villa Dei, the *Graecismus* of Eberhard of Béthune, the *Legenda Aurea*[5] *Sanctorum* of Jacobus de Voragine, the *Specula* of Vincent of Beauvais, the *Summulae* of Peter Hispanus and of Paul Venetus.

The "masters" who taught Vives at Paris were Gaspar Lax, a Spaniard, and John Dullard, who came from Ghent. Moreover, the Spanish teachers and students have received the reputation of being at that time the narrowest and most abstruse dialecticians[6], and it was amongst these that Vives

[1] These were the "honourable" nation of the Gauls, the "venerable" nation of the Normans, the "most faithful" nation of the Picards, and the "most constant" nation of the Germans, which included England.

[2] Bonilla, p. 46.

[3] The trivium of grammar, dialectic, rhetoric, and the quadrivium of arithmetic, geometry, astronomy and music.

[4] Bonilla, p. 50.

[5] For Vives' criticism on the *Legenda Aurea*, see p. cxlviii.

[6] Bonilla remarks that many Spaniards were amongst the most decided champions of the reactionary hosts and names the following: Juan de Celaya (from Valencia), Professor in the Collège de Ste Barbara at Paris; Fernando de Enzinas, a master in the Collège de Beauvais at Paris; the three brothers Coroneles, one of whom was rector of the Collège de

probably mixed during his residence in Paris. When the time came that he opened up his incisive and overwhelming attack on the Parisian schools, it is characteristic that Lax[1] and Dullard are mentioned with the affectionate respect and regard that Vives felt for teachers (and for old associations) whatever their intellectual limitations.

John Dullard struck the keynote of conservatism in studies when he laid down time after time to his pupil the *dictum*: The better a man is versed in the reading of authors the worse dialectician and theologian he will become[2]. The significance of the fight between Mediaevalism and the Renascence is often reduced to the question of pre-eminence between grammar and rhetoric on the one side and dialectic or logic on the other. It must, however, always be understood that couched in these terms grammar and rhetoric stand for the critical reading and study of authors.

Vives has entered into the fullest explanation of the whole conflict, and although it would take us too far afield to present an exposition in detail, yet a general account, gathered as far as possible from Vives himself, will enable us to understand what residence in Paris had meant to him in the years from

Montaigu in Paris; Juan Dolz del Castellar, Professor at the Collège de Lyons at Paris, and eight other Spaniards, leaders of the time in Paris.

[1] Gaspar Lax is one of the interlocutors in Vives' *Sapientis Inquisitio*, which gives a sketch of the studies of the time.

[2] Quoties illud mihi Johannes Dullardus ingessit: *Quanto eris melior grammaticus, tanto peior dialecticus et theologus.* (Bk II. chap. 2, *de Causis Corruptarum Artium.*) Vives explains himself, in another passage, that he means by a *grammaticus* the teacher who helps the pupil to understand what is to be learned from written books, e.g. poets, historians, etc. Hence, he says, the *grammaticus* is called *litteratus*. As an instance of the dignity which should attach to the *grammaticus* he instances the Spanish Antonius Nebrissensis "who for his varied and far-reaching erudition, versed as he was in every kind of writer, might have assumed any description or title he liked, yet preferred to be called and esteemed nothing so much as to be a *grammaticus*," *de Causis Corruptarum Artium*, bk II. cap. 2, Majansius ed. VI. pp. 84–5.

1509 to 1514, and its decisive importance in his intellectual development. For the result of Vives' quarrel with the dialecticians and scholastic philosophers of Paris, and his protagonism of the "reading of authors," was, as Lange says, that "he broke the bridge behind him," and went forward, in his intellectual outlook, to meet the future half-way.

In 1519, after he had left Paris five years, he wrote at Louvain (where the study of "good letters" counted) a treatise in the form of a letter to a young friend from Louvain, named John Sterck or Fortis[1], a student in the University of Paris. This book was entitled *In Pseudo-dialecticos*[2]. In it Vives gave examples of the obscurities and barbarisms which characterised the logicians or dialecticians, who tyrannised over every branch of knowledge as within their scope. He showed how they had hindered the advance of literature by their use of corrupt, and too often meaningless, terminology and language, all leading to wild and outrageous incorrectness of thought and speech. They cannot be understood by Latinists, nor even by one another. Yet the technical language of dialectic is a sort of Latin. Were it brought into the light of the ordinary vernacular, intelligible to the crowd, "the whole host of working men, with hisses and clamour and the clanging of their tools, would hoot dialecticians out of the city. For they would seem bereft of wits, and of ordinary common sense." If dialectic used the vernacular as its instrument, the true

[1] Félix Nève (*Collège des Trois Langues*, p. 387) can hardly be right in identifying this John Fortis with the John Fortis who was President of Busleiden's College at Louvain. For the latter was director of the Collège de Saint Donat in 1517, and was transferred to the headship of Busleiden's College in 1520, and could not, therefore, have been a student in Paris in 1519. The John Fortis at Paris may have been the President's son, in whom Vives may have been interested for the father's sake as well as for his own.

[2] The subject is also treated in the following works of Vives: the dialogue: *Sapientis Inquisitio* (1538), *de Disputatione* (1531), and of course in *de Causis Corruptarum Artium* (1531).

could be sifted from the false arguments by everybody. "But he who does not understand the jargon of the dialecticians is deceived in the beginning of his studies, and the further he proceeds the further he goes wrong. It is certain that the pseudo-Latin they employ would not be understood by Cicero if he came to life again. But, not only so, there is none of the pseudo-dialecticians who can possibly speak with such circumspection as not to sin constantly against even his own most empty rules and forms.

Vives is satisfied that in its origin the Disputation was justifiable. The earliest object was, rightly enough, the attempt to fix more deeply what had been taught by the teacher. There had been, amongst the older men, formerly, a comparison of opinions and reasons, not the intent absorption on victory, but on the elucidation of truth. The name "Disputation" bears witness that the original intention of the practice was that the subject-matter of thought should be pruned or purged of all falsity, so that the truth might emerge. Afterwards, praise and reward were bestowed by an audience on the best debater. From praise often came riches and wealth. "The depraved desire of honour or money penetrated the minds of disputants, and just as in a prize fight, victory alone, not the elucidation of truth, became the aim."

The Disputation had taken possession of the whole field of education as the prevailing method. It was not limited to the practical training of the theologian, the lawyer, the physician, as an instrument for the discovery of truth. And, to further complete its downfall in the universities, dialectic borrowed from metaphysics and clouded the minds of all kinds of students with disputations on "*realitates*, *formalitates*, *entitates*, *de modo significandi vocum*: on which Scotus, Albertus Saxo, and Boethius have written as well as the book whose title is *de Scholarium disciplina*[1], than which," adds Vives,

[1] This book, of pseudo-Boethius authorship, in the opinion of Sir William Hamilton, was written by Thomas Cantipratensis in the first

"I think nothing in the whole corruption of the arts was ever more inaptly or foolishly conceived."

By 1519, when Vives was writing the *In Pseudo-dialecticos*, he had already become a friend of Erasmus, and it was in this year that Erasmus had said to More that no man was better fitted than Vives "to utterly overwhelm the battalions of the dialecticians." Vives, indeed, almost rose to the high satirical vein of his friend and senior[1] when he wrote in his later work on *The Causes of the Corruptions of the Arts*, in 1531—on the way in which boys' schools had been polluted with the jargon and senseless trifling of the dialecticians who had managed with their endless terminology of definitions, divisions, argumentations, majors, minors, conclusions, etc., to invade the province of grammar, that subject, in the wide sense of the term, for which the humanists had such high respect. They waged their disputations around Donatus and Priscian, and worried the boys with their glosses and commentators, and practised the boy in wordy disputes on these subjects in the name of 'grammar,' "beginning his career of altercation from his birth and making no end of it for him until his death." Vives then continues in flood-like invective quite in the manner of Erasmus, "When a boy has been brought to the school, at once he is required to dispute, on the very first day, immediately he is taught to wrangle, though as yet unable to talk. The same practice is pursued in Grammar, in the Poets, in History, as in Dialectic and Rhetoric, and in absolutely every subject. Someone may wonder how the most apparent, simple, rudimentary matters can be susceptible of

half of the 13th century. It gives a sketch of the academic methods of the time (Sir W. Hamilton, *Discussions on Philosophy, Literature, Education etc.*, 3rd ed. p. 776).

[1] In considering the personal relations of Erasmus and Vives it is reasonable to take into account the fact that Erasmus was twenty-six years older than Vives. The letters of Vives are full of this affection and admiration of a younger for an older man.

argument? But nothing is so clear that some little questions cannot be raised about it, and even as by a wind, stirred into action. These beginners are accustomed never to be silent, to asseverate confidently whatever is in their mouths, lest at any time they should seem to have ceased speaking. Nor does one disputation a day suffice, or two, as with eating. At breakfast they wrangle; after breakfast they wrangle; at supper they wrangle, after supper they wrangle. In the house they wrangle; out of doors they wrangle. At meals, at the bath, in the sweating-room, in the temple, in the city, in the country, in public, in private, in every place, at every time, they are wrangling[1]."

But Vives himself not merely indulges in this vigorous onslaught; he also indicates the available remedies. He proposes the abandonment from early education of dialectic based on metaphysical terminology, and, instead, the introduction of pupils to the direct knowledge of the external world; for this comes first in the normal process of our knowledge. He points out that we cannot penetrate into "inner mysteries," except through those things which are external. He ridicules the action of the logicians in taking the raw boy straight from his studies in grammar and plunging him in the *Praedicabilia*, the *Praedicamenta* and the six *Principia*. For, says he, "the process is to the unknown through the known (*ad incognita enim itur per cognita*[2]) and *we can only attain the verdict of the mind's judgment by first employing the functions of the senses.*" The second remedy is that the youth should receive a sound training in Latin and Greek and in the various subjects of knowledge which have been best expounded in those languages. For the rest, he should then understand, or at least his teachers should realise, what the aim and scope of logic is. Vives maintains that students should not learn logic as an art for its own sake, but as an instrument for the acquisition of more

[1] *De Causis Corruptarum Artium*, *Opera* VI. p. 50.

[2] *Ibid.* VI. p. 131 (bottom of page).

important knowledge. Just so much Logic should be acquired as will be of assistance to us in pursuing what we ought to study in the other branches of knowledge. Who can tolerate the man who knows nothing beyond the boundaries of logic? Who would approve a painter occupying the whole of his life in preparing his brushes and mixing his pigments; or the cobbler in sharpening his needles, his awl, and knives, and in merely twisting and smearing thread, and then rubbing it? "If such expenditure of time is intolerable for good Logic, how far can we be expected to tolerate the babblement which has corrupted every branch of knowledge in the name of Logic[1]?"

But Vives is not only swayed by deep indignation and unrestrainable contempt for the corruptions of dialectic. He is also full of passionate longing and enthusiastic expectation of the change that must come. He recalls the fact that in the Middle Ages the Latin language had first become "moderately" degenerated, and then it found no avenger. At last its impurity became so unbearable that scholars arose in revolt and restored it to its splendour, beyond the reach of further obscurity or corruption. And then Vives adds: "I do not know whether it would not be better to pray that the obscurantists proceed in the heaping up of their insanities, accumulating them in every place with all possible swiftness, so swiftly that, as soon as possible, not only the most noble minds but even the lowest of the low may recoil in distaste from them, and all kinds of men may unite for the downfall of their stupidity." Suddenly, he turns from impassioned invective to the vision of the future: "I see as if from the depth that this change is strenuously in progress. For amongst all the nations, men are coming forward of clear, excellent, and free intellects, impatient of servitude, who are determined to thrust off the yoke of this most foolish and violent tyranny from their necks. They are calling their fellow-citizens to liberty. They

[1] *In Pseudo-dialecticos*, *Opera* III. pp. 58, 59.

will assert absolutely the claims of the citizen of the republic of letters to intellectual liberty, most delightful even far off—the liberty which has been lacking for so many centuries, and will train the students in genuine arts and sciences not by wild and violent masters, but by those most gracious and holy teachers...."

Vives had experienced the struggle of leaving the paths of the old traditions, and had made the "great refusal" which emancipated intellects have usually had to make. He describes the change from the old to the new in his own intellectual development: "I thank God most gratefully that I have left Paris, as if escaping from Cimmerian darkness into light. I have found out by experience what is in those branches of knowledge which are worthy of man and are thence called the 'humanities,' for I am not so demented, nor have I deserved so ill of myself as not to have weighed the value of these better subjects with great and exact care. I have clearly recognised that I was changing the old for the new, what I had already acquired in the way of knowledge for what had yet to be won; what was secured for what was uncertain. No one willingly puts on one side as frivolous or as mere trifling what he has already acquired by dint of great labour. No one can regard as mere child's play work which has occupied so long a period, and which has been the source of such anxiety for so many days, and of sleeplessness for so many nights. And thus at first the change was so odious to me that often I turned away from the thought of the better humanistic studies to my old studies, so that I might persuade myself that I had not spent so many years at Paris to no good purpose. And I do not doubt also that this message (of humanism) will be most hateful to many, though it behoves them to give it their best consideration if they will attach credence to the experience of others. Those who cannot be amongst the best and most accomplished scholars (such as by their own efforts attain all their knowledge) may be at least in that class of good men who give heed to the man who counsels them. For they may then learn that they can be saved from the worst class of men, who neither have knowledge gained by their own activity of mind nor listen to the men of intellectual experience who advise them in the better subjects."

The breaking-up of old associations, the cutting of the cables which bound him to the school of Valencia and the University of Paris, to the teachers and to the fellow-students whom he had met there, could not but deeply grieve his affectionate nature. The memory of this struggle becomes articulate[1] when Vives accepts the irresistible call to follow the light of the reading of authors and the knowledge of the great writers of antiquity. With Paris left behind, in the quiet of the intellectual centre of Louvain, and with the warm sympathy close to him of the one man for whom Vives had learned to care the most, and to reverence as the highest of humanists, he had achieved the honour, which balanced all his pains and struggle, in having Erasmus for his preceptor and friend.

### (3) *Vives at Bruges and Louvain.*

There is some doubt as to the year in which Vives first went to Bruges. But it is probable that he left Paris to take up permanent residence in Bruges at the beginning of November 1514[2]. This does not conflict with the statement

[1] *In Pseudo-dialecticos*, *Opera* III. p. 63. Vives has the satisfaction, however, of noting that his old teachers John Dullard and Gaspar Lax had come to lament most deeply the time they had wasted on dialectical studies.

[2] Vanden Bussche quotes the dedication of Vives' *Christi Triumphus* to show that he was still in Paris in Oct. 1514, and states that it is confirmed by other passages in his works. The Bruges archivist asserts that there is no record in the town archives, nor has he found any in Vives' works, warranting the 1512 date. Naturally Vives would wish in his dedication to the town authorities at Bruges to give the outside limit to his connexion with the town. On the other hand there is no reason to doubt his calculation as to the number of years since his first visit to Bruges. Vives distinctly states that his residence has not been continuous. See p. lxv.

that has been made that Vives was in Bruges in 1512. This seems to be founded on the dedication of Vives' public-spirited work—on *Poor-Relief* (the *de Subventione Pauperum*). This book was published in 1526, and shows the affection which had grown up in Vives for the city of his adoption, Bruges. The statement that he has been in Bruges for fourteen years, made in 1526, is intelligible, even if he only paid the city a temporary visit in 1512, and became a resident in 1514. The Prefatory letter reveals a spirit far removed from mediaevalism and is in touch with the modern citizen's ideal of the promotion of the public good by all men. Paris was the scene of the progress of Vives from the hateful morasses of scholasticism to the verdant pastures of "good letters." After another fourteen years of life mainly at Bruges, Vives has reached the resting-place of his intellectual development in the recognition that the most thorough scholarship is not an end in itself. The idea of "scholarship for scholarship's sake" is illusory. Scholarship is not the end of life; it is the glorious means whereby a man renders himself the most effective human agent in promoting the real ends of piety and the search for truth. The value of the results thus obtained from learning lies in the application of all knowledge to the common good of mankind. This vitally interesting letter is the *pièce justificative* of this further great change of standpoint in Vives' life. The following is a translation of the Prefatory Letter.

"Juan Luis Vives, to the Town Council of Bruges, all health.

"Cicero teaches that it is the duty of a foreigner and stranger to abstain from prying into the affairs of the state that receives him. This is sound advice, for to occupy ourselves with other people's business is hateful in any place. But friendly concern and admonition are not thereby to be disapproved. For the law of nature does not permit anything which deals with the interests of his fellow-men to be alien to any man. The love of Christ has united men to one another, may I say, with an indissoluble bond. To think that anything connected with this city is alien to me distresses me as it would if I were in my own city of Valencia. I do not esteem this city otherwise than my own country, since *I have been a resident here for the last fourteen years. Although I have not lived at Bruges continuously*, yet I have always been accustomed to return here, as if to my home. Your civic administration, the education and courtesy of your people, and the extraordinary neutrality and justice (celebrated throughout the nations) have been a real pleasure to me.

"Here, too, I married my wife—and so I would wish to consult the interests of this city, not otherwise than as that in which the goodness of Christ has decreed that I should pass what remains of my life. I count myself as its citizen, and towards its citizens the feelings in my mind are those of a brother. A sense of the needs of so many of the inhabitants of this city has driven me to write my opinion as to the manner in which it would, in any way, be practicable to relieve their distress. Whilst I was in England I had already asked what I had better do from Dominus Pratensis[1], the Mayor of your city, who, in matters concerning the public good of this city, ponders deeply and often, as, indeed, he ought to do. To you, the Town Council, this work is inscribed, because you are heartily disposed both to confer benefits upon, and to relieve the needs of, the wretched. For we see what a multitude of the destitute there is, as they flock hither and thither, to obtain assistance for their needs. It was the original cause of cities[2] that there should be opportunity in each of them where love (*caritas*) should unite citizens in the giving and receiving of benefits and in mutual help, and their association together should be strengthened. It ought to be the task and keen endeavour of the administrators of the city to take care that each should help each, so that no one should be overwhelmed or oppressed by any loss

[1] See p. lxxviii *infra*.

[2] Compare pp. 12–13 *infra*.

falling on him unjustly, that the stronger should assist the weaker, so that the harmony of the association and union of the citizens may increase in love, day by day, and may abide for ever. And as it is disgraceful to a father of a family, in his wealthy home, to permit any one to suffer hunger, or to suffer the disgrace of being without clothes or in rags, so it is similarly unfitting in a city (unless it were absolutely without resources) that the magistrates should tolerate a state in which their citizens are pressed hard by hunger and distress. Do not feel annoyed on reading what I have to say. At least consider the subject itself with as great care as you would punctiliously inquire into a lawsuit of a man in his private capacity, in which there were, say, a thousand florins at stake. I wish you and your city all prosperity and happiness. Bruges, 6th January 1526."

This long quotation is a historical document. Is there earlier than this any instance of the modern attitude towards civic duty and ideals, or of the sense of individual responsibility in concerning itself for the good of the entire population, the heart-felt need to confer for the good of the poor and to take practical measures for their amelioration; and, as the treatise proceeds to point out, for the removal of the causes of the poverty? Vives, I venture to suggest, was the first to regard poor-relief as both an individual and also as a civic task; not a question of merely ecclesiastical alms-giving, but as a matter of concern for social and municipal organisation. In other words, the economic and moral problems of city life required careful sociological study and trained, determined efforts on the part of all, to cooperate for the interests of all and for the good of all, utilising the power and resources of the town, and its executive, the Town Council.

This identification of himself as a citizen of Bruges with the town and with the Town Council; taking its problems to heart in the same loving anxiety as he would those of his own city of Valencia, surely entitles Vives to be called the first modern Christian socialist in the essentially humanistic sense of the term. We have seen him, at Paris, ploughing his way through the barren soil of scholasticism, and as the result of hard toil reaping the harvest of a knowledge of the new learning to be found in the best authors. But the essential characteristic of Vives was not love of scholarship in itself. He cared for his fellow-men, for the elemental pieties of life, in the home, the city, the nation, and profoundly believed in the best knowledge ascertainable, as the surest way of happiness in the solution of life's practical problems[1].

In this attitude of the good citizen Vives differs from Erasmus. It is true that Erasmus is called Roterodamus, as Vives is named Valentinus. But it was not the part of Erasmus to look back with longing affection to the Rotterdam he had left behind, and to pour forth his affection on the new towns of his sojourn, from their links of association with a joyful past. Nor in the social sense was he a man who loved his fellow-citizens. As he left one town for another he shook the dust from under his feet and passed on, absorbed in the serene heights of critical scholarship, and impatient of civic or other interruption.

We see, then, in Vives, that the five years of Paris life had transformed the Valencian youth from the mediaeval school-boy into the young man of staunch conviction as to the value of the New Learning, whilst the longer residence of fourteen years at Bruges (up to 1526) had aroused and strengthened in him the sense of the value of true scholarship for the needs of the world. He was destined, as he forecasts in the above dedication, to pass the remainder of his life—from 1526 to 1540—chiefly in Bruges as a permanent residence, though between 1522 and 1528 he spent part of the year in England. During all this later time Vives endeavoured to make clear to himself and others, in whatever branch of study he was engaged, the relation of scholarship to practical life.

[1] See p. xc *infra*.

Such was the general line of the development of Vives' life and character. A sketch of the main facts up to the time of his first visit to England in 1522 will divide the years equally between Bruges alone (1514–1518) and between Bruges and Louvain jointly (1518–1522).

When Vives had decided to leave the University of Paris towards the end of 1514 the attraction of Bruges must have been strong to prevent him from turning his steps back to Spain and to Valencia. There was a numerous Spanish colony at Bruges, and it combined the advantages of being not only a great commercial centre, but also the residence of men of literary culture[1]. Vives spent the first few weeks at Bruges in the family of a relative on his mother's side, Bernard Valdaura, whose daughter Margaret he afterwards married.

An attempt has been made to show that Vives met Erasmus as early as 1514[2]. This is improbable, since we know the movements of Erasmus, and he did not visit Bruges till June 1515, on his way to Basle. It is, of course, possible that Vives saw him on that occasion, but had that been so it is curious that neither Vives nor Erasmus refer to such a meeting. However, in July 1517 Erasmus removed from Basle to Louvain, where he stayed for three years, in connexion with the Collège des Trois Langues, recently established by Jerome Busleiden to further the new Renascence reading and study of the old authors, a task thoroughly congenial to Erasmus, at any rate, in its aim.

The Collège des Trois Langues was opened 1 Sept. 1518, and, pending the erection of a new building, lectures were

[1] Amongst the friendships Vives made at Bruges were those with Francis Craneveldt, in whose hands Vives' widow placed the arrangements for the publication of his posthumous work, *De Veritate Fidei Christianae*, and Juan Martínez Poblacion (see p. xlix *supra*), and the clergymen of the Church of St Donatian (in which parish Vives lived at Bruges), viz. the Dean, Marcus Laurinus, and the young Canon, Juan Fevino.

[2] See Lange, p. 780.

held in rooms lent by the Augustinian Fathers, close on the Fishmarket. The circular staircase leading to two halls, used as a larger and a smaller class-room by Erasmus himself, whose lectures Vives attended, are still to be seen, though until recently used for commercial purposes. Erasmus undertook to act for the executors of Busleiden's will, as the "promoter" of the College, which sought affiliation with the University (founded in 1426), placed in the building known as the Halles. There were other colleges, somewhat after the English system of Oxford and Cambridge, one of which, the Lilian College or gymnasium, is mentioned by Vives (see p. 209 *infra*). The study of the new "good letters," or literature, as the leaders defined the object of the Renascence educational movement, had much strenuous opposition to encounter. The students of the Faculty of Arts of the University proper took pleasure in going everywhere shouting out, "We don't talk Fishmarket Latin, but the Latin of our Mother-Faculty." The authorities had to intervene to prevent collision, a state of affairs not unknown in the high disputes between the Trojans and the Greeks in other academic institutions of the time.

The date at which Vives appeared as a pupil of Erasmus at Louvain is uncertain, but he had become fixed in that city from whence, in 1518, he dated his dedication of the *Meditationes in Psalmos Poenitentiae* to his pupil, William de Croy (nephew of the Duke of Chièvres, the celebrated minister of Charles V) Archbishop-designate of Toledo, and Primate of Spain, who was already a Cardinal of the Roman Church. In 1516[1], when Vives took him in charge, he was only a youth of 18 years of age. Vives was a student under Erasmus and in 1519 was a lecturer in the Halles of the University itself, where, in the mornings, he expounded Pliny's

[1] Lange offers good reasons for the statement that de Croy had been Vives' pupil from 1516.

*Natural History*, and in the afternoons, in his private house[1] in the rue de Diest, he lectured on the *Georgics* of Virgil. In 1522 he set himself to deliver a third lecture each day, on Pomponius Mela, the geographer. He is also said to have given public courses on Cicero's *de Legibus*, *de Senectute*, and on the fourth book of the *Rhetorica ad Herennium*; on the *Convivia* of Philelphus, and it is said on one of his own books, viz. the *Christi Triumphus*[2]. Amongst Vives' pupils were Honorato Juan, Pedro Maluenda, Diego Gracián de Alderete, Antonio de Berges, and Jerónimo Ruffald (Jerome Ruffault). There is extant a letter of an English student called Nicholas Daryngton[3], mentioning his attendance at Louvain of lectures on "cosmography" under Vives.

In 1519 Vives, accompanied by his pupil de Croy, went away from Louvain, on a visit to Paris, just at the time that his incisive *In Pseudo-dialecticos* was, as a new book, the subject of discussion, and Vives was surprised to find that in spite of his intellectual attitude there were scholars who were personally at any rate favourable to him. He tells Erasmus in a letter of his warm reception, and how John Fortis, to whom he had written the letter of attack on the dialecticians, brought together a company of scholars, amongst whom were important logicians who were prepared to condemn "those stupid follies" of the schools. But the great joy of the Parisian visit was to meet Guillaume Budé, Erasmus' friend of long standing, but, adds Vives, in a letter to Erasmus,

[1] By which were two fountains. In the *School-boy Dialogues*, *Vestitus et Deambulatio Matutina*, one interlocutor says: "Vives is accustomed to call the fountain close to the gate the Greek fountain; that one farther off in the garden he calls the Latin fountain. He will give you his reasons for the names when you meet him" (*Tudor School-boy Life*, p. 92).

[2] This list is given by M. Paquot, *Mémoires pour servir à l'histoire littéraire des Pays-Bas*, I. p. 117.

[3] *Calendar of State Papers* (*For. and Dom.*), Vol. III. No. 2052, under date 14 Feb. 1522. He says Louvain is a pleasant place, and he is less disturbed in studies than he had been in Cambridge.

"now mine, or rather ours." Vives' warmth of attraction to Budé personally was only equalled by his admiration for his mental gifts. He found expression for his affection for Budé in 1523[1], nearly four years after the meeting: "This man's sharpness of wit, quickness of judgment, fulness of diligence and greatness of learning, no Frenchman ever paralleled, nor in these times any Italian. There is nothing known in Greek or Latin but he hath read it over and discussed it thoroughly. In both these tongues he is alike, and excellently perfect. He speaks them both as familiarly as he doth French, his natural tongue." Vives' admiration for Budé's character was as complete: "He always gives to his religion the first place. Though he has a wife[2] and many children he has never been drawn from his true square by any profit or study to augment his state, but evermore swayed both himself and his fortunes and directed both." Budé established himself as the greatest Greek scholar of his age[3] by the publication of the *Commentarii Linguae Graecae* in 1529.

Towards the end of 1520, Vives began, at the solicitation of Erasmus, the edition of the text and *Commentaries on St Augustine's Civitas Dei*, which Erasmus desired to be made a companion production to his own editions of the text of St Cyprian and of St Jerome. Undertaken by Vives with the thought that it would exact only a few months' labour, it proved a heavy, almost intolerable task. On January 10, 1521, Vives' old pupil, Cardinal de Croy, died at the age of 23 years. Vives was bowed down with sorrow. Erasmus had left Louvain in 1520, and Vives' letters are full of grief, and he almost

[1] In the *Commentaries on St Augustine*, Bk II. Cap. 17 (Healey's translation), p. 74.

[2] As to the relation of Budé and his wife, see the interesting account by Vives in *Vives and the Renascence Education of Women*, p. 118.

[3] It is of Budé the story is told, to illustrate his absorption in study, that when some one announced that his house was on fire he replied as he went on writing: "Go and tell my wife, I never interfere with household affairs."

suffered paralysis of will before the continued labour of editing St Augustine. He fell into a serious illness and was taken to Bruges where he could be treated as an invalid more comfortably "amongst my Spanish countrymen according to their custom and fashion." He was received into the house of a rich Spanish merchant, Pedro de Aguirra, who treated him as a father, and after his recovery it is said gave him a house fully furnished for his personal use[1]. Vives was convalescent in June of this year, 1521, and stayed at Bruges, to await the fêtes in connexion with the visit of Cardinal Wolsey, who had received an invitation from Charles V to meet him at Bruges. There is no record of an interview of Vives with Wolsey, but Wolsey was ready to show friendly help in the near future when Vives came to Oxford. In 1522 Vives completed the *St Augustine*, which he dedicated to King Henry VIII, a fact which, as Vanden Bussche says, provoked the authorities at Rome as much as the work itself. Add to this, in the Preface, he wrote one of the most glowing recognitions of friendship, and one of the most sincere and emphatic tributes of admiration for his scholarship, ever bestowed on Erasmus. These grounds and the heterodoxy in some of his notes led eventually to the placing of the edition of the *St Augustine* by Vives on the Index of Prohibited Books *donec corrigatur*. The irony was complete, for no more attached son of the Church could be found than Vives, though no Church could constrain the strength and freedom of his thought.

In 1522 the Duke of Alva charged a Dominican monk to offer Vives the tutorship of his son at a salary of two hundred golden ducats. The commission was not fulfilled by the monk, and Vives was then without financial resources. In the meantime Erasmus wrote him doleful comments on the lack of sale of the *St Augustine*, informing him that

[1] Vanden Bussche gives the above particulars, taken, he tells us, from writing believed to be in Vives' own hand, in a copy of his work (the *de Officio Mariti*, published at Bruges 1529).

Froben reported that he had attended Frankfort book-market and not a copy of Vives' *Commentaries on the Civitas Dei* had been sold[1].

It was at this juncture that Vives came to England, said to have been called thither by Wolsey[2]. There can be no doubt that if Wolsey induced him to come to England, the project of Vives' visit was also welcomed by the King, by Queen Catharine of Aragon and by Sir Thomas More.

## (4) *Vives in Oxford and in London.*

The earlier years of Vives' annual visits to England were the most glorious of his life. For he lived in the sunlight of a Court in which Spain and the Spaniards were popular. He had the pleasant variety of lecturing in Oxford, where there was all the enthusiasm of cultured men spontaneously evoked by the new foundation of Corpus Christi College, and in that College he was allotted rooms. Above all he had the companionship and friendship of men like Sir Thomas More and those congenial people whom the Chancellor gathered round his Chelsea home.

The warm response of King Henry VIII to the compliment of the dedication by Vives of the *Commentaries on the Civitas Dei* was followed up by the royal favour. Henry VIII had been trained as a theologian until the death of his brother Arthur brought him to the throne. Both the King and the Queen helped Vives financially, and gave him the pleasing task of drawing up the plan of education of the Princess Mary. The loyal friend and patron of Erasmus, William Blount, Lord Mountjoy, extended his good-will to Erasmus' friend, and

[1] Erasmus adds: "I do not therefore look askance at the matter, except that the brevity which I formerly recommended you would have made the book more saleable." He suggests the poor comfort that Vives should undertake an "improved" edition of the *Civitas Dei*.

[2] Vanden Bussche, in *La Flandre*, 1876, p. 312.

induced him to write a *Plan of Studies* for Mountjoy's son Charles[1]. Sir Thomas More from 1519[2] onwards had been keenly attracted to the writings of Vives. More was twelve years younger than Erasmus, and when Vives came to London in 1523 was 45, whilst Vives was 31 years of age. Vives had just finished his *Commentaries on St Augustine's Civitas Dei*, a work on which More had himself lectured in the Church of St Lawrence Old Jewry in London. Sir Thomas More entered his manor-house at Chelsea, with its library, gallery, gateway, and garden reaching down to the Thames, in the year of Vives' first visit. More's manor-house must have been a home of more than usual fascination to Vives. For Sir Thomas More knew the life and homes of Flanders, and the friends of Vives there, even if he had not previously met the Valencian himself. As long ago as 1508 he had visited Louvain and afterwards stated his opinion that with all due respect to the Universities of Louvain (and to Paris), after personal observation of their work, he would still prefer to send any son of his to Oxford or to Cambridge. But this was before Erasmus had acted as the "promoter" of Busleiden's Collège des Trois Langues at Louvain[3]. In a letter of 1516 More informs Erasmus that he had made the acquaintance of Jerome Busleiden at Mechlin, and that he had been overwhelmed with admiration at the magnificence and taste with which Busleiden's house was

[1] Vives' *Plans of Studies* (*de Ratione studii puerilis*), were both written in 1523. Translations are given in *Vives and the Renascence Education of Women*, pp. 137–49 and 241–50. The Plan for the Princess Mary is dated Oxford, the Nones of October, 1523; that for Charles Blount, London, 1523 (no month stated).

[2] See p. xxii *supra*.

[3] In 1515, together with Tunstall and others, More was sent on an embassy to Flanders to the Archduke (afterwards Emperor) Charles to settle differences which had arisen between London merchants and the steelyard of foreign merchants settled in London. In 1517 he was sent on an embassy to Calais, and in 1520 was at the Field of the Cloth of Gold. In 1521 he was abroad on an embassy to Bruges itself.

planned and built, its delightful furniture, its varied collection of beautiful objects of interest, its monumental antiquities, especially ancient coins, and its library crammed full of books. But most of all More was amazed by Busleiden's mental application, which made him master of more than all his books. The thought of this Flemish Maecenas and his cultured home dwelt with More and found expression in three Latin poems[1], and not improbably furnished him with suggestions and stimulus in making the Chelsea home not merely "the School of More," for his own children, but also a literary centre, which served as the meeting-place for most of what was best in English humanistic scholarship and aspirations. More's *Utopia* had been written in 1515–16, and the spirit of social philosophy permeating both More and Vives must have afforded unusual opportunity for the recognition of common sympathies. The thought of More was not entirely absent from Vives when he was writing on the studies to be pursued in the "Academy," for we find the latter recommends the student of Political Philosophy to read the *Utopia*[2] of Thomas More, together with Plato's *Republic* and *Laws*. And it is interesting, though not without its pathos, to note that in the *Plan of Studies* he drew up for the Princess Mary, Vives suggests to her the reading of More's book. Another bond of union between More and Vives was their common devotion to their hero, Erasmus. But most of all would weigh with Vives the charming family life and particularly the culture of the daughters of the household. In 1523 Margaret was 18 years of age, Elizabeth 17, Cecilia 16, and More's son was 14 years of age. Three years after Vives' arrival came Holbein the painter from Basle, warmly commended by Erasmus and as warmly received by More into the household. It is from

[1] In More's *Epigrammata*, published in his Complete Works. These Latin poems on Busleiden are reprinted in *Félix Nève's Collège des Trois Langues*, 1856, pp. 384, 385.

[2] p. 260 *infra*.

his delineations we know so well the outward features of the More family, and from him we have the priceless picture of the family group. Colet and Grocyn had died by the time of Vives' arrival in England, but he probably met at More's house Linacre, Mountjoy, William Latimer, Lupset, Elyot, Croke, Reginald Pole, John Fisher, John Longland bishop of Lincoln, Cuthbert Tunstall, and John Leland. Vives, too, must there have met Richard Hyrde, who left Oxford about 1519 and became a tutor in More's household. Vives had been at work on a book commissioned by Queen Catharine, the *Institution of a Christian Woman*, before he reached England. He had finished it April 5, 1523. It had been published at Antwerp in Latin. Queen Catharine was greatly interested in it, and desired Sir Thomas More to write a translation of it into English. More was anxious to undertake the work, but his Chancellor's duties left him little time. Curiously enough the Queen's arrangement with More to provide an English translation of Vives' book was unknown to Richard Hyrde, who had been so impressed by Vives' views on women's education that, on his own initiative, he had devoted himself to providing an English translation, and on its completion consulted More on what he had done. More gladly yielded to Hyrde, but agreed to read over and "correct" Hyrde's manuscript. The translation (posthumously) published in Hyrde's name, therefore, must be recognised as having received both the general approval and the corrections of Sir Thomas More[1]. The names of Vives and More are thus closely linked in literary associations, with Queen Catharine in the background —the instigator and encourager of this work on the education of women.

Vives entered into the spirit of the Mores' household with his characteristic readiness to respond to all simple and sincere

[1] For a fuller account, and for Hyrde's translation, of Vives' *Institution of a Christian Woman*, see *Vives and the Renascence Education of Women* (Educational Classics Series. London: Arnold, 1912). See especially p. 31.

life. The nobility of the Chelsea School of More silenced the cavils and cynicism of the most callous and flinty of worldly-minded men; in Vives respect for More's family became another rooted affection. In 1536, his work on letter-writing[1] includes a letter to More, in which Vives sends his salutations and asks for his heartiest greetings to be passed on to More's children, and especially he adds to my "Margaret Roper, whom since the time you first brought me to know her, I have not loved less than if she were my very own sister[2]."

It seems to have been due to Wolsey that Vives was called to Oxford, where he was already in residence in Sept. 1523. Vives was evidently in his element at Corpus Christi College on the new foundation there of Bishop Fox. He would be happy in entering into the spirit of Fox who had designed his college in 1517 to be a "bee-garden, wherein scholars like ingenious bees are by day and night to make wax to the honour of God, and honey-dropping sweetness, to the profit of themselves and all Christians." Vives seems to have been appointed to a University Lectureship in Rhetoric in succession to Thomas Lupset, who had also been lodged in Corpus Christi College[3]. Vives duly continued and indeed added to the symbolism of the bees, for we are told that the bees had swarmed about his chamber and had associated such a tradition around Vives, who became known by the name of the "mellifluous doctor," that for more than a century the bees were left undisturbed to a permanent heritage of the roof over what had been Vives' study[4].

[1] Vives' *de Conscribendis Epistolis*, together with a work on the same subject by Erasmus, was published at Basle in 1536.

[2] *Opera* II. 308.

[3] For the details of Vives' connexion with Corpus Christi College see P. S. Allen, *Ludovicus Vives at Corpus* in the *Pelican Record*, Dec. 1902.

[4] Vives carried away the recollection of the bee simile, and used it in his work: see p. 55, end of paragraph, and p. 179, line 1. In the frontispiece of this book, at the top corners the bees are again associated with him.

In the year (1523) from Oxford, besides the two *Plans of Studies* already mentioned, Vives wrote the *de Consultatione*, the work from which Ben Jonson helped himself so liberally in writing on literary criticism. This was written by Vives at the request of Louis de Flandre, the Seigneur de Präet, ambassador from the Court of Charles V, who was in Oxford at the time[1]. De Präet was from 1522 onwards a magistrate of Bruges and suggested to Vives that he should write on *Poor-Relief*[2], a suggestion which bore fruit in 1526. It is probable that Vives also met at Oxford the group of men interested in Spanish studies[3] such as Sir Richard Morison and Thomas Paynell. John Twyne, one of the early Elizabethan antiquaries, was a student under Vives whilst he was at Corpus Christi College[4].

Vives' relations with Cardinal Wolsey were unbrokenly pleasant. In the first year at Oxford Vives, who did not easily forget benefits or kindness received, dedicated his translation from the Greek to Latin of two orations of Isocrates[5] to the great Cardinal, from whom, says Vives, "I have never come away empty-handed (*indonatus*) and whose kindness and good-will to students are 'incredible.'"

But this sense of universal good-will and protectiveness from all Oxford and London, 1522–1528, was counter-balanced by the drawbacks of residence in England, only too painful for a true son of the South. When in attendance on the Court in London he had poor, uncomfortable lodgings

[1] Vanden Bussche, p. 313.

[2] See p. lxiv *supra*.

[3] J. G. Underhill, *Spanish Literature in the England of the Tudors*, pp. 88–103. Morison translated the pupil's text-book of maxims of culture and religion by Vives called the *Introduction to Wisdom* c. 1540, and Paynell translated Vives' *Office and Duties of an Husband* in 1540. Both books were written in Latin. Underhill says that Morison and Paynell were students in Oxford at the time that Vives was lecturing there.

[4] Woodruffe and Cape, *Schola Regia Cantuariensis*, pp. 60–61.

[5] The *Areopagitica* and *Nicocles*.

at a distance from the Palace, so that his time was taken up in walking and petty employments, and studies became impossible. Life in his London lodgings, he has to admit, is wearisome in the extreme. Besides the discomforts of his rooms, the uncertainties of the English rains and fogs must have sorely preyed upon the Valencian whilst in London and Oxford[1]. But these drawbacks were only occasional and were minimised by the conditions of his occupations at Oxford and in London which permitted him to spend part of the year in Bruges[2]. On the whole Vives must have taken away with him many happy recollections of England.

Already we have seen[3] that Vives' expulsion from England was inevitable when the King became bent on his divorce from Catharine of Aragon. Vives had had the happiness of intercourse with, and much graciousness from, the Spanish princess for seven or eight years. He had had actual beneficence extended to him from her even before he met her. It has been suggested[4] that Vives was the private secretary of Queen Catharine, but there is no direct evidence on the point. Whatever the exact official relation was their close friendliness is undoubted. Thus in a letter[5] Vives mentions that he had accompanied the Queen Catharine from Richmond to Sion[6] where she was going to her sacred devotions, and in the

[1] Vives says in a letter dated Oxford, March 10, 1524 (?), "Here the sky is windy, thick, humid, and the kinds of food different from what I am accustomed to. As for the rest all is prosperous, thank God. My princes are loving, smile upon me, and show real kindness." *Opera* VII. 197.

[2] Erasmus puts it humorously, calling Vives *ζῶον αμφίβιον*, an amphibious animal, at one time swimming amongst the Britons, at another making a nest amongst the people of Bruges (in a letter 15 Oct. 1527).

[3] p. xxviii *supra*.

[4] A. Lange, p. 795.

[5] Vives Aegidio Gualopo suo (to Giles Wallop), *Opera* VII. p. 208.

[6] I.e. the Convent of the Order of S. Bridget in Sion House, Isleworth, near the Thames, ten miles from London. For a full account see G. J. Aungier, *The History and Antiquities of Syon Monastery* etc. 1840.

course of the Queen's conversation she expressed a concern for the good of Wallop. And again, in a text-book[1] written for the Princess Mary, Vives says to her: "I remember your mother, a most wise woman, said to me as we came back by boat, from Sion to Richmond, that she preferred moderate and steady fortune to great ups and downs of rough and smooth. But if she had to choose one or the other, she stated that she would elect the saddest of lots rather than the most flattering fortune, because in the midst of unhappiness consolation can be sought, whilst sound judgment often disappears from those who have the greatest prosperity."

We thus catch a glimpse of the communings of the Queen and Vives. The intercourse was destined to an abrupt end. Vives wrote in 1531 to his Spanish friend Juan Vergara: "There has been a great change for me in Britain...I joined myself to the Queen...I bore her all the help I could by word of mouth and by writing. This course offended the mind of the King so far that he ordered me to be detained for six weeks *in libera custodia*, whence I was dismissed on the condition that I would not engage myself in the Royal dispute. So as I was free, I thought it wisest to return home [to Bruges], and this the Queen advised me to do by papers sent secretly. After some months Cardinal Campeggio was sent into Britain as the judge of the case [i.e. in 1528]. The King in a great hurry sent to tell the Queen to seek her councillors and advocates for pleading her side of the case before the said Campeggio and the English Cardinal [Wolsey]. The Queen summoned me to her presence. I said it was not expedient for her to be defended before that tribunal by anybody, that it would be better to be condemned unheard than to accept the delusive pretence of such a trial, that the King was merely seeking a pretext with which to put a face on before his people, and to make it appear that the Queen was given a chance of defence, and that for the rest he did

[1] The *Satellitium Animi*, Bruges, 1524.

not greatly care. The Queen was then angry with me that I had not immediately obeyed her will rather than my own judgment. But to me my judgment is worth all the princes there are. And thus the King held me as his enemy and the Queen regarded me as dilatory and refractory. And both of them have taken away my salary."

We have seen the friendly relations of Catharine and Vives, the two Spaniards, the Queen and the Valencian scholar, not unlike the relations of Queen Elizabeth and Roger Ascham. When Ascham died the Queen declared she would rather have thrown ten thousand pounds into the sea than have lost her Ascham. When Vives left England, having lost Catharine's pension and her friendship, it would be hard to guess which felt the wrench more bitterly, the woman who asked his help or the man who thought the kind of help asked for was unwise to give or receive. Whether Vives' judgment was right as to the best course to adopt with regard to Campeggio's tribunal or not, he was sincerely convinced as to the futility, and worse than futility, of defence. He was not lacking in loyalty or affection, for the next year, in 1529[1], he wrote of Catharine: "If such incredible virtue (as Catharine's) had fortuned when honour was the reward of virtue, this woman had dusked the brightness of the heroes, and as a divine thing and a godly, sent down from heaven, had been prayed unto in temples; for there cannot be erected unto her a more magnificent temple than that which every man among all nations, marvelling at her virtues, have, in their own hearts, builded and erected."

Was nobler admiration from any man ever poured forth on a woman who a year before had withdrawn her pension from him, especially when we recall the fact that the writer, in the meantime, was on the verge of starvation. Vives had still the

[1] In the *de Officio Mariti*. See *Vives and the Renascence Education of Women*, p. 11.

refuge of his home and friends at Bruges, the city which Erasmus described as "prolific in minds worthy of Attica."

### (5) *Back to Bruges.*

Vives was a citizen of Bruges in a degree to which he could not belong to London or Oxford. Vanden Bussche discovered that he attended the meetings of the Guild of Saint-Luc, and amongst the fraternity made many friends. It is said[1] that a member who entered this Guild in 1528, by name Jan van Wynsberghe, painted a portrait of Vives. If so, this is possibly the source of the engraving by Edmond de Boulonois, on which so many later engravings of Vives were based, including the frontispiece to this book. Vanden Bussche has identified the sites of Vives' Bruges residences, the first being in the rue du Pont flamand, and the second in the Lange Winckel near the warehouse reserved for the Spanish merchants.

On one of the visits to Bruges, having first spent part of the year in England, on May 26, 1524, Vives was married to Margaret Valdaura, daughter of Bernard Valdaura, already mentioned as a relative, on the mother's side, of Vives. Vives was 32 and his wife 19 years of age. Few details of Margaret are known. The inscription on the tablet (in St Donatian's Church, Bruges) to her memory says she was of rare purity, and very like (*simillima*) her husband in all her gifts of mind, and that she was an ornament amongst women. She survived her husband twelve years, dying in 1552. Both the family of Bernard Valdaura, her father, and that of his wife, Clara Cervent, have been traced to a probable Valencian origin. Clara Cervent has been justly placed by Vives amongst heroic women. At 18 years of age she married Valdaura, a man

[1] Vanden Bussche in *La Flandre*, 1876, p. 309, states that the story comes from Cornil Breydel, monk of the Abbey of Saint-Bavon, who may have had it from Margaret Valdaura, Vives' wife.

of 46. Her husband was attacked by a loathsome disease. Physicians despaired of his life and advised his wife to pass over attendance on him to nurses for fear of infection, but Clara (and her mother joined her in the task) nursed Valdaura, never resting at night for more than from one to three hours, and even then in their clothes, and eventually plucked him from death, only for him to relapse into another long disease, which lasted for nearly seven years. Altogether for ten years, out of twenty years of married life she completely forgot herself and was absorbed in tending personally on the "doleful" body of her husband whom others shunned. It was to be near such a woman that Vives had himself removed to Bruges when he fell ill at Louvain, and his reverence for the wifely love which found its only possible satisfaction in utter self-devotion stirred him deeply. His earliest days at Bruges had been passed in the Valdaura household. At that time Margaret was a child of nine, and Vives must have watched her progress through the ten years until she became his wife with that particular interest which a scholar and educationist manifests in the development of a child whose parents are his especial friends. The sense of security for his affections was doubly guaranteed. His wife was part of the sanctities of life in having such a mother. This feeling established itself in the current of his thought. In 1529, in his book on the *Office and Duties of an Husband*, within five years after his marriage with Margaret, in his list of saints, by the side of St Agnes, St Catharine, St Margaret, St Barbara, etc., for, as it were, a revised book of saints, he included, we have seen, the names of Queen Catharine of Aragon and his own mother Blanca March, and in this same list of those worthy of saint-hood is included the name also of Clara Cervent.

Bruges was again, in fact, his unfailing home, when the English storm-centre of the Royal Divorce made removal from England necessary in 1528. There are indications that Vives was concerned in business transactions whilst serving

f 2

King Henry. For instance, licences were granted him to import 300 tuns of Gascon wine and Toulouse woad into any part of the king's dominions, excepting Calais, for three years[1]; and later he held a licence to export 100 quarters of corn[2]. These may have been commissions secured by Vives for his Spanish merchant friends at Bruges. It is not clear how Vives managed to pay the expenses of his wife and the home at Bruges. The details of his literary activity seem to leave little possibility for him to have engaged in outside work, though he earned but very slight remuneration by his writings. The supposition that his wife took up some remunerative occupation is not unlikely, for the Valdaura family, with the permanent invalid, had had no sources of income as far as is known. In the family there were Margaret's sister Maria, and three brothers, the eldest Bernard, then, Nicholas[3], well known later as a physician, and a third brother, to provide for; there must have been means for their support whilst young, the result of someone's earnings. The only available earners, as far as can be seen, were Margaret and her mother, by this time a widow. Vives himself bears witness that the three years immediately after his expulsion from England, 1528–1531, were years of great privation at home, and that it could only have been by a special Providence that they did not die of hunger[4].

During this beclouded period of his life is to be placed the interesting story of annual visits paid by Ignatius Loyola to Bruges, whilst he was a student at Paris, between 1528 and 1534, so as to beg alms from his compatriots, the Spanish merchants[5]. We hear of Vives inviting the future founder

[1] *Calendar of State Papers* (*Foreign and Domestic*) of reign of Henry VIII, No. 1293. Date 28 April, 1526.

[2] *Ibid.*, No. 1298. Dated 16 Henry VIII.

[3] Vives wrote a letter of commendation for Nicholas to Budé at Paris when the youth was entering as a student of medicine. The letter is undated but internal evidence shows it was after 1529.

[4] Letter to Vergara, *Opera* VII. p. 148.

[5] The incident is described by the biographers of Loyola, Ribadeneira

of the Society of Jesus to breakfast (though hospitality in the midst of his poverty must indeed have made the incident conspicuous to Vives), and the remark of Vives to a friend is recorded: "This man is a saint, who will, of a surety, found an Order." This account has sufficient validity on its face, especially as it comes from the Jesuits themselves, to justify the idea that Loyola may have received inspiration, and even suggestions in the construction of an educational plan for schools, from Vives. For in these years Vives was undoubtedly engaged in thinking out the problems of education. The results of his educational studies were issued in 1531 in the *de Disciplinis*, which not only was his own greatest contribution to educational thought, but, on the whole, was probably the most stimulative and progressive pedagogical work produced up to that date[1].

Vives had written on Poor-relief with keen sympathy in 1526, but with little anticipation that he was to experience in his own person two years later something of the sufferings of the poor which he had so realistically described. On the appearance of this book on *Poor-relief* the Collège des Echevins of Bruges had presented Vives with a silver cup, and his book had been translated from the Latin into the vernacular at the expense of the town authorities. But these marks of esteem had not paved the way to any means of securing a settled income.

These years (1528–1531) of darkest financial gloom are marked by incessant intellectual work. Vives duly paid his debt of gratitude to Catharine of Aragon in the *de Officio Mariti*[2] in 1529. This book was written in response to the request of Alvaro de Castro, a Spaniard of Bruges, who, in

1572, Garcia 1722, and Mariani 1842; and by historians of the Order, F. Sacchini 1842 and Genelli 1848.

[1] For the points in common between the educational views and the Jesuit educational system, see Lange, p. 843 *et seqq.*

[2] See p. lxiv *supra*.

1523, was a friend and fellow-lodger of Vives in his London lodgings. After de Castro had read Vives' *Institution of a Christian Woman*, he had eagerly urged him to supplement that work by writing on the duties of a husband. Vives then sketched the plan of the work and wrote out the chief portions of it in Spanish, as de Castro's acquaintance with Latin was only slight. He took up this manuscript again in 1528 and translated and completed the work in Latin. Vives dedicated the book to Francis Borgia[1], Duke of Gandia, a Spaniard of Vives' own province of Valencia, who was in high esteem with the Emperor Charles V. Borgia was particularly drawn to the Valencians in Bruges, of whom Vives mentions in his dedication Juan Andrés Straneus, Honoratus Joannius. It is said that Borgia acted generously to Vives in recognition of this dedication, though details are not mentioned.

In 1528, in the midst of the unhappy retirement from the service of the English Court, came a sign of growing coolness from his honoured teacher and friend, Erasmus. Certainly Erasmus was unfortunate in the moments at which he offered adverse intelligence, or worse, adverse criticisms, to Vives. Whilst Vives was still in depression[2], due to the reaction over the strain of forced labour on the *Commentaries on St Augustine's Civitas Dei* in response to the urgent requests of Erasmus to bring the work to a speedy conclusion, the latter had communicated to Vives Froben's statement that not a copy could be disposed of at Frankfort Fair, and this had suggested some reflexion on the reputation of Vives. As to the question of sales, Vives replied (May 10, 1523) that he knew Froben had sold very

[1] Charles V made Borgia Viceroy of Catalonia, but on the death of his wife he withdrew from the world, entering the newly founded order of the Jesuits, of which, against his desire, he was made general.

[2] Vives had told Erasmus, as he sent the last portion of the *Commentaries* in July, 1522, that his whole body was enfeebled, his nerves depressed, and on his head "there seemed to be placed the intolerable weight of ten towers."

many copies. "I know," he adds, "who have bought them." For instance, "within a few days over thirty had been sold in London." As to his reputation Vives says, "no one is more conscious of my literary shortcomings than I am myself, nor is any one less inclined to conceal them. I am often astonished to find myself so favourably regarded as I am." He goes on to say that even if he were able to write the greatest marvels of scholarship, he should still recognise that it would be owing to a certain gift of genius by which life is breathed into literary productions, and would not be due to any merit in himself personally. "When a man has had literary work placed in his hands, he acts wisely if he performs it with the utmost industry and carefulness. He should then submit himself with equanimity to the accidental fortune of reputation." If only he may pursue the true path of erudition and wisdom, Vives is content to be obscure. He declares he now sees things more clearly than previously, and that he has written a book for the Queen of England which will at least show the healthiness of purpose, and not the betrayal of himself by his voice like a shrew-mouse, or the shaking of dice to try his fortune and gain reputation.

That Erasmus was really attached to Vives there is no need to doubt. He wished his old pupil to come to the high reputation to which he was justly entitled. Erasmus made a mistake in accepting Froben's practical estimate instead of judging the book on its merits, a judgment which, had it been delivered *de plein cœur*, favourable or unfavourable, would have brought deep satisfaction to Vives[1]. In fact Vives' *Commentaries* on St Augustine were a considerable success. By 1661 the large folio had actually passed through sixteen editions. It may safely be said to have been, in actual circulation, more successful than even Erasmus' St Jerome.

[1] As he said himself in a letter: "I do not seek any other glory than to please you and others like you, if there are such....One Plato is for me worth the whole of the people of Athens."

As the adviser of Froben the publisher, Erasmus was, no doubt, disturbed by his adverse report, and probably much more hurt on account of the blow that it would be to Vives. But Erasmus had little self-restraint in mentioning unpleasant facts. He probably thought that Vives had far more modesty than was good for him, and in short that he ought to be roused from despondency by the sense of the necessity of attaining to the highest glory of literary position, from which Erasmus genuinely felt Vives was only withheld by his own self-questionings.

The annoyance of Erasmus with his friend continued. When the *Institution of a Christian Woman* appeared he took the opportunity once more to write to Vives for what he considered to be his good[1]. He complains with regard to that work that the style is too extemporaneous. The treatment of married women is somewhat severe; Erasmus hopes Vives is more gracious to his own wife. Lastly, the favourable mention of Vives' relatives is undesirable; other people must not be expected to like it. Vives replies that he had aimed at intelligibility rather than ornaments of style, because he was writing to women untrained in scholarship. If he had treated women too severely, had not Erasmus set him an example in the restoration of St Jerome's works? As to the other criticism Vives remarks, "Thrice altogether I have noticed members of my own family....I was persuaded to say what I did from its truth, and because, in my opinion, these examples are as worthy of narrative as the stories of women handed down to memory to us by others of long ago[2]." But he is unshaken in his friendship, and asks Erasmus to continue his criticisms. "There is nothing more blessed in life than to have a wise friend as one's admonitor."

Nevertheless, Vives was travelling in a direction taking him farther away from Erasmus, who seems to have felt that the

[1] *Erasmi Epistolae*, 1642 ed., column 835.

[2] *Opera* VII. p. 186. The letter is dated Bruges, St Margaret's Day, 1527.

Valencian had conducted his English court affairs as badly as he had lapsed in his literary aspirations[1]. In England Vives had kept up a pleasant correspondence with Erasmus, treasuring points of interest to him and including them in his letters. "Claymund and the best men of the University of Oxford send you their greetings." He has heard nothing with more pleasure for a long time than that Spanish compatriots find delight in Erasmus' works. The King has been reading Erasmus' book on Free Will, in answer to Luther, and manifested complete pleasure, especially in a passage which he pointed out. The Queen also was marvellously pleased, and characteristically ordered a greeting "to be written to you in her own words." The King has a commission for Erasmus to write annotations on the Psalms. Linacre has just died. His book, however, is published and in it he mentions the name of Erasmus, whence "you may see he not only loved but also revered you." And so on.

Yet when Erasmus published his *Ciceronianus*, in 1528, he included the names of those contemporary writers whom he regarded as the lights of the age for their ability in writing. He omitted the name of Vives at the time when his untoward English experiences must have made the omission particularly painful. Ursinus Velius expostulated with Erasmus on the lack of reference to Vives. Whereupon Erasmus wrote to Vives and assured him that the omission of his name was "an oversight." He asks Vives to accept his old age and his pressure of duties as the reasons for the oversight, and consoles him by saying that he had been more fortunate in "forgetting" Vives than in "remembering Budé, for the Budaeans are raging[2]." Vives replies[3] that there is no

[1] Erasmus carefully avoided offering any decisive opinion as to the divorce question, either before or after its settlement, and probably regarded Vives as an imprudent literary man in taking Catharine's part.

[2] *Erasmi Epistolae*, 1642, col. 1044, dated Calends of September 1528. Erasmus was 62 years of age at that time.

[3] *Opera* VII. 191, dated from Bruges, Calends of Oct. 1528.

wonder that Erasmus should have forgotten him when he had so many names and matters in his mind, and even if he had passed him by deliberately he would not have complained, "since I have discovered that nothing has been done by you to me with hostile mind."

Vives has found rest in a view of life in which fame is not an essential element. He tells Erasmus: "I would prefer to be of real service to one or two in promoting their virtue than to have a reputation, however great, without rendering service thereby to others.... I ask you, my teacher, after this, not to attempt to urge me on to personal reputation or glory. For I solemnly state that these aims move me less than you would believe. *I set my great store by the public good. Most keenly would I advance that good in any way I could. Those are the fortunate people, in my opinion, who are serviceable in that matter*[1]."

This was the parting of the ways. Erasmus lost his interest in Vives. Time was short and Erasmus had much to do. The claims of scholarship engrossed him more and more. In 1531 Vives writes begging a few words as to his old master's health. "It is due to the love we bear each other, and to the relief of my particular anxiety." On May 10, 1534, Vives wrote, reasserting his affection, and his continued trust in that of Erasmus. But he could not hide from himself that Erasmus was failing, and he was evidently aware that Erasmus was himself conscious of the fact. He can only pray that Erasmus may be given such strength of mind and body as will make his physical suffering more tolerable. Erasmus died July 12, 1536, a little less than four months short of completing 70 years of age.

[1] There is no wish on Vives' part to emphasise any difference of his point of view from that of Erasmus. For he adds his admiration of Erasmus as of one who has gained the satisfaction at which he himself would aim. "I think it a truer glory of yours to have made others better from their reading of your monumental works than to hear all those expressions of glory—'most eloquent,' 'most learned,' 'first of all.'"

Vives had indicated to Erasmus that his thoughts were becoming fixed on the public good and the public service—an aim by no means new to him. The work on *Poor-relief*, which seems to have escaped Erasmus' notice, or at least his attention, had shown that his interests were becoming hopelessly dispersed, or were widening in their human sympathies—according to the point of view from which this change is regarded. He had given up the ideal of "pure scholarship" as it is called, or "knowledge in itself, and for its own sake." Intellectual pursuits were valuable not simply as exercising the mind, not simply as increasing individual possessions, but as having social implications. As Swedenborg later declared, "all religion has relation to life," Vives announced that in his view all learning has relation to life. He desired that all scholars should place their trained minds, and their store of knowledge, at the service of their fellow-men, even at the expense of foregoing the solitary student's absorption in "universes of thought" which only touch on practical life at rare points.

Erasmus has been called "the literary chief of Europe." "Before the sickly scholar of Basle, throwing on every controversy of the age the light of his genius and his learning, all Europe bowed[1]." Nevertheless, Vives knew he had a distinctive work[2] to do, and that he could not withhold himself from it even if Erasmus extended to him no encouragement in the task. Hence his work on women's education, and the

[1] Charles Beard, *The Reformation* (Hibbert Lectures 1883), p. 64.

[2] Dr C. Lecigne wrote his thesis (1898) *Quid de rebus politicis sensuit J. Ludovicus Vives*. He bases the thesis on a study of seventeen separate treatises and letter-tractates of Vives. These include letters to D. Everard de la Marck, Archbishop of Valencia, to Cardinal Wolsey, to John Longland, Bishop of Lincoln, to King Henry VIII, to the Emperor Charles, and the treatises *Somnium Scipionis*, *Aedes Legum*, *in Leges Ciceronis Praelectio*, *de Europae Statu ac tumultibus*, *de Pace inter Caesarem et Franciscum Galliarum regem*, *de Europae dissidiis et bello Turcico dialogus*, *de Subventione Pauperum*, *de Vita sub Turca*, *de Concordia*, *de Pacificatione*, *de Sudore Christi*, *de Communione Rerum*.

work on *Poor-relief*, on both of which subjects he could write with more knowledge and absorption of interest than Erasmus. He also entered on the discussion of high politics. He boldly wrote a letter to Henry VIII to plead anew the cause of Catharine, and again to urge him not to divorce Catharine[1], and to beseech him to throw his power on the side of international peace. He protested against Francis I or any other king allying himself with the Turks.

In 1529 he dedicated his most typical political work to the Emperor Charles V, viz. his book on *Concord and Discord amongst Mankind*[2]. In sustained eloquence, and with concentrated thought, Vives brings all his powers to bear upon the subject of universal peace amongst Christians. He is full of passion in his desire for the wars of princes to cease, for disputes amongst learned men to disappear, for unity in religion to be promoted, and that loving piety should abound. He attempts to induce Charles V to use his vast power for the good of mankind, to become as it were in his own person the philosopher-prince of Plato, or, shall we say, to surpass the dreams of Sir Thomas More, by the transformation of the *Utopia* from the realms of fiction into an idealistic spirit which should animate the treatment of national and international problems in their practical issues in the whole life of Christian Europe.

Yet Vives was no sympathiser with the Anabaptists in their declaration against private property. In his *Communion of Goods*[3] he protests against the recent iniquitous wars making a demand for property to be held in common by a usurpation of the name of liberty and equality, whereas you cannot by any promulgation transfer the virtue of a man's mind, or his

[1] Cf. p. lxxxix note[1].

[2] *De Concordia et Discordia in humano genere* (Antwerp 1529), dedicated to the Emperor Charles V. Without satisfactory evidence Vives has been described as the tutor of Charles V. There can be no doubt, however, that the two, monarch and subject, highly respected each other.

[3] *De Communione Rerum* (written in 1535, published in 1538). A clear and able statement of what we now call Individualism.

wisdom, judgment, memory, into common property. Or even if you limit the demand to material things, the taking of the student's books away from him for the use of the soldier will not be recompensed by the student's joint use of the implements of war. Vives' social sympathies were based upon the educational doctrine of the differences of mental ability, the necessity of discovering the essential capacities of each individual, and by the help of teachers and others of strengthening those capacities[1].

Pursuing his constructive policy of using his scholarly thought for the public good, Vives threw himself into the study of educational problems and wrote the *de Disciplinis*, which he finished July 1531, at Bruges. This work was divided into twenty books, seven books on *the Corruptions of the Arts* and five on *the Transmission of the Arts*[2]. The seven books of the *Corruptions of the Arts* deal with the negative side of the educational problem, viz. the reasons why knowledge as a whole had degenerated from its active, vital search for truth, especially after the times of the great thinkers of antiquity. Vives traces the general causes of corruption of the arts, and then deals specifically with the corruptions of grammar, dialectic, rhetoric, nature-philosophy, ethics and civil law. In every subject which he discusses he critically examines not only the instances of old and contemporary methods of study, but he also suggests the sound and effective attitude to be taken for their rightful study. The *Causes of the Corruptions of the Arts* is the best contemporaneous account of the aims and methods of the teaching of the times, critically considered by a writer who wished above

[1] For the educational doctrine see the *Transmission of Knowledge*, Bk III. Chap. 3, "On the Choice of Pupils," p. 72 *et seqq. infra*.

[2] The remaining eight books consist of the treatises on the Arts: 1. *de Prima Philosophia*; 2. *de Explanatione cuiusque Essentiae*; 3. *de Censura Veri*; 4. *de Instrumento Probabilitatis*; 5. *de Disputatione*. The *Prima Philosophia* is divided into three books, the *de Censura Veri* into two books.

all things to free himself from illusions as to the golden age of past scholarship, or even as to any finality in the current Renascence standards.

The five books on the *Transmission of Knowledge* are the part of the *de Disciplinis* translated in the present volume. Their purpose was to provide a constructive system of Christian education on a critical, reasoned basis, which should show the aims, methods and resources of education as Vives found it, for the purpose of the development, by educational processes, of scholars thoroughly trained, physically, intellectually, morally; not only capable, but also eagerly desirous, of taking their part whole-heartedly in the affairs of life, and of devoting themselves in whatever career they chose, to making their profession an effective instrument of the public good.

In his Parisian days Vives had attacked the methods of the "Pseudo-dialecticians." In the last eight books of the *de Disciplinis* Vives endeavoured to show the constructive lines which he would advocate for logic teaching[1]. In 1533 he offered his detailed suggestions for the teaching of rhetoric[2]. This was followed by a treatise on letter-writing[3]. *The School-boy Dialogues*, to serve as material for learning to speak Latin[4], is one of the latest of his books, and shows that the mind of the writer, in its maturity, had not lost that spring and buoyancy which knew how to appeal to the child's interests.

The last educational book of Vives might be regarded by some students as the most important of his works, for it points to the psychological basis of education. This was entitled *On*

[1] See also on the subject of logic p. 163 *et seqq.*

[2] In his *Rhetoricae, sive de recte dicendi ratione, libri tres*, with which was issued the *de Consultatione*, lib. 1, so useful to Ben Jonson. Published at Louvain Sept. 1533.

[3] *De Conscribendis Epistolis*, Basle, 1536.

[4] Called the *Exercitatio Linguae Latinae*, 1538. Translated into English under the title of *Tudor School-boy Life*, London, Dent, 1908, in the Introduction to which an account is given of the significance of this widely-circulated school text-book.

*the Soul and Life*[1]. Here, in the territory of psychology, Vives shows that whilst studying Aristotle's views on this subject we must not be satisfied to rely on the ancients, but we must adopt the method of observation and experience, and thus step forth to progress in knowledge of the mind on our own initiative. He discourages discussions on the nature of the soul, and insists on the investigation not of what the soul is but what it does or suffers. Vives, thus, is the father of modern empirical psychology, and to name one outstanding theme on which he has anticipated later inquiry, the theory of the Association of Ideas is laid down with a clearness which has won the high recognition of those interested in the history of psychology[2].

In the province of religion Vives was also active, but here it was the side of practical piety which especially engaged his thoughts[3]. He published a collection of *Prayers and Devotional Exercises*[4]. The historians of the English Book of Common Prayer[5] point out that books of Private Prayers (put forth by Authority) displaced the old type formed on the plan of the Canonical Hours and even those of the Morning and Evening Services of the Prayer-book. They ascribe the origin of these domestic prayers to Vives, whose prayers were translated and

1 *De Anima et Vita*, 1538. This book was dedicated to the Duke of Béjar, and it is interesting to note that in 1605 Cervantes dedicated his *Don Quixote* to the contemporary Duke of Béjar. "Thus," says Bonilla, "the Dukes of Béjar were honoured by the first philosopher and the first novelist of Spain" (p. 247).

2 See *Collected Works of Thomas Reid* (ed. Sir Wm. Hamilton), Vol. II. pp. 890, 896, where Hamilton says in the note on *Association of Ideas*, "Vives' observations comprise, in brief, nearly all of principal moment that has been said on this subject, either before or since his time."

3 For this reason, and also on account of the rancour of the advocates, Vives had no sympathy with the Lutherans. Yet no man was more eager than Vives, not even Erasmus or Luther himself, for the reform of the abuses of the Church, and in requiring higher standards of living from all men.

4 *Ad animi exercitationem in Deum Commentatiunculae*, Antwerp, 1535.

5 F. Procter and W. H. Frere (1902 ed., p. 128).

adopted by John Bradford. After their use in several collections, Vives' prayers form a substantial part of the *Book of Christian Prayers* issued in 1578 by Royal Authority of Queen Elizabeth and apparently were used by herself[1]. Vives furnished prayers to be said at first waking in the morning, at uprising, at putting on of the clothes, at first going abroad, at returning home, at the setting of the sun, at the lighting of the candles, in the evening, on unclothing ourselves, at going into bed, when we be ready to sleep. These prayers, and many others of Vives, were incorporated into an official English Protestant *Book of Private Prayers*. Graces before and after meals were commonly said by boys and the old books of Manners and Morals make due provision for these, usually in Latin, and only in later centuries in the vernacular. Nor, probably, was Vives peculiar in his recommendation of saying a prayer before beginning studies. "We ought to pray," says Vives, "that our studies may be sound, of no harm to anybody, and that so we may be sources of sound health to ourselves and the community at large[2]." He regards it as desirable to offer prayer before proceeding to publish a book[3]. The fact of the Catholic source of these prayers must have been outbalanced in England by the sense of the fit expression in them of human aspiration.

The events of Vives' life from the time of his leaving England in 1528 call for only a brief account. In 1529 the sweating sickness broke out. Vives and his wife fled to Lille. Margaret had no fear and shortly returned to Bruges. Vives went on to Paris, after which he returned to his wife and wrote a religious manual on *The Sacred Diurnal of Christ's Sweat*. In 1531 he called his sister from Valencia to come and live with him. He gave lessons to Jacques de Corte, a distinguished jurisconsult. In 1532 he paid a visit to his friend Georges de Halewyn (at the Château de Comines), a great friend of good

[1] Parker Society, *Private Prayers*, ed. W. K. Clay, p. xx.

[2] p. 276 *infra*.

[3] p. 300 *infra*.

literature. Again heavy troubles began to overtake Vives. In 1533 already the gout had taken possession of hands, knees, arms, up to the shoulders. In 1535 came the deaths on the scaffold of his friends Bishop Fisher and Sir Thomas More. In 1536 Catharine of Aragon died in January and Erasmus in July.

In 1537 Vives found a home in Breda in Brabant, as tutor to Mencia de Mendoza[1], wife of Henry, Count of Nassau, well-known as an encourager of literary men. It is supposed that Vives lived at Breda from 1537 to 1539. In 1539 he finished his last book *On the Truth of the Christian Faith*[2]. Margaret, Vives' widow, secured the help of Francis Craneveldt in seeing the work through the press, and it appeared at Basle in 1543. It is an exposition of the Christian faith from the standpoint of the Roman Church. It treats of religion in general from the point of view of its application to life. It establishes Christianity as against the Jews and Mahometans, and as against the philosophical systems of antiquity.

H. G. Braam[3], in an analysis of Vives' theological works, declares that everywhere he bases his views on the rational attitude, and maintains that he is the precursor of the best of the 18th century rationalists. "God has given man reason, and he must therefore make use of it." It would probably be nearer Vives' view to say that he is a Modernist-Catholic. For he is an undoubted Catholic. He says: "I declare I submit myself always to the judgment of the Church, even if it

[1] Mencia Mendoza was the daughter of the first Marquis of Cenete and niece of Cardinal Mendoza. Vives had mentioned her as a girl in the *Institution of a Christian Woman*, "I see Mencia Mendoza growing up, I hope she will become distinguished some day." Whilst at Breda Vives published *In Bucolica Virgilii interpretatio* and *Censura de Aristotelis operibus*. For an account of his stay at Breda see "Mémoire de l'Abbé de Ram" in *Nouveaux Mémoires de l'Académie de Bruxelles*, Vol. XII. p. 79.

[2] *De Veritate Fidei Christianae*, published at Basle 1543.

[3] *Dissertatio Theologica, exhibens J. L. Vivis Theologiam Christianam*, Groningen 1853.

appears to me to be in opposition to the strongest grounds of reason. For I may be in error, but the Church never is mistaken on matters of belief[1]." But though a Catholic he is, as has been well said, more Johannine than Pauline[2].

The great labour bestowed on this last work increased the infirmity of his gout, now complicated by other diseases. He died at Bruges 6 May 1540. He was buried in the Church of St Donatian in that city[3]. On 22 August in the same year, at Paris, Guillaume Budé, the greatest Hellenist of that age, also died. Erasmus had died in 1536. Thus the three scholars known in the next century and a half[4] as the triumvirs of literature had passed away within four years. Erasmus was nearly seventy years of age at the time of his death; Budé, seventy-three; Vives was the youngest, viz. forty-eight.

We can now, in a brief form, give an answer to the question: Who was Vives?

Juan Luis Vives was a Spaniard of aristocratic descent, trained in the old paths of scholasticism both at Valencia and in Paris. He was a leader in the revolt of humanism against the Parisian dialecticians. Strengthened by the enthusiasm of the new movement of Busleiden's *College of the Three Languages* at Louvain and by intercourse with Erasmus in that city he came over to England and was attached to the first Renascence Oxford College of Corpus Christi. For the rest of his life with the stimulus of previous connexion with the new revolutionary humanistic institutions

[1] *De Veritate Fidei Christianae*, Bk I. Cap. 3, *Opera* VIII. p. 22. By Vives' desire this work was dedicated to Pope Paul III.

[2] The *Transmission of Knowledge* shows Vives' religious views applied to pedagogy. See Bk I. Chap. 4, p. 28 *et seqq. infra*. On the authority of the Bible see *ibid.* p. 89 *infra*.

[3] Vanden Bussche, *loc. cit.* p. 319.

[4] At the end of the 17th century A. Teissier can still describe these scholars "comme les Triumvirs de la République des Lettres de leur siècle," *Les Éloges des Hommes Sçavans*, Utrecht 1696.

of Louvain and Oxford—the most progressive universities in the world of that time—and in the forward movement of which he had played no inconspicuous part, he was caught up by a zeal for the public good, in which the best academic resources were to be brought to bear, if we may use the Platonic metaphors, to use their academic gold—for counterbalancing the silver and brass and iron of the denizens of the outside world individually, nationally, and internationally.

He was the central figure in the conflict with the dialecticians. In the extended use of the scientific method of induction, coupled with the concentrative employment of observation and experiment he is the precursor of Bacon. He is the pioneer in the observational treatment of psychology. He is the first writer to urge an organised system of poor-relief as a civic and national duty. He is an apostle of universal peace, a position by no means so popular in the days of 16th century Tudor absolutism and imperial ambition as it is at the present day. In this hatred of war, of course, his efforts were linked with those of Erasmus. Lastly, of all the humanists, it was Vives who gave the closest attention to the study of education and the after history of education, in its main principles and many of its details, is to be found foreshadowed in his *de Disciplinis*[1]. He was the great "way-breaker" in education, to use Lange's description.

He was, moreover, a man of noble personality in whom the inner springs of character were greater than any objective work which he produced.

Though he renounced ambition and the reward of fame his written works entitle him to high distinction, as we look back on his achievements. He was the first in the modern world to write a critical history of ancient philosophy, in which he passed beyond the method of biography and traced in

[1] See the elaborate treatment of the indebtedness of later educationists to Vives by A. Lange in Schmid and Schrader, *Encyc.* IX. Abteil. 3, pp. 843–51.

outline the development of scientific progress[1]. In logic, whilst he is chiefly known[2] as an iconoclast, and in this connexion anticipated the chief points of attack afterwards made by Francis Bacon, more emphatically than that philosopher he preserved the highest reverence for Aristotle, whom he recognised, in spite of all the adverse criticism he had brought against him, as "unique above all other" philosophers[3]. The directions of his intellectual activity were thus, in some respects, different from those of Erasmus and of Budé, but the record of Vives' achievements, as well as the great charm of his personal characteristics, all go to provide reasons for the insight of the 16th century in regarding him as one of their most important leaders, and to justify their opinion, from their own point of view, in linking his name with that of Erasmus and of Budé in their triumvirate without in any way intending to question the supremacy of each[4] in his own special province, or provinces, of mental greatness.

[1] In the *de Initiis Sectis et Laudibus Philosophiae*, written in 1518, published in 1521 (at Louvain). This work received high praise as a new departure from J. J. Brucker in his *Historia Critica Philosophiae*, v. 87 and VI. 696 (1767), who was apparently the first to recognise that Vives had written the earliest modern history of philosophy. This philosophical tendency can be seen also in the text, in Book I: "Educational Origins."

[2] T. Spencer Baynes in the Introduction to the Port-Royal Logic speaks of Vives as one of "*a few men of independent thought*" who had done more than follow in the beaten track of Logic since the time of Boethius up to the time of the Port-Royal Logic, 1662.

[3] See p. 8, ll. 8–10 *infra*. Dr T. G. A. Kater has written in the University of Erlangen a Dissertation on *Johann Ludwig Vives und seine Stellung zu Aristoteles*, Erlangen 1908.

[4] On the supremacy of Budé as a Greek scholar, see D. Rebitté, *Guillaume Budé: restaurateur des études grecques en France*. Budé, too, was the founder of the Collège de France. As to Erasmus see R. B. Drummond, *Erasmus, his Life and Character*, Lond. 1873. As to his pre-eminence in many directions all the world knows.

# CHAPTER III

## VIVES ON EDUCATION

**Vives "the second Quintilian."** Vives was often called the second Quintilian. In an age in which the return to antiquity was the only way to re-capture the intellectual enthusiasm which could make further progress possible, there could be no higher compliment paid to an educationist than to compare him on equal terms with the greatest of the Roman thinkers and critics on education. Nor must it be forgotten that it was only in 1416 that Poggio discovered in the Abbey of St Gall, MSS. of Quintilian's *Oratorical Institutions*, lost, in a complete form, for so many centuries. When the printing-press multiplied copies of this precious complete work[1] it became "the code" of the best educationists of the age. Quintilian was a native of Northern Spain, and Spaniards particularly prided themselves on the contribution to the theory of oratory and of education made by their countryman, first to Rome, and then in the 15th century fully restored again to the service of the whole learned world. But if the term "second Quintilian" were to be taken in the sense of reproducing the views of Quintilian or of authors of antiquity solely, a sense in which it was certainly not meant by the 16th century, it would be an inadequate description of Vives, and we should lose part

[1] The *editio princeps* was published at Rome by P. de Lignamine in 1470, and was followed by a separate issue in the same year by Sweynheim and Pannartz.

of its complimentary import. For Vives was to the Europe of his time what Quintilian had been in the first century A.D. to Rome. He was the modern Quintilian, prepared to incorporate what was best and permanent in humanity from the ancients, but to use the ancient writers as a starting place, and not as a goal, in education and in all other "arts" and branches of knowledge. He had passed over the bridge separating the mediaeval and modern ages, and had entered on the "way-making" side of the modern world. He was the Quintilian of the Renascence, in looking forward towards the conceptions of the golden age placed in the future, not in the past; towards scientific knowledge gained, not from time-honoured but obsolete authority, such as that of Aristotle and the scholastic philosophers, but from independent research and the direct interrogation of nature; and finally in looking forward to the rise and growth of separate nationalities and separate vernaculars. With all these possibilities before the future, Vives recognised that education must change the old moorings, and adapt itself not merely to the contemporaneous state of things but also that it must make due provision for the right spirit and the right methods, in advancing hopefully and buoyantly to meet the vaster possibilities of the developing knowledge and culture of the future. In short, Vives was Baconian in outlook, two generations before the great philosopher drove home to a steadily progressing civilisation the scientific aims and suggested the bases of modern advance, which had been, with Vives, only the prophet's vision.

**Vives a Modern Thinker.** Men, who mark transition-stages, are rarely understood by the later generations, who benefit so greatly by their labours. The modern claim of the right of inquiry and of freedom of thought and investigation, are clearly enough stated by Vives to his contemporaries, who would not, as we are apt to do, regard them as commonplace ideas, but who must have looked on them as revolutionary suggestions to depose the ruling monarchs of philosophy, and substantially as much if not worse intellectual treason, as it would be political treason, to dethrone an absolute king or emperor, say, Henry VIII or Charles V.

The modern key-note of Vives is struck in the dedicatory address to King John III of Portugal[1] of the *Transmission of Knowledge*. To live worthy of the nobility of his ancestors is a sufficiently onerous task for the king, since his predecessors had made Portugal the conspicuous sea-power that it then was, but King John must also transmit the glory of his predecessors' achievements in an increased and more splendid mass, to posterity. The whole dedication rings with the jubilant delight of a new era, where the only possibility of mediocrity of achievement, would be to expect too little of himself. The hour has come for great deeds; the king, and each in his degree, must play the man. So, passing from an individual king to the great band of scholars and teachers, all in Vives' opinion should dedicate their work to the service of mankind. The end of studies is not mere reverie, glory, or reward. The fruit of all our studies is to apply them to the common good[2]. Nor is it sufficient to be concerned for the increase of the happiness and welfare of the present generation only. Sound knowledge is to be gained and transmitted for the good of posterity, "for whom we ought to care as we do for our sons[3]." At Paris Vives had forecast that the time was approaching when the absolute claim to liberty would be made by students. In the noble passage quoted by Ben Jonson, Vives, following Seneca, acknowledged the leadership but not the autocracy of the best of the ancients. "*Truth stands open to all*," and Vives, like Bacon, afterwards, called upon all students and investigators to seek it and proclaim it for the good of all.

**Vives and Bacon.** It has been said of Bacon that at the root of his intellectual powers was his optimism. This is

[1] p. 1 *infra*. [2] See p. 283 *infra*. [3] See p. 210 *infra*.

characteristic also of Vives[1]. Add to this aspect, what is true of Bacon in spite of cynical paradoxes at his expense, he was a great philanthropist, and such a description of Bacon as that written by Dean Church, would apply equally well to Vives:

"Doubtless it was one of Bacon's highest hopes, that from the growth of true knowledge would follow in surprising ways the relief of man's estate[2]; this as an end runs through all his yearning after a fuller and surer method of interpreting Nature. The desire to be a great benefactor, the spirit of sympathy and pity for mankind, reign through this portion [i.e. the philosophical] of his work—pity for confidence so greatly abused by the teachers of man, pity for ignorance which might be dispelled, pity for pain and misery which might be relieved."

The parallel between Vives and Bacon can be best illustrated by the common belief in the greatness of the actual world which became so instinctive to the Elizabethan age. This it was which made Jonson so readily seize upon Vives'

[1] We should have thought that the discovery of America by Columbus might have stamped itself on Vives as the pre-eminent event of the times. But when he refers to it (p. 246 *infra*) he adds: "But since then vaster events have followed. These cannot but seem fabulous to our posterity, though they are absolutely true."

[2] So, Vives bids teachers, "pity the human race, blind and forsaken amidst so many dangers," p. 60 *infra*. He says: "What can we fix as the end of man except God Himself?...We must return to Him by the same way we came forth from Him. Love was the cause of our being created....From that love we have been separated, forsooth by the love of ourselves. By that love we have been recalled and raised up, that is to say, by the love of Christ." The perfect knowledge of the divine life, both Vives and Bacon laid in the "oracles" of Scripture. But Vives allows no fixed barrier between science and religion. "All things the more they are known the more they open the doors to the knowledge of the Deity as the supreme cause, through His works; and this is the most fitting way for our minds to reach to the knowledge of God." See pp. 29–30 *infra*. And again, Vives says: "By the possession of reason we become most like ...to the Divine Nature....This state was ordained by the Creator for men....But through sin all things were inverted" (p. 250).

declaration that nature was not so effete or exhausted as not to be able to bring forth, in his age, results comparable to those of earlier periods. "Nature always remains equal to herself." There are many such passages in Vives. Here from his *Causes of the Corruptions of the Arts* is a passage, which surely might have been written by Bacon himself. Vives is speaking of the authors of antiquity, and says: "Yet they were men as we are, and were liable to be deceived and to err. They were the first discoverers of what were only, as it were, rough and, if I may say so, shapeless blocks which they passed on to their posterity to be purified and put into shape. Seeing that they had such fatherly good-will and charity towards us, would they not be themselves unwilling to pledge us not to use our own intellects in seeking to pass beyond their gifts to us. The good men amongst them undoubtedly in the past stretched forth their hands in friendship to those whom they saw mounting higher in knowledge than they themselves had reached. For they judged it to be of the very essence of the human race, that, daily, it should progress in arts, disciplines, virtue and goodness. We think ourselves men or even less, whilst we regard them as more than men, as heroes, or perhaps demi-gods—not but what they excelled in many and great achievements. So we also might no less excel, in the eyes of our posterity, if we were to strive sufficiently earnestly, or we might achieve still more, since we have the advantage of what they discovered in knowledge as our basis, and can make the addition to it of what our judgment finds out. For it is a false and fond similitude, which some writers adopt, though they think it witty and suitable, that we are, compared with the ancients, as dwarfs upon the shoulders of giants. It is not so. Neither are we dwarfs, nor they giants, but we are all of one stature, save that we are lifted up somewhat higher by their means, provided that there be found in us the same studiousness, watchfulness and love of truth, as was in them. If these conditions be lacking, then we are not dwarfs, nor set on the shoulders of giants, but men of a competent stature, grovelling on the earth[1]."

Bacon's *Advancement of Human Learning* includes in the first book a discussion of the "discredits" then attaching to learning. The "discredits" correspond in many ways to the "corruptions" which form the subject-matter of the earlier portion of Vives' *de Disciplinis.* For instance, among the causes of the "corruptions" dealt with by Vives, are arrogance of scholars, search of glory, jealousy, covetousness, ambition, love of victory rather than truth, the depreciation in which mathematics were held, the futility of studies undertaken for gain, the ill-equipment and small repute of teachers. Still closer to Vives is Bacon's name for "that kind of Rational Knowledge which is transitive, concerning the expressing or transferring our knowledge to others; *which I will term* by the general name of *Tradition* or Delivery." Bacon must have known the title of Vives' book, the *de Tradendis Disciplinis*, when he wrote the *Advancement of Learning* in 1605; and in 1623 when the Latin version was issued under the title of *de Augmentis Scientiarum* libri ix, the only Latin text of the *de Disciplinis* ever

[1] *De Causis Corruptarum Artium. Opera* VI. p. 39. The latter part of the above passage is quoted more than once in a well-known 17th century work: *An Apologie or Declamation of the Power and Providence of God in the Government of the World*, 2nd ed., Oxford, 1630, by George Hakewill, Preface p. 6 and p. 229. This book combats the view that modern ages have "decayed," and vigorously asserts the progress of later as against ancient times. The controversy went on as can be seen in Joseph Glanvill's *Plus Ultra: or the Progress and Advancement of Knowledge since the days of Aristotle*, 1668, and in William Wotton's *Reflections upon Ancient and Modern Learning*, 1694, which gave rise to a controversy, made memorable by the intervention of Dean Swift with his *Battle of the Books*, published in 1704. Intermediate between Vives and Bacon was the work of Louis Le Roy, who wrote *Des Vicissitudes ou la Verité de Choses en l'Univers*, Paris, 1579, translated into English by Robert Ashley in 1594, under the title of the *Interchangeable Course of Things.* Le Roy urged that "we ought by our own inventions to augment the doctrine of the Ancients." This book must have been known to Bacon.

published in England had been issued in 1612, edited by Henry Jackson[1]. The term, which Bacon seems to claim as distinctive, of "tradition," for transmission of knowledge, whether consciously or unconsciously borrowed, is reminiscent of Vives. It is true he widens the use so as to include the critical apparatus necessary for the presentation of authors.

If we examine more closely the details included by Bacon in the pedagogical part of the art of "Transmission" (for this is the word by which his Latin *Traditio* is rendered) we find interesting points of contact with Vives. Bacon's shortest rule is "Consult the Schools of the Jesuits," and we have seen that apparently those Schools through their founder had consulted Vives. Bacon, like Vives, advocates a collegiate education (in preference to private tuition) not in private houses nor merely under schoolmasters, but in colleges. For in colleges there is more emulation, and "there is also the sight and countenance of grave men[2], which tends to modesty, and forms their young minds from the very first after that model." This is all in keeping with Vives' idea of the Academy.

[1] Henry Jackson (1586–1662) was the son of an Oxford mercer. He was a scholar of Corpus Christi College, Oxford (Vives' College when lecturing at Oxford), and, in 1612, was probationary Fellow of the College, and in that year, as Antony à Wood records: "he did diligently recognise and added marginal notes with a copious Index to the twelve books of J. L. Vives," i.e. the *de Disciplinis*. Wood adds: "He has also made a collection of several of the works of Pet. Abelard from ancient MSS of that author, and had revised, compared and collated them....The Grand Rebellion breaking forth in 1642, the soldiers belonging to the Parliament rifled his house, scattered the said collection and made it so imperfect that it could never be recovered" (Wood, *Athen. Oxon.* III. 577). Jackson's edition of Vives' *de Disciplinis* is a very scarce book.

The marginal descriptive Latin heads adopted by Jackson in his text together with his references to authorities have been included in the present text, in a translated form. These notes, at any rate, show the points of special interest felt by an English scholar in Vives' book at the beginning of the 17th century.

[2] Vives says in the Academy should be old men who would attract "by a certain majesty and authority." See p. 63 *et seqq. infra.*

For the "order and manner of teaching" Bacon says: "Avoid abridgments and a certain precocity of learning which makes the mind over-bold, and causes great proficiency rather in show than in fact." And, again, Bacon says[1]: "As for epitomes (which are certainly the corruptions and moths of histories) I would have them banished, whereto likewise most men of sound judgment agree, as being things that have fretted and corroded the bodies of many most excellent histories and wrought them into base and unprofitable dregs." Vives had treated these very books of summaries as a cause of the corruption of learning, for by stealth, he says, students think from them to gain their pseudo-knowledge, whereas real knowledge can only be acquired by inquiring into the grounds of things and understanding their causes[2]. Instead of studying authors themselves, their works have been turned into *centones*[3], a term which may reasonably represent Bacon's "unprofitable dregs." As to the "precocity" which Bacon ascribes as the cause of the use of epitomes, Vives also had observed it: "Students, content with these 'little flowers,' 'summaries,' and as they are called 'pearls[4],' hastening along to the end which their mind desires, despise as superfluous what is necessary for true erudition, whilst those counterfeits and fictions which they affect, are inconsistent with it." Bacon advises encouragement of the individuality of the pupil's mind and tastes; and full freedom to pursue them. Vives, providing scope for the private reading of the pupil, when left to himself, is especially modern in his recognition of the adaptation of training to each individual pupil. The next subject dealt with by Bacon must be quoted at length: "The application and

[1] *De Augmentis Scientiarum*, Bk II. cap. 6.

[2] *De Causis Corruptarum Artium*. *Opera* VI. p. 61.

[3] A Cento was an attempt to make a new work by a hotch-potch of the words in a well-known author strung together usually in the form of verse.

[4] i.e. *Margaritae*. The best known is probably the *Margarita Philosophica* (Friburg, 1503), by Gregory Reisch, an encyclopaedic text-book on a mediaeval model.

choice of studies according to the nature of the mind to be taught, is a matter of wonderful use and judgment; the due and careful observation whereof is due from the masters to the parents, that they may be able to advise them as to the course of life they should choose for their sons. And herein it should be carefully observed, that as a man will advance far faster in those pursuits to which he is naturally inclined, so with respect to those for which he is by defect of nature most unsuited there are found in studies properly chosen a cure and a remedy for his defects. For example, if one be bird-witted, that is, easily distracted and unable to keep his attention as long as he should, Mathematics provides a remedy; for in them if the mind be caught away but a moment, the demonstration has to be commenced anew." Vives devotes nearly a whole chapter to this subject[1]. Down to the detail about Mathematics, Vives had had the whole subject in his mind: "Mathematics are particularly disciplinary to flighty and restless intellects which are inclined to slackness and which shrink from the toil of continued effort....In this subject there is the necessity...of the idea of series and a perpetual string of proofs. We can easily let them slip, unless they are frequently made use of and thoroughly impressed on the mind[2]."

Lastly, Bacon advocated stage plays, an educational method which he confessedly adopted from the Jesuits. Vives[3], in dealing with the *Causes of the Corruption of Rhetoric*, had urged the value of the declamation[4] and had suggested the importance of oral repetition as an exercise for the memory, and had insisted on voice-training, and even required the student to regard gesture as a constituent part of the oration. The training of the youth to a "little assurance and to being looked at," points which Bacon considered the acting in stage

[1] See Bk II. chap. 3, pp. 73–80 *infra*.

[2] See p. 202 *infra*.

[3] *De Causis Corruptarum Artium*, Bk IV. chap. 4.

[4] See also pp. 186–7 *infra*.

plays would help to develop, certainly are not to be found in Vives[1].

One further parallel in the scientific domain may be mentioned, especially since it brings out another link of Vives with modern developments of knowledge. Bacon says: "Astrology is so full of superstition that scarce anything sound can be discovered in it." He proceeds, however, to inquire how it may be "purified, rather than be altogether rejected[2]." Vives holds that astrology is a "thorough product of ostentation and impostures." He will not even pursue its history as a "corruption," for he contends that it is not an "art" at all, but a *fraud*, and he must, therefore, pass it by[3]. In the manual which he prepared for all youths who proposed to proceed to scholarly studies, his *Introduction to Wisdom*, he writes: "Crafts must be shunned that fight against virtue; all crafts that work by vain conjectures as palmistry, pyromancy, hydromancy, necromancy, astrology, wherein much pestilent vanity lieth hid[4]."

There was thus common ground between Vives and Bacon (even if there were in the latter reserves as to its total rejection) in their condemnation of the study of astrology. The rejection of this subject was a sufficiently noticeable attitude in Bacon, for he was living in the days when Queen Elizabeth extended her royal favour to the astrologer John Dee. Melanchthon accepted astrology. What is more remarkable, Tycho Brahé (d. 1601) and Kepler (d. 1630) cast nativities[5]. Nevertheless,

[1] Vives distinctly deprecates play-actors' realism—in leading to imitation in life, of what is bad as well as what is good. "The exposition of authors should be made in the words of the vernacular and by degrees in Latin, pronounced distinctly and with gestures which may help intelligence, as long as they do not degenerate into the theatrical" (ad histrionicum), p. 104 *infra*. See also *de Ratione Dicendi*, *Opera* II. p. 220.

[2] *Works* edited J. M. Robertson, pp. 462–3.

[3] *De Causis Corruptarum Artium*, *Opera* VI. p. 206.

[4] *Opera* I. p. 11. See also *de Causis Corruptarum Artium*, *Opera* VI. p. 19.

[5] On the question of casting horoscopes we can gather Vives' opinion.

much earlier, Vives, followed by Bacon (less decisively), took what was to be the modern view[1].

**Vives on Nature-Studies.** But, apart from these general educational agreements between Vives and Bacon, Vives had already, two generations before Bacon, formed his conception as to the importance of Nature-studies on the lines of observation and experiment[2], and, what is more, had included them in his system of school-education[3].

Vives saw as clearly as Rousseau later that the chief ground for the "corruption" of the study of Nature was the absorption of pupils in book-learning. Students of the natural sciences in the 16th century could not keep away from Aristotle, or Pliny, and whatever the erudition or even power of observation of those authors might be, they clearly abounded in hasty generalisations. Instead of limitation to the reading of ancient authors on natural science, there must be substituted direct observation and investigation, and instead of disputation there must be "silent contemplation of nature," and instead of metaphysical discussions, observation and the consideration of the actual phenomena of Nature. The whole question of Nature-studies in their higher aspects was knit up with the training of the

In a note on the "angles" of the heavens used in casting nativities or horoscopes, Vives gives the Greek names, shows his knowledge of the pseudo-art, and then adds: "But we have angled long enough for any good we have gotten: Forward." Vives' *Commentaries on St Augustine's Civitas Dei*, Healey's translation, p. 193.

[1] On the teaching of astrological views in the 16th century, see Foster Watson, *Beginnings of the Teaching of Modern Subjects*, pp. 361–89.

[2] It may be observed, without, perhaps, being regarded as more than an accidental coincidence with Bacon, that Vives uses the word "exploratio," in the sense of finding out by search (see p. 216 *infra*), so that Bacon's well-known phrase "exploration" of Nature was not unparalleled.

[3] It is somewhat curious that Bacon in his treatment of pedagogy says nothing about the introduction into the curriculum of any kind of nature-observation. Vives was driven to the necessity of including some form of observational study, for in his psychology (i.e. in the *de Anima*) he had recognised the senses as "our first teachers." See p. cxxii *infra*.

student of medicine, and the "corruptions" which had beset medicine had fallen with redoubled force on Nature-studies[1]. Vives had realised the significance of the training of the senses[2] in training observation. By the senses, he remarks, we come to the discrimination of similars and dissimilars, and in this process we are helped by experience of and by experiments on things. We must first apply our own concentration and other powers of our minds to phenomena. When these fail, we can call in the expositions handed down by others. We all of us have for the purposes of observation the "light of nature," and this may be concerned with the senses, in visual discrimination, with the judgment, as intellectual discrimination, and with the intellect, in reasoning through causes and effects. "The youth," says Vives, "will find Nature-study easier than an abstract subject, because in it he only needs alertness of the senses, whilst for ethics he needs experience in life, knowledge of historical events, and a good memory. What we know of Nature has been gained partly through the senses, partly through the imagination, though reason has been at hand as a guide to the senses. On this account we have gained knowledge in few subjects, and in those sparingly, because of those shadows which envelope and oppress the human mind[3]. For the same reason what knowledge we have gained can only be reckoned as probable, and must not be assumed as absolutely true[4]."

But there are dangers in Nature-study particularly for those who are incredulous of the discoveries of others, whilst they

[1] *De Causis Corruptarum Artium*, *Opera* VI. p. 185 *et seqq*.

[2] Vives refers to the part played in education by the training of the senses in the *de Anima* and also in the *Causes of the Corruptions of the Arts*, as well as in the *Transmission of Knowledge*.

[3] i.e. through the Fall of Man.

[4] p. 166 and p. 168 *infra*. "In all natural philosophy the scholar should be told that what he hears is only thought to be true, i.e. so far as the intellect, judgment, experience and careful study of those who have investigated the matter can ascertain, for it is very seldom that we can affirm anything as absolutely true."

assert their own, although often founded on insufficient evidence; or for those who accept the authority of others without investigation, on their own account. Especially must Nature-study be undertaken in connexion with genuine religious convictions. Vives held that Nature must he examined with "the torch of Christ," and not with the "poor light of heathen authors." This passage[1] impressed Comenius who adopted it as the motto of his *Natural Philosophy Reformed by Divine Light* (*Physicae Synopsis*).

The remedies proposed are characteristic of Vives. Nature-study, like all our studies, should be applied to the needs of life, to relieve some bodily or mental pain, or to the cultivation within us of the feeling of reverence. "The contemplation of Nature is unnecessary, and even harmful, unless it serves the useful arts of life, or raises us from a knowledge of His works to a knowledge, admiration and love of the Author of these works[2]."

Vives' plan of Nature-study is as follows[3]:

The teacher begins with the easiest topics, viz. those natural objects which are evident to the senses. The outlook is then extended to a general survey of the whole of Nature, as if it were presented as a picture—the *Orbis Pictus* as Comenius[4] afterwards called his book. This will involve a general knowledge of the celestial as well as the terrestrial sphere[5]. "In these studies there is no disputation necessary; there is nothing needed but the silent contemplation of Nature."

Only promising and capable students are to proceed past the stage of descriptive cosmography. Such will go on to astronomy, ancient and modern geography, the study of animals, plants, herbs, the agricultural sciences. Vives, as became a

[1] See, at length, p. 172 *infra*.

[2] p. 166 *infra*.

[3] p. 168 *infra*.

[4] The question of the indebtedness of Comenius to Vives has been discussed by August Nebe: in *Vives, Alsted, Comenius, in ihrem Verhältnis zu einander*. Elberfeld, 1891.

[5] The text-books are fully stated p. 168 *et seqq*.

native of Valencia, laid considerable stress on the study of the great variety of fishes, and their different names locally. Gems, metals, pigments, can be studied in Pliny, and in Raphael Volaterranus. But over and above all the book study there must be the close observation of outward Nature. The student will observe "natural objects in the heavens, in cloudy and in clear weather, in the plains, on the mountains, in the woods." Then for further knowledge, following the example of Pliny, he will consult the practical experience of gardeners, husbandmen, shepherds and hunters[1]. Eyes, ears, mind, all must be intent. The practical application of knowledge to husbandry, should keep the students from metaphysical fruitless speculation. Finally, Vives points out that Nature-observation will be a pleasant resource to the aged, and a recreation at all stages of life. "It is at once school and schoolmaster."

When we remember that it is only within the last decade that Nature-study has won its place in present-day schools, we cannot help regarding Vives, the pioneer of nearly four hundred years ago, as showing remarkable insight into the educational possibilities of the subject. As we have seen, in his *School-Dialogues*, he at least brought the subject of Nature-study attractively before the minds of generations of school-boys[2].

The first modern writer to treat psychology empirically was not likely to overlook the necessity of training sense experience. Thus, Vives declares "the senses open up the way to all knowledge[3]," and again, "whatever is in the arts was in Nature first, just as pearls are in shells or gems in the sand[4]." It could

[1] Vives expands Pliny's suggestion so as to include other directions of practical activity. He would have the boy visit shops and factories and inquire from craftsmen as to their work (see p. 209). In the *Janua Linguarum* and in the *Orbis Pictus*, Comenius makes use of this idea, including amongst his topics descriptions of trades.

[2] See pp. li–lii *supra*. The *Exercitatio* (School Dialogues) had an unusually wide circulation. Over 100 editions have been noted (see Bömer: *Die Lateinischen Schülergespräche der Humanisten*, Berlin, 1899).

[3] See p. 168 *infra*.

[4] See p. 20 *infra*.

hardly be expected that Vives should have thought out a scientific method of investigation, when two generations later Bacon failed to establish that New Instrument of research, which should infallibly rise from being the servant of Nature, to becoming her Interpreter, and thence proceed to bring her into subjection.

**Vives' use of the Inductive Method.** Vives, like all students of Nature who proceed by the way of observation and experiment, and do not submit themselves to the dictation of Aristotle or any other authority, was bound to stumble upon the Inductive Method. For we cannot study the facts of Nature from syllogisms, and if we wish to reach to any law of generalisation, we must first observe particular facts exactly and methodically. In Vives' account of the origin of arts, the Inductive Method is introduced. Arts were due to observation joined with reasoning. "In the beginning, first one, then another experience, through wonder at its novelty, was noted down for use in life; from a number of separate experiments the mind gathered a universal law, which, after support and confirmation by many experiments was considered certain and established. Then this knowledge was handed down to posterity. Others added subject-matter which tended to the same use and end. This material collection by men of great and distinguished intellect, constituted the branches of knowledge, or the arts[1]."

In describing the method of teaching to be adopted by the school-teacher, Vives has a clear insight into the principle of the Inductive Method:

"In teaching the arts, we shall collect many experiments and observe the experience of many teachers, so that from them general rules may be formed. If some of the experiments do not agree with the rule then the reason why this

[1] p. 20 *infra*.

happens must be noted. If the reason is not apparent, and there are some deviations, they must be noted down. If there are more deviations than agreements, or an equal number, a dogma must not be established from that fact, but the facts must be transmitted to the astonishment of posterity, so that from astonishment—as has been the case in the past—philosophy may grow." Vives insists that all generalised knowledge has developed from particulars of experience. So-called inventors and discoverers had a "certain unusual force of nature" perhaps, but starting without an "art" to guide them, they put together particulars of experience by the conjoint use of their observation and reason, to form the basis of an art, which already they found originally from material in nature. The Inductive Method had produced the art of rhetoric. For it was from the study of the practice of Cicero and Demosthenes in writing good Latin, that examples of the use of rhetorical expressions built up the "rhetorical precepts." Nevertheless, however complete an art may have become, "he who studies it or expounds its rules must withdraw his eye from experiments and direct his sight to Nature herself....For in Nature there is an absolute model, which each mind expresses as well as his genius and diligence will allow him; some more than others, yet no one completely and perfectly."

The perception of the inductive basis of the art of rhetoric was the outstanding instance in which the humanist could see the force and validity of induction generally. If rhetoric as an art was built up of the generalisations from instances of figures and tropes in Cicero and Demosthenes, grammar was only, in its source, the collection of the usages of the people in their ordinary speech, and the rules of grammar the short and precise statement of the common factors and principles in the people's own language. By comparison with the practice in other languages, there issued the knowledge of common principles between languages themselves, i.e. philology. Nor is it too much to say that, having once obtained an insight into the

Inductive Method, Vives applied it consistently through his writings in nature-studies, language, medicine[1] and law[2].

Great is the change from the mediaeval reliance upon the authoritative *dicta* of Aristotle and his commentators, and the deductive method of showing the application of his principles to the explanation of some fact of nature, of language, or of some other "art" or "science," to the position thus taken up by Vives. He was logically driven to realise that when he gave up the principle of authority, his only resource was the appeal to experience, through observation and experience, the reconstruction in thought along historical lines, of each of the arts, combined with the individual testing, by each student, by observation and experiment, of what was recorded in human experience. Hence he was impelled to write the section entitled[3] "Educational Origins," a book which the modern reader may regard as dry and lifeless. On the other hand, the student of *Culturgeschichte*, or of education, will find in this section the first modern attempt to read the past history of the race in terms of an interpretation of experience, in all the

1 "Out of how many practical experiences on all sides has the art of medicine to be built up like rain-water composed of drops" (p. 233 *infra*).

2 Vives considers that a jurisconsult should realise for each law what its life-giving force is and what its preservative force is to the community (see p. 262 *infra*). He also says: "Amongst legal systems which differ from one another, each has a reason of varying degrees of logical value for its own view." The jurisconsult is required, in Vives' opinion, to discover *the good and the right* in all the varying laws of different communities, and the resultant principles to be constituted into an *Ars Justitiae* (pp. 252–3 *infra*). The qualifications of the jurisconsult are given (p. 268 *infra*) and include power of psychological observation, experience in life and the study of history. Such a man has then, together with the knowledge of law, such *prudentia* (wisdom in the experiences of life) as to qualify him to be a student of jurisprudence, a view which places jurisprudence as an emphatically inductive study.

3 The descriptive titles of the books have been supplied by the present translator, and are not those of Vives, who simply distinguishes the book by ordinal numbers.

directions of civilisation. In fact this book contains the first modern descriptive history of civilisation. Encyclopaedic as were Vives' interests, he brings his empirical, inductive method to the reconstruction of each. In his *Causes of the Corruptions of the Arts* he had shown in multitudinous detail the stupefying effects of authority. But in his *Transmission of Knowledge* he supplies the alternative method of appeal to experience as offering an explanation of "origins" of the arts and sciences as well as providing the basis of a vitally new method of education. When, nearly three hundred years afterwards, Pestalozzi expressed his aim in the memorable words, "I want to psychologise education," his attitude was in continuous development from the starting-point first established by Vives. The appeal away from authority to experience involved the application of the inductive method. It demanded a psychology on empirical lines. Vives gave it the new direction. He was the last of the Mediaevalists; and also, the first of the modern scientists.

But distinctive as this achievement was, and more progressive still as was Bacon's contribution to the scientific impulse, as Dean Church pointed out, Bacon's views were only "poetical science" compared with the "mathematical and precise science" which was brought to its development by Sir Isaac Newton. In the hands of the latter, scientific method rose to a standard, a *censura veri*, for which Vives groped in vain, and towards which Bacon apparently did all that was at his time possible, without a deeper grasp than the mathematics[1] of his age could provide, and in which he, to his own loss and to the loss of his age, was by no means well equipped. Bacon devised the modern scientific method, but it was developed to fruition by

[1] It will be noted that Vives advocated the study of Mathematics (see p. 201 *et seqq. infra*). He wishes them to be pursued so as to obtain from them such help "as will be useful" in the student's life (p. 207 *infra*). For the distinctive position of Vives in connexion with the teaching of Mathematics see Foster Watson, *The Beginnings of the Teaching of Modern Subjects*, p. 254 *et seqq*.

Newton. The forerunner who heralded the appeal to experience in the study of man and nature, and made the bold bid for the empirical, inductive method in both scientific investigation and in teaching, as the only refuge from the survival of mediaeval authority, was Juan Luis Vives.

**Vives and the Study of Psychology.** The *de Anima et Vita* of Vives was published in 1538[1]. It was, however, written prior to the *de Disciplinis*, i.e. prior to 1531[2], and Vives borrows passages from it, in dealing with the adaptation of educational training for the various dispositions to be found amongst different pupils, and to the training of sharpness in observation, capacity in comprehension, and power in comparison and judgment. Vives' views as to the "choice of wits," and the methods of judging boys' powers and character (the "trial of wits") evidently influenced Ascham and Mulcaster as already noticed, and probably stirred Juan Huarte a compatriot of Vives to write a comprehensive treatise on the *Examination of Men's Wits*[3], as Richard Carew, the English translator, called it. Huarte thought that an examination of children by experienced physicians, watching the earliest activities and efforts of children, might be so conducted as to determine the occupation in life to which they might most usefully be trained. The right seed might thus be sown in the right soil of children's minds. Vives discusses several tests of boys' abilities, as e.g. arithmetic shows sharpness or slowness of mind. Memory

[1] The title-page says: "Opus insigne, nunc primum in lucem editum." (Basle, September, 1538. Robert Winter.)

[2] See p. 73 *infra*. This point is not unimportant, since it shows that Vives had specifically studied Psychology before writing on Education.

[3] Huarte's title is *Examen de Ingenios para las Ciencias*, written in 1557. Carew's translation (1594) was not taken from Huarte direct, but from the Italian translation of Camillo Camilli (Venice 1582). Huarte's book was translated into German by the great critic G. E. Lessing. A second translation into English was made by Edward Bellamy in 1698, with the title *The Tryal of Wits*. Dr J. M. Guardia: *Essai sur l'Ouvrage de J. Huarte* is an able and thorough treatise on Huarte, Paris 1853.

indicates natural ability, both in the aspect of ready comprehension and in that of faithful retention. The play of children reveals their real mental inclinations, for they show their real nature when at play.

This psychological study is to be turned to practical account. "Every two or three months let the masters deliberate and judge with paternal affection and grave discretion, concerning the minds of their pupils, and appoint each boy to that work for which he seems most fit....When unwilling minds are driven to uncongenial work, we see that almost all things turn out wrong and distorted[1]." Boys with minds unsuited for "letters" should not be unduly trained in them, and even those who have been admitted into the school should not be advanced to those parts of a subject for which they manifest no aptitude[2]. In the treatment of *Higher Studies*, speaking of spiritual subjects, Vives advises the teacher[3], or shall we not say in this instance? the priest, to study psychology[4]. Could the argument be better put: "The study of man's soul exercises a most helpful influence on all kinds of knowledge, because our knowledge is determined by the intelligence and grasp of our minds, not by the things themselves." Vives' inclusion of the consideration of the psychological attitude of the jurisconsult is parallelled by his description of the psychological adaptability which should distinguish the physician in his treatment of the sick man[5].

The *de Anima* is a comprehensive treatise founded on Aristotle's book with the same title, but written in the spirit of one "accustomed to give his assent to reason rather than to human authority[6]." It deals with a large number of subjects,

[1] p. 82 *infra*.
[2] As e.g. in Nature-Studies—see p. 169.
[3] The actual word used by Vives is "doctor."
[4] p. 211 *infra*.
[5] p. 225 *infra*.
[6] p. 213 *infra*.

amongst which are: sensation and the separate senses, cognition, reason, judgment, language, contemplation, will, sleep[1], dreams, old age, death, immortality[2]. In addition Vives treats of the feelings and passions including love, hate, joy, hope, anger, envy, jealousy, grief, fear, shame and pride[3].

The independence of Vives from Aristotle may be demonstrated by his illustrations. When speaking of two associated ideas [*recordatio gemina*] he says, "it often happens that our mind travels more readily from the lesser to the greater than *vice-versa*, meaning by the greater, the more excellent. For instance, as often as I see a house at Brussels, which is opposite to the Royal Palace, Idiaqueus comes into my mind, for he is the occupier of it. It was in that house very often, as far as his business would allow, we talked for a long time over matters most pleasant to both of us. Now, as often as I revolve the idea of Idiaqueus in my mind, I do not think of the Palace, because the memory of my friend and his house is more noteworthy to me than the idea of the Royal Palace. It is the same with sounds, tastes, smells. When I was a boy at Valencia, I suffered from fever. Whilst my taste was perverted, I ate cherries. For many years afterwards, whenever I tasted fruit, I not only recalled the fever but also seemed to experience it again.

[1] There are at least eight quotations from Vives' *de Anima* which I have noted in Robert Burton's *Anatomy of Melancholy* (1621). One is the passage where Vives wonders how schoolmen could sleep quietly, "and were not terrified in the night, or walk in the dark, they had such monstrous questions and the thought of such terrible matters all day long." Burton also quotes from Vives' *de Institutione Christianae Feminae*, the *Commentaries on St Augustine's Civitas Dei*, the *de Causis Corruptarum Artium*, and the *de Veritate Fidei Christianae*.

[2] On the above topics of the *de Anima et Vita* Dr Gerhard Hoppe has written: *Die Psychologie des J. L. Vives*, Berlin 1901.

[3] On this part of Vives' *de Anima*, a monograph has been written by Roman Pade: *Die Affektenlehre des J. L. Vives*, Münster-i.-W. 1893. Vives strikingly says in his Preface to the *de Anima*, Psychology presents special difficulties "because we have nothing above and beyond the mind, which can look down and judge on it below."

Wherefore it behoves us to let the 'clues' intended to stir up our memory, be quite bare of importance, lest they should destroy the significance of what they are to suggest to us."

Interesting as Vives is on the subject of Association of Ideas, pedagogically he is still more significant in his declaration that "the senses are our first teachers[1]." Sight is, says Vives, the chief of the senses, from the point of view of knowledge. But after a certain stage of knowledge has been reached, the sense of hearing teaches us in a wider reach, on greater subjects of thought, and in less time, than sight. For we receive in a minimum of time, through teaching, what took a vast time to become a matter of knowledge at all, and hearing was therefore well termed by Aristotle, "the sense of learning." It is at this point that Vives introduces a reference to a deaf and dumb man who became a student. The incident was told by Rodolph Agricola[2], who stated that he had seen the man. Vives expresses amazement, since he recognises that nothing is easier than to learn by listening to a teacher, *if one has the sense of hearing*. But God has wonderfully extended the power of learning that it is possible to become self-taught, and *a man may become his own teacher*.

**Language-teaching in Education.** There was unanimity amongst the scholars of Vives' time, whether they belonged to the old order of mediaevalism or to the new order

[1] In the section *de Discendi Ratione*, in the *de Anima*, Bk. II. cap. 8. Precisely the same statement from Rousseau in his *Émile* has received high commendation.

[2] In the *de Inventione Dialectica*. In connexion with the story of the deaf and dumb man quoted by Vives, it is worth noting that the first known systematic attempt to educate the deaf, was made in Spain, where Petrus Pontius, a Benedictine monk, taught the deaf to speak by instructing them first in writing, "then pointing out to them the objects signified by the written characters, and finally guiding them to the motions of the tongue, etc., which correspond to the characters." (Quoted from the *Philosophia Sacra* of F. Vallesius, 1590, by Sir Wm. Hamilton: *Discussions*, etc., 1866, p. 177.)

of the Renascence as to the necessity of training scholars in the use of Latin. But this unanimity was apparent rather than real. Accordingly, in his attempt to lay down the conditions of Latin teaching, Vives was beset with difficulties behind and before. The mediaeval teaching of Latin was soaked in corruption by its inseparable connexion with dialectic. In his treatise against the *Pseudo-dialecticians* and in the *Causes of the Corruptions of the Arts*, Vives had copiously and irresistibly illustrated the barbarity of diction and incorrectness of grammar of the mediaeval Latinity. Erasmus tells us that the very schoolmasters delighted in hitting upon such words as "bubsequa, bovinator, manticulator, or other obsolete crabbed terms." One of them after twenty years of the study of grammar made it the chief part of his prayers that his life might be spared till he had learned how rightly to distinguish between the eight parts of speech, "which no grammarian, whether Greek or Latin, had yet accurately done." Vives, as we have seen, had bemoaned the Latinity of the dialecticians and had asserted that Cicero would not know or understand their conversation if they spoke their "Latin" in his presence. Erasmus puts an answer to the criticism of their Latin into the mouths of the divines, that it is not for the dignity "of Holy Writ, our profession, that we should be compelled to follow any grammar rules." For it was a "great majesty of these Duns doctors, if *to them only* it be lawful to speak false Latin." They had no need to pride themselves on this power, adds Erasmus, "for many cobblers and clouters (patchers) can do that as well as they."

The satirical account of Latin as it was learned and taught at the beginning of the 16th century given by Erasmus in the *Praise of Folly* was a whip and a scourge to the schoolmasters and dialecticians and divines of the old order, on account of their crude and corrupt Latin. It is easy, in the light of later knowledge, to under-estimate the ostentatious official strength of the mediaeval forces in the days of Erasmus and Vives. It was only satire of the boldest stamp that could make reform of studies possible. The *Praise of Folly* was trenchant and eloquent enough to become popular, and to turn the forces of scholasticism into ridicule. But Erasmus' book did not stand alone. The *Letters of Obscure Men* has been called the national satire of Germany, for which country Herder held that this book "had effected incomparably more than Hudibras for England, or Gargantua for France, or the Knight of La Mancha for Spain[1]." But the extent of the influence of the *Letters of Obscure Men*, whilst no doubt intensively greatest in Germany, was not only wide as humanism itself, but so subtly clever and innocent (on the surface) were these *Letters* that the very foes they attacked, the masters, preceptors, doctors, licentiates, cursors in theology, members of orders, were half in doubt whether the attack was not directed against the "poets" as the humanists were called.

This triumph of literary art which gives the most realistic picture of contemporary academic and literary life of the first part of the 16th century outside of the humanistic camp, was, to quote the words of Mr F. G. Stokes, "the mirthful trumpet blast heard within the ramparts of mediaevalism, that announced if it did not cause their impending fall[2]."

Naturally no subject of school-teaching suffered so much as the Latin language from the mediaeval oppression of corrupt dialectics and grammar. In a concrete form this can be illustrated by citing a work written by Henry Bebel, called the *Misuse of the Latin Language* (1500), in which a list is made of corrupt Latin words then used. This was followed by a more

[1] Sir Wm. Hamilton, *Discussions*, 3rd ed. p. 203.

[2] F. G. Stokes, *Epistolae Obscurorum Virorum. The Latin Text, with an English Rendering, Notes, and an Historical Introduction*, 1909. This excellently edited work now renders accessible to the English reader a remarkable book. No books for the student are comparable in the light they throw upon the problem which met the humanists in their struggle against mediaeval survivals, with the above work together with the *Praise of Folly* of Erasmus.

comprehensive list compiled by Cornelius Crocus[1], with a view of improving spoken Latin by supplying words to be avoided.

On the positive side of correct and eloquent expression in Latin speech and writing, one book of special influence had been published, before Vives wrote his *de Disciplinis*, viz. the *Elegances of the Latin Tongue* of Laurentius Valla. This work dealt very fully with Latin syntax, inflexions, and synonyms of expression, and although Vives criticised it, as he felt bound to do, on points of scholarship, yet it made a notable advance[2] on all its predecessors in the possibilities of Latin teaching. And Erasmus, for the profit of teachers and students, provided the valuable and widely-spread little book on *Variety of expression* (the *de Copia*) in 1511.

Humanism, therefore, stood for Latin as the language of scholarship, as did mediaevalism, but it was for pure Latin, for conversational purposes and for writing. Pure Latin meant Latin such as Cicero or any other educated Roman would have spoken, and therefore in the Renascence view, must be associated with the reading of classical authors, who alone contain what can be known as to Latin usage in speech and in composition, since the mediaeval tradition of the old written Latin was utterly untrustworthy, and the continuity of the old rustic dialects of Latin had developed in accordance with the needs of the daily life of the people, and outside of literary usages. In other words the Renascence view demanded that classical Latin should be brought back to life again. In the next generation to Vives, Sturm keenly laments the disabilities of the modern compared with the Roman child. "Cicero was but twenty

[1] The title is *Farrago sordidorum verborum, sive Augiae stabulum repurgatum*, c. 1520. See L. Massebieau, *Les Colloques Scolaires du Seizième Siècle*, p. 43.

[2] Hallam says: "If those who have done most for any science, are those who have carried it farthest from the point whence they set out, philology seems to owe quite as much to Valla as to anyone who has come since.' *Introd. to Lit. of Europe*, Part I. chap. 3.

years of age when he delivered his speeches in behalf of Quintius and Roscius; but in these days, where is there the man, even of eighty, who could make such speeches?"

Erasmus, as he did not hesitate to make known, wished to be "a citizen of the whole world, not of a single city," and regarded Latin as practically the only possible language for literature and education. His opinion was, as Mr Woodward puts it, "that nothing justifies the abandonment of a universal, highly developed and historic speech such as is Latin, for a series of local, rudimentary and obscure jargons[1]."

Vives showed a distinct independence on the subject of language teaching. Like Erasmus he hated the barbarism of the Latin of the old schools. Speech is the instrument of human society, for the exercise of the social instinct. Hence the particular language used, this or that, will primarily depend on its effectiveness as a means of communication and secondarily on its resources for eloquence and brilliancy[2].

**A universal language.** The original language which Adam spoke was probably perfect. Hence that would be the desirable universal language, had not sin led to the punishment of a Babel of languages. Vives considers that as things are, a common language, at any rate amongst Christians, is a unifying force for religion, for commerce and for general knowledge. And the Latin, above all languages known to him, seems to satisfy best most of the suggested conditions[3]. For the Latin language, formerly spoken when so many branches of knowledge were best known, the mother-tongue of so many distinguished men of intellect and activity, who by their writings enriched its vocabulary, provides the condition of "a man who has the good fortune to be born in a well-taught state." Two considerations have special weight in connexion with Latin, first the wealth of

[1] W. H. Woodward, *Erasmus concerning Education*, p. 63.

[2] See p. 39 and p. 90 *infra*.

[3] Book III. chap. I, beginning p. 91 *infra*, gives the full discussion of the question.

knowledge contained in it, and secondly its diffusion through so many nations, that to give it up would cause confusion in the world of knowledge, and a great estrangement amongst men, on account of their ignorance of any other languages[1]. This objection specially applied to scholars of the time, who either did not know any other language, or at least, like Erasmus, were unwilling to use them. Vives shows solicitude also for the value of a common language for what we call now missionary purposes. If only Mahometans had some language in common with Christians, he believes they "would cast in their lot with us[2]." It is *some* common language that Vives desires.

**Latin and other Languages.** Though the practical advantages of the adoption of Latin as a common language attract Vives, compared with Laurentius Valla he is cold in its praise[3]. For Vives there is no special, or at least, unique formal discipline in Latin to warrant the depreciation of other languages. Speech is given to satisfy a need, and is for use, developed by use, not for display of erudition[4]; therefore that language should be used by any student in which he can

[1] p. 92 *infra*.

[2] pp. 92–3 *infra*. Vives had an especial interest in the Arabic of Mahometans through being a native of S.-E. Spain. He leaves Hebrew for the study of the Old Testament as optional, if the student is strong-minded enough to withstand Jewish falsification. See p. 95.

[3] Naturally the Italians were the keenest protagonists of Latin. Laurentius Valla said:

"Our ancestors have given to the nations the Latin language, a divine present, true food of the mind. We have lost Rome, lost the Empire, and lost domination, not by our fault but through the misfortune of the times. However, thanks to this domination, still more glorious, we now reign over a great part of the earth. Italy is ours, ours is France; ours Spain, Germany, Pannonia, Dalmatia, Illyria and many other countries. For the Roman Empire extends wherever the Latin tongue is spoken....How long, Quirites (for thus I call all those who use the Latin tongue), are you going to permit your city to be occupied by the Gauls, i.e. pure Latinity to be overwhelmed by barbarism?" *Elegantiae Latinae Linguae* (Praefatio).

[4] p. 96 *infra*.

best communicate his thoughts and knowledge. Vives steps apart from his brother humanists, from Laurentius Valla, from Erasmus, and enters a territory almost entirely his own, in the early Renascence, when he says: "We ought to welcome a good sentence expressed in French or Spanish, whilst we should not countenance corrupt Latin[1]."

For the rest, with his mind bent on the utilitarian aspect (in the best sense of the term) of speech, Vives demanded that, whatever language was used, the real matter of importance was the learning of the "solid things[2]" written in it. "Let students remember," says Vives, "that if nothing is added to their knowledge by the study of a language, they have only arrived at the gates of knowledge, or are still hovering in the entrance-hall. Let them remember that it is of no more use to know Latin and Greek than French or Spanish, if the value of the knowledge which can be obtained from the learned languages is left out of the account[3]." And, again, to the same purpose he says[4], "What are languages other than words? Or what importance is it to know Latin, Greek, Spanish and French, if the knowledge contained in those languages were taken away from them?"

Vives' doctrine of the equality of languages as instruments for the adequate communication of the knowledge of "solid things," as well as of the thoughts and judgments of one individual to another, is too remarkable in a writer of the early part of the

[1] p. 296 *infra*.

[2] Vives has been suggested as a source of many of the educational views in the *Tractate of Education* (see *Nineteenth Century*, Oct. 1909) in an article: "*A Suggested Source of Milton's Tractate.*" With the passages cited from Vives above, may be compared from the *Tractate*: "Though a linguist should pride himself to have all the tongues that Babel cleft the world into, yet if he have not studied the solid things in them as well as the words and lexicons, he were nothing so much to be esteemed a learned man, as any yeoman or tradesman competently wise in his mother dialect only."

[3] p. 163 *infra*. [4] p. 274 *infra*.

16th century, to be established upon what might seem to be a chance utterance. For it emphasises to a still higher degree the realistic aspect of his educational ideas, which we saw he had developed in his advocacy of Nature-studies. It may perhaps be said that nothing more distinctive as to the position of Latin, relatively to other languages in education was written even by John Locke[1], than the following, which may be regarded as Vives' manifesto on the subject:

"'To be eloquent,' says Quintilian, 'is to express all the thoughts which you have conceived in your mind, and to convey them to those who listen.' Unless this is done, all the higher parts of Rhetoric are superfluous, and it is like a sword, hidden within, and sticking to, the sheath. *What particular language is employed is of no consequence.* For in the Scythian, French, German and Spanish languages there are many eloquent men. If a man is learned and fluent in Latin and Greek he will not appear to be so, to a man who speaks some other language than those. For Latinists and Graecians are *barbarians* to the Parthians and Medes. Livy was more eloquent than many who had been born at Rome, though Pollio said of him that he talked with wisdom, but in the dialect of his native Padua. Perchance, he was more eloquent than Pollio himself! The same Asinius Pollio said of Latro Portius that 'he was eloquent in his own native Spanish.' How much more fluent and eloquent was Anacharsis than many Athenians, whether he was discussing subjects of nature or of morals, in Scythian or in Greek, though he committed solecisms, or rather Scythicisms in the latter? No one, indeed, ought to like or approve of what is filthy or vicious in a language. From the readiness to

[1] Lange (pp. 850–1) deals with the comparison of Locke's general views on education with those of Vives, disclosing considerable differences through the fact that Locke no longer regarded Latin as a spoken common language, and the separation of the principle of utility from the religious factor, which includes in its scope the future as well as the present world, in Vives view.

pass by the bad have proceeded many of the disasters which have befallen the arts, as well as degeneration in the power of judgment. But, assuredly, if the option is offered, who is there who would not vastly prefer impure and faulty speech, concerned with great and lofty material, rather than the most elegant and ornate language elaborated over trifles[1]?"

**The Teaching of Latin Grammar[2].** Having adopted the general principle of utility Vives regards grammar teaching in Latin as desirable just so far as it furthers the end of acquiring the practical ability to use Latin, viz. for speaking purposes, the reading of authors and the "solid things" in them, and for composition. He is in entire revolt against the mediaeval importation of metaphysical conceptions into grammar, and the laborious compilations of grammatical rules and exceptions with which the boys of the time were plagued. All the arts, in Vives' opinion, arise from nature, and accordingly grammar originally is only the statement of ordinary usage in ordinary natural speech. It is an inductive art, and the failing of the contemporary schoolmasters was in regarding the rules of grammar, only to be gathered by long processes of induction, as if they were the commands of artificial dictatorial authoritativeness, or *à priori* prescriptions which the boy was to learn first, and then deductively apply them to the accidence of the words and the syntax of the constructions which he found in the authors he read. Hence the custom had arisen of learning the whole art of grammar first, with rules and exceptions before proceeding to reading authors, who, apparently, were chiefly of

[1] *De Causis Corruptarum Artium*, *Vivis Opera* VI. p. 180.

[2] Vives states his idea of a grammar-teacher (*grammaticus*): "The office of a grammar-teacher is to form the mouth and the hand of the child; thence to build up his intelligence, so that he may be delivered up to the pursuit of the other arts supported by the greatest help possible from the authors whom he has studied under the guidance of the grammarian." *Vivis Opera* VI. pp. 78–9.

use for the verification of the grammar rules. Against this type of procedure, Vives vigorously protested.

We have seen that he regarded the name of grammar-teacher as most honourable, and required him to be a man "furnished and adorned with literature." Only such teachers, he thought, could duly train youth. Often the old type of teacher, says Vives, attempted to draw "the immeasurable stream of linguistic usage through their grammatical formulae," whereas Grammar, Logic, and Rhetoric were all observed and derived from the speech employed in ordinary conversation. Usage, in Roman times, was not determined by the grammatical rules. He is quite explicit as to the "corruptions" which have followed on the perversity of these grammarians. "Grammarians have not only weakened and broken the compass of speech by reducing it into the meagre and penurious prescript of grammar rules; but they have also corrupted it with many errors, in that they have spoken otherwise than they ought to do; *well, in respect of rules, but ill in respect of ordinary usage, which is the lady and mistress of speaking.* You may see full many exact masters of grammatical art in this manner pollute their speech with foul enormities, whilst they follow grammatical art which cannot by any devices include every usage, through the variety of usage, and through the liability of language to change. Nor does usage always follow analogy. Accordingly, grammarians could not duly collect and bring every detail into their categories. Add to these considerations the fact that changes constantly were taking place at the arbitrament of the multitude, in whose hands is the spoken language. Now, of course, since we have no people of the Latin or Greek speech, the laws of those languages can only be gathered from the writings of authors[1]."

[1] The *Causes of the Corruptions of the Arts*, *Vivis Opera* VI. p. 79. The translation above is given almost entirely in the words of Joseph Webbe who quotes (with acknowledgment) from Vives very freely in his *Appeale to Truth*, 1622. For an account of the controversy about the teaching of grammar, see the chapter on "The Grammar War" in Foster Watson, *English Grammar Schools*, p. 276 *et seqq.* Vives seems to be the source

The war was to come between Grammar and the Reading of Authors. It was to be a long war, and was not settled even by the time of John Locke, who still had to complain that grammar-teaching almost monopolised the attention of the school teacher[1]. But Locke still considers that Latin is absolutely necessary to a gentleman. His remedy is substantially the application of the method suggested by Vives, and afterwards by Montaigne, i.e. let children learn Latin as they learn French "by talking and reading[2]."

The difficulties of applying this simple sounding alternative of reading of authors in the place of grammar, even at the early stages, were, in the time of Vives, undoubtedly formidable. Vives' own statement, which seems to have greatly impressed Webbe, in 1622, shows how Grammar had so to say absorbed literature. Webbe thus translates from Vives:

"This little creeping fountain (of grammar) having in time,

from which the discussion started in modern times, though, of course, Quintilian had pointed out to the grammarians of his time that "custom" is the best schoolmistress for languages. The position of Vives and of Webbe (who is one of the most emphatic of all English writers on teaching Latin, by reading and speaking it, rather than from the preparatory training of text-books of grammar) is that, on the whole, the method for learning a foreign language is in principle that by which we learned our vernacular. The most valiant pioneer in our own generation of the new movement (which indeed is the old movement of Vives) in language teaching was the late W. H. Widgery, in that excellent brochure *The Teaching of Languages in Schools* (1888), which even now in the large multiplication of books for the teaching of languages, no thoughtful educationist should omit to consult.

[1] Locke says (1693): "When I consider what ado is made about a little Latin and Greek, how many years are spent in it and what a noise and business it makes to no purpose, I can hardly forbear thinking that the parents of children still live in fear of the schoolmaster's rod, which they look on as the only instrument of education; as a language or two to be its whole business."

[2] See Ascham's *Scholemaster* (Mayor's ed.), p. 6. Locke however regard the method of learning Latin by conversation as having become practically impossible, and advocates the device of interlineal translations of Latin authors.

through continual and universal employment, gotten credit, wealth, and patronage, grew ambitious; and, under the first title of entire simplicity, hath at last engrossed rivers, streams, and branches, out of Orators, Poets, and Historians; yea, and almost out of all the greatest arts and sciences; and is become a full, swollen, and overflowing Sea; which, by a strong hand arrogates unto itself (*and hath well near gotten*) the *whole traffic in learning, but especially for languages*[1]."

**Latin-speaking.** Whatever the difficulties might be of overcoming the dominant tradition of preparing for language-teaching by grammar text-books, Vives was perfectly clear as to the rightness of his plea for at least minimising their use. The way we learn our mother-language contains within it the principle for acquiring any second language. "If we lived amongst a people speaking Latin or Greek, I should prefer to observe their linguistic usages and to converse with them for one year than to bestow ten years to this purpose under the best and most reputed schoolmasters[2]."

Latin-speaking, therefore, formed a main feature of Vives' scheme of early instruction in Latin[3]. Pronunciation is first to be carefully taught. Correctness here is essential, for those who speak good Latin and Greek will understand one another, but the Spanish speaker of his particular kind of dog-Latin is not understood by the German speaker of some other sort of jargon Latin[4]. The minimum of Grammar is laid down by

[1] Webbe, *Appeale to Truth*, p. 3, translating from Vives.

[2] Vives also writes with his accustomed urgency to the same effect in the *Against the Pseudo-Dialecticians*, in a passage which should be quoted: "Latin and Greek speech came before grammatical, rhetorical, dialectical, formulae....We do not speak Latin in a particular way because the Latin grammar orders it to be so spoken, but on the contrary, the Latin grammar orders us to speak a particular way because the Romans spoke in that way." *Vivis Opera* III. p. 41.

[3] See Book III. chap. 3, p. 107 *et seqq.* For training in Latin-speaking Vives composed the *Exercitatio* or School Dialogues (see p. li, note[2] *supra*).

[4] p. 96.

Vives[1]. Then begins the reading of books, all much as Ascham planned for students afterwards.

Latin-speaking in the pupil requires observation of the master's speech, and calls for the system of note-books already referred to[2]. Memory is to be deliberately cultivated[3] so as to retain correct and elegant expressions for speech and writing.

Speech is learned by the pupil speaking, together with the master's corrections of the pupil when he pronounces wrongly and speaks incorrectly[4]. So in composition, in the early exercises of letter-writing, of free composition, or of translation, all can be reduced to practice on the part of the pupil, together with direction and correction of mistakes by the teacher[5]. Vives' whole treatment is to throw the substantial work on the boy, to exercise his activity of mind, his ingenuity, his judgment. The paper-books, double translation, repetition of his new knowledge to others—all serve this purpose[6]. The secret of all advance is the boy's own self-activity. Therefore Vives' maxim is, whatever knowledge is attained, whether by one's own unaided efforts, or from instruction, "turn it to use."

**Mental discipline of linguistic studies.** The application of this principle of self-activity to rhetoric was of great significance. Vives by dispensing with the old obsessions of logic and grammar made room for the study of rhetoric, with

[1] p. 97 *infra.* It is of interest to note that when the boy has need of a grammar Vives recommends the text-book "passing under Erasmus' name," but which as Vives tells us was "composed by Lily and revised by Erasmus." This was the earlier form of "Lily," and is a distinctly progressive *short* grammar.

[2] p. xxxviii *supra.* [3] p. 109. [4] p. 111.

[5] Book III. chaps. 3, 4, 5, 6.

[6] "Whatever the boys have heard from their master let them first repeat to fellow-pupils more advanced than themselves, or to an under-master and afterwards to the master himself," p. 110 *infra.* Sir Wm. Hamilton says that all authority acquiesces in Vives' conclusion that "nothing is so conducive to great erudition as to teach what one knows." *Discussions*, etc., 1866 ed. pp. 776–7 n.

emphasis on the "inventions," viz. collections of subject-matter of composition made by the pupils themselves, and with forms of eloquence, to be best cultivated in any language which gave the writer the most spontaneity of expression. This was the principle of the reformed logic and rhetoric of Pierre de la Ramée, in the second half of the 16th century, and in the development of these subjects after him. These reforms led to rhetoric becoming the basis of a training which proved of high significance, for instance in England, in preparing our literary men, statesmen and gentlemen in the latter part of the 16th and through the first half of the 17th century[1].

In the time of Vives, no satisfactory Latin Dictionary existed for school purposes[2]. The teaching of vocabularies therefore had to be undertaken as part of the school-work[3], and the teacher was required to make notes in his readings, so as to supply his pupils with the names of objects not likely to be mentioned in the simple books he was reading. The turning-point of Dictionary facilities came with the great Dictionary[4] of Robert Estienne (Stephanus) which appeared in 1531, the very year of the publication of the *de Disciplinis*. Besides compiling his great Latin Dictionary, Estienne prepared a small Dictionary for boys (1550). It was after this date that school-dictionaries for Latin became available[5]. Vives declared[6] that the absence of adequate Dictionaries was a "great lack." But in the same way that, at the present time in the science-studies of schoolboys, educationists often suggest the predominant value of apparatus made by the teacher and the pupil for their own experiments and demonstration purposes, so with the

1 *English Grammar Schools*, chap. XXVII.

2 p. 134. The books for the advanced student for consultation as to the meaning of words are named—for Latin, pp. 141–2, and for Greek, p. 150.

3 pp. 133–4.

4 *Thesaurus Linguae Latinae*, published at Paris.

5 In England John Withals published his *Short Dictionarie for Yonge Beginners*, c. 1554.

6 *Vives and the Renascence Education of Women*, p. 247.

early 16th century Latin studies, the necessity for the pupil of finding out for himself and noting down in his Paper-book the Ciceronian usage of a particular word or phrase, must have resulted in a kind of self-made Dictionary. From the necessary search and research, there must have arisen an educational value in the intellectual activity, which is often lacking in present-day classical teaching, on account of the comprehensiveness of text-books provided; leaving little for the pupil to do, but to appropriate the material placed in his hands by the labour of others. Vives' methods are therefore more analogous to those by which elementary science is studied, practically, to-day.

**Latin School Authors.** The early Latin studies comprise the easy reading in Latin stories and little verses such as those of Cato or Michael Varinus, then the letters of Pliny Caecilius and, of course, those of M. T. Cicero. Vives does not hesitate to introduce the letters of Ægidius Calentius, though he was not an ancient but a Renascence writer, on the ground that his letters were suitable for boys' interests in reading. Erasmus' *On Variety of Expression* (*de Copia*) and on *Correct Pronunciation* (*de recta Pronunciatione*) follow. Then elementary rhetoric from Quintilian, Diomedes, Mancinellus, or John Despauterius, whilst the *Tables* of Peter Mosellanus will be found useful. Then the boy begins composition seriously—first, by choosing the author's own words and descriptions for subject-matter on his theme, mixed with passages of his own. Then Erasmus' *On Variety of Expression* will help him to vary his phrases. Vives then introduces a general sketch of universal history, and a presentation of geography such as Pomponius Mela affords[1].

The student then comes to the "purer" writers whom he must study so closely that he will be able to follow them as standards in his own writing: Caesar, Cicero's Letters to his Friends, particularly those to Atticus.

[1] For the details of this plan, see p. 134 *et seqq*.

The dramatists, important for their conversational Latin, will include Terence and chosen parts from Plautus, with Seneca's *Tragedies*.

From the poets are to be read Virgil's *Æneid*, *Georgics* and *Bucolica*, Lucan, Horace's *Odes*, Persius and some of Martial's *Epigrams*. The *Metamorphoses* and the six books of the *Fasti* of Ovid should be read for a knowledge of mythology. Of Christian poets, Prudentius and Baptista of Mantua are to be read. And, here again, amongst the poets, a modern work is admitted, the *Rusticus* of Politian.

Of historians, Vives names parts of Livy and of Valerius Maximus. Lastly, Cicero's *Orations*.

In addition to the above books which the teacher will read with the boys, the pupils are expected to read the following authors privately: Thomas Linacre, Antony of Lebrija, Mancinellus, Laurentius Valla, a critic like Servius Honoratus. Cardinal Hadrian should be read for his collection of examples; and Guillaume Budé on the *Pandects* and on *Coinage*.

In further historical studies, the rest of the books of Livy should be read, Tacitus and Sallust. For mythological poetry, Vives recommends Boccaccio, who borrowed considerably from Ovid.

For purposes of extension of the student's vocabulary (as we have seen, in the absence of dictionaries, of great importance), he should read: Cato, Varro, Columella, Palladius, Vitruvius, and Grapaldus. The student should read all the orations of Cicero and the declamations of Quintilian.

Finally, as standards of style, to be kept before the pupil, Vives names the modern writers: Longolius, Pontanus, Politian and, it is interesting to notice, Erasmus.

Vives' method makes great demands on the reading of teachers and scholars. He advocates, therefore, a library for the Academy, and the teacher is to train the pupil in the choice of books[1]. He was probably the first educationist after the invention of printing to advocate the formation of school libraries.

[1] p. 124. See also pp. 141, 149, 271.

**The Greek Language.** Vives says the value of Language-study is for application to life and he would by no means admit all pupils to Greek studies. It will be quite sufficient for many to learn Latin and a little Greek, just so far as to be able to converse on Greek subjects. An ill-founded affectation of higher studies in Greek is injurious to the student and to the learned world. Men going into official and public life should have a working knowledge of Latin and Greek sufficient for the reading of authors. Such a grounding will assist their work and also be a resource to them in old age. Those intended to become scholars will proceed to the higher authors in Greek[1]. The treatment of both Latin and Greek authors as subjects of study is, like that of Milton, realistic. Latin and Greek are to be studied because the best knowledge on every important subject, in the time of Vives, was thought to be, and largely was, only to be found in authors who had written in those languages.

**Modern Languages.** In one of his letters, Erasmus bears testimony to the ability of Vives in speaking French almost as well as his native Spanish, and to his understanding of Flemish. There is no evidence as to his knowledge of English, but his description of the lodgings in which he lived in London makes it sufficiently probable that he possessed such a minimum as was necessary for dealing with his landlady, and for the ordinary affairs of daily life. For it is certain that the ordinary Londoner of the time, whom he would meet, would speak to him in no other language than English. At Oxford Latin was the College language, and in the house of Sir Thomas More the family, and most of the friends gathered there, could speak Latin, and he would find little opportunity for practising

[1] The whole course in Greek is detailed in Book III. chap. 7, p. 143 *et seqq*. Chapter 8 contains an account of interpretative or critical studies, styled by Vives, "Classical Philology," in connexion with the subject-matter of authors. He also devotes an interesting chapter (chap. 9) to estimates of some of his predecessors and contemporaries.

his English there. At the Court, with Queen Catharine and her friends, probably Vives would speak in Spanish chiefly. Moreover, during the six years of his visits to England, Vives was only in this country for portions of the year. At any rate it is clear that Vives had an interest, from his personal experiences, in the problems of the learning of foreign languages. When he discusses the teaching of rhetoric, he insists that in speaking or writing on public and civil affairs, in their own or other countries, scholars should have direct knowledge of the subjects on which they write, whereas he complains that often contemporary writers have not seen for themselves, "even in a dream," what they venture to write about. "*They do not know the very country, or even the city, in which they are living.* Whilst they are always meditating on ancient Rome, they remain in this age of ours no more than pilgrims to it, as far as language is concerned." Men cannot be called eloquent when they become mute, directly they attempt to speak in another language, and when they cannot apply "three words from the learned and polished language they affect[1]."

Vives has keen enthusiasm for pure Latin-speaking and writing, and he has optimism enough to believe that such men as Politian and Erasmus had won the position of freemen of the Roman Republic, although living so long after the Fall of Rome, but he was also practical enough to realise that a man "competently wise" in a modern language also deserved well, not perhaps of the Latinists, but certainly of humanity at large. For practical wisdom in the affairs of life seeks the instruments—linguistic or otherwise—best fitted for individual competency. Vives knew from his own life in Spain, France, Flanders and England that real knowledge in civil and public affairs could alone come from that intimate relation which can only exist in speaking the language of the country in which one lives. He was unable to write his book on Poor-relief in Flemish, but the Town Council of Bruges took steps to prove the acceptability

[1] *De Causis Corruptarum Artium, Vivis Opera* VI. p. 179.

of his gift by having the work translated into that language. They paid Vives the acceptable compliment of believing that he had written "not for ostentation, but for use." It was appropriate that the popularly conceived works of Vives, e.g. *The Institution of a Christian Woman*, the *Introduction to Wisdom* and *The Colloquies* were called for so early and so often in various vernaculars. The "extemporaneous" characteristic of *The Institution of a Christian Woman* which troubled Erasmus, meant, looked at from another standpoint, its adaptability to the needs of the people as distinct from those of the scholars of the time, in a degree not easily to be attained by elaborately composed treatises, contrived to run the gauntlet of Ciceronian critics.

As for methods of learning foreign languages, Vives had one directive principle. "In a language which is in continual use there is no necessity to frame systematic rules. The language is learned better and more quickly from the people themselves[1]."

Further, it may be said that Vives saw clearly the necessity of the individuality of nations, of which a separate language is one of the outward manifestations. He did not regard it as satisfactory that a man should know far more of the age of Cicero or Pliny than of his grandfathers, "in respect of food, attire, worship and dwellings[2]." Thus, he explicitly states that national customs must differ; some customs would be suitable enough to Germans which would be unsuitable for Spaniards[3]. These customs will have their due effect upon the national education in each country[4]. It is clear, therefore, that when

[1] p. 96 *infra*. Vives, probably, would have warmly approved of Latin-speaking colonies and "cities" to be established of those who could speak Latin, Greek, Hebrew, as a plan for educational teaching of languages, a project of the seventeenth century. See *English Grammar Schools*, p. 313.

[2] p. 209.

[3] p. 256.

[4] p. 252.

he argues for a universal language, i.e. Latin, it is not with a view of superseding national training but with the aim of supplementing that training by affording a medium of international culture. One great unifying element for the people at large, as well as for scholars, amid the diversities of the nations, was for Vives, undoubtedly, "the light of our religion," and the Latin language through which its services spoke, supplied a confirmatory reason for bilingualism—to consist of the vernacular and the international language, Latin[1].

**The Vernacular.** Three great events happened for Spain in 1492, the year of Vives' birth, first Granada was wrested from the Moors by Ferdinand and Isabella, secondly, the discovery of America, under Spanish auspices, by Columbus, and thirdly, the publication by Antony of Lebrija of a Spanish grammar and dictionary. The strain of patriotism in Spain grew intense, and although Spain was divided, like other countries, into districts with different dialects making a common standard difficult, thus early, in 1492, Antony of Lebrija (Antonius Nebrissensis) had attempted to show what Castilian really was. He was the first humanist scholar to produce a grammar of a romance language. It was part of a national movement. Don Diego Hurtado de Mendoza (1503–1575) is the type of the very best Spaniards of the age. First, a statesman and erudite classical scholar, with a library renowned throughout Europe, he retired from active life and composed his vernacular classic *Guerra de Granada*, and, of course, wrote his romance of *Lazarillo de Tormes* in Spanish. The feeling spread that it was, as one critic said, better to be useful to a great number in the vernacular than to a few persons in Latin[2].

Though Vives had left Spain, he was still a Spaniard. His boyish opposition to Antony of Lebrija had changed into

[1] Cf. the Jews, who have always remained bilingual in their educational system.

[2] Quoted by Massebieau, *Les Colloques Scolaires*, p. 163.

admiration both for the latter's classical scholarship and for his pride of nationality. Vives became the first humanist-scholar who advocated the serious study of the vernacular by the teacher. His insistence on the mother's part in the education of children was accompanied by the conviction that the vernacular should be carefully taught to the child by the mother, who should thus in addition become nurse and teacher, and concentrate in herself all the maternal claims of affection. Accordingly, for her children's sake, if not for her own, she must be a book-reader, that she may teach her children and "make them good[1]." As we have already seen[2], for three hundred years the Valencian mothers had passed on the language intact to Valencian children. Mothers are the guarantee of a national language, and it is therefore incumbent on them to impart that language, purely, and to see that, as far as they can control the surroundings, no "rude and blunt" speech gets a hold on the child. When children go to school, they are to speak "in their own tongue, which was born in them in their home, and if they make mistakes in it, let the master correct them." But the school problem we must remember, in Vives' view, was a bilingual one. The children therefore having gained at home and at school the basis of their native tongue, must gradually add the speaking of Latin. There must needs be the pitfall of mixing up the Latin and the vernacular. Vives makes the concession that boys should be allowed to speak the vernacular out of school, "so that they may not accustom themselves in any way to make a hotchpotch of the two languages[3]." As the pupil advances in his study of Latin, he must be required to express his thoughts in

[1] *Vives and the Renascence Education of Women*, p. 123.

[2] p. xlvi *supra*.

[3] p. 110 *infra*. On the relation between classics and the vernacular in Jesuit schools, see T. Corcoran, *Studies in the History of Classical Teaching*, pp. 212–13. Professor Corcoran is one of the few English writers who have appreciatively quoted Vives in their account of methods.

Latin, for nothing is so important in learning a language as practice in speaking it.

It is necessary to bear in mind the fact that in the early part of the 16th century only too frequently the masters knew less of the vernacular than they did of Latin. That this was the case in England is distinctly stated by John Palsgrave, the tutor of the Princess Mary Tudor, sister of Henry VIII. This remarkable man, whom Vives not improbably met at the English Court, was a classical scholar, who knew French so intimately that he practically furnished the French people with rules for their own language[1]. English schoolmasters, according to Palsgrave[2], could write an epistle "right Latin like," speak Latin, and indite Latin verses; "yet for all this, partly because of the rude language used in their native countries [i.e. counties]...and partly because, coming straight from thence to the universities, they have not had occasion to be conversant in such places, where the purest English is spoken, they be not able to express their conceit in their vulgar tongue, nor be sufficient, perfectly, to show the diversities of phrases between our tongue and the Latin (which in my poor judgment is the very chief thing that the schoolmaster should travail in)[3]."

This description of the English schoolmasters was applicable to those of other countries[4], and the only possible way in such circumstances of improving the vernacular teaching of the boys in the schools was to insist on the better training of the teachers themselves in their knowledge of the vernacular. This is precisely what Vives urges in the following important passage:

[1] See Sir Sidney Lee, *French Renaissance in England*, p. 80.

[2] In his translation of the *Comedye of Acolastus*, 1540.

[3] Such a passage throws light on what has presented difficulty to some students of educational history—viz. the fact that the Authorised Latin Grammar was issued in Latin, and the even still more striking fact that some English Grammars were written in Latin, e.g. the *Logonomia Anglica* (Alexander Gill, *c.* 1621).

[4] See p. 14 *infra*, l. 12 from bottom of page, sentence beginning "It is a great advantage."

"Let the teacher know the mother tongue of the boys exactly so that by means of the mother tongue he may make his instruction more pleasant and easier for them. Unless he knows how to express aptly and exactly in the vernacular what he wishes to speak about, he will easily mislead the boys, and these mistakes will accompany them when they are grown up." But even this demand on the teacher is not sufficient. He must also understand the historical growth and development of the vernacular; the words which have come into the language, those which have gone out of use, and those which have changed in meaning. In short, he should be "a Prefect of the treasury of his language," otherwise, in the multitudinous changes of a language, books written a century before in it, will become unintelligible to posterity[1].

Constant to his purpose of making all knowledge available and effective in every direction, Vives deserves credit for his advocacy of the use of the vernacular as far as possible for legal purposes. "All laws should be written in the vernacular, and in intelligible and clear language[2]." As language changes, and old forms become obscure, the state should re-frame the old phrases to the usage of the later generation. Every individual should be made acquainted with what is expected from him in the society in which he lives.

Nothing, perhaps, shows more clearly the practical aspect of Vives' attitude towards the vernacular than his advice to the maid in her prayers, to either make use of the language which she understands, or else to get someone to interpret the Latin in the vernacular for her[3].

[1] p. 103 *infra.*

[2] p. 265. In England, French and Latin were for centuries the legal languages, and discussions on legal cases, "readings in the Moots," were issued in French at any rate up to 1680. Sir John Fortescue, writing on the *Praise of the English Laws* (*c.* 1463), composed his work in the Latin language.

[3] Even then he wishes the maid to be quite clear that speech is for the expression of thought. "Let her not ween that prayer standeth in the

**History.** In dealing with the reading of authors Vives had already made provision for a general sketch of universal history[1] from Adam to the Flood, to Abraham, to Moses. From the Trojan War, the Founding of Rome, on to the Downfall from the Gauls. From Alexander of Macedon, on to the Punic Wars, on to Sulla and Marius, and to the Birth of Christ. From Christ to the Goths and Huns, to Charles the Great, to Gottfried of Bouillon, to the Invasion of Europe by the Turks, to the recent retaking of Granada, and an account of Charles V. Along with the history a general sketch of ancient geography is required, an alliance well in keeping with modern pedagogy. Such courses were to be studied by all boys, as necessary parts of a study of language and literature. After the higher studies of logic, nature-study, rhetoric, the mathematical sciences, the professional subjects for the Church, medicine and law have been discussed, Vives requires the advanced student to consider the conditions for acquiring practical wisdom in life. This is gained, if not by personal experience, in the last resort, at any rate, by the experience of some man or men, now living—or who lived in the past. In this pursuit of wisdom we must make use of the experience of others as well as of our own. We must follow other men's experiences in past ages as well as in the present. Hence we need to study history, which is the source of so much of our knowledge, and prepares us in so many ways for life[2].

Vives is interested in the psychological aspect of historical study, disclosing the essential nature of human beings, and in the study of the manifestations of the affections and passions of the human mind in history[3]. Still more valuable is it to study

murmuring and wagging of the lips, but in the heart and mind." *Vives and the Renascence Education of Women*, p. 89.

[1] p. 135 *infra*.

[2] Vives deals with History-teaching, p. 231 *infra*, and historical writers, pp. 237–49.

[3] p. 232 *infra*.

the achievements and development of the rational judgment. He is so much struck with the unique significance of history as a practical training that he asks: "How are we to account for the fact that our philosophers have not been suited for ruling cities and peoples, except on the ground of their deficiency in historical knowledge, which is the nurse of practical wisdom?" Vives demands attention away from wars and slaughter to the triumphs of peace[1]. He has already shown the value of the historical study of the arts, law, medicine, theology.

The most noteworthy passage in his treatment of history, probably, is his realisation of the value of the study of recent and contemporary history, his power of detachment from the ancient writers, his willingness to consider the modern historians on their merits[2]. "I have not mentioned," he says, "those writers who have written on some small race or state, such as Flanders, Liège, Utrecht. Nor have I included those writers who used the vernacular language such as the Spanish Valera, Froissart, Monstrelet, Philip de Comines, *of whom there are many not less worthy of being known and read than the majority of Greek and Latin historians*[3]."

Vives also wrote critically on the "corruptions" of history. He was impatient with what he called "the lies" of Greek history. "It would be truer to call Herodotus the father of lies than of history." He desires a clean-cut division between history and myth, and is keenly alive to the dangers to historical accuracy from poetical licence. He wants a more exact chronology. He passionately objects to praising Caesar for robbing men of their lives by war[4].

[1] p. 236 *infra*.

[2] Mr W. H. Woodward says: "Vives is almost alone amongst humanists in finding a place for Monstrelet, de Comines and Froissart in historical study" (*Erasmus concerning Education*, pp. 64–5).

[3] Highly as Vives praises these historians, he pointed out what he considered shortcomings in them, in the *de Causis Corruptarum Artium*, *Vivis Opera* VI. p. 108.

[4] *De Causis Corruptarum Artium*, VI. p. 105. "Shall Julius Caesar be

The idea of war amongst Christians aroused Vives' sternest indignation. The glory, as it is called, of war impels men to the slaughter of peoples and races—to horrible crimes. Accounts of wars should only be introduced into histories briefly, barely, and without approval, but rather with detestation. We should not ascribe commendation to a victor, after a long war, but "such a warrior should become an example to us of what a depraved passion of ambition, anger, or lust can bring to birth, and should reveal to us on what a slight and uncertain turning-point the affairs and fortunes of men are based, when we place our trust so completely in the hands of such men[1]." In the *Causes of the Corruptions of the Arts* Vives observes that all wars are civil wars[2]. In the *Commentaries to St Augustine's City of God* he declares: "Men have expelled peace wittingly and of set purpose imagining our whole felicity to consist in the tumults of wars and slaughters. And so we brave it that we have slain thus many men, burnt thus many towns, sacked thus many cities, founding our principal glories upon the destruction of our fellows[3]." Again, in the same work, he says: "Truly fighting belongs neither to good men nor to thieves, nor to any that are men at all, but is a right bestial fury and therefore it was named *Bellum* from *bellua* a beast[4]." So in the *Transmission of Knowledge*, in the chapter on the teaching of history, Vives discountenances sympathy with wars and battles which "equip the mind with examples for the performance of evil and show the ways we may inflict injuries one on another[5]." Finally, in the little *Introduction to Wisdom*, the student's guide

praised because he sent so many thousands of men to violent death, when he could not give life to a single one?"

[1] *De Ratione Dicendi*, *Opera* II. 206. Cf. Kuypers: *Vives in seiner Pädagogik*, pp. 68–9.

[2] *Opera* VI. p. 106.

[3] Healey's translation, Bk XIII. Chap. 19.

[4] *Ibid.* IV. Chap. 4.

[5] p. 236 *infra*. There is a similar condemnation of sympathy with war, p. 31 *infra*.

to study, he admonishes the young pupil: "War, that is to say, robbery without punishment, is a great advancer of men to honour, such is the madness of foolish people[1]."

In accounts of the lives of saints he demands the absolute exactness of truth that he would wish had been observed by the Greek historians, and metes out severe blame on the stories of the saints as told in the *Legenda Aurea*. "How unworthy of saints and Christian men is that history of saints called the *Golden Legends*. How can it be called golden, when it is the composition of a man of iron-countenance and leaden heart? What more disgraceful can be said of that book? How shameful it is for us Christians that the most noble acts of our saints are not handed down to memory more truly and accurately, whether from the standpoint of accurate knowledge or with a view to imitation of so great virtue, when Roman and Greek authors wrote with such great care about their generals, philosophers and wise men[2]." Vives, we have seen, declared his allegiance to the Roman Church. But he also manifests his independence of mind, and makes his protest against what he regards as abuses and corruptions in ecclesiastical traditions.

**The Academy.** The idea of an Academy probably was suggested to Vives' mind by the "School" of Sir Thomas More at Chelsea. At any rate, this thought had occurred to Erasmus in his well-known description of it. "You would say that in More's house Plato's Academy was revived. But I do the house injury in comparing it with Plato's Academy....I should rather call it a school, or university, of Christian religion[3]." Similarly, Vives called his work on *The Transmission of*

[1] Moryson's translation, Chap. III. 57.

[2] Cf. the paragraph on the subject of the history of the Church, pp. 248–9 *infra*.

[3] Erasmus, *Epistolae*, 1642 ed., col. 1506. Erasmus continues: "In it [More's Academy] is none, man or woman, but readeth or studieth the liberal arts. Yet their chief care is that of piety. There is never any one idle. The head of the house governs it, not by lofty carriage and frequent rebukes but by gentleness and amiable manners. Every member of the

*Knowledge* by the alternative title of Christian Education (*de Institutione Christiana*).

So many different associations are clustered round the term "Academy" that it is necessary to see exactly what Vives means by it. "A true Academy," he says, "is an association and harmony of men, equally good as learned, met together to confer the same blessings on all who come there for the sake of learning[1]." No doubt Vives kept in mind his experiences of the College of the Three Languages at Louvain, and Corpus Christi College at Oxford (that institution with the bee-like diligence of the students), as well as the more domestic, family type of training of More's "Academy[2]."

One feature of Vives' Academy is the intellectual advantage to the young from being associated with the old, in whose company they are educated more "liberally and purely[3]." The ordinary branches of knowledge, "the arts," may be taught by masters of different ages, but the training for "service to their country and for civil life" should be in the hands of "wise, old men, as formerly at Rome[4]." Whilst, thus, youths can receive help from old men in the wise practice of life for which Vives cares so deeply, on the other hand the Academy will serve as

household is busy in his place, performing his duty with alacrity, nor is sober mirth wanting." Cf. Vives' account of Economics (p. 257 *infra*).

[1] pp. 63–4 *infra*.

[2] Household education was an important method in the Middle Ages. See details in *Manners and Meals in Olden Times*, ed. Furnivall, p. xvii *et seqq*. Sir Thomas More e.g. had himself been trained in the household of Archbp. Morton, who had prophesied a distinguished career for him. A prototype of More's Academy is to be seen, on the pietistic side, in the household education of Elzear, Count of Sabran and his wife Delphina (see A. T. Drane, *Christian Schools and Scholars*, pp. 536–7). Vives was familiar with a similar tradition in Spain. Talavera, Mendoza and Jimenez made their houses centres of intellectual progress.

[3] p. 70 *infra*.

[4] p. 72 *infra*. See also pp. 258–9. Vives, following Cicero, gives the preference to old men in their social circles and clubs, for their practical wisdom, as compared with learned men "in their schools" (p. 209).

a "haven" to receive those advancing in years, "driven hither and thither in a great tempest of ignorance and vice" in the outside world[1]. Nor is it improbable that the presence of Sir Thomas More's father, Sir John More[2], in the Chelsea home, where four generations lived happily together, was also in the background of Vives' mind.

Pupils were to be admitted to the Academy from seven years of age, and the complete course occupied up to twenty-five years of age. The institution thus was a primary and secondary school, a college and university combined, and included aged men of sound experience and wisdom as a body guard of the best general mature interests of life.

Nothing is more calculated to surprise us than the negative aspect of Vives' Academy, i.e. the entire absence of any suggestion of ecclesiastical control or oversight. It is probably the first proposal of an institution to undertake university work without the aegis of the Church. Vives suggests that teachers should receive their salaries from the State, though he does not seem to have realised that such a proposal involved some degree of state control.

John Calvin's Academy at Geneva has at least common points with Vives' idea, whether suggested by it or not, first that it included a school for children as well as a College for advanced students. Secondly it was independent of any authorisation, either of Regal Charter or of Papal Bull. If it seems unwarrantable to connect Calvin's ideas with Vives as a source, it is at least a striking coincidence that there is so much more in common between the two men's ideas than the name, "Academy."

[1] p. 63. Cf. Izaak Walton's account of Sir Henry Wotton, on his appointment to the Provostship of Eton College. "The College was to his mind, as a quiet harbour to a sea-faring man after a tempestuous voyage."

[2] Judge of the Court of King's Bench. After Sir Thomas More became Chancellor, on passing this Court, on his way to the Chancery, he would enter the Court and ask his father's blessing on his knees.

The site of the Academy is regarded by Vives as of the first importance[1]. The air must be bracing, though the country round should not be too alluring from studies. There must be a good food supply, and the buildings must be well apart from all disturbing noise. The school should not be near any royal or ducal court[2], nor within "the neighbourhood of girls." The buildings should be outside of a town, not too near a public road. Nor should a site be chosen near the boundaries of a province, which would suffer longest and most by the outbreak of war, a consideration not to be overlooked in Vives' remembrance of the wars with the Moors in his native country.

Mulcaster showed close similarity to Vives in his views as to the site of a school[3]. We can hardly help thinking that Milton had Vives' Academy before his mind, when he suggests the "spacious house and ground," to be "at once a school and university, not needing a remove," but to be "absolute" for all studies[4]. Vives prescribes courses for the physician and the lawyer in their studies. The first Academy in England in some respects resembling Vives' views, appears to be that of Thomas Gataker[5] at Rotherhithe, in the first half of the 17th century.

After the Act of Uniformity, there were many schools or academies founded in England after the Gataker type, and of these some few developed into more or less public "Dissenting

[1] p. 53 *et seqq.*

[2] This is a contrast to the Italian tradition when the most renowned of the Renascence Schools were in connection with Courts. It is pointed out by Wychgram that G. W. Leibnitz, the German scholar, held the exact opposite to Vives, viz. that an Academy should be placed in a residential town so that youths could gain an experience in ducal courts, which, he thought, would be of service to them in their training for after life.

[3] *Positions* (Quick's reprint), p. 229.

[4] See *Nineteenth Century*, Dec. 1909, in the article on *A Suggested Source of Milton's Tractate of Education*. Samuel Johnson speaks of "the wonder-working Academy" in Aldersgate Street referring to Milton's own private school there.

[5] Erasmus Middleton, *Biographia Evangelica*, III. p. 290.

Academies," as they were called in the 18th century. They accepted, in the early days, pupils of all ages and stages, and eventually equipped men in the preparatory culture for all professions, by no means restricting themselves to denominational limits. It is claimed that their aim was "to make students thinkers, open their intelligence and give an impetus to further knowledge[1]." The success of the intellectual and moral stimulus afforded by the Dissenters' Academies did much to balance the effect in England of the low standard and stagnation of the English Universities in the 18th century. There is no doubt these Academies, if they consciously represented to themselves any model, would have pointed to the Genevan Academy. But, once again, it is to be noted that Vives' idea of an Academy was *en évidence*[2].

Vives is many-sided, and the chapters on schools[3] present suggestions which will appeal with different emphasis to different readers. Sound education is for the culture of the mind, not the instrument for acquiring honours or money. The boy has no prescriptive right to higher education. The school is an

[1] Alexander Gordon, *Early Nonconformity and Education*, 1902.

[2] An educationist, John Dury, proposed a scheme for an "Academy" which is interesting for comparison with that of Vives. In his *Reformed School* (1650) Dury suggests that an "Association" should be formed of "free," grown-up persons, who should live together, to worship God and for profitable employment and mutual assistance. They are to engage in occupations suitable for each sex, and, as far as possible, to devote part of their earnings to the relief of the poor. There are to be two separate schools, one for boys and one for girls. The Associates act as "tutors" to the children, for whom "ushers" are appointed for the teaching. The Governor is at the head of all Associates, ushers and children. The object of the Association is to aid the sense of continuity in all stages of life. The scope of the education provided is "to know God in Christ and to become profitable instruments of the Commonwealth."

[3] Vives uses the following terms for educational institutions: *paedagogium*, *schola*, *ludus literarius*, and *academia*. The *paedagogium* seems to be the preparatory school where ability is first tested. *Ludus literarius* is a grammar school, and the Academy an institution in which every aspect of educational work is included and brought into perspective.

atmosphere of development, in which only those boys should enter, or be allowed to remain, who are suited to it, and whom it suits. Whilst opportunities should be open to all, Vives recognises that often the poor boy has more ability and application than the rich boy. Only those, rich or poor, who will benefit thoroughly from its help should be allowed to remain in the school. "In trade, and in the manual and mechanical arts, we see fewer persons spending their labour in vain than in the pursuit of learning." Once admitted, patience as to results must be shown, and a difference of ability, temperament and disposition of pupils involves a different speed of acquisition of knowledge and re-active disciplinary processes of mind. With true insight, Vives remarks: "It is not expedient to expect *one time* for all. *Nothing could be more unequal than an equality of that kind.*" Given that the pupil has sufficient tested mental ability, the one thing needful on his part is the right attitude towards his work. Let the scholars enter the schools as if about to worship in temples. Similarly, the teacher's work is intensive rather than extensive. "Who can bewail the fewness of his scholars, when the Creator of the world was satisfied with a school of twelve men?" Hence Vives would have the payment of the teachers in no way dependent on capitation fees. The teacher's salary should be just as much as a good man would desire, but a sum such as a bad man would despise. In other words, the reward of a teacher is intrinsic, not extrinsic. It is for the public, who profit so unspeakably from his services, to make secure the teacher's welfare and comfort. It is the teacher's part to do his work with his thoughts concentrated on the good of pupils and others through them—like Christ, who taught "for our service, not for His own ostentation."

**The Final Aim.** Vives had come to regard education as conterminous with life. "There is no end which can be fixed to the pursuit of wisdom," he says, "in the whole of our life." As long as life lasts, these three objects must occupy us:

"to obtain sound wisdom, to give right expression to it, and *to put it into sound action*[1]." To be approved of God is the great aim of both the present and the future life. Nothing can be more acceptable to Him than the devotion of our mental gifts, our erudition and knowledge, to the use of our fellow-men, who are His children. Studies must not be our sole occupation and delight. "The fruit of all studies is to bring our knowledge to the common good[2]." Every study is of unlimited extent, and might lead us to complete absorption in it, but there is always some stage at which we are able to make it available for "the use and advantage of other people."

Comenius, in speaking of Nature[3], wishes to get beyond the conception of that corruption which has befallen all men since the Fall of Man, and quotes Vives: "What else is a Christian but a man restored to his own nature, and, as it were, brought back to the starting point, whence the Devil has thrown him[4]." Bacon, we have seen, looked on the knowledge which was to come as the "relief to man's estate." Milton declared the end of learning is "to repair the ruins of our first parents by regaining to know God aright, and out of that knowledge to love Him, to imitate Him, and to be like Him." With Milton, Vives held that the love of God came through knowledge of Him, but even the power of this perfect knowledge of the divine life lies in the resultant actions of piety, i.e. in its practice rather than in mere knowledge. Milton speaks of man becoming like God; Vives says man is to be changed into His Nature. In the *de Anima* he says, "Man ascends above the heavens to God Himself," and this proves his divine origin. Love was the cause of our

[1] *Introductio ad Sapientiam*, *Vivis Opera* I. p. 16.

[2] p. 283. It will be noticed that in such a subject as Astronomy which might readily lead the thoughts to reverie, Vives insists on the practical aim in the study of the subject, p. 205 *infra*.

[3] *Great Didactic*—Keatinge's trans. p. 192. See August Nebe, *Vives, Alsted, Comenius, in ihrem Verhältnis zu einander*, Elberfeld, 1891.

[4] *De Concordia et Discordia*, Bk I.

creation. We have been separated by the love of ourselves. But we have been recalled by the love of Christ, and are now able to return "to our source, which is also our end."

The supreme end of life therefore is God, and education is the right practice of the art of living. The way of life and the way of education is to seek God's approval, and as He is the Father of all, we must treat all human beings, and especially our pupils, as His children. It is inconceivable, from such a point of view, that religion should be disjoined from education[1]. The foundations of piety, in so far as they are built up on knowledge, must be taught in the home, and still further developed in the school. The Scriptures are to be impressed "with great majesty" on pupils, so that in reading them they feel that they are listening to the great God Himself. In addition a short but careful text-book of directive precepts concerning the elementary principles of practical piety and wisdom should be used, and for this purpose Vives compiled his *Introduction to Wisdom.*

Two points connected with this religious aim had special influence on his educational views. Firstly, the hatred of war, as incompatible with the doctrine of love in which he whole-heartedly believed. We have seen that this attitude influenced his teaching of history and reading of authors. He also insisted that physical exercises and recreation should be kept free from any ulterior purpose of military training. Secondly he desired that in the reading of classical poets by boys, selections should be used to include only subject-matter thoroughly consistent with Christianity and above all with the development of a moral and pure tone of mind[2]. The desire of truth in historical

[1] See p. 34 and p. 84 *infra.*

[2] pp. 49–50 *infra.* After Vives many followed in the protest against harmful heathen authors. About 1560, Thomas Becon, in a *New Catechism*, protests against the use in schools of wanton and unhonest authors like Martial, Catullus, Tibullus, Propertius, etc., and the "wicked and ungodly" Lucian. Lawrence Humfrey, in the *Nobles*, 1563, complains of

writings had led Vives to condemn the *Golden Legends.* Similarly he discountenanced the reading of the mediaeval romances of the Knights of the Round Table, Florisand, Amadis and Roland[1].

Accepting the final aim of Vives as the return of man through knowledge to his source, viz. the love of God, and his special means of advancing educationally towards that end, the learning of all knowledge which is pure and true, and the application of all a man's gifts and erudition to the honour of God and to the service of his fellow-men, we must modify the description of his position as that of a utilitarian, in the ordinary sense of the term. No man was less self-centred, less selfish. Usefulness in his terminology meant purposefulness, not only for this life, but also for the next. Education implicitly in Vives concerns itself with the whole outlook of the soul on its way back to God, in this world and the next, as a continuous process, and involves as its intimate impulse the discipline of the will. His work may thus be regarded as one of the most thoroughgoing expositions of the later pedagogical doctrine of the training of the good-will[2], constantly employed on the lines of self-activity, morally, intellectually, physically; the soul bent upon the good of others.

the "foul error" of reading Ovid and Boccaccio, and would not have the pupils made acquainted with poets "nipping in taunts and wanton in talks." In the Commonwealth period, William Dell, Master of Gonville and Caius College, Cambridge, asks: "What should Christian youth have to do with the heathenish poets, who were, for the most part, the devil's puppets and delivered forth their writings in his spirit." Finally, Comenius dispensed with the reading of the Latin and Greek poets and substituted authors who gave "real" knowledge and helped to supply vocabularies of useful words describing "things."

1 *De Causis Corruptarum Artium, Vivis Opera* VI. p. 109.

2 Since writing the above opinion I find that this aspect has attracted the attention of the Germans. Dr George Siske has written a monograph on the subject: *Willens- und Charakterbildung bei Johann Ludwig Vives.* Langensalza, 1911.

The charm which the work of Vives possesses for the student of Renascence life is the unrestrained expression of his thoughts, without *arrière pensée* as to whether Cicero in antiquity, or Erasmus as a contemporary, will agree with him or not. He has won his own judgments—he would rather we did not call them merely opinions—in a struggle against authorities all along his path. He has won the peace of piety at the same time. There is, therefore, a sense of consistency in his life and his writings. He speaks directly what he thinks, without regard for consequences and without regard to effect. He is absolutely simple and absolutely sincere. He is under none of the illusions of ambition or avarice. He is a follower of the truth, and of piety, assured that these are the most certain of all knowledge, and that the arts only gather their value, as seen in their light, and judged by their standards. He is well aware that he has set out on an adventurous journey in his work on education, and, in his Preface, he asks pardon for the errors to be found in an undertaking "so new" in its scope. But whatever its errors his attitude is that of all noble research. "I would not desire that anyone should yield his opinion to mine. I do not wish to be the founder of a new sect, or to persuade anyone to swear by my conclusions. If you think, friends, that I seem to offer right judgments, see well to it that you give your adherence to them, because they are true, not because they are mine....You, who seek truth, make your stand, wherever you think that she is[1]."

[1] p. 9 *infra*.

F. W.

*March* 1913.

JOANNIS LODOVICI VIVIS VALENTINI

# DE TRADENDIS DISCIPLINIS

LIBRI QUINQUE

FIRST PUBLISHED, IN LATIN, BY MICHAEL HILLENIUS, AT ANTWERP, IN 1531. NOW TRANSLATED INTO ENGLISH FOR THE FIRST TIME, AS

*The Transmission of Knowledge*

# (DEDICATORY ADDRESS)

## JUAN LUIS VIVES

### TO KING JOHN III THE RENOWNED KING OF PORTUGAL AND ALGARVE, LORD OF GUINEA, ETC.

THE splendid deeds of thy ancestors have brought glory to their descendants, and at the same time the pressing necessity not to fall below the standard which they have set. For what else are those great deeds than the sure marks of noble descent so that all people may know what is to be expected from such a family, and may demand greatness from each representative, as if by right. As we often see shepherds and husbandmen fix a mark on mute animals, plants, and on trees that are specially beautiful, and regard their offspring and offshoots as having a sure promise of distinction and excellence beyond the rest, so when I consider the achievements of thy ancestors which are all gathered together and super-imposed on thee alone, it is clear to me that thou wilt have to exercise great and keen judgment, diligent watchfulness and care, so as not only to maintain thy heritage, but also (as is frequently expected from the indications already shown) to transmit thy predecessors' achievements on a larger and yet more splendid scale, to thy posterity. Thy progenitors dared to set out from Portugal to explore new seas, new lands, new and unknown climes. First they overthrew the Arabs and took possession of the Atlantic Sea. They were carried away beyond the path of the Sun (i.e. the Equator) and having traversed the Southern Sea south of Ethiopia, they penetrated to the territory opposite to us; hence to the Red Sea, and even up to the entrance of the Persian Gulf, where they erected fortifications. Then they travelled north of the mouth of the

**Deeds of the Portuguese.**

Indus, and established their authority over the fierce and blessed shores of all India. They have shown us the paths of the heaven and the sea, before not even known by name. They have also discovered peoples and nations who perform marvellous religious rites and are in a state of barbarism, though possessing wealth, on which our people so keenly cast their affections. The whole globe is opened up to the human race, so that no one is so ignorant of events as to think that the wanderings of the ancients (whose fame reached to heaven) are to be compared with the journeys of these travellers, either in the magnitude of their journeyings, or in the difficulties of their routes, or in their accounts of unheard-of conditions of life of the various nations who give us a rude shock by their differences from us in appearance, habit and custom.

But far beyond these matters in importance is the fact that our religion has been propagated far and wide, with such glory to the Christian name, and so much service to those whom thou hast brought into subjection, that the conquered are in a better condition, because conquered by thee, than thou art, because thou hast conquered them. For what hast thou obtained through thy victories? Nothing, except thought, toil and anxiety of affairs, in both undertaking the enterprises, and in maintaining the power thus acquired. A great example has been set for the emulation of Christian Princes, that they should only take up arms and seek victories of this kind, so that they may, by this means, make conquests for themselves and for God, and at the same time give cause to the conquered to rejoice in their defeats, since they have resulted in so ample a reward to themselves. Yet in the wars in Ásia and Africa, it was not a question of fighting for a small territory of land or for a small state with vast provision and supply of forces; but for the vastest provinces and kingdoms, so that the greatest part of the whole earth was at stake, in the fortune of war. Thy forefathers are to be congratulated, that although they accomplished so much from such small beginnings, their efforts have been followed by so rich an issue in respect of their many toils and their indefatigable activity. And as for thyself, entering the first steps of thy life-course, thou must not so much be congratulated as exhorted that, for the future, thou run with alacrity thy course, and press forward in their steps, towards the noblest deeds, of which within thy palace walls thou hast such examples. Thou must maintain what thou hast received from them, and by the same means, those of carefulness, industry, gentleness, magnanimity, greatness of deeds, constancy, fidelity. If thou dost this, then in the same way that we spur thee on, to rise to the virtue of thy ancestors, thy descendants will be able to cite and plead thy example for imitation. We can fairly expect that this will be the case from some of the deeds thou hast already accomplished, as if thou hadst been put on trial; deeds in spheres worthy of a prince, of sacred and uncorrupted justice, and where necessary, deeds of sternness and inflexibility. Through these means thou hast brought it about, as in many places is the custom, that not only laws and right, are of service to men, but that also men obey the laws, and act justly, and do this recognising that thus they will obtain the greatest freedom. This is a foretaste of thy mind, to show thou dost not merely please thyself; and at the same time, as it were, it is a pledge to all thy people, from which they look for great and noble works, as if due from thee, and they will be troublesome reminders in the future, unless thou perform what thou hast led them to expect.

Also thy good-will towards the learned and towards learning is evidence of thy disposition towards wisdom and the culture of the mind. Nor is thy benevolence bare and sterile, as is the case with many princes, who think they have done enough and to spare by learning, if they praise it, or avow that they wish it well. Thou addest also friendliness to scholars and magnificence of help to learning proportioned to thy royal wealth. The proofs are thy gifts to Paris and other Universities, in which so many troops of thy scholars are maintained at thy cost. Naturally, thou favourest those who are like thee, those who will be of great use to thee. With fullest justification the boast was made throughout Spain that there was no father of families more wise than thy father Emmanuel, who would have no one in his family without fixed employment, and would not allow his sons to be idle; he made all of them, as becomes princes, learn the military art, and he made them study literature. You also understand how great is the similarity of gifts in princes and learned men, so that these are not two different kinds of men, but they are rather such as should be more friendly to each other and more closely joined than they are. The one is made strong by the other; they are as it were mutual helps. Both are given by God to states and peoples, that they may have wise regard for the common good of the state; the learned by their precepts; princes by their edicts and laws; both by their examples. Learning requires freedom and leisure. This can be given by the royal power. In return, princely power will receive counsel in dealing with the difficult matters of business. Such advice is afforded to princes by the learned, in the practical wisdom gathered from learning, so that it is clear if either is lacking to the other, that his particular gift cannot be obtained and preserved. The association of thyself with the duties of those whom thou cherishest will be of such a kind as to help and support thy skill and thy power. This will be the amplest reward of thy liberality. For to what others couldst thou listen with more right, or whose counsels of a more careful and faithful kind couldst thou use than those of men who have acquired wisdom through thy kindness so that they might worthily be with thee when thou art deliberating about the most important matters? This thy so great and singular good-will to literature and the learned has led me, without hesitation, to dedicate to thee my books *de Disciplinis* which I have recently written. They treat of subjects which interest thee greatly, and if my work should not please thee, in the treatment of its topics, yet at least the subject with which it deals will give thee pleasure. Farewell.

BRUGES, *July*, 1531.

# PREFACE

## OF J. L. VIVES OF VALENCIA TO THE *DE DISCIPLINIS*[1].

WHEN I reflected that there is nothing in life more beautiful or more excellent than the cultivation of the mind through what we call branches of learning (*disciplinae*), by means of which we separate ourselves from the way of life and customs of animals and are restored to humanity, and raised towards God Himself, I determined to write on the subject, as far as my powers let me, and to do so, if I am not mistaken, in a manner different from what most of our predecessors have done. In the first place I have attempted to write spontaneously and clearly, so that my words may be easily understood, and the meaning retained, and as suitably as possible to the nature of the topics, so that knowledge may be gained with a certain delight, and thus that the fruitfulness for the learner may be increased. For I have attempted to so adapt the work that noble minds may be attracted to studies of this kind. Moreover, I have tried to clothe my matter in a certain grace of style, partly because it is not fitting that such noble subjects should be presented in a mean and base manner; partly that the students of elegant literature should not remain always hanging over the expressions of words and speech, as has been constantly necessary in previous writers on these subjects, through the fruitless and

[1] The *de Disciplinis* is the title of the two works taken together, viz. the seven books of the *de Causis Corruptarum Artium*, i.e. the Causes of the Corruptions of the Liberal Arts, and the five books of the *de Tradendis Disciplinis*, i.e. the Transmission or Teaching of the Subject-matter of Knowledge. The first edition included other works. See p. xii *supra*

horrible difficulties of language and matter which had to be gulped down, however long a student read. Thus will be perceived the usefulness of the learned languages, which we learn with so much toil, since on the one hand they contain the subject-matter of the sciences, and on the other, are fitted for providing full expression for them.

I have also sought to free the sciences from impious doubts, and to bring them out from their heathen darkness into the light of our faith. I shall show that the old writers were mistaken, not through the limitations of the human intellect, as some have thought, but by their own fault. Therefore I have produced my reasons from Nature, not out of divine oracles, so that I should not leap across from philosophy to theology.

If I have accomplished this purpose in some measure, I shall have obtained the richest of fruits for my labour. For what employment of thought could be more useful than that of bringing men out of darkness into light, to that light which, when it is seen, makes all people happy; but without which, we should ever be most wretched men? And if any are conscious of their dimness of insight, then I trust I may lead them to see the light more clearly and openly, and in the way in which they themselves may realise that they have come to a clearer vision. We shall not let the earliest studies be infected with heathen errors, and thus contaminate our religion, but, from the beginning, we shall accustom ourselves to right and sound views, which will then by degrees grow up with us. But because the authority of the ancients in the transmission of arts has been firmly established, I have had to state clearly in what matters I am of opinion that they have fallen into error, so that I in my course as teacher as well as those students who have willingly committed themselves trustfully to me as their leader, should not find hindrances at the threshold of learning. By this means I thought I could with more convenience and correctness discuss the arts themselves. In the treatment of these questions I have had often to oppose many of the old authors; of course, not all, for that would have been an endless as well as a useless task, still I have had to controvert some which have been received and have been generally approved for a long time. I must confess I have often been ashamed at what I have ventured to undertake, and I condemn my own self-confidence, in thinking that I should dare to attack authors consecrated by their standing through the centuries. Especially is this so, in connection with Aristotle for whose mind, for whose industry, carefulness, judgment in human arts, I have an admiration and respect, unique above all others.

I beg therefore, that no one condemn me of ingratitude and rashness on this score. For I have always held that we must render the ancients our warmest thanks, for not withholding from us, their successors, the results of their study and industry. If they have been mistaken, in any matter, we must excuse it as error due to that frailty, which is part of the human lot. Moreover it is far more profitable to learning to form a critical judgment on the writings of the great authors, than to merely acquiesce in their authority, and to receive everything on trust from others, provided that in forming judgments we are all far removed from those pests of criticism and assertion of one's views—viz. envy, bitterness, over-haste, impudence, and scurrilous wit. Nature is not yet so effete and exhausted as to be unable to bring forth, in our times, results comparable to those of earlier ages. She always remains equal to herself, and not rarely she comes forward more strongly and powerful than in the past, as if mustering together all her forces. So we must regard her in this present age, as re-enforced by the confirmed strength which has developed, by degrees, through so many centuries. For how greatly do the discoveries of earlier ages and experiences spread over long stretches of time, open up the entrance to the comprehension of the different branches of knowledge? It is therefore clear that, if we only apply our minds sufficiently, we can judge better over the whole round of life and nature than could Aristotle, Plato, or any of the ancients, who spent their energies in so prolonged an observation of the greatest and hidden things, as to bring forth in them rather the wondrous admiration of newness than fresh contributions to real knowledge. Further, what was the method of Aristotle himself? Did he not dare to pluck up by the root the received opinions of his predecessors? Is it, then, to be forbidden to us to at least investigate, and to form our own opinions? Especially as Seneca wisely declares: "Those who have been active intellectually before us, are not our masters but our leaders." Truth stands open to all. It is not as yet taken possession of. Much of truth has been left for future generations to discover.

I do not profess myself the equal of the ancients, but I bring my views into comparison with theirs. Just so much confidence should be given to my opinions as the cogency of my reasoning justifies. When, on the other hand, the weights of arguments are equal, it would be impudent for anyone to refuse precedence to the old authors over myself, or over any recent writers, for ancient opinion has been put to the test by long experience, whilst the new and unknown has not received the confirmation of experience.

For my own part, I would not desire that anyone should yield his opinion to mine. I do not wish to be the founder of a sect, or to persuade anyone to swear by my conclusions. If you think, friends, that I seem to offer right judgments, see well to it that you give your adherence to them, because they are true, not because they are mine. This attitude is useful to yourselves, and would be of help generally, in all your studies. To contend fiercely for my opinions would not do any good to myself, whilst it would injure others, by leading them into dissensions and parties. You, who seek truth, make your stand, wherever you think that she is. Leave me, whether I am still living, or whether I have already met the fate of death, leave me, to my Judge, to Whom alone my conscience will have to justify itself. I do not doubt that I have often made mistakes in what I have brought forward, as is naturally the case, with anyone who seeks to point out the mistakes of others, with whose minds, intellectual zeal, knowledge and experience, he cannot for a moment compare. But like as Aristotle begged for gratitude in respect of what he had discovered, and pardon for what he had omitted; so I ask that my good-will in the attempt to pursue the good be recognised, and that you pardon with ready good-will the errors of an undertaking which is so new. No knowledge is at the same time discovered and perfected. If anyone, perchance, should think it worth while to polish up these rude efforts of mine, and to supply what is defective in them, then, perhaps, there will be supplied a work which may be studied with some fruitfulness.

# BOOK I

## EDUCATIONAL ORIGINS

# CHAPTER I

## BEGINNINGS OF SOCIETY

Man naturally is induced to prepare for himself those things which he sees to be necessary. What inventions therefore did he first devise? The Beginnings of Society. The rise of human Needs and their Satisfaction. The consequent earliest inventions.

**The three operations of the Mind: (1) Simple apprehension, (2) Composition and division, (3) Exploration of Nature.**

MAN has received from God a great gift, viz. a mind, and the power of inquiring into things; with which power he can behold not only the present, but also cast his gaze over the past and the future. In all this, man considered the chief use of so great an instrument to be to examine all things, to collect, to compare, and to roam through the universe of nature as if it were his own possession. Nevertheless, man has wandered further out of the way than he has advanced in the way. If anyone looks at the steps he has accomplished and the results at which he has arrived, by themselves, they seem quite marvellous. If he compares them with what has yet to be attained, he must conclude that man has scarcely put his foot beyond the threshold, so few and so obscure are those facts which he possesses. Indeed, we will expose the rags of this beggarliness, since our riches appear so very ample to us only through ignorance, or at any rate through want of reflexion upon what is still greater. First of all, the love of self-preservation which nature planted in man, stimulated him to pay attention to

**Means of Sustenance.**

the fact, that he could not subsist even for a moment if the nourishment of life was wanting; therefore before all else, he had to attend to those things which he must have in order to nourish and sustain himself; of course in matters of eating and drinking, he had to understand how to distinguish the beneficial from the harmful foods, and how to prepare and preserve them. And, since the body was liable to many diseases, and, as it were, to an ever recurring tyranny, he sought means to fortify himself against disease, so that it should not attack him, and that he might drive it out if it did attack him. Then he reflected that his tender body, exposed as it was to injury from the weather and the sun, was affected harmfully by these vicissitudes, and he invented a means of protecting himself from the violence of cold and heat, from winter and storms[1]. So, first, covering was applied to the body. Then, since clothes afforded too little protection against the greater forces of Nature, man heaped up things impenetrable to those dangers, stones, mud, fragments of rock, wood, hard substances, with which to protect himself. But since even then men were not sufficiently secure from wild beasts, who might make an attack upon them while they were careless and unaware, or weighed down by sleep, they sought means of sheltering themselves, so that their rest might be more secure. Since, through his great helplessness and need of so many and such varied things, no one was sufficient for himself, at first, many people lived together in the same cave: then as affection narrowed its bounds, a man and his wife seceded with their children; they came out of the caves, and built for themselves huts and tents of small pieces of wood, and covered the roofs with small twigs of trees[2]. At first these huts were built here and there as if spots widely spread over the open plain; just as now, cities and

**Medicine.**

**Clothes.**

**Buildings.**

**Caves.**

[1] Cf. J. L. Vives, *de Causis Corruptarum Artium*, near beginning of bk I.

[2] Cf. Aristotle, *Politics*, bk I, chap. i.

towns are built. But soon, because affection exhorted those who wished each other well not to go farther away, and because need of mutual help urged them, certain persons brought their own huts together into a kind of village[1]. But, however much simplicity flourished among them, yet, in men exposed to, and suspicious of, injury, some complaints existed. Naturally they all referred these to the oldest man, just as sons to their father, and he, since man's nature at this time was less corrupt, obtained power over the rest, because he was older; and for that reason, he was believed to surpass every one else in experience and wisdom. But when they discovered that there were not wanting some to whom white hair and wrinkles did not bring much goodness of mind and heart, and others whose cunning increased with years, they sought out someone who was the wisest and the best. In this also they made mistakes; for a decision cannot be made as to who is wise except by a wise man. If for any reason they reverenced greatly a particular man, to him they submitted themselves; of course it was for that reason which seemed to them most powerful in human affairs; to some this was money, to others, beauty; to others, strength of body and mind; to others, eloquence; to others, birth; to others, knowledge; to others, the reputation of justice. But since there were many who strove for that honour, and the worse claimants would not yield to those who were better, because pride persuaded each that he was the best, then there arose parties in the multitude who did not act by the dictates of reason, but with excited passions, and to settle the discord, one was elected by common agreement to be the judge; or at any rate, after conflict one was proclaimed the victorious claimant[2]. In those primitive times it was sufficient to state what ought not

Villages.

Judgments.

Government by the oldest man.

[1] Aristotle, *Politics*, bk I, chap. i.

[2] Homer, *Iliad*, II 204 οὐκ ἀγαθὸν πολυκοιρανίη· εἷς κοίρανος ἔστω εἷς βασιλεύς.

to be done; the ruler's word restrained both the hands and the wills of the people; so great among them was respect for right and justice. Contumacy grew; then laws were passed, and penalties were attached to their violation, since now it was not sufficient to forbid; punishment was threatened for the terror of all, lest insolence should spread itself abroad. The wish to do evil seized not only one or two persons, but multitudes of men, and whole peoples: so that the general animosities sought to glut themselves in general bloodshed. To ward off these sudden risings, those who were united by community of interests, surrounded themselves with walls, and sought weapons with which to repulse hostile attacks. Changes in these conditions were brought about in the course of time according to opportunities; daily business brought men together, and speech bound them to move as closely as possible amongst one another in an indivisible, perpetual society. By the help of speech, their minds, which had been hidden by concentration on bodily needs, began to reveal themselves; single words were attended to, then phrases and modes of speaking, as they were appropriate for use, i.e. as they were marked by public agreement of opinion, which is, as it were, what a mint is to current coin[1]. It is a great advantage to have a common language, for it is a bond which holds society together, since if there are peculiar ways of speaking among sections of the same nation, the effect is that of using foreign tongues; men do not understand each other thoroughly. Nothing is more troublesome to those who have business to transact, or who have much social intercourse. In human society, in which it is right for men to use moderation and reason, it was fit that each person should act, not rashly, nor violently, nor in the manner and fashion of wild beasts, but modestly and moderately, as far as reason, well and fittingly trained, might prompt him. It is from reason all practical

Laws.

Walls.
Arms.

Speech.

[1] See Cicero *de Oratore*, bk I.

wisdom springs, and practical wisdom is like a rudder for guiding a ship, and its use is exceedingly great all through life, both in regard to food, clothing, habitation, and in regard to a man himself, his wife, children, household; towards his fellow citizens, in a private position, towards the magistracy and the chief officers, or towards inferior citizens if he himself is the magistrate or chief. By it the whole order of his life ought to be regulated, and at no stage of his life should he be without it, nor indeed can he be if he lives humanly; for all the humanities come under the head of wisdom; from it spring those sciences which the Greeks called Ethics, Economics, and Politics. These are subjects which the human intellect and the whole nature of man with impulses aroused by the Creator, necessarily found out and built up into organised knowledge. If they were excluded entirely, man would not live at all, and if removed in part he would live not a human life, but the life of a wild beast or a savage.

Practical Wisdom.

When men had duly provided for the necessities of life, the human mind passed from necessities to conveniences, so that having acquired them, man might not only have something by which to protect himself from such great and constant danger, but something pleasant in which he might delight now that the sense of want had been driven away. For while the whole of man's nature was oppressed by the vast power and uncertainty of necessity, everything had been changed into an enemy; nor could man think of anything except of raising this blockade[1].

Conveniences.

Arts of necessity and of pleasure.

But when everything seemed quiet and peaceable, bodily pleasure and mental pride showed themselves, and they sought and, as it were, claimed the greatest portion of sovereignty over man. Men became slaves of pleasure, and planned many delights; they became the slaves of pride, and made many inventions to serve as vain ornaments, whereby was gained a reputation for superiority.

Pleasure.

[1] See J. L. Vives, *de Causis Corruptarum Artium*, bk I.

Then those remedies against necessity, and the devices for convenience, were either transferred to the service of pleasure, or dragged over to the most bitter tyranny of pride, so that they might either delight the body, or perform as it were a play on the stage before the eyes of the beholders. For man's needs it was enough to have few things, and such as could easily be procured. Luxury added more, and pleasure and pride united, found no bound or limit. Man's mind, freed from anxiety for the needs of the present, began to live again, and to contemplate leisurely, as it were, this theatre, in which man was placed by God; to examine separate objects, which were in the heavens and in the elements, earth and water: namely constellations, living beings, plants, gems, metals, stones, and the contents of his own mind. Curiosity led him forward, and when he thought he had made a discovery, he felt great joy as if from a victory. That pleasure was constantly increasing, since some things seemed to follow from the finding of others, just as when the beginning of a thread is secured, it is found to be connected with another set of things quite different from those which were being examined. Then, in showing his inventions as if they were children born from himself, he derived pleasure by no means small in imparting them to others. From the admiration of others for him, he felt at first great joy, but when all eyes were turned towards him, an idea of superiority and pride grew in him. A violent desire for display exciting greater admiration, increased to such a degree, that some persons neglected all the duties of life, so as to devote and give up themselves entirely to investigation; and then if anyone contradicted them, there arose strife, factions and sects. This desire impelled others to know what no one else knew;—what was going to happen, or what was buried or hidden in great darkness. Then came men, who through desire for money, or the possession of the pleasures which they coveted, ventured most impiously to learn from an evil spirit those secrets which they could not learn from a mortal.

Pride.

Curiosity.

"Sects."

# CHAPTER II

## BEGINNINGS OF STUDIES

Of what importance and value Religion is to other branches of practical life. The reputed conventions of arts and of those knowledges which had the name of arts, or rather those which are worthy of being known. The influence of Religion on other branches of Knowledge. The Origin of Sciences: their discoverers.

Now, this unbridled eagerness for knowledge had been carried very far, when, in the midst of the course, that on-rush of mental energy began to be checked by the most capable minds, while they considered what at length was to be the goal of such a wide and anxious course, what was to be the reward of such continuous labour—a question particularly worthy of the attention of the human race. For what is the good of fatiguing oneself with this effort, if nothing is gained by desires except fresh desires; if the end of one longing is the beginning of another; if we work continually, and there is no end or rest? For what is more wretched than man, the most excellent of the animals, if, in this manner, he seeks after and desires the things which are exposed to his senses, and which are connected on all sides with his life, and then they bring him no rest or delight, and produce no pure, solid, or lasting joy? That, as I said, is a very excellent inquiry, and one far more worthy of, and suitable for, our intellect, than an investigation as to the measure or material of the heavens, or the virtues of plants or stones; and yet one hard to explain, which by its difficulty has exercised the greatest minds more

The *summum bonum*.

than it has instructed them; in truth, because the human mind, provided with its small lamp, is not able to attain to the conception of that ultimate end, unless it has been enlightened by the end itself; as happens to those who go into dark places by help of a light. Therefore, there was need of God, not only to teach us how to come to Him, but also to lead us by the hand, since we are weak, and constantly liable to fall. This is the function of religion, which we receive from God Himself, a ray from His Light, strength from His Omnipotence. This alone brings us back to the source from which we came, and towards which we are going. Nor is there any other perfection of man, seeing that when this is accomplished, every end for which he was formed is obtained[1]. For who is there who has considered the power and loftiness of the mind, its understanding of the most remarkable things, and, through understanding, love, and from love the desire to unite himself with the things of knowledge, who does not perceive clearly that man was created, not for food, clothing and habitation, not for difficult, hidden and troublesome knowledge, but for the desire to know God more truly, for a participation in eternity, and in His divine nature? Wherefore, since that is the perfection of man's nature, and the consummation of all its parts; and since piety is the only way of perfecting man, and accomplishing the end for which he was formed, therefore piety is of all things the one thing necessary. Without the others, man can be perfected and complete in every part; but—not without this. He can even do without food and daily sustenance, but not without piety, unless he is in the future to be most miserable. This is what the Lord said to Martha, who was anxious not only about unnecessary things, but about the daily food—"thou art careful, and troubled about many things; one thing is needful, which Mary hath chosen, to sit

**Religion.**

**Perfection of everything constituted by its end.**

**Religious Piety the way to the goal of happiness.**

[1] Aristotle, *Ethics*, bk I.

at the feet of the Lord and to hear His words[1]." Wherefore all arts and all learning, without religion, are childish play. For, just as the human mind has invented and occupies itself with what we call games, of small dice, or cards, or balls; or as with fiery energy it tries to be intent upon some pastime, but knows nothing better or has nothing better to do; or is slothful and lazy, and does not rouse itself to the labour of the good arts; or as it withdraws its attention from more difficult matters, so as to return to serious studies afterwards, refreshed by relaxation—so the mind of men has exercised itself in the arts and in the investigation of different kinds of subjects. Hence, partly through ignorance of religion and partly because it is fettered by the weight of studies, the mind cannot rise to religion or, through laziness, does not try; and thus neither bestows refreshment on the body to which it is attached, nor collects its renewed powers to efforts in the territory of religion. And just as among us, those who are not clever at games, but do possess experience of life and practical wisdom of life, are not blamed—but we hold him who plays games, but is untrained in practical wisdom, as disgraceful and blameworthy—so he who knows none of the arts but yet has a practical knowledge of virtue, and has formed and ordered his life by its rules, is so far from being blamed that he is deserving of praise. On the other hand, he is worthy of ignominy and dishonour who is learned and instructed in human arts, but is destitute of virtue. Socrates, a pagan, made this clear in many of his disputations, and other pagans followed him. Wherefore the sons of Lamech are said to have found out profane learning and to have recorded it in literary works; "the children of this generation are," as the Holy Gospel says[2], "in their generation wiser than the children of light." But all our knowledge is a kind of close inspection which either consists in the contemplation of each particular object, e.g. when the eye observes closely the distinctions in a variety of colours, and again when

[1] S. Luke x. 41—42.

[2] S. Luke xvi. 8.

the mind ponders over the memory of events, or considers closely and seeks after some end; if it collects general aspects or norms to a definite end, it is called an art. In the beginning first one, then another experience, through wonder at its novelty, was noted down for use in life; from a number of separate experiments the mind gathered a universal law, which after it was further supported and confirmed by many experiments, was considered certain, and established. Then it was handed down to posterity. Other men added subject-matter which tended to the same use and end. This material, collected by men of great and distinguished intellect, constituted the branches of knowledge, or the arts, to use the general name. Now, whatever is in the arts was in nature first, just as pearls are in shells, or gems in the sand, but because the dull eyes of many men passed them by without notice, they were pointed out by men, more alert, and the latter were called discoverers, not as if they themselves had made something which previously had no existence, but because they revealed what had been hid. Therefore, the first observers who hoped that something could be brought into some art are the first discoverers of the arts. Seneca says that "each person who has hoped to discover something has greatly aided discovery." We award also the same honour to those who have collected rules from experiences, e.g. Hippocrates, who, as is related by M. Varro, collected the rules of medicine which were found in the Temple of Aesculapius and from them made formulae, and in fact formed a conception of the art. But those who bring together scattered facts and make clear what is confused, and explain the involved, and bring light and clearness to what is obscure, have also obtained the name of discoverers, e.g. Aristotle[1], in his *Dialectic*. Therefore, as Manilius[2] sings, "Experience through various applications has made art." Yet

**The manner in which arts were discovered and developed.**

**Arts.**

**How men became named discoverers in the arts.**

**Experience.**

[1] See last chapter of the *Elenchi*. [2] *Astronomicon*, bk I, l. 61.

experiences are casual and uncertain unless they are ruled by reason, which must preside over them like the rudder or the pilot in a ship; otherwise they will be risky, and the whole art will be fortuitous and not certain. This may be seen in the case of those who are led by experiences alone without a standard as to their nature and quality, and without respect to the place, time, and the remaining circumstances, for it ought to be as Plato says in *Gorgias*, "let experience bring forth the art, and let art rule experience." As a certain power is given to the earth to produce herbs of every kind[1], so our minds are as it were endued with a certain power of seeds over all arts and all learning; and a certain proneness to those first and most simple truths, by which tendency the mind is carried on; a wish for the aims that are most clearly good; a quickness of mind for the most manifest truths, just as there is a sharpness of the eye for green and of the ear for harmony. Aristotle perhaps would have called this tendency "power" whilst Plato calls it "seeds"; and I have nothing, of course, to say against the name. Others apply the name προλήψεις, i.e. anticipations and monitions impressed and fixed in our minds by nature. That is the reason why the boy agrees at once to the most evident truth which he has never seen before, just as the lamb flees from the wolf which it has never before beheld. Idleness and sloth crush these seeds and destroy them; but exercise, through the use of things, produces from them a plant and fruit. The judgment cultivates and directs them, just as natural fruits are rendered better by the hands and the care of men. Wherefore if there is no judgment, or if it is clearly deceived, they degenerate into fraud and lying, in exactly the same way as the whole mass becomes sour from sour leaven or rennet. Nor do certain false impostures deserve the name of arts or knowledge, e.g. the tricks of demons or of diviners: for judgment does not govern their laws, but desire; and these tricks are handed down in

**Experience deceptive.**

[1] Genesis i. 12.

pyromancy, necromancy, the art of judging from lines in the hands (chiromancy), from astrology, as they came into the minds of certain peoples. Thus, they are different among the Egyptians and the Chaldeans; and are not the same among the Greeks and Arabians. Assuredly, these can no more be said to be "observations" than if anyone were to say he saw a stick in the water broken when it is whole, or many colours in the rainbow when there are none.

**What knowledge is.**

But I only call that knowledge which we receive when the senses are properly brought to observe things and in a methodical way to which clear reason leads us on, reason so closely connected with the nature of our mind that there is no one who does not accept its lead; or our reasoning is "probable," when it is based on our own experiences or those of others, and confirmed by a judgment, resting upon probable conjecture. The knowledge in the former case is called science, firm and indubitable, and in the latter case, belief or opinion. Not every kind of knowledge is called an art, but only that which becomes a rule for doing something; e.g. those things which happen at random or by chance are not done by art as, for example, the representation in a picture of the foam of a horse, which owed its origin to the painter having thrown a sponge at the picture, in anger[1]. For art is the means of attaining a sure and predetermined end. Every art, first of all, has an end, which it keeps in view, towards which it aims everything, like arrows to a target, either directly or indirectly. Further it occupies itself with the material with regard to which the end arises; and it does not occupy itself with that material otherwise than by teaching those precepts which, being practised, lead to the end of the art.

**What arts are.**

**The "end" of an art.**

**Its subject-matter.**

[1] See Pliny, *Nat. Hist.* xxxv, 104.

# CHAPTER III

## ARTS AND SCIENCES

On the number and variety of the arts; whence they were taken. An inquiry into what pertains to the arts, one by one, and the teachers of them. The number and variety of arts and sciences, and their subject-matter.

**The end of an art.**

IN the arts, as in every kind of work, the end is first brought to the mind by reflexion; then follows the carrying it out. But not so in the invention of each art. For there are arts in which the material is sought because of the end, as in agriculture, where all things are brought together to sustain life. In others, the end is desired because of the material, e.g. in the contemplation of nature, when this most beautiful work captivates us while gazing in admiration of it, and the prospect itself and an understanding of so great a work are the aims sought, and in this pursuit, the subject-matter allures men. In other cases, the art is discovered by a kind of accident, as when a piece of work is done in an art, beyond the design set before himself by the workman, e.g. in many ornaments, in the inlaying of tables, and lately in artillery[1]. In others, the end of knowledges is knowledge itself, and these are called "the contemplative arts": such as the contemplation of nature, and that of quantities which is called geometry. The end of other arts is action, as in music when, after the action, nothing is left. These are called "active arts."

**Its subject-matter.**

**The differences amongst arts according to Aristotle.**

[1] See Polydore Vergil bk II, chap. xi and bk III, chap. xviii.

The end of other arts is some work or effect besides the action, as in building, medicine, which are termed "practical." Some are instruments for effecting other objects, e.g. grammar and dialectic, which for this cause are called by the Greeks *ὄργανα*. Those which are not brought together under rules and precepts are not arts at all, but, to use a general name, are experiential knowledge, e.g. the knowledge of history or the contemplation of God. Wherefore an art is defined for us as a collection of universal rules brought together for the purpose of knowing, doing or producing something; although oftentimes certain things in an art are not sufficiently universally observed, e.g. in the contemplation of nature. Therefore the expression "an art" is sometimes used in a wider sense, i.e. for "observation" and also at times for a kind of knowledge in which there is nothing presumptuous or dangerous. But we have to be warned; the material of the arts is not of one kind or description. In some it is single and simple, as in theology, God. In others, single but composed of various things, e.g. in statuary, a statue may be formed of metal, stone, mud, clay. One kind of material is quite natural, as in agriculture; another, quite artificial, as in economics and politics. There is another kind of material, natural indeed, but cultivated by us through use, e.g. in painting, building, oratory. The practice of an art is nothing but the carrying out of its precepts; that indeed is the part of the pursuer of the art, and the precepts are his instruments rather than those of the art itself. The end of the artificer is the carrying out of its precepts. The end of the art is always a very excellent work which will surely be the result of that action if nothing prevents, e.g. the end of the medical art is health, but that of the doctor is the application of drugs according to the rules of the art. Thus that which is for the art itself only the means, viz. the precepts, is, for the practiser of the art, the end, and for this cause neither art nor artist can be deprived of their separate ends. For an

**What an art is.**

**The differences in subject-matter of the arts.**

**The practice of an art.**

art does not regard the separate cases, but all in common, which are bound together by that method by which the art teaches: whilst, what the artificer does is concerned with separate cases. The art performs nothing, but only teaches.

**In practical arts we meet with the individual and the particular.**

Wherefore the art of medicine does not concern itself with the health of this or that person, but considers in general the health which ought to be the consequence of its precepts and laws. These are afterwards applied by the doctor in the case of individual men, as from a fountain. Wherefore if the rules of the art (when there is nothing from without to prevent), fail to produce health, the art is not yet perfectly established; but, if health necessarily follows, then of course it is complete and perfect: and it directs the eye to some certain end, which is always attained if the most suitable way has been taken towards it.

**Art and the artificer.**

Therefore this discussion of ours is not about that art which is pursued amongst men, but with that whose perfection is founded in the nature and power of things, and in the minds of men. For that which we discover, attain and practise, by our own stupidity, is generally not an art, but the image of an art or some slight portion of an art. I will say the same thing about the practiser of the art who laments that he has had very little success in this or that case; it is not through the fault of the art, which ought not to and cannot show the hindrance to actions; nor should he himself be blamed if he has duly carried out and applied the precepts of his art. As in Rhetoric, it is the business of the art to show the rules of persuasion, but it is the orator's function to apply them so as to persuade. Wherefore, just as desires and roads are all separated from one another and

**How arts are distinguished.**

denoted by their end, so all the arts are distinguished by their end, not by the subject-matter. For diverse arts may deal with the same material, e.g. the arts of the coiner and the smith use iron; those of the carpenter, the coach-maker, the maker of statues, use wood. Artificers, also, differ in their mode of action, in the material they use and in their instruments.

Besides the ends of the art and of the artificer, there is the human end. The end of everything good is covered with a veil; because it is reached only as a last point. But nothing can be sought unless it is believed to be good. Men consider that what benefits them is good, and what injures them is evil. But they believe that they can be benefited in mind and in body; and on that account, many external things are counted as useful; whence it happens that since the opinions of men are different, through their opinions their desires are different, one fixes on one end in his pursuit of arts; another on another, each for himself. In the case of some, the consideration of money has great influence; everything has reference to that[1]. Others prefer reputation, glory, dignity, power. There are some who seek the arts for the sake of pleasure and luxury. Others long for knowledge and the enjoyment of things. Others desire the cultivation and increase of piety: some desire some one of these things; others, many; others, very many. There are some who wish to acquire knowledge of arts for themselves; others who wish to share them when they are acquired; some, for themselves alone; others, for those who are dear to them—for instance, their children; thus, Zenobia studied Greek that she might teach her sons; and Aristotle is said to have spent much labour on the art of medicine, that he might help his friends: so, some labour for the state; many for posterity, which stands to them in the place of sons. It is thought that evil is to be avoided instead of seeking the good; for to escape evil is considered as a profitable thing, just as it is to obtain good. And just as many study so as to be of use to those whom they wish well, so not a few study in order that they may injure those whom they hate, even in the act of conferring on them those things to which the name of benefits is given.

**The end of arts.**

[1] See Aristotle, *Ethics*, bk I.

**From whom and how we are to learn arts.**

I think, too, that we ought to notice how and from whom we are to learn: then, to consider the results of learning. For God teaches us, and also those whom He has sent, the prophets of old: then, the Apostles and holy men. Then we are taught by means of schools, some to whom the duty was commanded; sometimes angels teach; heretics teach; bad and wicked men teach; devils teach—fathers, mothers, old men, young men, boys, women, skilled and unskilled persons—even dumb animals teach us; e.g. the Egyptian ibis, the clyster; the hippopotamus, the cutting of a vein; the swallows, in their building; other animals, in the use of herbs[1]. Now some learn in such a way that they leave no time for the affairs of the citizens, their friends, relations, family, parents, children: every moment is entirely devoted to their studies. Others study so that they cut off the time which nature requires, and endanger their health and minds. There are not wanting some who (which is most impious) leave no time for piety, or less than they ought, but readily follow after other things. There are some who wisely attend to everything, and distribute to each employment its proper time. Many however are slothful, just as if the only business entrusted to them was to be lazy. Everything is done at odd times, and carelessly. That which instruction effects in the pupil, or through him on others, I call the issue of learning: namely, that he becomes in mind, better or worse, wiser or more foolish; in body, stronger or weaker, more beautiful or more ugly. In short, the value of the study of an art to a scholar may be judged by the development in him, or through him to others, of one of these classes of advantages or disadvantages.

[1] Pliny, bk VIII, chaps. xxvi and xxvii.

# CHAPTER IV

## GOD OUR HIGHEST GOOD

Since it is God to Whom, as our Supreme Good, it behoves us to refer ourselves and all that is ours, we must study those arts which cherish our love towards Him, and reject immediately the study of those which either diminish or extinguish it. God is the Highest Good. How this proposition affects our view of the Arts and Sciences.

Now we must show what arts are harmful to men and to what extent, and which, on the contrary, are beneficial. Man, like everything else, is to be judged by his end: for he is fruitless and most miserable if he does not attain his end, but most perfect and most happy if he does attain it. What can we fix as the end of man, except God Himself? Or where can man more blessedly repose, than when he is, as it were, absorbed in God and changed into His nature? We must return to Him by the same way we came forth from Him. Love was the cause of our being created; for no sign of His love can be more evident than that He created us, in order that such great happiness might be communicated to us. From that love we have been separated, forsooth by the love of ourselves. By that love we have been recalled and raised up, that is to say, by the love of Christ. By love, i.e. by our love to God, we are to return to our source, which is also our end; for nothing else is able to bind together spiritual things, nothing is able to make one out of many, except love; but knowledge must precede love. God loved us before we were born, because He knew that we had already

**The end of man.**

**Love of God and of ourselves.**

proceeded from Him; we exercise love after we are born and have obtained the power and habit of knowing. But faith will show what things ought to be loved, since the first and simplest elements of piety have been handed down to each person from God the Father of all and His Son Jesus Christ Who, for the redemption of our sinful bodies, took upon Himself our same body, but was without sin. How the same things are to be known and loved is declared very clearly, not by any writings invented by men but by the divine oracles, which writings have come from the Holy Spirit and in which there is perfect knowledge of the divine life, which is called piety or religion; but its power is comprised more in action than in knowledge.

**Piety or Religion.**

Those first elements are not so simple that they do not suffice for action; no one should be utterly ignorant of them. But the perfection of piety is that of those who exalt themselves through their love, which not only is fiery, but like a fire lifts up on high those whom it takes possession of. These are like him to whose charge the flock was committed, and who heard from his Lord, "Lovest thou me more than these[1]?" Such as these should be powerful in sound doctrine and resist those who contradict it, as Paul the Apostle says[2]. This knowledge of the divine life rests on its own strength and is consistent with itself; nor does it need any supports at all; rather, in it alone all the treasures of knowledge and wisdom are locked up. All other things whatever written by heathen authors on other subjects, or, to a certain extent, on the same subject, are childish stammerings and utter ignorance when compared with this holy and admirable wisdom. This ought to be the standard of other principles, just as God is of spirits and man of living creatures; so that every kind of learning may be valued to the extent that by its matter, its end taken as our end, its teachers, its method and its results, it agrees or does

**Piety, the "rule" for arts.**

[1] S. John xxi. 15. [2] Titus i. 9.

not agree with this standard. No subject-matter, no knowledge is, of itself, contrary to piety. I call that contrary which is at variance with faith and love, that namely which takes these virtues utterly away, or certainly lessens them by bringing into the mind wickedness and sin. For materials of study are taken from things which the good God has made, and therefore they are good. Neither is piety adverse to anything good, since it becomes itself the crown of everything good and nothing in us can be good without it, nor can anything be inimical to it, since its author is He whose worship and religion piety professes, and for which it prepares man's will.

**Knowledge *à posteriori* through the "creatures."**

Indeed all things, the more exactly they are known, the more do they open the doors of entrance to the knowledge of the Deity, i.e. the supreme Cause, through His works; and this is the most fitting way for our minds to reach to the knowledge of God. Philo Judaeus[1] writes that it was thus Abraham came to find out God.

**The Book of Nature.**

For, from the heavens and the elements, from their eternal motions, their invariable order, the fixed regularity of the years and the seasons, he came to understand that there is some wisdom by which all these sure and constant things are ruled. Therefore, casting aside and despising the follies of the gods, which man had created for himself so that he might adore his own handiwork, he sought and worshipped it. The great Basil[2] relates that Moses so trained his mind by the knowledge of Egyptian learning that he arrived at the contemplation τοῦ ὄντος. Hence the holy Psalmist sings, "The heavens declare the glory of God and the firmament sheweth his handiwork[3]," and Paul, "I have learnt the invisible things of God through the visible[4]." I pass over what John Pico writes about natural magic, which serves the useful purpose of making us understand how the miracles of Our Lord clearly exceeded all the power and skill of Nature.

[1] *De Migratione Abrahami*, bk I.
[2] Homil. (to Youth) 54.
[3] Psalm xix. 1.
[4] Romans i. 20.

I, for my part, think that proud ignorance is more inimical to piety than modest knowledge. We generally see that where there is a lack of knowledge, there true and sincere piety does not flourish at all. But I call knowledge true, according as it lies near or is like the truth. For crude and false conjectures laid down as the foundations of knowledge may do injury to piety; to this class belongs the opinion of the Epicureans, that pleasure is the highest good of man; then, concerning our mind and concerning the gods, affirmations as impious as they are senseless, have been made by Epicurus and by others. These are all impostures of evil spirits which I have just removed from the rank of branches of knowledge. The goal of knowledge is sometimes harmful to piety, e.g. in arts which aim at injuring men, of which kind are philtrations, incantations, and that part of the military art which belongs to the attacking and slaughtering of men; and the whole class of war machines, and also other arts which are bad because they are maleficent[1]. Now, when we learn for the purpose of injuring, our ends are impious.

War wrongful.

And those ends which we seek for the sake of ostentation, cannot but lessen our virtue; and to this class all arts may belong, but necessarily sophistry, since it cannot be set forth except for some vain display or caprice. Also a curious delight in examining that which is of no use for life, effects nothing for piety. Paul, the Apostle of the Gentiles, does not suffer us to be led away by curious arts; and in the *Acts of the Apostles*[2], many of those who followed arts which were not evil or impious, but only curious, being persuaded by that same Apostle, publicly burnt their books, the price of which was a sum not to be despised. To this class belong jugglers' tricks, alchemy, transmutation of metals, divinations and other impostures. These things, indeed, through all the senses, bring shameful pleasures to the body, but inflict a great blow on piety; they absorb the whole strength from the mind, to the

[1] See Horace, *Odes*, I, xxvii.

[2] Acts xix. 19.

body, and compel it to become brutish, so that from the first it can only uplift itself and think about God with difficulty, and soon cannot even do that.

Those from whom we must not learn.

It is dangerous to learn from one whose words and companionship send us away worse than we came, and so much the more when the corruption of our nature makes us inclined to his persuasion. But it is impious to learn anything from an evil spirit, with whom God wishes us to have no communion: in fact, his cunning and artful ways, which are many and multifarious, are all planned to deceive us and turn us away from that good for which we were created. Of this class are arts taught or invented by a demon: they have in them some abomination either open or concealed, which will not be absent from those who practise them, as e.g. in most oracles, divinations by lots, prophecies, to which the human mind, eager to know abstruse or future events, easily listens[1].

Evil compact: concealed or expressed.

The manner of learning arts.

In the manner of learning or practising arts, we must strongly condemn any relaxation of piety either wholly or in part, through absorption in the study of human arts, nor should that time be given to them, which we need to finish our journey to a happy immortality. When we are attacked by physical disease, even as soon as we observe its approach, not only have the exercises of learning to be discarded, but also the peremptory functions of life, at home and in the state.

The effects of the study of arts.

Besides all these considerations, the issues of the study of an art ought not to be neglected. Of course in many cases, arts and erudition hinder the progress of religion; e.g. in the inquiry into the nature of things, and of abstruse things which are either hidden in secret places or are involved in the future, which the Lord has reserved for Himself alone, so that He did not think fit to

[1] See S. Augustine, *de Civitate Dei*, VIII, 1021.

reveal them to the Apostles[1], but forbade them to search into the times and seasons which the Father had put in His own power, for men have been wont to transfer their trust in God to the things which He has made. There are some things which almost always increase vice, and detract from virtues, e.g. disputations, quarrelsome, contentious books, in which the intellect arms itself against truth, and by an impious affectation of commendation of the truth prefers to hide the truth, rather than to yield to it.

To the same class belong books which praise vices, such as cruelty, war, love of money, tyranny, fraud. But of licentious writings, such as the Milesian Fables, than which there is nothing more silly or more impure, there are many among the poets; very many in alluring popular songs, and in books written in the vulgar tongues. And all these things are judged by each person according to his own intellect; for some things suit some minds, and some things others, just as certain foods suit certain palates and stomachs. For there is no knowledge so good that we cannot corrupt it, just as there is no food so healthy that it cannot become unhealthy, if it gets infected with disease. But although there is no learning and skill which is not of itself of service to piety, yet this is not the only thing to be considered; it must also be of use to us; since we do not learn arts and sciences for their own sakes, but for our good. All things in this world as they were made by God, are good and beautiful. But these good things are not all to be appropriated by everybody. They are indeed all good in themselves, but we cannot each of us have all that is good. So, in learning and in all kinds of knowledge we must make a choice.

**Goodness: (1) absolute, (2) relative.**

Different subjects of study require, in each case, a distinct type of natural mental ability for its successful pursuance. It is possible, however, to obtain a judgment as to which

[1] Acts i. 7.

studies a particular person would wisely refrain from undertaking. Just as a skilful medical man can pronounce with regard to the bodies of men after he has had them under his examination, so the man of practical wisdom (*vir prudens*) can form a judgment as to the special excellencies of mind, judgment and learning of a particular person, if he be called in, to act in this so important a function.

**Arts suitable for Christians.**

Now we will show what arts are suitable for Christians, and constitute the sure guardianship of their piety. For this (piety) as we have often said (and it needs to be often repeated) ought to receive the first close observation, and the keen attention of the mind should never be removed from it. If anyone, either at the very beginning of life when he was shaped by Nature, or afterwards through some most bountiful gift or favour from God, should devote himself to religion, so great would be the outstanding excellence of mind bestowed upon him, that he would rise upward to that height of divine sublimity in which he would repose as in his most happy and natural home. And then, having despised and disdained all human things, he would become as it were an inhabitant of that inaccessible light, in which that holy and all-powerful Being dwells. Hence it would happen that man, having attained a higher than human fate, would spend in this body a life more angelic than human; he would have no need of arts or any knowledge; no want would threaten him; nothing would terrify one who was superior to all misfortunes or need. We see that such as have, to a certain extent, attained to this perfection of life, were those who, in solitude and remote regions, spent a life apart from human intercourse, made pleasant and sweet by communion and conversations with angels; men like Paul and Antony, and the two named Hilary who, despising their own bodies as if they were things external to themselves, always adhered and clung to Him with Whom they were going to spend an infinite eternity. But these were very few, selected by the great favour of God, on account of their very high, and clearly godly character.

Idleness is to be shunned.

But the rest, to whom it is not given to aspire to such great happiness, when they cast down their eyes from that sublime view, ought not to betake themselves to the torpor of ease, so as to do absolutely nothing. The Lord, at the beginning of the world, sentenced the sons of Adam to labour[1]; in accordance with this judgment Paul in his Epistle to the Church at Thessalonica[2] writes: "If a man will not work, neither shall he eat." Solomon[3] by the example of the ant stimulates the lazy to work: and David[4] says that "he is happy who eats bread which he has procured by the labour of his hands." Our Lord, in his Gospel[5], does not do away with work, but with anxious care about results, which is *μεριμνᾶν*. Therefore it does not become anyone in the Church to live in ease and idleness. For even those holy hermits, when sometime in the day they relaxed the ardour of contemplation, exercised themselves in various works, sometimes of the hands, and sometimes of the mind.

What the Christian arts are.

But what then should these arts and sciences be? What other than those which are necessary for the aims of either this or the eternal life. They will either advance piety or be of service to the necessities, or at least the uses of life, for the latter are not greatly different from the necessities. By piety I understand either our own personal piety or that of others. So by "necessities," I mean our own and those of others. So marked is the shortness of time determined to each one, and in this shortness of time, so quick is the flight of life, and those things of which we have need for the cultivation of mind and body, for

Those things which are useful are to be studied.

[1] Genesis iii.
[2] 2 Thess. iii. 8, 9, 10.
[3] Proverbs vi. 6.
[4] Psalm cxxviii. 2.
[5] S. Matthew vi. 34.

our sustenance, or that of others, all those things are so numerous and varied, that it would be the height of madness, to reduce in any degree the short allowance of time, by spending it on what is superfluous. For useful undertakings we have not time enough, how then can there be a superfluity of time which anyone can afford to lose? For the necessities of the body there comes to man's help the study of foods, medicine, clothing, dwelling. Knowledge founded on experience is necessary to determine in what manner these means should be secured and preserved, as also is the knowledge in what it is each of these has its value. The soul is nourished and made pure by that which brings light or zeal to it, so that it may know how to pursue what should be desired in life, or to escape what ought to be avoided. To this end we must partly learn and accept what has been handed down to us, and partly think it out for ourselves and learn it by practising it. For God has given our soul one power, the intellect; and our body another power, in the hands. With these two powers, we surpass all other living creatures. For as our intellect raises us high above the souls of beasts, so also our body excels that of beasts, through the uses to which we can put our hands[1]. But as to what the hands can accomplish there will be elsewhere a further opportunity of showing. Now let us speak as to the activities of the mind.

[1] Cf. Aristotle, *de Anima*, III ἡ χεὶρ ὄργανόν ἐστιν ὀργάνων.

# CHAPTER V

## DIVISIONS OF KNOWLEDGE

Concerning the twofold power of the mind, and whatsoever is dealt with in either of the two orders. Then as to human society, whence and how it is derived, by what it is preserved and by what, on the other hand, it is undermined. Lastly the fit and exact divisions of different kinds of knowledge. Variety of man's powers and activities. Knowledge and its divisions.

**Divisions of all the arts.**

In the mind there are especially two functions, the power of observing, which is said to be the eye of the mind, or its acumen, and the power of judging and determining with regard to those things which the mind has seen. The former is concerned merely with observation but the latter has regard to men's actions. The human mind ranges over the heavens, elements, stones, metals, plants, animals, man; the last named it regards not merely in a single relation, but it investigates man's mind and body and those things which happen to both these, in their permanent states, and in their vicissitudes at various stages. Then the mind passes to consider human inventions, which open up a wide field for observation. Thence it goes on to study spiritual things, and eventually is led to the supreme and all-powerful God. All these subjects as far as human ability can receive them, are submitted to the judgment. The judgment compares one thing with another and shows which is useful, which harmful, which indifferent to the body; in matters of food, clothing, health, dwelling, what things are

**The Judgment.**

adapted to our necessities, conveniences, resources; in what manner they should be prepared, preserved, and put to use. Similarly the judgment provides for the soul and advises what things are helpful and what harmful to the development and illumination of the mind, whence it may issue better or worse by those means which we have, earlier, described as necessary to be prepared, preserved and used. We men are born for society, and cannot live thoroughly without it[1]. Nature has wisely made provision for this, both so that the arrogance of the haughtiest animal should be repressed when he sees that he has need of so many things, and also when he recognises the necessity for the winning of mutual love, which increases by intercourse and exchange of thoughts. This takes place so much the more easily and thoroughly, as there is less arrogance. For arrogance is the destroyer of the whole of the bond of human harmony. Goodness is the bond of society; its guide is the sound judgment, in which are to be found practical wisdom and wise leading of the whole life. Practical wisdom is increased by experience, which is supported by the memory, for the knowledge of many and great things would be less useful, if there were not something which preserved them and produced them before the mind for use, just at the time of need. Experience is either our own individually, or that obtained by others, which may serve to warn us, by the example of actual past occurrences, or it may be in the form of supposed occurrences such as are contained in histories, fables, stories, and similitudes. Briefly, experience may be gained from all accounts of those things which are handed down as having been said or done, or, again, from those writings which have been composed and are suited to instruct men in wisdom. So, too, with adages and sentences, in a word, all those precepts of wisdom which have been collected from the observations of the wise, which have remained amongst

**Society.**

**Man is a political animal.**

**History.**

[1] Aristotle, *Politics*, I, 2.

the people, as if they were public wealth in a common storehouse.

Speech.

For the exercise of the social instinct, speech has been given to men, how otherwise could society exist, since our minds are hidden away in so dense a body? How completely dead and torpid would the mind be if it only found expression in the look of the eyes, if we could only express our manifold thoughts by mute nods! This would not be expressing ourselves, but rather kindling in others a desire to understand our thoughts, as we see happens with those who do not understand one another's speech. Amongst people absent from one another, writing takes the place of speech whether they be separated by distance of place or time. This is a great aid to memory and a faithful witness of past events. In speech are two arts, the first that of practical necessity, a use which depends on its effectiveness for the intelligence rather than for polish and brilliancy; the other art of speech serves rather for pleasure and delight. In the latter is to be studied all elegance, polish and splendour of diction. To this is to be added the adaptation of appropriate style of treatment to things, places, times, persons. This art arises out of practical wisdom and is called rhetoric.

Letter-writing.

Division of arts.

Rhetoric.

Laws.

But because uncurbed minds not infrequently rush forward to the hurt of others, laws were instituted[1], and the limitation of rights promulgated, i.e. barriers were imposed on all license, when it was not restrained by the reason which was so near at hand. Certain instruments, so to say, also were sought for, with which we should be more easily and pleasantly led to the paths of reason. For the examining of masses and magnitudes; for moving them into a particular place, or establishing and fixing them where there was need, an art was thought out which is called *geometry*; for counting by numbers, an art in which no part of life lacks instances,

[1] Aristotle, *Politics*, I, 2.

*arithmetic* was devised. In the close investigation of truth, which has become so obscured to us, the judgment is advanced by a canon of probability; in forming an opinion which is based on conjecture, the instrument of dialectic is useful. It is called an examination as to the true (*censura veri*). To all these arts is to be added Music, as a relaxation and recreation of the mind, through the harmony of sounds. Under this head, comes all poetry, which consists in the harmony of numbers. Prose oratory, however, has its rhythms, though they are not fixed by definite and constant law, like poetry. These matters have been thought out in the human mind by industry, in accordance with the mind received from the great Artificer God, the gift we receive through Nature. This special favour bestowed by God, surpasses all others which can be compared with it. But since God has not allowed us on account of the magnitude of our sins, to have this imparted as a gift, for all the details of experience, we have to apply diligence so as to seek out what is useful, whilst we are lighted by that Lamp, which He has bequeathed to the human race. These are therefore the material and boundaries of those subjects of knowledge, which are not inconsistent with piety, and are of deep advantage to the body. Not only are they of great service to the body, but also many of them serve the cause of piety most thoroughly by the cultivation of the mind. These sciences, or if anyone prefers the name, branches of knowledge (*cognitiones*), can be divided from more points of view than can be here explained; according as it seems necessary to fix ends and aims, so the ground of division is changed. For some which are separated from one another can be joined, and vice-versa. So that if anyone makes Nature, one general science and kind of knowledge, this science can further be divided into the observation of plants and animals, and from plants into herbs, fruits, trees.

**The acumen of human nature.**

**The natural light of the mind must be increased by diligence.**

Another division of arts.

Observation of Nature.

Our division, if I am not mistaken, for the convenience of students should be as follows: those things which serve for observation and knowledge involve first the exercise of sight on the external face of Nature, which means, clearly, the use of the senses, like as, for instance, we gaze at a picture, and just in the same way as we look at a map on which cities, peoples, mountains, rivers are placed before the eyes. This is called inspection (*aspectus*) or reflection (*contemplatio*) and he who is skilled in it is called *aspector*, or *contemplator*. Let the keenness of sight of the mind descend from its height to the intimate working of Nature which is concerned with the inner essence of everything. For in this study an entrance is found to the essential heart of things more readily by the mind than by the eye, although observation begins through the eye. The man who thus penetrates with his mind into Nature is the first or intimate philosopher (*primus philosophus, seu intimus*) and his knowledge is "first philosophy" or knowledge of the innermost work of Nature (*prima philosophia vel intimum Naturae opificium*). From both mind and eyes, the wise man seeks for the outward causes which lie near to the eyes and the other senses. This kind of skill is called *scrutatio* or *investigatio*. The one who is skilled in it is called a *scrutator* or *investigator*. Afterwards let him proceed to those studies which escape every observation of the senses. For it is by thought alone that what we call spiritual questions (*res spiritales*) are investigated and this branch of study is called *spiritalitas*, and its students *spiritales*. From all these subjects is collected a far-reaching and comprehensive description of subjects, in which not only are appearances noted, but also the causes themselves. This is accomplished more by unravelling (*explicando*) than by mere observation (*inquirendo*). The latter study is called Natural History (*historia Naturae*) and

First philosophy.

Scrutinising of Nature.

Spirituality.

Natural History.

the man versed in it is termed a *Historicus*. Reflexion (*contemplatio*) must succeed to actual sense experience. This study will prescribe e.g. what foods should be brought on to the table, what not. This is called by the Greeks, Dietetics, and he who studies it is called a *Dieteticus*. You may if you wish use other names such as *vescus*, *esu*[*ri*]*alis*. Make your choice of names if only you let the study of things themselves remain. Then for the establishment and maintenance of health, we have Medicine. After Hippocrates, Dietetics became a part of Medicine and led to the institution of physicians. Now we have surveyed sufficiently the interests of the body, and we must pass to those of the mind and to the ordinary relations of men with one another.

**Dietetics.**

**Medicine.**

Included in this subject-matter are precepts such as every man ought to have properly established and fixed in his mind. This art of morals is called ethics and he who professes it is an *ethicus* or moralist. Some precepts teach how a man should bear himself in his private relations at home; others, how he should conduct himself in public relations, in the state. The former are called Economics, the latter Politics, from which the students, respectively, are termed Economists and Politicians. The words are Greek and were not unknown amongst the Romans, as borrowed words. For our speech, there are rules which have for their aim correct expression. These rules constitute the art of Grammar. Other rules are adapted to the needs of discourse suitable for various persons, times, places. This subject is called Rhetoric. The careful investigation of the contents and style of ancient authors and the diligent observation and annotation of them, a subject properly joined with grammatical study, is termed Philology and the student of this subject is a Philologist. Practical experience in life, gained through the examples of

**Ethics.**

**Economics.**
**Politics.**

**Grammar.**

**Rhetoric.**

**Philology.**

our ancestors, together with the knowledge of present-day affairs makes a man, as the Greeks name him, a *Polyhistor* as much as to say *multiscius* (a many-sided man). Such a man, however, we, following a better nomenclature, term a man of practical wisdom (*prudens*) and his province we call practical wisdom (*prudentia*). Then follow sciences which are useful to other branches of knowledge: geometry, arithmetic, students of which are called geometricians and arithmeticians. He who is concerned with the discovery of the probable is called an *Inventor*, and he who passes judgment on what has been discovered by probability is called a critic (*censor*). The musician (*musicus*) as he is called, deals with Music; the poet (*poeta*) with Poetry. In matters of divinity and sacred subjects we ponder deeply as far as is permissible to mortal men, on the Nature of the Holy One, or on those precepts of His, which lead and point the way to Him. He who is skilled in the first of these studies is termed a theologian (*theologus*); and he who studies the second is called a *Theonomus*. We will treat on both of these subjects elsewhere. We will now only say as to these subjects mentioned above, how we think they ought to be taught and learned one by one.

**Practical Wisdom or Polyhistoria.**

**Geometry, Arithmetic.**

**Exposition of Probability.**

**The Musician. Poet.**

**Theologian. Theonomist.**

# CHAPTER VI

## CHOICE OF BOOKS

In so great an abundance of books, which should be read in class, and which by private reading. Then the author offers to estimate the especial value of each, but he does this rather to incite others to the same labour, than because he hopes to be able to carry out the plan fully himself. Should the books of the heathen be read? Books and their place in the acquisition of knowledge.

**Books.**

To books we must refer for knowledge in every subject. For without them, who could hope that he would attain the knowledge of the greater things? The direct inspiration of God teaches only very few, and to those whom He teaches, He merely gives what is serviceable and necessary to their own eternal welfare. Certainly only very rarely, do men show themselves worthy of, i.e. suited to receive, so great a favour from God, and it is not fitting that the teaching of the Divine Master should stoop to the manifestation of activity amongst the unsuited. Therefore the man desirous of wisdom must make use of books, or of those men who take the place of books, viz. teachers, otherwise there only remains for him to talk foolishly. As in everything connected with observation there are no limits, for there is nothing so manifest to the senses that it would not require many minds to be most lavishly exercised for a very long time, for a complete record, so we find books have increased to such uncountable numbers. Some writers publish what they

**Learning: (1) Extraordinary, (2) Ordinary.**

themselves have written; others limit themselves to compilations from other writers. So much is this so, that, now, a man's life would not suffice, I do not say for the reading what has been written on many arts and sciences, but on any one of them—let alone the time for understanding them. Seneca remarks that Cicero maintains that if his own life were doubled in length, time would not suffice for him to accomplish the reading of all the poems of the lyric bards. But if everything written by those old philosophers, historians, orators, poets, physicians, theologians, had reached this age, then we could put nothing but books in our houses; we should have to sit on books; we should have to walk on the top of books; our eyes would have to glance over nothing but books. Even now there is a terror fallen upon not a few people, and a hatred of study, when they find offered them in any subject of study the volumes which will need indefatigable industry to master. They instantly depress the minds of those who look at them, and the wretches moan inwardly, and ask: Who can read all these?

**The great multitude of books might deter men from study.**

There must, therefore, in every science and art be appointed set books which must be read and explained in the schools, and others to be read privately, so that the course of life, so short and fleeting, may not be consumed in what is superfluous, and (as also is not infrequently the case) in the positively harmful; and so that life may not flee away before it has come to the bearing of fruit. He who would thus settle the choice of books, supported by a great knowledge and discriminating judgment would, in my opinion, truly confer a great benefit upon the whole race of mankind. But such an one must not be satisfied with merely making a note of the worth of the books, but he should also indicate the passages in the books where topics one by one should be sought. This task I will, to some extent, attempt to perform; with what success I shall not greatly distress myself, at any rate I shall manifest the strong desire to stir up many others,

**Certain books must be read.**

especially those who will be far better able than myself more comprehensively to promote the interests of the race of students, either because they are gifted with greater mental energy, or because they are equipped with a richer knowledge of things. I shall not be envious of the gifts of any man, who may confer either this or any other good on the human race, and it will be very pleasant to me to be pushed back into the last place, or even into no place, in the commonwealth of letters, if I may only see the progress of human wisdom, a wisdom which our mortal race needs in this our age, if never before, sunk as it is in the depths of shame and crime. It cannot be expected that I should be able to treat of all writers worthy to be read. It would be an almost insuperably difficult task for me, not so much because of the crowd, as because of my ignorance and forgetfulness. The liberty I take in making any attempt to do it you will excuse in me, when you remember that the undertaking has particular reference to rendering studies useful, and at least my opinion must not be estimated at so great a value that it is to be regarded as sufficient for removing any author even of the lowest class from his recognised position, much less for degrading an author of the highest rank.

**We must study the useful sciences.**

I will speak of the sciences one by one, and in what manner, as it seems to me, they should be taught, and will mention what I think has been well and usefully written on them by various writers.

Before everything, we must remember that the needs of life are varied and numerous, since they pass by in single moments, one need arising out of another, so that if we rightly spend our time, there is no moment remains over for trifling, and all branches of knowledge must be applied, not to any empty dilettantism but to the practice of life. Galen[1] says rightly that those sciences which bring no usefulness to life have no claim to the name. Wherefore although the aim of some sciences, as I have shown above, is observation, yet this

[1] *Oratio suasoria ad artes*, chap. vi.

must not be the student's end, but must lead to some further practical issue. If there is no other aim proposed to a science (than that of observation) it is certainly fitting that the learner should have one himself. The observation of Nature is so immense, so unlimited, that if anyone steeps himself in it, he will not attain what he desires, and will lose the whole fruit of his life's labour, unless he applies the knowledge which he has acquired in his studies either to the uses of life, or to the admiration and worship of his Creator. Nay, even the contemplation of God, than which nothing can be termed more wonderful, more comprehensive, or more excellent, should be turned to some use, so that we may be inflamed, and seized by it and absorbed by it. Let me give a warning, now, at the threshold, since human sinfulness has matured all over the world, and the depraved affections of the soul have become so strong, it has become necessary that the sciences should be handed on more purely, more simply, and that they should be less infected and imbued with craft and impostures. For it is only by this means (as far as this may be possible) that Christian people may be taken back to the true and native simplicity, and thus all branches of knowledge may scatter fewer sparks by which minds are inflamed wrongly—only too much inclined of themselves, to great and cruel fires of passion. Wickedness is too much heaped up, and the judgment sharpened on the whetstone of depravity. There is no need of greater sharpness of criticism, (but rather as it were of some blunting), not that men should become devoid of practical wisdom, but that they should develope more sincerity and simplicity, and for that very reason, become wiser, not more astute. Our life will become so much the more happy, the less it is stained by deceit and sophism, the more like it becomes to the life of men of old, whose rectitude and simplicity of mind rendered them worthy of conversation with God. Add

**The end of an art and of the student of the art.**

**The study of arts should lead to piety.**

**Arts should lead Christians back to the early Christian knowledge.**

to this, that branches of knowledge demonstrated briefly and purely, aid sharpness of wit, judgment, practical wisdom, and the enjoyment of common things, whilst a long treatment of these subjects dulls mental vigour and is most harmful. On this subject it is said, in the words of a very wise man, "In much wisdom is much grief, and he that increaseth knowledge, also increaseth sorrow."

**Should heathen literature be read?**

At this point we are met by the very pertinent question as to profane literature, e.g. of the heathens, Agarenes[1], Jews. Should these writings be read, or should they be entirely rejected? There is, indeed, in them much wickedness and deceit and a great deal of poison for those who are inexperienced and for the vicious. It is a somewhat serious question, and well worthy of careful thought, as anyone may easily imagine, and no single solution can be universally pronounced. I have previously taken up the position that no knowledge of things can be a hindrance to piety. The right reading of Gentile (i.e. heathen) works did no harm to (amongst the Greeks) Origen, Justinus, Basilius, Nanzianzenus, Chrysostom, and amongst the predecessors of our faith, no harm was done to Tertullian, Cyprian, Lactantius, Jerome, Ambrose, Hilary, Augustine, Gregory, Isidore, Thomas (Aquinas). Even some heathen writers proved of great use to them as the *Hortensius* of Cicero to Augustine[2]. Many have been harmed by heathen authors, e.g. Lucianus, the Emperor Julianus, Domitius Calderinus, Codrus Urceus, Pomponius Laetus[3]. Many experience in themselves that their piety was, in some cases, invigorated by this sort of literature, in other cases, it has been weakened. These books therefore must be regarded as a great field, of which one part is useful, and another hurtful; in which useful herbs spring up in one place, and noxious weeds in another; whilst

[1] i.e. Arabs.

[2] Augustine, *Confess.* III, 4.

[3] Vives, *de Conscribendis Epistolis*, near the end, says of one writer: "*He abhorred the name of Peter because it savoured of Christianity.*"

in a third part the field is planted with flowers, which serve for pleasure and adornment. They contain what is useful. The observation and inquiry into natural objects promotes the serviceableness of food, of health, or some other use of life. They contain also mathematical knowledge which is of service in so many directions. Do they not contain the knowledge of antiquity and of all human memory, of so many words and deeds, keenly, seriously, gaily, and piously expressed, by which practical wisdom is cultivated and helped? In a word, they contain all that knowledge, that encyclopaedia which leads to the life of greatest usefulness, in which what has been observed and thought has been diligently consigned to posterity.

**Useful books.**

**Books contain the vigour of men's minds and learning.**

Hence it comes to pass that unlearned men, however intellectual they may be by nature, cannot be pervaded by so great a vigour of mind as those who are of average intellectual power, when furnished with learning, for they have many others to help them, whereas the unlearned, however great their untrained intellects, certainly are units, and stand alone. Here avail the instruments of truth, of discovery, of judgment, which help us towards practical wisdom. The heathen, moreover, present effective judgments of great weight against vices, and praise for virtues, which we are permitted to use for our good, and against our vicious inclinations. These judgments are found in their teachings and precepts, which have been composed through some great impulse of natural good, which has been handed down to us for our practice, and which offer to us many helps in our affairs. The heathen, in the last place, possess every ornament, grace, elegance, and splendour of discourse. Yet amongst these so healthy characteristics, they mix up dangerous gifts, not a few, like as sometimes honey or the sweetest wine is mixed with poison. Of this kind are the scruples and doubts raised about

**Value of heathen writers.**

**Harmful books of heathens.**

matters of our faith, and what is worse than these, even more pernicious, open derision, and sometimes also railing, since purblind and weak-sighted eyes cannot bear to turn their gaze to so great a splendour of light. Then we find praise of many vices, e.g. pride, anger, cruelty; the admiration and worship of power, wealth, pleasures; the story of vices which breathe contamination in their very recital as, e.g., the stories of lust, revenge, vainglory. These recitals open up schools of slyness, deceit, imposture. Whence, the soul, whether it wills or not, must get much deceit and fraud clinging to it, which will only await the opportunity for being put into practice. For when men's care and thoughts are directed towards ambition or gain, only those things are pursued which bring money or glory. For him who knows how dangerous these books are, and who understands the subject-matter, there would perhaps be no harm on entering upon these studies and plucking from them what might seem good to him. Nay, even wise men need at times to know of what is harmful, in their contest against the harmful, just as skilled physicians use poisons against poisons. In this way they can compare the dangerous writings of the heathen with our own, to show the impurity of the former and the excellence of ours, and by the comparison with darkness, make our light appear the brighter. In short, they may well peruse all sorts of writings either for their intrinsic merit or to point out their deficiencies, as e.g. where our age has written against the heathen so as to defeat them with their own weapons. A catalogue of such works has been drawn up by Jerome when he answers that orator Magnus to whom Calphurnius Lanarius had given his aid. For this reason when Julian the Apostate was strenuously persecuting the Christians, he ordered that they should not be taught the liberal arts, lest they should pluck feathers from the eagle with which they might transfix the eagle itself[1]. This simile he is

[1] See Juliani, *Epistolae*; Socrates, *Histor. Eccles.* bk III, chap. x and Nicephor, bk X, chap. xxv.

said to have used when he found himself at a loss in the liberal arts.

Harmful books are dangerous to those of a curious disposition, such as those who do not hesitate to taste hemlock, and try what its flavour may be, and thereby bring about their own death. So, too, with the ignorant and careless, who do not know the right use to make of books. It certainly would be very fitting, if, on account of the weakness and darkness of our mind, hurtful passages could be cleansed, so that there should be no pitfall of harm left, and we should only then wander about in those fields in which grow wholesome or pleasant herbs, sown by some honest and wise husbandman, and taken from the sure vineyards of holy religion, or only those things approved as satisfactory, and transplanted there away from dangerous fields, as the treasures of the Egyptians were converted to the adornment of the Temple[1]. How much more fruitfully and pleasantly do we take our journeys in the meadows if we fear no snares from plants or serpents, than we should in the doubtful and dangerous districts of Asia and Africa. S. Ambrose has wisely and piously adapted Cicero's work *de Officiis* (which is full of good thoughts and of what is useful for life) into a form consistent with our faith, since he thought it was safer for people to quaff what trickled from a Christian than from a heathen source. Knowledge and experience of evil are of service to a few, if only it has been shown how we can make use of the evil to some satisfactory purpose, or as we say, commonly, when they are "turned to use." For this reason, the Lord, considering our infirmity, forbade that we should within ourselves have anything to do with the hidden and deceitful snares of the devil, or any commerce with him. Perhaps to some it might be permitted without danger. But a common danger is to be avoided by all in common. Therefore I think that a good man will not go into

[1] See Augustine, *de doctrina Christiana*, II, 4.

dubious tracts, and that it is better to accept the Christian teaching handed down through Christian tradition from Christ than to learn from monumental works of the impious, even if we cut out those things which might injure the integrity of good morals. If this cannot be done, at least, let some man show us the way, a man not only well furnished with learning, but also a man of honour and of practical wisdom, whom we trust as a leader; who will remove us from danger either quietly without explaining the danger, lest he rouse the desire of curiosity; or, will openly show to those for whom it is fitting, what danger lies hidden, and knowing thoroughly the minds of those whom he is leading, will explain as much to every one as it may be expedient for him to know. In this manner the heathen woman will be received into marriage, with nails and hair duly cut, according to the rite of the children of Israel, even as S. Jerome expounds[1].

**The reading of heathen writers.**

[1] Epistle ad Magnum oratorem Rom. Vol. 2, p. 326, ed. Basle (1516).

# BOOK II

## SCHOOLS

# CHAPTER I

## SCHOOLS AND TEACHERS

Where schools should be erected. Who should be chosen to the task of teaching, how and by whom; concerning the salary or reward of teachers; also other matters which pertain to the economy of schools. The erection of schools. The choice of schoolmasters. Their position and payment.

It is necessary, next, to say what things, in what manner, to what extent, by whom, and in what place, each subject is to be taught. Above all things it is especially to be considered how instruction may be given well, so that good morals may not be corrupted, or in any way impeded or dimmed.

**The site for the Academy.**

First of all, something must be said about the site, for that is usually the first consideration in erecting a school. Careful attention should be given that the air be healthy, so that the scholars may not have to flee thence, smitten with a fear of pestilence. Thus, Alexinus, the philosopher of Elis, who taught in an unhealthy place and in a place which lacked many things which were necessary for use, was deserted by all his pupils: and that indeed, though he met with the greatest approval and acceptance[1]. Nevertheless, I would not choose a verdant or pleasant place, which

[1] Laertius in his *Euclid*, bk II.

may often tempt the scholars to venture forth unless, perchance, the attention is absorbed in delightful studies, such as poetry, music, history. I consider that this unhealthiness of climate was chosen by Plato for his Academy in the suburbs of Athens. Yet if he deliberately aimed at unhealthiness, he would scarcely bring me to approve of his plan. For those who are going to accomplish good and accurate work in studies must be in health. Let it be secured, then, that plenty of nourishment (and all that is helpful) is at hand, so that fruitful minds may not be compelled through slender equipment to give up letters, and so be without great good, both for themselves and for many others, especially when youths who strive after learning are too often in poor rather than opulent circumstances, and the vanity of riches allures those who possess riches to far different desires, such as hunting, horses, war, play, voluptuousness, and every kind of pleasure, in the pursuit of which they think they apply their riches to the most fitting use[1].

**The poet rightly says that not easily do men develope, to whose virtues the straitened circumstances of the home stand in the way.**

**Almost all young men give their mind to some pursuit, either of rearing horses or dogs for hunting or else give themselves to philosophy.**

Let the site be apart from the crowd, and especially from workmen who produce a noise and loud sounds in their work, such as smiths, stone-cutters: in short, all who use a hammer, a wheel and lathe, and a weaving-comb; yet let not the place be altogether uninhabited, lest there should be wanting witnesses and, as it were, spectators of their faults, if they are addicted to any. Therefore I should like the inhabitants to be earnest and upright, whom the scholars may reverence; not innkeepers or wicked people who may urge them on to vicious practices; not sordid, or hunters after petty gains: for grasping people make others anxious and sordid, and to become such as those who are called by the Greek word μικρολόγοι, and nothing is more inimical to wisdom. Also let

[1] So Terence in *Andria* I, I.

the site of the school be far from the retinue of a court, and from the neighbourhood of girls ; the former, by ease and evil arts, incites their minds, unformed and flexible, to any shape, and the latter by their beauty allure the student at a time of life exposed to that attractive form of evil. It would be certainly better to have the school built outside the town, especially if that is by the sea or if the inhabitants are devoted to merchandise, provided that a place is not chosen where idle people are accustomed to stroll about for pleasure. And do not let it be near a public road, lest the minds of the scholars should be drawn off from the work they have begun by the diversion of watching the passers-by. Nor should the site be on the boundaries of a country which is wont to be infested by war, lest the fear of war should not allow pupils to give their attention to their studies in security. Let a public academy be established in each province of a country. I define a province not by its natural limits, such as mountains, rivers or the sea, but by the fixed rule and sovereignty under which it is. I suggest this so that if the youths are shut in on the borders of the territory by a neighbouring war, either because of their own danger or the anxiety of their friends, they may not have to take refuge in another kingdom or else be compelled, on some emergency, with great waste of time, to interrupt studies well begun. Let no one wonder that the place where wisdom is to be born and grow should be sought with this care, when we so anxiously look after a place where the bees can get honey, the price of which is how much below wisdom?

**The masters should be of good moral character.**

But most of all it is the men who are of service to the school: therefore not only let the masters have such learning that they may be able to educate well, but let them also have skill and aptness in teaching[1]. Let their characters be pure. The first care is that they may neither say nor do anything which may leave an evil example for the hearer, nor anything which it

[1] Quintilian I, I.

is not safe to imitate. If they have any faults, let them strive to put them away and eradicate them entirely, or what is next best, let them carefully and strenuously keep their faults away from the notice of the scholar, for the latter ought to bear himself in accordance with the example of his master. Nor must the teacher be of proved character only, but he must also be practically wise[1]. Let him have a disposition fitted to the art which he professes and to the kind of pupils whom he instructs, for the better his methods, the better they will understand. As a grammarian, let him not be rabid. As a physician, let him not be of the obstinate sort who will not give way before one who offers better advice than himself. As a moral philosopher, let him not be arrogant and a mere discoverer of the faults of others. Practical wisdom, the directress of the whole of life, has the greatest and most effective power in teaching good ways, in correcting faults, in reproving, and in showing the use of punishment (and how far it should go), for these things, employed in their own time, and place and manner, have great effect; but if they are inopportune, they are all odious and inefficacious. Let the master be good, and a lover of letters: for, because he is studious he will gladly teach so that he may exercise himself, and because he is good, so that he may be of service to others. He will be of a fatherly disposition towards his pupils, so that they may be to him in the place of sons, nor will he be on the look-out as to how much payment he may obtain from them or from his profession. Instruction which is sold is never well given. Xenophon[2] in his *Commentaries* is the authority for the statement that Socrates specially avoided the selling of instruction.

**Two faults should be driven out from learning.**

Two faults are to be driven very far off from all learning and from learned men—avarice and ambition. These both spoil the arts, and bring literary men and letters into contempt. For they drive learned men to what is most unworthy, in that

[1] Quint. I, I and 2, and II, 2.

[2] *Memorabilia*, bk I.

they assent to the most absurd opinions and ignorant judgments; in that they admit the disgraceful parts of the arts to the honours of study; in that they pertinaciously support what is false. Such men prefer that all knowledge should be turned upside down and annihilated, rather than that they should confess themselves vanquished or ignorant of anything. In short, the teacher should not do, say, seek and pursue those things by which money or glory may be obtained. Otherwise he brings about the results: deceit, quarrels, perjury, hatred; finally, principles weakly defended. How can a teacher rule his pupils when he looks to them for praise or money? Therefore let every opportunity for personal gain be removed from schools. Let teachers receive a salary from the state, such as a good man will desire but a wicked man disdain; lest, if it be large, ignorant and wicked persons may insinuate themselves into posts through greed for gold, while good and learned men who do not know how to canvass for posts, and do not wish to do so, may be excluded. Let them receive no fees from pupils and thus avoid seeking money from them, or treating them too kindly and indulgently through hope of gain. Do not let the pupils buy their food from the masters, but one of the scholars may be chosen every week, who shall be, as it were, the steward (*architriclinus*). Let him every day see after the buying of the meals; and when the week is ended and the account drawn up, let him bring together tokens, having added in the account a payment to the servants for their work. Let the food be such as is readily procurable, pure and easy to cook; for this kind of food keeps the body healthy and the mind vigorous. Also let every occasion of boasting, arrogance and ostentation be removed. Wherefore, let public disputations in which the truth is not brought out, be rare; where nobody agrees with the person who speaks with greater keenness for truth: only

(1) Arrogance.

(2) Avarice.

The scholar's way of living.

The hope of triumphing in disputations should be removed from scholars.

praise for wit or cleverness is sought. And out of this struggle for praise grow quarrels and wrangling and dissensions. What is more pernicious, the intellect takes up arms against truth and, in order to subvert it, uses all kinds of secret devices and applies every contrivance it can, so that it wishes truth to be overthrown and overcome by it, instead of submitting itself to the truth. And a strife so nefarious and impious as this does not become good men, much less Christians, whose minds ought to be most pure,—followers of the truth, of Christ Himself. Finally, many go away from these disputations still more full of railing and more obstinate, and no one is any wiser or better than when he came.

**Degrees of honour in the Academy.**

Would it not be better not to have any degrees of honour in an academy, according to the word of the Lord: "Be ye not called Master, for One is your Master[1]"? Might there not be some temporary reward of learning rather than a lasting dignity? Or is it better to have some honours, as distinctions of learned men, lest all be measured by the same ten-foot rod of approbation or reprobation? For that saying of Christ refers to heavenly doctrine of which he is the only Master. Therefore it does not seem right that the title should be abolished simply because it has been abused, but rather that it should be restored to its right use and value. No laws are good enough if the wickedness of men chooses to twist them to suit their own desires. Nevertheless, the best laws are to be as unalterably fixed as possible. Yet let only a few be admitted to these honours, lest a mark of the greatest distinction become worthless through becoming too common: and also because the pride of many people increases, and through a swollen kind of dignity they refuse to learn from those who are wiser. Hence S. James[2] gives the advice, "My brethren, be not many masters."

[1] S. Matthew xxiii. 8. [2] S. James iii. 1.

Let all be kept at each kind of study for a certain and fixed time, lest anyone who has tasted but slightly of learning shall trumpet himself as one who has finished a course of instruction, and completed the circuit, as they say in the Greek contests. Let some extra time be added for those who are somewhat slow, for it is not expedient to have one time for all; nothing would be more unequal than an equality of that kind.

Learners.

Those who learn should be called 'students' or 'learners.' Then after a certain time, when they have gained experience, they will become 'professors.'

Professors.

For some time they should teach before a public audience, among which there will sometimes be those who are able to pass judgment on what is said. If they are approved, let them cease to be 'professors,' and become 'doctors' or 'masters.'

Doctors or Masters.

From these men, who have the necessary aptness, teachers will be chosen. These we call 'master-professors,' and they will be held to have the highest honour in the whole academy.

Master-Professors.

And if anyone is unworthy of the 'Doctorate,' either through ignorance or through a disgraceful and wicked life, his dignity should be publicly taken from him, just in the same way as the magistrates of the State used to be lowered in rank.

Character as well as knowledge necessary in teachers.

Let those who are raised to the office of instructors of youth be judged, not only by their learning, but also by their characters. Teaching with which the life does not correspond is harmful and disgraceful. A life without learning may merit much praise, but cannot be approved in the teacher. Therefore the school is not the place for it; elsewhere it has its high and honourable place. Those who are appointed to, or are entering upon, a post of honour should pay nothing for it. Let them not give a banquet or influence by any appeal to greed the minds of those about to appoint them to any honour. Let recipients of honours feast together, if they like, and pay for their feast by money collected amongst themselves, as a proof of their hilarity. But let them be merry in such a way as not to forget that they are devoted to wisdom.

**The choice of professors.**

Let them make those men professors or masters who by their learning, their judgment and their character are able both to teach others and to gain the approbation of the public. Among this class there must not be men who are a disgrace to learning, or who perversely abuse it, nor those who disturb the peace of others, nor those who think so much of gain that for the sake of it they are ready to strike a blow at the public good, by giving the control as the guides of scholars to those who will throw down headlong their students into the whirlpool (of ignorance). Let them pity the human race, blind and forsaken amidst so many dangers; let them remember that their heavenly Lord and Master is calling to them: "Ye are the salt of the earth"; "Ye are the light of the world[1]." And if the light is obscured who will be able to see; and if the salt hath lost its savour, wherewithal shall it be salted? Therefore let professors and masters—avoiding disputation with one another, and divesting themselves of pride—be good, learned and practical, and spend their lives harmoniously, so that they may mutually help each other, knowing that they are doing God's work. For he who helps a brother who is labouring for the truth, not only helps a man but also the truth, and shows himself a servant of God, from Whom proceeds all truth and Who is indeed the highest truth Himself, pure and perfect[2]. Those who know that most things are obscure and uncertain to learners will be far from divisions and quarrels amongst themselves, and that man is mad who hates his brother on account of what is no more revealed to himself than to the other. I know not how little greater is the very faint glimmer of truth which shines more on one than on another.

Do not choose the professors from those scholars in whom the desire of favour or of money is very powerful. It is not

[1] S. Matthew v. 13, 14. [2] S. John xiv. 6.

the most useful men who would be chosen from among them, but the most favoured and the most popular and obliging, or those who have given or promised most, or from whom license may be hoped for. Much less do I approve of what I learn is done in some academies—that at the same hour two masters teach the same subject, whom they call 'concurrentes,' and I have never heard a more appropriate word, for they do run together assuredly, and meet and fight with violent abuse, bitterness and fury. There is a pandering to the audience, as it were to the public in the theatre, who are pleased not with the best man, but with the best actor. For the hearers cannot pass an opinion on what they are ignorant of. Hence strife is received by the audience with great applause, for the spectacle of a fight is most pleasing to them. All respect and reverence for the teacher vanishes, and with it disappear the tranquillity of philosophical thought and the progress of studies. Masters as well as pupils become accustomed to envying, anger, offensive language, want of restraint in deeds and words, and other vices extremely unbecoming a good man. Wherefore, they proceed to public affairs, to private affairs, to councils, in short, to every function of life, ignorant and senseless, because of their minds being constantly irritated, and are like wild beasts. Therefore let professors be chosen and approved, not by the votes of the inexperienced and uncouth crowd, but by a few out of the academy who are respected for their learning and the uprightness of their lives.

**Election of professors.**

*'Concurrentes.'*

**The election of professors to be made by delegated wise men of the Academy.**

# CHAPTER II

## THE IDEAL SCHOOL

With what end in view boys should be sent to school. What should be the mental ability in each. How mental ability may be estimated. Whether it is best to educate at home or in schools. This is indeed a very old question but it is one treated by Vives, both acutely and thoroughly. Aims of school life. The ideal school. Public and private education.

**The entrance of the boy into the School.**

WHEN a boy is brought to school by his father, let it be made clear to the father that learning ought not to be sought as a means of making an easy living, for that would be a reward unworthy of such extraordinary labour. If teachers gave expression to this opinion actually in their lives, others would readily believe it to be true. If the contrary were the case, what hope would a father have of practical wisdom and piety in his son, if he saw that the teacher, i.e. the example set to his son, was imprudent or wicked? It should be made known that the end of learning is that the boy may become wise and therefore better. Let the boy remain one or two months in the preparatory school that his disposition may be investigated. Four times a year let the masters meet in some place apart where they may discuss together the natures of their pupils and consult about them. And let them apply each boy to that study for which he seems most fit. Apollonius of Alabanda, who is spoken of by Cicero[1] as a master of rhetoric, although he was paid for his teaching, would not suffer those

[1] Cicero, *de Oratore*, bk I.

whom he thought would not become orators to waste their labour with him, but used to dismiss them, and exhort and urge them to devote their time to some other study which he considered more suitable. Let the gratuitous teacher do his work as thoroughly as the man who is paid, whether he be a rhetorician, philosopher or theologian. Let him as a Christian do what the heathen did, and not allow a boy to lose time and money by having him as a teacher when the pupil is unable to profit by instruction, lest nothing else should be looked for in learning but disgrace and a seed-plot of errors, and the scholar, as it were, have the wild beast aroused in him and be thus sent out as a source of injury into the state[1]. If these precautions be taken, then the unlearned will honour the learned as if they were gods fallen down from heaven, and their academies as holy places and full of sacred awe, inhabited by a divinity, as were formerly Helicon and Parnassus. How shameful it will appear to the thinking man that our characters and our ignorance should be laughed at and despised by the unlearned, and, what is the most serious, that this treatment should not be undeserved? For indeed it is not to be tolerated that husbandmen, shoemakers and carpenters, and men of the lowest class should generally be more temperate in their dispositions than very many learned men. To a school of the right kind, not only should boys be brought, but even old men, driven hither and thither in a great tempest of ignorance and vice, should betake themselves to it as it were to a haven. In short, let all be attracted by a certain majesty and authority, and let the teacher accomplish more among his pupils by inspiring trust and veneration than by blows and threats. Admiration of the intellects and characters of the teachers will be the greatest stimulus to study, and a powerful influence in producing obedience. This is a true academy, namely, an association and harmony of men

**The source of contempt for learning.**

**What an Academy is.**

[1] Quintilian I, 3.

equally good as learned, met together to confer the same blessings on all those who come there for the sake of learning. For it is not enough for one or two in that academy to be good, if there are many bad who are marked by plotting and by audacity. For the bad will overcome the good, as we often see it happen. Pupils will flock over to the teacher who pampers them the most.

**Private and public education.**

Is the question asked: Are boys better educated at home or in public institutions[1]? If there be any such academy as I have depicted, it would certainly be best to place boys there from their infancy, where they might at once imbibe the best morals, and evil behaviour would be to them strange and detestable, as he who was educated by Plato, when he saw his father angry, wondered very much and affirmed that he had seen no such offence in Plato[2]. But as academies are now, the question requires more consideration than one might think. For we must consult the interests of the home, the fatherland, and beyond it.

Above all, boys must be accustomed to delight in good things and to love them, and to be grieved at evil things and to detest them; yet their ideas (of good and evil) should be suited to their mental grasp, for they cannot at once apprehend the highest and the absolute[3]. The fact is that habit is most pleasant, and opinions received by us as children follow us very far on the road of our lives, and so much the more if they have been fixed and confirmed in the earliest age by conduct. In this respect boys are naturally apes; they imitate everything and always, especially those whom they consider worthy of imitation on account of their authority, or because of the faith they place in them, such as parents, nurses, masters and school-fellows. Hence, we find a corrupt disposition in many pupils from whom it ought to have been swept away, certainly in those whom I have just mentioned.

[1] Quintilian I, 2. [2] See Seneca II, 2 *de Ira*.
[3] See Quintilian I, 1.

The father's anxiety for the morals of his children.

It is fitting that a father should have great anxiety about the morals of his son, greater than about his inheritance, in proportion as morality is more important than inheritance[1]. And whether he is going to bequeath any inheritance or none, the first thing to be possessed is an upright disposition. Nay, rather, there is no need of inheritance, but of virtue: for "the good man will quickly make a fortune, and the wicked man will quickly spend it." When the demand comes from parents for a method of education for children, then Nature herself speaks to us, and sacred learning teaches us by examples and precepts. If for no other reason, certainly for the sake of his son—especially when he is deliberating about the instruction of his son—it is most important for the father to acquaint himself with the state of his house and the whole family, even if he knows nothing about them at any other time. If he sees that anyone is moulding the waxen mind of his boy to evil, let him remove him if he can conveniently do so. If not, and if there is no one in the family whose character the boy could worthily imitate, let the father commit the care of his son to others away from home[2]. Thus the Romans formerly used to send their sons to some old and distinguished man, very serious and pious, for the sake of learning. For instance, Cicero was taken to Q. Scaevola, a man of high and noble family, of dignity and wealth[3]. For old men do not shrink from trouble, when they see that it is useful, and especially when it is necessary for the republic, since the republic will be after their death exactly as they have left the boys or youths. At the present time, when the thought of the common good affects few and almost none, this office is despised by all when indeed it ought by no means to be avoided but for love of one's country ought to be eagerly desired and embraced. But, to-day, in many of the nations,

Children the seed of the republic.

[1] Quint. *Institutiones Oratoriae* X, 10.

[2] Quint. I, 2.

[3] See Cicero, *Philip.* 8.

love of the fatherland is not even understood, to such a degree does each live and care for himself alone. Therefore if a father is able, let him appoint as teacher for his son a holy and pure man. Let the boy be taught by him, if he is able to teach, only not alone, for, as Quintilian[1] shows, he will in that case make less progress. If it is not possible to obtain such a man, from whom the boy may receive good instruction, or if there are not fellow-pupils to be found, let the father send the boy to the public gymnasium of the State, and choose out some relative or neighbour or friend, to whom the boy may be sent from time to time, so that he may be examined as to his studies and the progress of his manners. But it is not good for boys to board in the school, for there they are not nourished so healthily nor provided for so liberally, as at home, unless the parents are despicable and sordid men and of dissolute life, or men who ruin the disposition of their sons by lavish indulgence. For those who now send their sons to certain schools for the sake of a courteous, polite and noble education are very much deceived, for in nearly all of them the masters are greedy, sordid, low, as well as morose, hard to please, passionate, and of most evil dispositions not to mention their effeminacy. Since the master cannot always be with them in all they do, the boys, in fact, are promoters and examples to one another of obscenity and certain false opinions about things. Therefore they go out from the schools as youths whom no one can see in society without nausea, nor brook without aversion.

**The Academy.**

Indeed, in the present state of scholastic morality, it is not expedient to send boys to a public academy without careful discrimination.

In the first place, one must find out from friends in the country some one who knows the natural disposition (of the master), and whether he is sufficiently learned. He himself will every day give many indications of himself. Next, whether he will make a proper use of his learning. For nothing is worse

[1] Bk I, cap. 2, where all things are found best explained.

than the abuse of good things, and learning—the instrument of the greatest value—may be turned to atrocious crimes, if it is lodged in a wicked disposition. Rightly does Quintilian[1] say that living honourably seems to him better than learning well. Those who are wicked and silly are rarely made good; on the contrary, rather through the degeneration of their nature, many who were originally good become bad. For men are changed by the companions whom they hold most dear, by a certain rubbing against them, as it were an infection, while they do not persevere in resistance to it. They are polluted by the taste of pleasures. In short, they are changed, because the body always exerts an influence upon the mind and represses it by its weight, unless it is supported by the mighty stimulus of teachers and right exercise. Wherefore it was said by Solomon, "Uncertain is the course of youth." In public academies the boy of an age prone to vice naturally, is pushed on either by depraved companions and friends or by a certain vicious inclination of the mind; and when once he has begun to go to ruin, whatever things meet him hurry him forwards, and struggle to tumble over with him. If they have teachers or masters, severe, diligent and watchful in their duty, these youths become hardened to their warnings of word and rod, and treat them as of no account. They are goaded on by their companions to endure chastisement or the sweetness of pleasure impels them to incur it. Hence the schoolmaster is hated as the cause of the hindrance of their desires, and when the boy is somewhat freed from restraint he shows himself troublesome to the teachers, as says Horace[2]. For he is not kept to his duty, but to a certain pretence of duty, at which fear—the worst guardian of duty—compels him to remain, and when fear prevails in the mind it makes him a worthless slave. For he does nothing under the influence of the beauty of

The causes of corruption of pupils.

The morals of youth shattered.

[1] *Institutiones Oratoriae* bk I, cap. 2, and Lactantius I, I.

[2] "Monitoribus asper," Horace, *de Arte Poetica* l. 163.

virtue, or of what is next best, the hope of praise. Therefore he does not take pains with his studies, nor does he concern himself with that which ought to be done; but the body being the chief thing, his mind wanders to its wishes and even drags the body along with it, if only fear departs for a little while he is exactly like a young colt who is perpetually trying to shake off his bridle, his horse-cloth and his rider. If by any means he is able to rid himself of his master or tutor, he thinks he has won a great victory and is freed from burdensome slavery. What joy he feels! what congratulations and applause does he receive from his abandoned companions! Then he wanders about, and strays unrestrained in the indulgence of every kind of vice, and dashes against the rocks of pleasure, like a ship in a great tempest of waves with its rudder broken and its pilot drowned. Youths pretty well grown up are not checked in academies by teachers and masters. Perhaps the latter do not dare, for fear the pupils may change their school and transfer their paltry money to another; how much less do they restrain the rich? For many learned men have regard to their own profit, and not to the instruction of the pupil. As the result of these conditions, besides the corruption of the minds of the youths and the passing on of vice, which is a great and special evil, further consequences, which are by no means trifling, ensue—the loss of the property of the poor father, who perhaps was providing for other children by the sweat of his brow. For to the eldest son the father, so far as his narrow income allows, is generous, and brings him up carefully and cherishes him to be as it were the staff of his old age and the support of the whole family; and he hopes that by-and-by this son will pay back with good interest to his brothers what was taken away from them in order to give him, alone, leisure for study. Then after a long time, when all the money is spent, the real state of things appears, and all the hope of the old parent is futile and vain. To the loss of money there is added the irreparable loss of time. The best

**Evils arising from bad bringing-up.**

years of life, and those most fitted for learning, have slipped away without fruit. The youth himself is growing in years,—and in ignorance and in hatred of learning. Nor does he who was once a scholar, that is a *dominus* and free, allow himself to be entered upon some trade or to do any work with his hands. He returns home, a coarse and savage beast, steeped in ignorance, arrogance, incivility, want of knowledge, and baseness, with a mind eager for every kind of wilfulness and vice; and in consequence of that life, given over entirely to all kinds of obscenity, he is worn away by diseases. Before he left school he had shaken off all shame and reverence, first for teachers, then for parents, then for friends and for his whole country; both because of his daily habit of sinning, which cast out all regard for virtue from his breast, and also because he frequently received from all his relatives in the country most loving and respectful letters, written as to a "man distinguished for his learning." And if such youths have had recalled to their minds a better course of conduct, they resist it and despise other people as if they were rude and ignorant, and cannot bear to be advised by anyone of those who, so many times, in their humility have confessed themselves to be their inferiors in knowledge and practical wisdom. In order that they may act more freely and be under no superior, they buy some degree of scholastic honour, (and this is a piece of unbridled and unrestrained arrogance), while the father of the scholar often applauds and rejoices, taking the semblance for the reality and not knowing the significance of what is taking place. When the course of their insolence is quite completed they leave the country, and they fear and hate the parents who have begun to realise their disgrace. They are the enemies of learned men, by whom they see themselves equalled and surpassed not only in estimation but also in learning, and the light of the learned reveals more clearly their own darkness and, as it were, convicts them of guilt. They

**The morals of vicious pupils.**

**Academic grades of honour.**

are the very worst class of men, because they are ignorant and insolent.

The more favourable conditions of the home.

More favourable conditions obtain in the home; tender bodies are nourished more healthily, and the home is more beneficial for the health and for developing growing strength. Children are educated more liberally and purely amongst old and prudent men. There are also lesser advantages. Daily intercourse with their parents will not suffer respect for them to pass away. The father will easily preserve and guard reverence for himself in his son, whom he sees every day and to whom he gives his command, with the authority of his fatherhood. Every single day that right will be renewed, as it were by use and custom of possession[1]. Love also will be increased if either the son is naturally good, or sees in his parent some tokens of uprightness and wisdom. The piety, which characterises the parents, will diffuse itself in those who are joined to them by blood. Therefore if their disposition is evil, there is need for fear; for what has more influence than the disposition of parents and relatives, imbibed with the milk and confirmed with age? But if the disposition be noble, it will be led on by love. What influence is greater than that of parents and relatives? Many have been led to do well from no other cause than respect for their parents, and a desire to make them happy: as Plutarch[2] writes concerning Martius Coriolanus. The memory of such men as these is, even to the remotest regions, an incitement to many to conduct themselves in accordance with the sentiments of such heroes.

Relatives must sound a boy's disposition.

The disposition of the boy and what he is specially fitted for, can be found out by relatives and friends, and the boy himself will every day give many signs of it. If he is not apt at his letters but

[1] Rightly says Terence in *Andria* I, 126: Qui scire possis, aut ingenium noscere, Dum aetas, metus, magister prohibebant.

[2] Plutarch's *Lives*, Justin, bk VI, Valerius Maximus III, 2.

trifles with the school tasks, and what is more serious, wastes his time, let him be early transferred to that work for which he seems fitted, in which he will occupy himself with more fruitfulness, and will be amongst the thoroughly trained, whom the Greeks used to call παιδομαθεῖς. In young boys also, budding faults will be met with; the flexible mind must then be formed in accordance with what is right. Parents, relatives and the father's friends may by their authority easily preserve reverence for teachers and country. Those of the same age as the boy have less influence to corrupt him; for he and his companions, wherever they go, meet with those in whose charge the boy is, and he is dragged back by them before he falls. If he begins to slip, love will take hold of him with its gentle hand. If this does not suffice, reverence and fear will come to his help, and these having been imbibed from earliest infancy and confirmed by habit, there will not be the hope or even a wish to be released from them. Thus the son is so devoted to his father by influence and authority that he loves and reverences him, and would not think it right to wish not to reverence him. The rod of discipline will be constantly raised before the eyes of the boy and around his back, for it has been wisely declared by Solomon[1] that it is specially good for that age, and extremely salutary. At the same time, through this manner of life, love for his parents and his country will burn very brightly in his heart, and he will wish to consult the interests of his country in whatever is most pleasant and dear to it, and whenever he has an opportunity, he will do all the good he can for its progress.

**The method of bringing boys into order.**

[1] Proverbs xiii. 24.

# CHAPTER III

## CHOICE OF PUPILS

When and by whom boys should be instructed before they proceed to the Academy. Under what conditions they should be admitted. A wonderful variety of dispositions is shown in boys. Reception of boys into the Academy. Choice of wits. Varieties of dispositions. Abilities. Methods of judging boys' powers and character.

For these reasons and considerations, the course I advocate is as follows:

**A school (*ludus*) to be established in every township.**

Let a school (*ludus literarius*) be established in every township, and let there be received into it as teachers men who are of ascertained learning, uprightness and prudence. Let their salary be paid to them from the public treasury. Let boys and youths learn from these men those arts which are suited to their age and tastes; but let their training for service to their country and their whole education in civil life be given by wise old men, as formerly at Rome. For, as it is recorded by Plutarch in his *Problems*, "the ancients considered it an honourable thing to educate their relatives and friends." If any

**When youth should be sent to the Academy.**

youths, on account of alertness of wit and goodness, are quick at their studies, when the transition stage from boyhood to youth has been reached, when their minds are now strengthened by right opinions about affairs, and are now prepared and fortified, let these be sent under auspicious circumstances to the Academy. And if anyone is sent earlier, because it is thought that he cannot be conveniently taught at home, let him go with a tutor whom he can reverence as his father; on the other hand, let the tutor show himself worthy of reverence by his practical wisdom and ability, and worthy of love by his kindness, but let him beware above all, to the utmost of his power, not to bring upon himself the dislike of his charge. Now let us go on to speak about the instruction itself.

**What the father ought to be clear about in his own mind regarding his son.**

When a boy is taken to school, let the father know what he ought to consider as the fruit of studious labour; surely, not honour or money, but the culture of the mind—a thing of exceeding great and incomparable value—that the youth may become more learned and more virtuous through sound teaching. Therefore if he brought with him to the school any baser idea, let him return home persuaded that he now expects higher and greater things of his son. Let the boy be taken under the condition that he is to be tried for some months; for when this is done in the case of men-servants and women-servants, and those who place plates and dishes on the table, how absurd it is that it should not be done in the case of those who can only become learned at so much greater cost both to themselves and others. In determining the instruction to be given to each person, the disposition is to be regarded; the close consideration of this subject belongs to psychological inquiry[1]. I will therefore borrow some remarks from the treatise I have written on this subject (*de Anima*). Natural powers of the mind are: sharpness in observing, capacity for comprehending, power in comparing and judging. Nothing physical is more similar to understanding than the eye; the one is the light of the mind, the other of the body. In the eye is the power of seeing all those things which are dim in colour, and that is called sharpness. There are some who have very great power in discerning separate and scattered things, but cannot grasp many things together, or if they do grasp them for a short moment, yet do

**Concerning mental ability.**

[1] Quintilian, *Instit. Orat.* I, 3.

not retain them. But often those who see, who grasp and retain images of things, cannot bring things into relation with one another; nor can they judge what the quality of a thing is by comparison of it with others. Just so is it with natural abilities of the mind. For, some minds are acute and see separate things clearly, but cannot grasp them nor retain them when they are connected; their comprehension is narrow, or their memory short and fleeting. Others grasp, but do not reflect on those things which are intuited, so as to judge and determine their nature and properties. And just as eyes are blind or weakened by recurring injuries, so minds partly become stupefied through folly and perpetual torpor, and partly at certain intervals they are scarcely sane; only that he who suffers from blindness or a defect of the eyes knows it, but he who is sick with a disease of the mind does not know it, and if it is pointed out to him, does not believe it. In a disease of the body the mind which is able to judge about it is not sick, it is otherwise in the disease of the mind—the mind itself being affected—it is not able to pass judgment concerning itself. The understanding is not to be trained by means of evil things, or by small and trifling things. The eye does not always discern acutely, even when it looks keenly, if it is late on in the day or in the darkness. So the mind is not to be considered acute because it abounds in small and light things, but because it keeps in the light and exercises itself about great things. For it is not to be doubted that our minds are now less powerful than they were before that first transgression. Now, we are more crafty in our wickedness: as saith the Lord, "The children of this world are in their generation wiser than the children of light[1]." Therefore noble minds do not give themselves up to trifles, but keep their eyesight even in the darkness and remain prudent men, in the midst of their playing.

**Variety of minds.**

**Comparison of the eye with the mind.**

**The object before the mind.**

[1] S. Luke xvi. 8.

In the mind are observed *its action and its material* (or content), partly separately, partly conjointly. From these are formed the desires and character. In action there are to be distinguished intension (or concentration) and extension, i.e. how great or small, how short or long; how quick or slow the action is. There are some minds who look intently and diligently at what they are doing, and who rejoice to get bound up in their work; there are others who look remiss and as if they were doing something else, and who, loose and free, do not wish to exert themselves; such were Ovid and Lucilius as Horace[1] bears witness. Such are those who are of an airy (flighty) constitution or who are enervated by extreme heat, or who, oppressed by flesh and the heavy burden of the body, avoid the labour of attention or cannot bear it. Some discern dimly, others clearly: the latter look deeply into things, and are said to have "acumen" (or sharpness of mind); the former come to a stop at the most obvious part of things, and are said to be, mentally, dull and blunt.

**The action of the mind.**

**Variety and kinds of minds.**

Some scholars find the first beginnings of things easy but soon are perplexed, over whose mental eye, as it were, a kind of mist spreads while they are working, which was not present when they came new and fresh to the work. Others, eager and strong, most happily continue steadfastly. Some accept as joined those things which they see together; some analyse things into their separate parts by a close examination, which is called *subtlety*. There are some who at the right moment, by their concentration, strike at the root of things, hasten on through many fields of knowledge and do not stop to rest; others linger and, as it were, leave their footprints behind. There are some, free and unrestrained, who quickly pursue what they want, e.g. men of well-balanced powers, whose minds are endowed with such vigour that they see at a glance through everything needed, and have it ready to hand, of which kind was Vinicius,

**Subtlety.**

**Swiftness of some minds.**

[1] *Satires* II, I.

of whom Augustus said that "he had the various powers of his mind as ready as coins in the hand[1]": such as these excel generally by their skill in extemporising, more than by writing and taking pains, e.g. Cassius Severus and Sulpitius Galba. Cicero[2] and Seneca testify that this happens with men who are not so much studious as gifted; for the mind when it is excited with heat brings many things before the eyes which, when it has cooled down again, steal themselves away. Some advance tardily and slowly, but at length arrive at their goal, and of these, some with their slow steps advance further than those who were before them in their course. The duration of action in some is very short and they soon come to a stop, e.g. impassioned and jejune races, such as the Egyptians and Persians; in others it is longer and more persistent, as in that painter "who did not know his hand from his picture," and in Didymus the grammarian, who, on account of his stubborn industry, was nicknamed χαλκέντερος. There are some whose alternations of leisure and activity are short but frequent. Others work a long time and then rest an equally long time—like Portius Latro[3], of whom Seneca writes. When such men burn persistently like fire they fasten on resinous material, but when they have burnt themselves out, they remain cold for a long time. They experience these frequent or daily changes from their food or drink, from the state of the weather or the place, or from the condition of their bodies. That man who was always equable they used formerly to call a "man of every hour[4]." Variations of mind arise from the different nature of each person, i.e. of the constitution and temperament of their

**Changes in the mind.**

**Causes of changes in the mind.**

[1] Jerome, Epistle to Pammach taken from Seneca II, *de clamat.*

[2] See Cicero, *Brutus, seu de claris oratoribus.* See also Seneca, *Ep.* 53.

[3] *Declamationes*, bk X.

[4] See Galen, *de Temperamentis.* Said by Quintilian of Asinius Pollio and Tiberius Suetonius; said also by Erasmus of Sir Thomas More.

bodies. The consequence is, that a man one moment may be great and keen-witted, and the next moment may no longer remain so. There are also other long lasting changes, which are resultant on the time of life. For certain persons become better with years, e.g. Scipio and Polemon, and those of whom Valerius reminds us; others become worse, e.g. Hermogenes, an orator in the time of Antoninus Augustus who, though he was most eloquent as a boy, became a most childish youth[1]. Precocious minds, in whose childhood there was a moderate glow, change for the worse, and presently if either excess of drinking or corpulence overwhelms them, they become stupid; but if their precocity is sharpened or there is a growth, especially around the brain, they become insane. It is better, however, in the case of those whose fervour in the beginning is excessive, if it is gradually tempered and becomes lukewarm; or if those whose bodies overflow with too many and noxious humours are soon purged of them. It is well the most delicate and lucid spirits should become thickened; lest their minds, sharp before the time, fly where they ought not and lest they should not be able to continue at work[2]. I believe this is the reason why Plato chose for his Academy a dense and heavy climate, advantageous to the subtle and light Attic minds: restraints, forsooth, were put upon them. Those persons do not change whose bodily constitution is in harmony with each stage of their course of life.

**The subject-matter about which minds occupy themselves.**

As to mental material (or content), some persons are exceedingly clever in things which are done by the hands. (These people the Greeks call χειρουργικοί.) Such boys you always see painting, building, weaving, and they do all these things so well, and with such great pleasure that you would think they had learnt them a long time. Others are devoted to the more

[1] Of Trapezuntium as is stated in his life by John Noviomagus. On Hermogenes, see C. Rhadiginus XI, 40.

[2] From Quintilian I, 3.

sublime matters of judgment and reason, incited by a greater and higher mental impulse, and from their boyhood they perform those manual arts ineptly, yet they understand already every word which they hear, and promptly and quickly discover the reason for a thing. A very few are good at both activities, though there are some of this kind. Some are suited to a particular branch of learning, e.g. poets who find themselves embarrassed in attempting fluent prose. I have known men who could narrate most wittily, yet in their reasoning were most absurd. Of rare quality are those who are equally capable in all the material of the mind, not only in hand-activities, but also in those which require a special intellectual activity; Plutarch[1] has shown that the mind of Cicero was of this quality.

**Subject-matter and action of minds.**

Again, minds are to be regarded in their material and in their action. Some are wonderful in trifles and small things, captious, cavillers, subtle—in great and solid things they do nothing; e.g. those who in matters of jest are talkative and of ready wit, but in serious matters you would say they were quite stupid; of this class are certain epigrammatic poets and scurrilous men; of such a man one of the ancients is related to have said "that he would more easily become a rich buffoon than a good father of a family." Of this number are those whose minds fly over the tops of things, and perceive certain minute details which escape the notice of others, but yet do not penetrate into the very heart and nucleus of the thing. Certain minds are acute, but their sharpness is very like the sharpness of a needle, which can separate into four or five fibres the width of one hair; not like the sharpness of a sword, which can cleave asunder a hard and solid thing. Those men are like swords, who do not excel in jokes and light affairs yet are great in serious and solid matters, e.g. Demosthenes. Cicero was admirable in both directions. There are some who

**Epigrammatists.**

**Minds: (1) Light, (2) Solid.**

[1] In his *Life of Cicero*.

cannot endure anything serious. They were not so by nature but they have accustomed themselves to slack ways, such as were the Milesians and Sybarites. Thus, in arts and learning some are made and fitted for some things, and very little fitted for others. Some follow their teacher quickly, being naturally gifted and thinking modestly of themselves[1]. Others run on before, some foolishly, being led into futile conjectures which they consider absolutely established, others proceed dexterously and happily, being good interpreters, such as they say Chrysippus was, who required from his teacher nothing but dogmas[2]; he used to say that he would himself find out reasons to support them. Certain persons make good use of what is found out by others, but produce nothing themselves. Such are devoted to imitation which is a bad thing if they get no further, though, if we believe Quintilian[3], it is a sign of genius in boys when they imitate what is good. Some people are better at inventing views of their own than at using other people's, e.g. certain acute men who are yet unwilling to devote their mind to understanding and examining the discoveries of others. There are some who, when there is need, can do both, and these Hesiod the poet places in the first rank of good men. Those men, who carefully pay attention to the works of others, are sharp-witted. For most of these phenomena in connexion with the mind, we can find parallel examples physically in the sight of the eyes. For, as I suggested in the beginning, there is nothing which so helps us to realise the reason and force of the mind as the eyes.

**The power and sway of affections.**

Morals also change the natural disposition in many ways, for the constitution of the body has a great influence on the strength of the mind and it is from the body that the passions take their rise. But the ground of morals is twofold, for they spring either from the nature of the body or from habit. Some have easily aroused feelings, others more tranquil ones; and

[1] Quintilian I, 3. [2] Diogenes Laertius in the *Life of Cleanthes*.
[3] Bk I, cap. 3.

in the latter, all affections, as it were by turns, rule and then have their fling. In the original feelings arising from the constitution of the body some are inclined to what is good, others to evil. In some men, certain feelings occupy the kingdom of the whole mind to such a degree that they drag to themselves everything that enters the mind. Just as when the stomach is diseased it turns whatever comes into it into noxious humours, so those minds which are ashamed to learn in the presence of witnesses are twisted aside to pride, arrogance or ostentation. Wisely did Bion[1] say that Pride is an impediment to great achievements. Such students give way to lust or evil desires, or to depraved ideas or sinister interpretations. Some have minds partly right, but suddenly a feeling rises up unexpectedly which lays its hand upon them and compels them to turn from the right way. Some are simple, upright, good; some crafty and crooked; some who constantly hide themselves; some who, on the contrary, always push themselves forward. With some minds, fear only effects anything; with others, kindness. Some minds are sensible, sober and temperate; others insane and furious, and this either habitually or at intervals. Some are gentle, others fierce and eager; some even are of an unbridled nature. Some sustain the movements of their minds by just and great undertakings, and these we call manly; others by slight enterprises or none at all, and are turned aside by a slight whiff of air: these are called childish and fickle. O admirable Author of such great variety! Thou Who alone hast created these conditions of mind, alone knowest the causes. There are indeed other differences of minds, but this treatment suffices for the present.

[1] See Diogenes Laertius, bk IV.

# CHAPTER IV

## TEACHERS AND TAUGHT

By what means and how far the mind and nature of the boy may be clearly perceived. For there is scarcely anyone of such a stupid disposition that he will not profit by some teaching, if there be sufficient care given. How teachers should bear themselves towards their pupils and what they should first teach. Trial of wits. Strong points of weak boys. The relation of teachers to scholars. What should be first taught?

**How the mind reveals itself.**

SUBJECT-MATTER is to be presented to the boy so that his mind may elevate itself by movement and action. For nothing of this nature can be judged of when it is quiescent. Pythagoras introduced Arithmetic, which his shrewdness discovered. Nothing displays the sharpness of the mind so much as a ready method of reckoning, and slowness of mind is proved by slowness in reckoning, as we have seen in the case of the feeble-minded, and Aristotle is our authority that the very stupid race of Scythians cannot count beyond the number four, while we name the numerals beyond ten. Therefore, there were followers of wisdom among the Greeks who considered that a man, simply because he knew how to reckon, might for that reason be called *λογικόν ζῶον*. As in Latin, *ratio* means both 'reason' and 'computation,' so with the Greek word *λόγος*.

**Arithmetic is, as it were, the Lydian stone of wits.**

**Memory a sign of ability.**

Quintilian considers memory to be an indication of natural ability; he says it consists of two parts—viz. ready comprehension and faithful retention[1]. The former is undoubtedly a proof of keenness, the latter of capacity. Judgment follows gradually afterwards.

[1] Vives, *de Anima*, bk II.

Therefore the child is ordered to learn by heart, then to imitate, according to what I have said above. Children should be exercised in play, for that reveals their sharpness and their characters, especially among those of their own age and who are like them, where nothing is feigned but everything natural. All emulation brings out and discloses the state of the mind, scarcely otherwise than the heating of the plants or the roots or the fruits brings out their special fragrance or the force of nature[1]. The boy should be taught, through play, both to rule and to command. As says Bias, "the office proclaims the man[2]." The Spaniards rather wisely say in a proverb that "office and play are the touchstones of minds." Every two or three months let the masters meet together, and deliberate and judge with paternal affection and grave discretion concerning the minds of their pupils, and send each boy to that work for which he seems most fit. If that is done, incredible advantage will ensue to the whole human race. Nothing would then be done badly and perversely by those who now do it under compulsion and against their desires, concerning whom is the advice of the wise poet, "say and do nothing against your natural bent[3]" ("Invita Minerva"). All things indeed will be performed in the best manner and with wonderful happiness by those who are naturally fitted to do them. When unwilling minds are driven to uncongenial work, we see that almost all things turn out wrong and distorted. It is not right to think too much about having a great number of scholars; how much better it is to have a little salt of good savour than a great deal that is insipid? How many philosophers have been content with a small audience[4]? and with this audience they

[1] Quintilian I, 3.

[2] Diogenes Laertius in his life of Bias, "Magistratus virum ostendet."

[3] Horace, *de Arte Poetica* l. 385.

[4] When Zeno understood that Theophrastus was held in the highest honour on account of the number of his disciples he said: "His chorus is greater but mine sings better." Theophrastus had 2000—as Laertius says in bk V.

used to discuss most acutely and wisely, great and weighty subjects. Our Lord, when He brought to the world the wisdom and salvation of God, contented Himself with a company of twelve men. In truth an audience of any size whatsoever will suffice to bring glory and profit to a teacher. I do not deny that in speaking a crowd is a stimulus to the mind, but speaking is a different thing from teaching[1]. In speaking, I observe that orators are stirred by I know not what goads, from the desire of glory. With regard to doubtful natural dispositions, I think we should not despair about the evil in them nor yet trust too much in the good. Both in the state and in the school there are many examples of change of disposition and character; still, when the will is defective, more frequently changes are for the worse. Because a boy's mind is not sufficiently apt, it is not therefore a matter for despair. For there are some minds which have been despised and yet they have brought forth fruit, sometime later. When a father has many sons, let him not at the beginning destine for study any one he likes, just as he would take an egg from a heap to boil or to fry, but the one who in his own opinion, and in that of his friends, is best suited for study and erudition. Some parents (and there is nothing more ridiculous) send to school those boys who are unfit for commerce or war, or other civil duties, and order them to be taught; and, what is a most impious deed, they devote to God the most contemptible and useless of their offspring, and think that he who has not judgment and intellect for the smallest and most trifling matters has quite enough for such great duties. When the boy is destined for study, as the father ought to conceive the highest hopes of his son, so should the teacher of his pupil[2]. But there will be a difference, because a father's love is generally dim-sighted and even blind, while it is fitting that the kindness of the teacher should be combined with the keenest eyes. No boy who has just been sent to school

**Wits should be tested as to their future ability.**

[1] Quintilian I, 2. [2] *Idem* I, 1 at the beginning.

should be regarded as so hopeless that he ought to be instantly expelled, but teachers should seek to help his progress, if not in learning, at least in his course of life.

**Begin with the foundation of piety.**

First of all the fundamental truths of our religion should be taught, that the boy may know how weak and ready for evil he is by nature; that nothing is, or can be, of any value without the help of God, to Whom he must pray frequently and sincerely, and without Whose help he must not hope to accomplish anything. How great is the blindness and error in the minds of the multitude who judge concerning what is good and the value of things! Virtuous opinions must be instilled into the empty breast, that we are the enemies of God, reconciled to Him through the cross of His Son; that he must fear God as being almighty, reverence Him as omniscient, and love Him as a beneficent Giver. For the expounding of these things I have written a little book called *Instruction in Wisdom*[1], and it will be easy for the teacher to pick out for the use of his pupil little flowers from the philosophers and sacred authors, as it were from the most verdant meadows. Let him show, again and again, how it is recorded that this life is a perpetual struggle, fierce and vehement; that the passions of the soul, in opposition to reason, are always girded and prepared for battle, and that if they conquer, the result is the bitterest perdition to man; therefore, much must be said and done against them constantly, lest they beat down our strength[2]. It cannot be told how many bad passions foolish boys let arise within them, thinking that there is no harm in them, and when, after they have become more noticeable, they try to uproot the habits, they find they have undertaken a task by no means easy; for the passions put forth roots, and frequently sprout forth anew. And since indeed all actions are pleasant when one is accustomed to them, what folly and what hopeless madness it is, not to become accustomed to what is best, especially when there is equal labour

[1] *Introductio ad Sapientiam*, 1524. [2] Quintilian I, 2.

in accomplishing good and bad projects, often even less in the good. Even if the effort be somewhat great, yet the reward of a noble character is great. Moreover, the habit of doing right becomes natural. Let the boys know that God is the Rewarder of all right actions[1]; and that our minds and thoughts are manifest to Him, so that as far as their age permits, they may become accustomed to do nothing for the sake of human gain, but rather for that divine and eternal reward.

**Minds which are unsuited for letters.**

After this, let the teacher see who are fit for learning; who are not. There are some minds which are stupid, very dull, rough and distorted. It is wonderful and pitiable to relate, that human minds produce good fruit more easily in the commoner and more worthless, than in the more liberal and distinguished arts. For in trade, in the practice of artificers, in weaving, finally in the manual and mechanical arts, we see fewer persons spending their labour in vain than in the pursuit of learning. What shall we say are the causes of this? Is it because in humbler pursuits the mind is not so greatly molested by the passions, whilst they join battle with it when it attempts the greater and more noble pursuits? Or is it because the mind is less strained in light and easy pursuits than in profound and lofty matters, so that in the former it seems to roll down a slope, and in the latter to have to climb up steep places? If in gaining learning the mind threw off all care, it would be unrestrained and would wander into the constant degeneration of pleasures and other unsuitable states for study. Nor are those persons fit for study who suffer from natural defects, e.g. mad people or imbeciles. These will soon give proof that they should be sent somewhere where they could be coerced by fear and blows. A boy of a depraved disposition, or a corrupter of others, must be reformed before he may be joined in the company of boys. Minds that have too delicate and fine an edge, without a solid background,

**Those suited for letters.**

[1] Quintilian I, 2.

or those of narrow capacity should not be fatigued and overwhelmed by study; just as a lancet is not to be used for cleaving wood, and as a weak eye should not be fatigued by intent gazing. Some boys are not fit for study at one time but are at another, and *vice versa*. A crafty man or one given to deceit, or one who will turn everything to wickedness, is better kept away from studies, which will be in him only the instruments of many evil deeds. He who is by nature ashamed to learn is not always unfitted for it, but he learns little; he must be shown wherein his ignorance lies, and be made to recognise it, so that he may wish to learn. If even thus his arrogance is not weakened, he must be put to those arts, the ignorance of which he is not able to hide and which he must learn, whether he will or no; and in his hearing, pride should frequently be confuted and censured as a most foolish thing. Those who despise their masters are most impudent, more fit for the plough than for books, for working in the field and the woods than for the company of men. He who does not at first respect his master, at length will come to reverence him as another parent of his mind. A frolicsome boy must be recalled to his duty, not expelled[1]. Of the different kinds and forms of mind, some kinds of discipline suit one, some another, as we have shown above; certainly there will be none which is incapable, at least of learning languages. Up to this point, the boy has been prepared for religious knowledge and for initiation into learning. Now he is to be admitted to the mysteries.

**Reverence for the teacher by his pupil.**

The affection of the master for his pupil will be that of a father; he will love him truly and from his heart, as if he were his own offspring. Does he indeed who gives birth to the body do more for the child than he who stirs the mind to action? In truth, in so far as the mind is more truly the essential part of the man than the body the teacher may be said to be more truly the parent. For we are not men because of our bodies which we

**Affection of the master for his pupil.**

[1] Quintilian II, 2.

have in common with the brutes, but in consequence of the likeness of our mind to God and the angels. For this reason Alexander of Macedon[1] acknowledged that he owed more to Aristotle than to Philip; from the latter he derived his body, but from the former his mind. The Apostle Paul says that he "had begotten in the Lord" those whom he led to virtue. But this paternal love will not be blind, but observant and even keen, so that it may detect all tendencies in the pupil which ought to be strengthened, or changed and amended.

**What opinion and feeling the boys should have respecting the office of education.**

Let it be firmly fixed in the boys' minds that what they are going to receive at school is the culture of the mind, i.e. of our better and immortal part; that this culture has been handed down from God to the human race, as the greatest gift of His fatherly indulgence, and that it could not have been given from any other source, and that assuredly this is the pursuit and way in following which, they may please God, and attain to Him in Whom is their highest happiness. In this way they will love such culture of the mind and recognise it as necessary for them, and reverence and adore it as sacred and sent down from heaven. They will then enter into their schools full of reverence, as if into holy Temples. Wherefore the masters will take all the precautions in their power, that the schools shall not be allowed to become worthless through play or to be contaminated by any disgrace. Boys will love, cherish and trust the masters as ministers in the service of God and as the fathers of their minds. Masters will easily gain love by their pleasantness of manner, reverence by their worth as teachers and by their upright life. It is incredible what great influence the affections of the master and the pupil exercise upon both good teaching and good learning.

**Whence the precepts of arts are to be collected.**

In teaching the arts, we shall collect many experiments and observe the experience of many teachers, so that from them general rules may be formed. If some of the experiments do not agree with the

[1] Plutarch, *Life of Alexander*.

rule, then the reason why this happens must be noted. If the reason is not apparent, and there are some deviations, they must be noted down[1]. If there are more deviations than agreements or an equal number, a dogma must not be established from that fact, but the facts must be transmitted to the astonishment of posterity, so that from astonishment[2]—as has been the case in the past—philosophy may grow. All the arts connected with doing, or making things, are best acquired from observing the actions and work of those who have been best instructed in them by nature, study, and habit. From such inventors, as we have shown, the arts were born. They even brought them forth without art, but were instructed by a certain unusual force of nature, aided by their own diligence and practice. Thus from their use by Cicero and Demosthenes, rhetorical precepts were gained; poetry from Homer and Virgil. But he who writes on every art and expounds its rules must withdraw his eye from experiments and direct his sight to nature herself, so that he may learn and teach more accurately than is customary[3]. Cicero himself said that this would be his method for training the best orator. For in nature there is an absolute model, which each mind expresses as well as his genius and diligence will allow him: some more than others, yet no one completely and perfectly.

**The order of teaching precepts.**

In teaching the arts the most effectual order must be followed, so that the hearers may easily learn and easily retain. The material being rightly arranged they are led naturally, and since they see that what follows grows as it were out of what precedes, they receive all as being quite certain. What this method is and how it is to be used in orations, has been shown to us in books on the art of speaking (*de Dicendi Methodo*). But since everything

**(1) On the method of speaking. What should be inculcated.**

[1] As Aristotle teaches, *Metaphysics* I, 1.

[2] This Aristotle teaches in *Metaphysics* I, 2. Plato in the *Theaetetus* and Plutarch in the *de Auditione*, Horace, *Epist.* 6.

[3] Arist. *Metaphysics*, I, 1.

should lead to piety, let the master remember, whatever he is doing, that he is a Christian, and let him turn away and hide whatever is contrary to a good mind, and always say what is conducive to good morals. Poets, e.g. Virgil and Lucanus, in the midst of their works introduce pleasant fables, even when they are dealing with serious topics, so that the reader should not forget that still they are writing as poets. Should it not then occur to us when teaching in every subject that we always are sworn to Christ?

**The authority of the Holy Scriptures.**

The authority of the Holy Scriptures is to be impressed with great awe on the hearts of the pupils, so that when they hear anything out of them, they may think that they hear the almighty God Himself. From them the master will choose some passages to be as it were remedies of diseases, as far as he thinks will suffice. When a trained power of judgment is necessary, he must not choose unsuitable passages which are beyond the understanding of the boys' age. And if Plato, Aristotle, Xenophon, Cicero, and other philosophers cite evidence from Homer and other poets to confirm their own opinions, how much more fitting is it for us to seek in the oracles of God, not only evidence, but supreme authority, in which we cannot be deceived, since it springs from infallible wisdom? But although in teaching an art, the most perfect and absolute parts are always to be propounded, yet in teaching, those parts of the art should be presented to the audience, which are most suited to their capacities. For the follower of an 'art' ought to fix his mind on the highest parts of it, and from them form its standards, and every student should hasten in pursuit. But the teacher in the school ought to look at his audience, not that he may turn away from the art, or teach the false instead of the true, but that he may teach those topics of the arts most suited to the capacity of his pupils. The sacred history of the Gospel declares to us that the Divine Artist and Master adopted both methods of teaching[1].

**Their supreme authority.**

[1] On the subject generally, cf. Quintilian.

# BOOK III

## LANGUAGE TEACHING

# CHAPTER I

## LATIN AND OTHER LANGUAGES

Speech the index of the Mind. The mother or vulgar tongue should be learned as perfectly as possible; also (in Spain) the languages of the Arabs and Saracens. The Latin language is praised. At what age and in what order it should be taught to boys. To this knowledge the study of Greek is a great additional treasure. An opinion on Hebrew. Language Teaching. The Mother-tongue. Latin. Hebrew. Greek. The ages of learning and the order of teaching Languages.

**Speech.**

THE first thing man has to learn is speech. It flows at once from the rational soul as water from a fountain[1]. As all beasts are bereft of intellect, so they are also lacking in speech. Discourse also is the instrument of human society, for not otherwise could the mind be revealed, so shut in is it by the grossness and density of the body. Like as we have the mind by the gift of God, so we have this or that language, by the gift of art. And so, both at home by parents, and in school by teachers, it is a necessary task to give boys facility in good enunciation, as far as their age permits[2]. In which task parents will be a great help, if for the sake of their children they take care to express the feelings of their minds in chaste words and in sound and apt oration; and secure that nurses and governesses do the like, and those amongst whom they dwell, so that they do not

[1] Aristotle, *Politics*, I, 2.

[2] Quintilian I, I.

speak perplexingly, absurdly, barbarously, and do not manifest those faults of pronunciation, which, if imitated by those of tender age will cling to them. Chrysippus, on this account, even wished to have educated women chosen as nurses. It is of great importance, says Cicero, what each one hears every day at home, and with whom the boy speaks, for he will speak in the manner that the father, pedagogues, mother, speak[1]. This has no slight influence on the learning of those languages which are acquired by art, in its effects both upon the understanding of the thoughts of others and upon the expression of our own.

**A universal language;**

Language is the shrine of erudition, and as it were a storeroom for what should be concealed, and what should be made public. Since it is the treasury of culture and the instrument of human society, it would therefore be to the benefit of the human race that there should be a single language, which all nations should use in common[2]. If this could not be effected, at least most nations and peoples, certainly we Christians, might use such a language for the purpose of being initiated in the same religious worship, and also for furthering commerce and general knowledge. It was for the punishment of sin that so many languages became current. Such a language as that universal one, just suggested, should be sweet, learned and eloquent. Its sweetness is in the sound of words whether simple and separate, as well as in the combination of words. The educative value of a language is in proportion to its apt suitability for supplying names to things. Its eloquence consists in its variety and abundance of words and formulae; all of which should make it a pleasure for men to use. It should have the capacity to explain most aptly what they think. By its means much power of judgment should be developed. Such a language it

**namely, the Latin.**

[1] Quintilian I, I; Galen, *de Temperamentis* II, 2 and Plutarch, *de Liberis Educandis*.

[2] Augustine, *de Civitate Dei*, bk XIX, chap. 7.

seems to me is to be found in the Latin tongue, above all those languages which men employ; above all which are known to me. For that language, whose words should make clear the natures of things, would be the most perfect of all; such as it is probable was that original language in which Adam attached the names to things[1]. For these are the true appellations of things, as to which it is written in the sacred psalm[2]: "Great is the Lord, Who counteth the multitude of the stars and calleth them all by their names. Great is His power, and of His wisdom, there is no end."

The *Cratylus* of Plato points to this opinion, though Aristotle gives another signification to it in his book *De Interpretatione*[3]. This discovery of the right appellations of things, beyond everything else, caused the admiration of Pythagoras.

But let us return to the Latin language. That language is already diffused through so many nations; almost all sciences are committed to its literature. It is rich in words on account of its cultivation by so many men of intellect in their writings, for they have increased its vocabulary. It is of sweet sound and is weighty in utterance, neither rough nor crude, as is the case of some other languages. It is like a wise and brave man who has the good fortune to be born in a well-taught state. It would, therefore, be wrong not to cultivate it and preserve it. If it were lost, there would result a great confusion of all kinds of knowledge, and a great separation and estrangement of men on account of the ignorance of other languages, since, as S. Augustine says, each would prefer to converse with his dog rather than with a man of an unknown tongue. Also for the spreading of piety it is most useful that men should understand one another. Would that the Agareni (i.e. Arabs) and we had some language in common; I believe that within a short time many of them would cast in their lot with us.

1 Genesis ii. 19, 20; Conrad Gesner, *Mithridates*; Augustine, *de Mirabil. S. Scriptu.* I, 9.

2 Psalm cxlvii. 4, 5.

3 Chaps. 2 and 4.

For the cause that the Lord conferred on his Apostles the gift of tongues was this—viz. to help on the unification of races in the same faith. For faith, as Paul says[1], is through what is heard, for which language is the instrument. Therefore earnestly would I wish that in most of our states, schools of languages should be established not only of those special three[2] but also of Arabic, and of those languages which may be the vernaculars of Agarenes, which men of no easy-going kind should teach, not for the glory thence to be snatched, and for applause, but men most ardent in the zeal of piety, prepared to spend their lives for Christ, that, through their instruction, Christ should be proclaimed to those nations, who have learned very little, or almost nothing, of Him.

**The language of teachers.**

Besides, it is also useful that there should be some language sacred for the learned, to which might be consigned those hidden things which are unsuitable to be handled by everybody, and thus become polluted. Probably another language different from the common language keeps these matters more separate. Although, of course, in that common language, there are retreats by way of metaphors, allusions, enigmas, and methods of assertion of that kind, inaccessible to ill-conditioned and sluggish minds. But for the grounds and reasons stated, the Latin language should be learned, and learned exactly, and not in a corrupted form. For if corrupted, the language forthwith ceases to be a unity, portions of the country one by one will have its own corruptions of dialect Latin. Hence it will happen that men do not understand one another, and do not understand those branches of knowledge, which are contained in the Latin. We have found by experience that this has already happened. The boy should give his attention to learning Latin whilst as yet unfitted by the feebleness of his wits to the understanding of other branches of scientific knowledge, i.e. roughly from the seventh to the fifteenth year. But as to the age the teacher

[1] Romans x. 17.

[2] Latin, Greek, Hebrew.

must determine more exactly by the boy's power and progress. If anyone has joined Greek to the Latin language, from the two he will receive many seeds of the material of knowledge remaining to us, so that from the study of those languages, he will come neither crude nor new to any kind of knowledge. Moreover he will derive discourse from those authors in which there are not and cannot be mere words; for much knowledge of different kinds of studies is necessarily brought together in the words of their books. By the same application to labour as the Latin is learned he will gain the Greek language. Add the fact that Greek makes a man cultured and well-stored. And just as the Latin language is able to build up and increase his store of vocabulary, so the Greek increases and adorns the knowledge of Latin itself and sometimes in other directions. It is necessary to the perfection of Latin, not otherwise than Latin is necessary to the Italian or Spanish languages; nor was anyone ever thoroughly skilled in Latin speech unless he was imbued with Greek. For from Greek discourse came the Latin; from the Latin, the Italian, Spanish, French were derived; for which nations formerly the Latin language was the vernacular. So we recognise that, in its usage, the Latin language became more fruitful and eloquent from the Greek, and the remaining languages of Europe from the Latin, but especially those three languages which I have just named. It would especially help on these nations if they became accustomed to Latin speech, and through speaking Latin they came to understand thoroughly the language itself, and through it came to learn thoroughly all the kinds of knowledge in it. From the knowledge of Latin, too, they would render the native language of their fathers more pure and rich, even as a copious stream is derived more purely from its source. How many matters are handed down to memory in Greek literature, in history, in nature-knowledge, private and public morals, medicine, piety, which we drink in more easily and more purely from those very sources themselves? If

**Greek.**

anyone should wish to join to these languages the learning of Hebrew, for the study of the Old Testament, there is nothing to hinder him, provided that he has time for all, and if he has confidence that he can acquire it, without becoming corrupted, for I hear that many things have been falsified in Hebrew writings by Jews, partly through their hatred of Christ, partly through inertia, since these people so often change their abodes, and have not leisure to bestow due labour on literature. Certainly if you consult two Jews as to the same passage, rarely do they agree. I would wish the Latin language to be known thoroughly, for this is a benefit to society and to the knowledge of all the sciences.

**Hebrew.**

In Greek there are great labyrinths and very vast obscurities not only in the variety of dialects, but in any one of them. Attic and those dialects nearest allied to Attic, are the most necessary, because they are the most eloquent and cultured, and whatever works the Greeks wrote, worthy to be read and thoroughly known, are consigned to these dialects. The poets make use of the remaining dialects for their songs, but their knowledge is not so weighty, especially since there are not only such great differences in the dialects, but also in the names of things and between the language of their prose and poetry, that they do not seem to be the same language. Not undeservedly does Antonius say in Cicero, that he dare not meddle with the poets, since they spoke in quite another language. The best of the poets and those from the reading of whom comes the highest reward, are the Attic poets, Euripides, Sophocles, Aristophanes, and what is left of Menander. If anyone be gifted with ability and memory, aided by his time of life and leisure, with knowledge built up by diligence and study, I would not have anything denied him. On the contrary I exhort such a man, under such happy conditions to undertake the labour of learning languages and the study of all kinds of sciences, whatever effort he may have to make. If anyone of crude powers, or without sufficient

**Study of dialects.**

leisure, or defective in ability or memory has taken to letters, for him the Latin language will suffice. For nothing should be given over to ostentation, which spoils the noble fruit of virtue, as with a pestilent breath, but learning should serve for use and necessity. Nor let anyone cite me the example of M. Cato[1], the Censor, who is said to have begun Greek literature when advanced in years, and to have acquired not merely the elements and beginnings of discourse, but also the power of the reading of authors. This is shown by the words Cicero makes him say in the dialogue *De Senectute*. For when he had quoted some passages from the principal Greek writers, which he could not have understood unless well advanced in that language, he adds: "I study Greek, so that I may be able to make use of such passages as those I am now quoting."

In a language which is in the continual use of people there is no necessity to frame systematic rules[2]. The language is learned better and more quickly from the people themselves. In the case of Latin, there are some points noted by the more learned who have inferred what the Latin language was, when it was a vernacular and mother-tongue. But rules are throughout for the guarding against mistakes, and speaking inaccurately, in dead languages. For when a language has been provided by nature, so that people can mutually understand each other in it, grammar will have this use, that by its means you can avoid the mistakes which might stand in the way of a mutual understanding. Those who speak Latin and Greek correctly will understand one another, but it is otherwise with those who speak those languages wrongly; the Spanish *barbarissans*[3] is not understood by the German *barbarissans*, and *vice versa*.

Grammatical science, like all other sciences, must proceed from those who themselves know the language better than those who learn it. At first the single sounds (vowels) must

[1] Cicero, *de Oratore*, bk I.

[2] See Horace, *de Arte Poetica*; Gellius I, 10.

[3] One who speaks the Latin language incorrectly.

be learned, and then the combination of sounds together, i.e. consonants, which are formed of a vowel together with an incomplete and imperfect sound. Then, syllables. Afterwards the boy is to be made accustomed to name letters speedily and sweetly, and to combine them. Next, you may show him in a rough way, by analogy of meanings, what are called proper nouns, common nouns, substantives, adjectives, then verbs, participles, pronouns. To these should be added some systematised scheme of adverbs and of other parts of speech according to their meanings, as before. Hereupon follow the declensions of nouns and the conjugations of verbs. Then will begin the concordance of substantive and adjective, noun and verb. Then will follow the rules of inflexions, then of gender, then of the conjugations of verbs. When all these things are duly understood, let a little Latin book be put in his hands. Let this be in free, conversational style, pleasant, easy, and of terse discourse. Let him learn at once the order of words, that the vocative is first, then the nominative, then the verb, and the other parts of the sentence. For this is the best and most natural method, which shows that what was enunciated without order and somewhat unintelligently can be taken with ease and reduced to order. This is done, although in a less boyish manner than the masters of trivial schools are accustomed to do it, by Donatus, Servius, and other expositors of the Greeks and Latins. After these outlines, so to say, have been taught, all things must be gone through again from the beginning more exactly and more accurately. Herein Theodore Gaza[1] has shown much skill, having followed the teaching method of Aristotle. And so let there be a fuller treatment of the eight parts of speech; then let syntax be expounded; let some more difficult and more solid Latin author be added, who may render the knowledge of the language richer and

**Grammatical art and how it must be learned.**

**The method of teaching grammar.**

[1] Bk I, caps. I and 4.

more polished, not indeed in the single words so much as in the conjunction and composition of words. Afterwards there should follow the treatment of prosody, to which should be joined the detailed exposition of some poet. But I wish this knowledge of grammatical science to be learned without being wearisomely troublesome, for whilst it is injurious to neglect rules, so it also injures to cling to, and to be dependent on, them too much, although the evil of too much carefulness is the more tolerable course. Quintilian places the study of Greek before that of Latin literature, but this was with boys whose vernacular was Latin. Since Latin with us must be learnt by instruction, the exact contrary is necessary, viz. the learning of the Latin language with more exactness should proceed with the rudiments of Greek. If anyone should consider the matter with close attention, he will see that my view of teaching and that of Quintilian are alike. For when boys formerly first came to the school, many things learned at home were already known in the Latin language. After the harder authors in the Latin tongue have been expounded, and the tropes and the main figures of speech in them have been pointed out, boys should pay attention to the greater exercises of speaking and writing Latin. At the same time, let philology begin to be opened up, i.e. some knowledge of the circumstances, times, places, history, fables, proverbs, sentences, apophthegms; domestic and rustic affairs; also foretastes of civil and public questions, all which topics bring the greatest light to their minds. I wish them first to imbibe Latin, so that those subjects, the need of which is the greatest, may stick fastest. I wish the whole manner of expression to be pure Latin, and not to be tinged with Greek. If I say this of the Greek language which is so clearly allied to the Latin, it will be evident that the same principle will hold still more of the Hebrew, which, through the roughness of sound and its whole method of expression, is so different from them both. In the study of Grammar I would wish the application of diligence, for sloth has ruined all sciences. Yet study should not be immoderate, lest the minds of students be overwhelmed with details. There should be leisure for the mind to be occupied with higher and more fruitful subjects, a view which approved itself to Fabius Quintilian[1].

**Order of study.**

Let there be in studies a selection, so that the first care may be given to the signification of words and the rules (formulae) of speech. Next let regard be had to the mind of the author, not so much as to his matter of instruction, as to the idea which he wishes to convey, so that the boy may learn to bring out the sense of those passages which are written obscurely and perplexingly. This sharpens the judgment greatly. In the third place, observe the precepts, taken from life, which are called in Greek γνῶμαι, together with noteworthy expressions and proverbs; fourthly, historical passages; and lastly, and needing only slight treatment, the consideration of the mythology contained in the author.

[1] Bk I, cap. 19.

# CHAPTER II

## THE VERNACULAR IN TEACHING

Teachers are admonished to avoid faults which will diminish their effectiveness of teaching. In exposition the teacher should pass by the inane and useless. How great a need there is that those things which they honour should be passed on to their pupils. The culture of the teacher and its relation to instruction.

**The faults of grammar teachers.**

THE master of the grammar school should be a stranger to those faults which the long exercise of grammatical art is accustomed to produce. When grammar teachers spend their time in trifling amongst the boys who drag them into ineptitude and puerilities as if by contagion, they lose all seriousness and moderation. They are compelled to attend to the faults of the boys, which are innumerable, and repeated over and over again (nor can their manly stomach tolerate these things), so that they are almost driven to anger and ferocity; and, thrust down in that pounding-mill, as it were, the common sense of teachers becomes greatly diminished[1]. Hence in their life and habits there exist moroseness and unpleasantness of manners. Jokingly someone has said that it is no wonder that grammarians should have such manners, for they get them straight away from the first verse of Homer: *μῆνιν ἄειδε θεά* ("Sing to us, goddess, the wrath..."). Since nobody in the school contradicts the teacher, he puts on supercilious airs and arrogance, and particularly brooks no opposition, and perseveres pertinaciously

[1] Quintilian II, 2.

in what he says lest he should lose any of his authority by giving way. For his audience, which consists chiefly of boys, awards the palm not on his merit, but because he never seems to be gainsaid. Schoolmasters often hope to be great by attacking and saying biting things of all kinds of other men. This at least is how the matter is estimated in the judgment of boys and boyish men, in accordance with whose humours the teacher endeavours to speak so as to retain his followers. Some of the latter, with their childish wit, make fun of the counter-sophist, and overwhelm him with maledictions and despise him. The rest pursue him as they would chase an escaped dog, as if quoted revilings had reference to him, whoever may have been the men on whom they were actually originally poured. In addition the scholars transfer to their ruler, with their boys' cruelty, those threats, terrible words and malevolent, abusive epithets which they find in their colloquies and written exercises: *nebulo*, *tenebrio*, *scelerosus*, *error fuste eluendus*, *monstrum majoribus hostiis expiandum*, *cerebrum in Anticyram mittendum*, so many and so atrocious tumults of syllables wrongly composed, or bits of stories or myths, not in every point exactly reproduced, are thus set in motion against the teacher, that you must agree that Ausonius rightly said that no grammarian ever is, or ever was, happy[1]. From all such misfortunes the prudent master will keep himself far removed by carefulness at all points. Let him accustom himself to sociability and friendliness; let him enter into the company and conversations of men in moderation and pleasantly, and as much as possible; he will free himself from annoyance, not by being distant, but by the careful cultivation of his manners. He will keep himself uncorrupt and holy, affable to his pupils, as a father, not as an ill-regulated companion. His erudition will be ample, accurate, diligent, careful in those things which we have mentioned; his instruction will

**The grammaticus ought not to rule tyrannously over his pupils.**

**The grammarian's duty.**

[1] Felix grammaticus non est, sed nec fuit unquam, *Epigrammata*, 128.

preserve the same order—that his pupils shall learn the words, then enter on the understanding of the authors. His memory for words and things must be good and rich, and he must keep it sound by carefulness and constant devotion to learning. The teacher may instil great learning in the minds of his pupils in a short time, if he is himself well at home in a wide range of authors, not searching them one by one with great labour, as places where he may find something here and there, as if a stranger, but as a lord who knows where every single thing is, and one who can always lay his hand on any matter he wants in a short time. In this power, before all, Rhemnius Palaemon[1] was held the prince of grammarians and was thoroughly acceptable to his age, when, in other respects, he was intolerable on account of his many disgraceful deeds.

**It should not be considered wrong for a grammarian not to know everything.**

It should not be regarded as a crime if the teacher does not know every myth and trifle. This does not necessarily indicate a lack of study of a particular subject nor of knowledge in general; as e.g. a man may be ignorant as to: Who was the real mother of Aeneas? Who was the nurse of Anchises? Who was the Penelope whose son was Pan, with Mercury for his father? What is the feminine form of the name Achilles? and other questions with which Tiberius Caesar was wont to plague the grammarians. As to which questions, the man of leisure Didymus[2], has disputed in his immense set of volumes. As in a state or in a well-conducted home, the magistrate or paterfamilias is worthy of blame if he hands over a post to a bad and useless man, when he could fill it with a good man, so it is a grave offence if in one's mind the space be filled with trifles when there might be in it those ideas which would be of high value. It fares badly with letters, and a very painful cross is imposed on studious toil, if these petty matters also are supposed to belong to the task of culture. Wretched

[1] On whom see Suetonius, *liber de Illustratis Grammaticis*.

[2] See Quintilian, bk I, cap. 13 at the end.

are the grammarians who busy themselves with them. When the urbane Virgil was asked what he meant in the Third Eclogue,

> Dic quibus in terris, et eris mihi magnus Apollo,
> Treis pateat coeli spatium non amplius ulnas,

he answered that he had written the lines so as to give the grammarians a cross to bear when they should come to that passage.

**The teacher should know the vernacular language of the boys.**

Let the teacher know the mother-tongue of the boys exactly, so that by means of their vernacular he may make his instruction easier and more pleasant for them. Unless he knows how to express aptly and exactly in the vernacular what he wishes to speak about, he will easily mislead the boys, and these mistakes will accompany them closely into later life, even when they are grown up. Nor do boys sufficiently understand the use of their own language unless things one by one are explained to them with the greatest clearness. The teacher should keep in his mind the earlier history of his mother-tongue and the knowledge, not only of the more recent words, but of old words also, and those which have gone out of use. Let him be as a Prefect of the treasury of his language; for unless this is the case, books written a century earlier will not be understood by posterity, since every language in the course of time undergoes multitudinous changes [1]. For which reason many points in the Twelve Tables escaped the notice of Marcus Cicero and the great law-scholars, for many things even daily slip out of a vernacular language. The teacher should have an ample and copious equipment of Latin words so that his boys may be truly able to draw from him as from a fountain. Let him not drive them to express what they wish to say by roundabout terms or, what is more reprehensible and unpleasant, to point out objects with the finger. This direct naming of things which present themselves to the senses is necessary for those undertaking the first rudiments, but copious expression is more useful

[1] See Conrad Gesner, *Mithridates*.

to the more advanced, that they should be accustomed to express clearly the more abstruse thoughts of their minds. For in this one rule is centred the whole force of eloquence.

**The exposition of authors.**

The exposition of authors should be marked by ease and clearness. In the beginning it should be in the words of the vernacular, and by degrees proceed to Latin, pronounced distinctly and with gestures which may help intelligence, as long as they do not degenerate into the theatrical. Let the teacher quote passages from authors, by way of illustration or in confirmation of what is said, and let him take care, as far as possible, that these should not merely consist of words, but also of short sentences or something which may be of service to either the boy's wits or his manner of life[1]. When the boy is expounding the signification of words, let him produce quotations from approved authors, in which as far as possible he will see to it that he declares most openly the force of the word, then at the same time, if it may be, let the sentence contain something worthy of knowledge. If he cannot find such for himself, let him make use of such as the teacher gives him. Sometimes, so that he may bring the matter better into view, he himself may make an example of his own, which may be changed in form, according to the need for a short sentence, or a fable or story, or a proverb, so as to express himself effectively. Whilst lecturing on a story or fable, the teacher should not describe the whole of it from the beginning, but give as much as is satisfactory for understanding the passage considered. But if the pupils have heard it before, it will be sufficient to remind them about it in a few words. Yet sometimes pleasant subjects must be sought out, and diverting matter for speaker and hearer be chosen, e.g. stories or fables may be related fully for the sake of taking away tedium. I would rather the grammar teacher should err in this direction than that he be dry. It is a mistake to suppose that a subject has been taught sufficiently,

**The pains-taking method of teaching.**

[1] Quintilian I, I.

when the teacher follows the Stoic manner, by indicating a few points. If the name of a man be stated, and he is renowned for warlike deeds, or for wisdom and is distinguished for his knowledge of things, or even if the man named was notorious by his hateful deeds, let it be shown where he was born, who were his parents, and the principal matters which have connexion with his reputation, at any rate those things which chiefly are necessary for the understanding of the passage. Let the teacher deal thus both with what is praiseworthy and what is blameworthy. Let the teacher state the most important chronological dates, as I will presently explain. Then he will point out, so as to make all easy, those things which have connexion with the subject-matter about which he is speaking: the city, mountain, river, fountain; where is the site, how far it is distant from some well-known place, e.g. from the Alps, Pyrenees, from the city of Rome, Athens, Rhodes, Jerusalem, the Nile, Rhone, Euripus, or from the Adriatic or the Etruscan Sea; what notable man the place has produced, what special products are to be found there, then if anything remarkable has happened in that place. An animal, or plant, or stone should be briefly described, and anything concerning its nature and qualities should—as far as possible and in the most attractive way—be noted and described; whether it is rare or unknown in our district, and where it may be found, should be taught. A precept (in Greek γνώμη) is said to be made clearer by some example, or by another sentence or a more striking illustration, or by giving it the support of a greater authority. If there is anything in it of a depraved tendency, it should be corrected by the standard of our religion. The origin of a proverb and its essential meaning should be elucidated as far as possible, then should be stated what its applied use is, and at the same time an instance of its use by an author should be quoted from a passage in which the author seems to have introduced it most appropriately and effectively. The teacher may also borrow

**How to bring in illustrations whilst reading authors.**

some easy illustrations from the study of higher knowledge, as long as it is appropriate to the capacities of the minds of his pupils, and so far as the quotations serve to elucidate the author under consideration. The rest of the more difficult parts which require a deeper foundation for their comprehension should be left over to the time of higher studies themselves. The author's plan should be expounded by the teacher, as was done by Donatus[1], though in this direction he goes too far. Then the obscure passages of the writer should be explained through other passages like them, but somewhat clearer. But if there are none of these passages to be found, then the explanation should be based on other passages of the same period or the one next to it, so that the teacher may show that this way of speaking or feeling of the author can be made clear by the reference to his period as a whole. For all which methods an example in my opinion can be found in Servius Honoratus[1]. I will not here discuss the truth of his judgments, but I approve, in the highest degree, his methods of interpretation, and would wish them to be taken as a standard by the teacher for the purpose of instruction; though it is fitting that the teacher should be more copious and prolix in interpretation than Servius was in writing. More minute points should also be brought before a class in teaching than are done in composing a book. Let the teacher remember that very apt image by which Quintilian describes the boy's mind, viz. that it is like a vessel with a narrow neck, which spits out again the too large a supply of liquid which the teacher attempts to pour in. Let instruction therefore be poured in gradually, drop by drop. Similarly let the teacher offer his pupils in the beginning few and easy matters of instruction; then the boy may become accustomed so as to understand further, greater, and more solid topics. In the first beginnings let the teacher often ask questions, and let him often supply the reasons for what he has got in answer. For great is the help to memory if reasons are associated with the matter taught.

**Method of the interpretation of authors.**

[1] Donatus (fl. 353 A.D.) wrote on Terence; Servius (b. 355 A.D.) on Virgil.

# CHAPTER III

## LATIN SPEAKING

The right attitude of pupils under instruction. Let them have paper-books, in which they carefully note down both what they have privately observed themselves and also what the master in his exposition suggests. On memory and its value, how it can be aided and at what age it can best be exercised. On pronunciation and style.

How the boy should listen to the teacher.

He should place implicit faith in his teacher.

THE boy should listen intently to the teacher and fix his look on him except when he has to look at his book, or when he has to write. He must recognise that hearing is the medium of learning, that those living beings who lack the power of listening are not capable of learning, and that nothing is more easy or more fruitful than to hear much. Whatsoever he has received from his teacher, let the scholar regard as if pure oracle, and since he will think him to be perfect and full of the highest excellence he will keenly wish that he himself should be like his teacher as far as possible. The disciples of Plato have stated that their master was round-shouldered, and the disciples of Aristotle that their master stammered. They thought these defects beautiful and worthy of imitation, because they were to be found in their master. I do not commend the imitation of faults, but I prefer that faults be taken along with virtues, rather than not to regard the master's virtues at all[1].

[1] Quintilian, bk I, cap. I.

Let the pupil learn to write correctly and quickly. The foundations of writing ought to be laid while pupils are being taught to read; they must know what letters, what syllables, what sounds ought to be separated or combined, and keep them ready for use. Let them be convinced that nothing conduces more truly to wide learning than to write much and often, and to use up a great deal of paper and ink. Therefore let each boy have an empty paper book divided into several parts to receive all that falls from his teacher's lips, since this is not less valuable to him than precious stones. In one division let him put down separate and single words. In another proper ways of speaking and turns of speech, which are in daily use; and again, rare expressions, or such as are not generally known and explained.

Rules for writing notes.

In a separate division, let him make history notes; in another, notes of anecdotes; in another, clever expressions and weighty judgments; in another, witty and acute sayings; in another, proverbs; in other divisions, names of well-known men of high birth, famous towns, animals, plants and strange stones. In another part, explanations of difficult passages in the author. In another, doubtful passages, which are still unsolved. These beginnings seem simple and bare, but later he will clothe and ornament them. The boy should also have a larger book in which he can put all the notes expounded and developed at length by the teacher, also what he reads for himself in the best writers, or the sayings which he observes used by others; and just as he has certain divisions and heads in his note-books, so let him make indexes of these places for himself and distinguish them by headings in order to know what he shall enter into each division.

Memory.

Let the memory be exercised at an early age; it improves with practice; let many facts be often commended to its care[1]. For that age is not so fatigued by remembering, because it has no labour of reflexion. Thus the

[1] See Vives, *de Anima*, bk II.

memory is strengthened without any labour or trouble and it becomes very capacious. Let, then, the tender mind be instructed in the rudiments of knowledge, for although rudiments may create aversion they must be learnt and are of great importance. Thus what would be disagreeable to censorious men is often even pleasant to children: therefore what a man would be disinclined afterwards to learn, must be learnt as a child.

**Memory from Quintilian.**

Memory consists of two factors: quick comprehension and faithful retention; we quickly comprehend what we understand, we retain what we have often and carefully confided to our memory. Both are helped by arrangement of facts, so that we can even recall what has passed away; this is just that art of memory which beasts are said to lack[1]. What we want to remember must be impressed on our memory while others are silent; but we need not be silent ourselves, for those things which we have read aloud are often more deeply retained. In the same way we remember better what we have heard from others than what we have read ourselves. In reading aloud two senses aid the subject-matter in finding an entrance into the mind, sight and hearing. If the thoughts begin to wander on account of a very small noise, then we must retrace the whole and exclude all that interrupts. As food which has just been eaten oppresses the stomach more than it increases the strength, until it has been transformed in the blood and digested in the body, so a discourse directly after it has been heard is of little profit until it has been, as it were, digested. What one learns just before one goes to sleep is far more vividly reproduced in the morning than what one learns at any other time, provided one has gone to bed, neither oppressed by drinking, or by eating to excess, nor weary and exhausted for want of food. It is a very useful practice to write down what we want to remember, for it is not less impressed on the mind

**How memory is to be cultivated.**

[1] See Vives, *de Anima*, bk III.

than on the paper by the pen, and indeed the attention is kept fixed longer by the fact that we are writing it down. Thus the time taken in the writing helps the idea to stick in the mind.

**Method of teaching.**

Whatever the boys have heard from their master, let them first repeat to fellow-pupils more advanced than themselves, or to an under-master, and afterwards to the master himself, lest awe of the master should confuse them while they are still inexperienced and timorous. At first it will suffice for them to repeat it word for word; but afterwards let them change the passage into designations and words similar to those which they have been taught. Let them be bidden to produce whatever words they think they have noted among their master's sayings which they may use in their own exercises. Then let them change the words and keep the same idea. Let the better-informed pupils repeat to those who are less well-informed what they have heard from their master, and explain it privately. This will both practise the elder boys and spur on the younger. It seems that boys more easily raise themselves to the intelligence of their elder schoolfellows than to that of their masters, for what is small and weak clings more quickly on its upward course to what is nearest than to what is highest, as we see happens in the case of trees. Let them at first speak in their own tongue, which was born in them in their home, and if they make mistakes in it, let the master correct them. From this start gradually proceed to speaking in Latin. They will mix up in the vernacular what they have heard from their master or read themselves in Latin, so that at first the language in the school will be a mixture of the mother-tongue and of Latin. Let them speak their own language out of doors, so that they may not accustom themselves in any way to make a hotch-potch of the two languages. The instructor must take all possible care that the expressions used are pure, and good Latin. The pupils are to be warned in this as in every other exercise, that they must trust more to rules than to practice or their own judgment, since the two latter are very feeble supports and easily mistaken. By the gradual increase of knowledge at last they will become Latin conversationalists. Let them try to express their thoughts in Latin words, for there is nothing which is equally important as is practice in the learning of a language. But if a pupil is ashamed to speak in Latin, it is hopeless to expect him ever to become fluent in that language. Whoever refuses to speak Latin after he has been instructed in it for a year, must be punished according to his age and to the circumstances. A mistake in a difficult passage should be pardoned and corrected so that the correction shall prove useful in the future, but if the mistake is made in an easy passage, the boy should be punished for it. Let the pupil diligently endeavour to imitate in his expressions and conversation, first, his master and then those learned authors, whom his instructor has pointed out to him, and also those men whom his master approves of as learned, but in speaking with those whose Latin is bad, it is better to use a language which cannot be so easily corrupted.

**Pupils to speak Latin.**

Since language was given to men that they might exchange ideas, it is fitting that it should be simple and clear, so as not to require an interpreter[1]. Clearness is of course considered from the point of view of the language itself and not from the understanding of the listeners, for if anyone is ignorant of the language and therefore is not influenced by our words, it does not follow that we have used obscure language. Nay, we may have spoken fluently and simply, if we have employed phrases which belong to the common usage of speakers and if the arrangement was clear, that is, if it followed a certain natural order[2]. Therefore avoid phrases which have long fallen out of use on account of their antiquity, and which are difficult to translate, phrases which are new and

**Faults of speech.**

[1] Quintilian I, 10.

[2] As the most frequented way is a good way, so is the most usual speech a good one. See Aulus Gellius I, 10, and Quintilian VIII, 2.

unusual and those which come from poetical translations, especially from Greek,—drawn out into long sequences of idiom—all these forms of expression should be rigorously avoided[1]. In Greek we need not be so anxious about speaking the language as about understanding it, as we only want to know the literature. But if anyone has sufficient leisure and his intellect permits of it he may also habituate himself so as to gain the power of speaking in that language.

**The faults of hearing.**

The faults in boyish ways of speaking must be noted so as to be corrected, as when the voice is too thin and the pronunciation of the letters too feeble. Those who commit this fault are called ἰσχνοθέται; he who commits the contrary one, whose voice is too thick and the pronunciation of the words rather broad, is called πλατειασμός, as for example Lucius Crassus in the works of Cicero, Sulpitius and Cotta. When the words come as it seems from the hidden depth of the throat, as in the Arabs and Hebrews, they are said λαρυγγίζειν, but when the voice is heard in the hollow of the mouth it is κοιλοστομία[2].

Aristotle divides the faults of speech into three kinds: (1) ἰσχνοφώνους, those who cannot pronounce a certain letter (they are called *blaesi*, lispers, in Latin); (2) ψελλούς, viz. those who entirely omit a letter or a syllable (in Latin they are called *balbi*, stammerers), Cicero in his letters to Papyrius Paetus contrasts them with men of eloquence; (3) τραυλούς who are called stutterers (*haesitantes*). Correct speech and a pronunciation free from faults are called ὀρθοέπεια by Aristotle. *Lambdacismus* and *Jotacismus* are the terms applied when the words are uttered with unnecessary emphasis. In certain nations there are peculiar letters, as for example among the Eretrienses[3], who very often mix up their letters, and the Germans, who pronounce the hissing "s." Faults which are the result of habit can be overcome, those which are the result

[1] See Quintilian I, 19. [2] Quintilian I, 5, 32.

[3] Inhabitants of Eretria, the principal town of the island of Euboea.

of nature can at least be improved, if they cannot be completely eradicated. For they can at all times be cautiously concealed, so that they need not be objectionably noticeable.

**Not to speak too quickly when learning.**

It is necessary to be careful that a boy does not pronounce the "s" sound in a lisping fashion from want of teeth, and that he should not get into the habit of speaking too quickly. The master himself must set him an example in the speed and fluency of his language. There are some teachers who hope to be considered perfect grammarians if, instead of uttering the words clearly, they pour them out in a perfect stream; this gives rise to much ignorance in life and is a great evil, for the mind cannot possibly follow the number of ideas suggested by the flying tongue, and thus one is obliged either to be silent or to utter absurdities so as to keep up the flow of language. For there is nothing considered worse form in that style than for a man to hesitate. It shows the difficulty under which he labours, although he wants all things to seem as if they were clear, or rather as if easy, to him. It is better to err by speaking too slowly than by speaking too quickly[1]; for in slow speech a man can think out beforehand what he is going to say, but in quick speech he can scarcely ever do this. There is, however, a certain golden mean between the two, which it is most desirable to maintain; and a certain quick and fluent way of speaking which I would not blame in a boy, even if the phrases were sometimes unthought out, for it is not out of keeping with his boyishness; yet, as he grows up, the practice must be softened and restrained, so that he may not acquire the habit of pouring forth words which have no thought behind them and merely spring to the lips thoughtlessly.

Practice in writing is a great help. "The pen," says Cicero, "is the best teacher and producer of speech[2]." Therefore, as soon as they have learnt syntax, let the pupils translate from the mother-tongue into Latin, and then back again into

[1] Quintilian I, I. [2] From Quintilian.

the mother-tongue. Let them begin with short passages, which can be gradually increased in length day by day. The same kind of exercises can be done in Greek, although I should prefer that pupils learned to translate from Greek authors rather than to translate from our language into Greek. It is right to draw attention to the fact that a translator must be well equipped in both languages; still he must receive most practice in the language into which he is translating. But it is impossible to fully translate words, of which one does not know the meaning. The works of Aristotle will be badly translated by a man who is not a philosopher and those of Galen by a man who is not a doctor.

**Translation.**

The pupils should likewise be well exercised in explaining difficult passages of great writers. For this requires great attention. Concentration is thus strengthened and the mind is sharpened, and the judgment becomes more active. Strange to say there are some people who do not understand how to write down what they would be well able to speak; this happens, as far as I can discover, because a wandering and unsettled mind is capable of sufficient attention for speech, but not for understanding what is written; it cannot support the strain of collecting and, as it were, compelling itself.

Added to this there must be practice in comparing writers, together with the expressions in which they agree, and in which they differ; for the general practice of language cannot be all limited to fixed rules. Let pupils write an easy letter, or tale, let them amplify a short sentence or a maxim, render a proverb into another language, and write a poem in prose, stripping it of all metre, an exercise which Crassus often practised, as we find mentioned in Cicero[1]. Laurentius Valla and Raphael Volaterranus employed the same method when they were translating Homer. Though I approve of this practice for boyish ignorance, I do not sanction it as an adequate rendering of a great writer, since in such a translation

[1] See Dr Lawrence Humphrey, *de Interpretatione*.

the greatest part of the beauty of the words is taken away. Let the pupil write at first few exercises, but let the master see that those are done correctly, then let him proceed to further exercises; style does not come by painful labour, but rather by careful and diligent exercise, so that the small beginnings which conduce so greatly to the whole (more than we believe even) may not escape our careful notice. Let scholars keep what they have written in earlier months, in order to compare it with that written in later months, so that they may perceive the progress made and persevere in the way in which they see they have made improvement.

# CHAPTER IV

## THE COURSE OF TRAINING

Disputations. Correction of mistakes in the process of acquiring knowledge and in morals. Attraction of studies. Boys' play.

**Disputations.**

THE boy who is brought to school ought not to engage in the disputations at once, for how can he know what to say when he is ignorant of everything? rather let him silently watch the ways of the school and carefully consider every single exercise; then let him begin to question his schoolfellows about any matter, rather than to judge or to contend about it.

With this consideration in his mind, Pythagoras of Samos used to command his scholars to be silent for some years so as not to get into the habit of asking frivolous and foolish questions[1]. Then they were permitted to have slight contests on small matters of debate; (these were somewhat frequent at first)—and the subjects of discussion were such as they had heard expounded[2]. Emulation in discussion excites youthful minds and does not suffer them to stagnate in idleness. For that reason the Lord called forth the Jews, as though they were boys, to fight with the heathen for the Kingdom of Heaven, as we read in St Paul's Epistle to the Romans. Therefore boys ought to be urged on by means of praise and small rewards which suit their age, and even by reproof and the pointing out of a comrade who has spoken better[3]. But

[1] See Laertius: *Pythagoras*. [2] Quintilian I, I.

[3] Horace, *Serm.* I, Sat. I.

one must be careful lest the matter should grow to hatred, and quarrels should arise. Let the boy contend eagerly but without any bitterness. Gradually these contentions should turn to a comparison of studies and the excitements of childish minds should subside. Indeed it is better for a young man to know nothing than for him to become the slave of ambition and pride. No one will easily believe, unless he has had experience of it, what wild and savage passions an ignorant young man will cherish, like serpents, in his bosom. Small rewards and praise should indeed be allowed to those of childish age, but these should be shown as childish trifles to the youth (as are nuts or horses of reeds or wood to those who have just put off the name of child), who would blush to desire them for themselves. The words of his instructor and his ways will greatly help to make pupils wish to despise such things, for while he often and vehemently inveighs against them and declares them to be ridiculous, he also will confirm what he says by his life.

**The bringing together of material from various subjects of study by pupils.**

The following are problems which youths may discuss: How to harmonise rules of subjects of study with practice; obscure and difficult passages in the authors; the explanation of maxims, proverbs, parables, fables, historical events; what is their origin, their meaning, their relation to other things; the name of a man, a city, a mountain, a river, a spring, a province, an animal, a tree, a stone, a metal; the force of a word and its etymology, its pronunciation and spelling; the expression, construction and laws of verse; all these subjects should be chosen according to his age, and in keeping with the extent of his studies. And since a man is taught nothing by nature, but everything is evolved by instruction, by hard work, habit and diligence, he often errs and goes in the opposite direction to what he ought, so that correction is necessary at all times and at all ages, and we ought not to allow any fault to cling and grow strong. There are, however, some things which the pupils

**Correction of mistakes.**

cannot yet grasp, and the master should postpone them to a later age, warning the pupil, however, that what he has done is not approved, though it is not blamed, and that it is pardoned on account of his stage of progress, but that the time will come when the teacher will have to show him where and why mistakes which are now overlooked, must be avoided when he shall come to understand higher standards[1]. There are things which we approve in boys but disapprove of when firmly established in men. In teaching it is well to dissemble a little, and not to censure everything that presents itself. Morals however must be kept free from blemish; not as though everything could be perfect at that age, but lest boys should be perverse and the beginnings of progress be spoilt. The wise teacher will remember what a difference there is between the beginner, the one who is getting on, and the one who is fully accomplished; that he cannot require from a boy, who is beginning, that which he expects from a youth, who has made progress in self-control and moral character. Nothing is so foolish as to expect ripe fruit when the trees begin to bud in early spring. Let the master not be angry with the boys, if they cannot do what youths can after having been instructed for a long time. Much less should the master get angry, as he sometimes does, if the boy cannot do what he can do himself. Although there is nothing more senseless, yet there are teachers who demand such tasks from little boys with cruel threats, blows and stripes. Such teachers themselves are more worthy of being beaten. Let the teacher observe moderation in his censure lest he should let anything slip himself, or lest he should arouse the fierceness of his pupils; do not let him crush their spirits by the harshness of his words, or confuse them by his severity. At the beginning of any task, suppose they are beginning to speak Latin or learning to write, certain mistakes which can easily be remedied in the course of time may be overlooked;

**Method of treating pupils.**

[1] Quintilian I, I.

urge the pupils by praise and approval as though with a pricking spur to a race, that they may not be made ashamed by the constant strange and subtle derision of their teacher and companions, and thus despair before they have tested their powers, for those who are hindered by the possibility of being exposed to ridicule never venture to make any advance. Those who are progressing ought never to be praised for anything for which the teacher sees he will one day have to substitute censure. Moderation in emending and correcting will also help, so that even if he silently passes over some inaccuracies, he can at least assert that there was nothing of which the pupils could say that the correction was wrong. This will greatly increase his authority.

**Punishment.**

Again, since the mind of man is misled by passions, every thoughtless action must be checked and restrained by reproof, and blame expressed in words, and if necessary in blows[1]; so that as with animals pain may recall boys to the right, when reason is not strong enough. For all that, I should prefer this beating to be done as amongst free men, not harshly or as amongst slaves, unless the boy is of such a disposition that he has to be incited to his duty by blows, like a slave. The master should not be too familiar with boys and those who are still childish, for the comedy says of them "Too much familiarity breeds contempt." Let the master then be grave without being harsh, and kind without being weak; do not threaten unless the matter requires it; do not abuse the boys, for this would give them cause for contempt and occasion of practice for it. If the boy will not comply with threats let the master beat him, but in such a way that while his still tender body suffers a sharp pain, it does not endure a permanent injury. Never let the master act in such a way as to accustom the boys to despise his threats or punishments; these I should wish him not to dispense lavishly, but to reserve them for special and rare

[1] But see Quintilian's views, I, 3.

occasions. Masters will thus secure dignity and value in all matters and not produce insensibility by repeated blows. Older boys indeed should be more rarely checked by blows, but still it should be done sometimes[1]. Boys should chiefly be restrained by awe and respect for their master and the important men of the academy, who are present as witnesses and the observers of both virtues and vices. So also respect for their fathers and relations, is a restraining factor.

**Commendation of learning by the teacher.**

The teacher must also point out what delight there is in learning, what deep, lasting and permanent pleasure, to which nothing else can be at all compared; all other things pass by and vanish before its presence; knowledge is a provision for old age, and serves as a safeguard over the whole course of life, whether joy asks for embellishments or sorrow for comfort; on the other hand what shadows, what dangerous evils spring from ignorance; to illustrate all these matters too many examples could not be produced! Further, boys must be reminded not to accept what they read about morals, as though it were a little story and it were sufficient to have heard it; but they should look on it as the most strengthening pasture for the mind which must be chewed, digested, and converted into the substance of the mind. Unless this is done it injures the mind just as undigested food upsets the body. Let them frequently remember that God is the Director of the world, that we shall all come before His judgment-seat at death, and that no one will be exempt; death comes to all alike, threatens all, is present everywhere and imminent; it carries off young and old at the same time. The teacher will have some short, general arguments ready, specially effective against particular faults which are usual to that age, for his task is to bring all his instruction and training so to bear upon the youth as to make vice hated or despised.

**Pupils must be encouraged to piety.**

[1] "When you drive a child by blows what will you do with the youth"? (Quint. I, 3.)

But inasmuch as the powers of our minds and bodies are not only limited, but are sometimes weak and feeble, we must give them some food and recreation, so that they may be able to accomplish further work, otherwise they are exhausted in a very short time, and then become good for nothing. Boys must exercise their bodies frequently, for that age demands growth and the development of the strength which has been acquired. In the same way they must not be pressed too much or driven to study, but they must be allowed some respite from attention, "lest they should begin to hate work before they begin to love it[1]," but still in such a way that they do not glide into mean pleasures. The human mind is wonderfully inclined to freedom. It allows itself to be set to work, but it will not suffer itself to be compelled. We may easily gain much by asking, but very little by extortion, and that little with difficulty.

Recreation.

There are games, which combine honour with pleasure, such as throwing the javelin, playing ball or running[2]. If Cicero recommended profitable and serious games to his fellow-citizens, how much more ought they to be recommended by us to anyone who is a philosopher. Everything ought to take place before the eyes of older people, who are reverenced by the pupils. The aim of such games is to promote the growth of the body, not to make boys wild and ferocious. The whole care of the health is directed to making the mind vigorous and to attain to what he (Cicero) most desired from the gods, "mens sana in corpore sano"; then to strengthen and refresh the mind so that it may be made fit for its daily work. Let the boys speak Latin while they are playing. He who speaks in his native tongue should be mulcted by losing a point in the game. In games boys easily speak Latin, and in this way more freely, if whatever is

The best games.

[1] As Quintilian says: I, I.

[2] Quintilian I, 3, and the dialogue *de causis corruptae eloquentiae* ascribed to Tacitus.

required in the way of speech in the game is first explained by the teacher in good and suitable Latin; for we speak unwillingly when we fear to say something wrong or inappropriate.

When the weather will not allow them to exercise their bodies out of doors, or in the case of those whose health will not permit them to take part in games, then happy and pleasant talks will afford great delight, such as tales or histories or narratives of a pleasant, witty, lively and merry kind. Similarly, it is suitable to quote either sayings which have elegance long drawn out or witty and laughable brevities. Sometimes also a fairly concentrated indoor game should be permitted, which will exercise their minds, their judgments and their memories, such as that of draughts and chess. They should have porches or wide halls in which to recreate themselves in rainy weather. But the chief care should be paid to the mind and the memory, which are injured by too much attention to the body. Some wise man has said, "Great care of the body is great carelessness for the mind." Nevertheless the body must not be neglected and brought up in dirt and filth, for nothing is more detrimental both to the health of the body and to that of the mind.

**Right method in nourishment.**

A system of good nourishment conduces very much in every way to the sharpness of the mind and the strength of the memory. Food should be taken at suitable times of the day and should be varied to suit the constitution of every individual, so that no noxious humour may strike its roots in the body. Weak-blooded (*exsucci*) people must take fluids, phlegmatic people what is warm and heating, melancholy people what is opposite to their nature, what will lighten their spirits and make them more gay. To these wine may be given a little more freely for as the Jewish wise man said, "Wine should be given to the afflicted[1]." Those who are too ardent (*biliosi*) should be cooled

[1] See Ecclesiastes x. 19; I Timothy v. 23.

down. For very fine minds, somewhat fatty foods are beneficial for health, as well as for keeping in check their force of intellect, that they may not suddenly collapse; to which danger the fineness of their mind too much exposes them. The youths should not be allowed to withdraw themselves by stealth, for according to the disposition of each they will either go and drink, or gamble, or resort with undesirable women. Thus much as to instruction in languages.

# CHAPTER V

## THE READING OF AUTHORS

On different classes of authors, the reading of whom is valuable and those the reading of whom is harmful, and especially as to virtue and vice in the poets.

**Differences in the value of authors.**

I SUPPOSE that I am now expected to set forth from what sources I consider this erudition is to be gained; I will do so as far as my powers allow. But I will first make a few general remarks about writers. All writers are not to be judged by the same standard. There are some who have followed a certain order in their writings, and have a short and clear style, which is easy to be understood; these ought not only to be read, but also learnt by heart. Others have carefully followed up the subject treated, but either too discursively or too confusedly for it to be any help to the pupil; these ought to be read, but are not to be learnt by heart as the former, or to be read repeatedly. Other writers it is sufficient to have read. There are some that it is not necessary to read, but which should be kept in a library for reference when occasion requires.

**1. Necessary to know.**

**2. Unnecessary authors.**

**From which authors boys should be kept.**

Above all things a boy must be kept from those writers, who might foster and feed any fault to which he is inclined, for example a sensual boy must be kept from Ovid, a jeering boy from Martial, an abusive and mocking boy from Lucian, a boy inclined to impiety from Lucretius, and most of the philosophers, especially Epicurus and his followers. Cicero will not do much good to a vainglorious boy unless it is pointed out to him under what conditions one can praise oneself without exciting aversion, or unless such a boy understands that we ourselves cannot tolerate even in the greatest man, or those who are greater than all praise of ours, the taint of self-glorification.

**Writers who cherish and inflame vices.**

Let the scholar begin the reading of the heathen, as though entering upon poisonous fields, armed with an antidote, with the consciousness that men are united to God by means of the reverence which has been given them by Him; that what men think out for themselves is full of errors; that whatever is opposed to piety, has sprung from man's emptiness and the deceits of his most crafty enemy, the devil; this will be generally sufficient without further explanation. Let the scholar remember that he is wandering amongst the heathen, that is, amongst thorns, poisons, aconite, and most threatening pestilences, that he is to take from them only what is useful, and to throw aside the rest, all of which they are neither to carefully examine themselves nor is the teacher to attempt to explain that which is hurtful to them. Laurentius Valla excellently says of a certain offensive word, "I would rather a man remained ignorant of it than that he should learn it through me." Thus the teacher should rather divert the pupil as far away as possible from it and lead him to a better word.

Having said this I will proceed to consider writers in both languages. Amongst them there are some who write in verse, others write in freedom from metre. This is called prose or in Latin, *pedester*[1]; the former are called poets, the characteristic of their art is music; they have no fixed subject, any more than the other arts, which are called "ὄργανα" by the Greeks, as grammar, dialectic and oratory.

**Poets.**

[1] i.e. on foot, not rising above the ground, not elevated like the language of poetry.

From the former the mind draws great refreshment on account of its harmony and character. But because of the subjects which the early poets have chosen to put into song, poetry is suspected by many of corrupting the morals and is openly hated by certain people. Although there has been a long and varied dispute on this subject, I will disclose my view on the subject in a few words.

**The usefulness in poetry.**

As far as verse is concerned, I consider it very charming because of its harmony, which corresponds with the melody of the human soul, of which I have already spoken. The words proper to poetry, whether original or adapted, are lofty, sublime, brilliant; poems contain subjects of extraordinary effectiveness, and they display human passions in a wonderful and vivid manner. This is called *energia.* There breathes in them a certain great and lofty spirit so that the readers are themselves caught into it, and seem to rise above their own intellect, and even above their own nature. But amongst all these, so charming virtues, very fatal faults are mixed, disgraceful subjects are partly described and expressed and partly even commended. Faults of this kind can do great harm, if the reader has confidence in the writer, and if his verses gain a lodgment in the listener's mind, unconsciously through the sweetness of the verse. The subjects are taken partly from the spiritual, and partly from the bodily, life. They do not harm the mind, unless authority and example from the author are added to them, for which reason Homer was banished from Plato's *Republic*; Pythagoras says that he saw his soul in the lower world hanging from a tree and surrounded by serpents, because of what he had feigned about the gods. This is much worse than what Silius Italicus fables Scipio Africanus to have seen. But if these tales could formerly injure students, they can do so no longer, for we know that those gods were bad and wicked beings, who deserved ruin and not heaven; but still it may injure some students when it is added that wicked people attained their ends through crime, as when a man gained a kingdom by treachery or murder. Physical crimes corrupt the mind by even mentioning them.

**Plutarch on the reading of the poets.**

Someone will ask, "How then ought we to read? How are we to gather healthy plants from amongst so many poisonous weeds? What are to be our precautions in stepping amongst the thorns? Or should we rather despise and reject them all?" Plutarch of Chaeronea wrote a book on reading the poets, in which he does nothing but arrange and soften the poison so that it may be less hurtful to those who take it, as when a poisonous mushroom is counteracted by an antidote. What need is there of this? Is it not wiser to leave the poison untouched altogether? Perhaps this is particularly the course to adopt with the poets referred to, and all the more because they add very little to knowledge of the arts, or to life, or indeed to language itself. Plutarch wisely and sensibly, as his manner is, gives precepts whereby the study of poetry may be made less harmful (although there are not a few things which afford a weak antidote) as when he bids us to point out to boys that poetry is not real life but a kind of painting. What then? If that very picture which we are gazing at, is obscene, does that not contaminate our minds, especially if it be subtly and artistically depicted? Not undeservedly did wise men wish to banish from the state such artists together with their pictures. Plutarch adds that poets by no means indicate that they themselves approve of their own disgraceful subjects. But not all; indeed some openly approve them fully, as Ovid, Tibullus, Catullus, Propertius, Martial and others of this type. Others however treat the subject most obscurely and show their disapproval by hints which only a very few understand. Further, Plutarch advises that the maxims of the moral poets should be opposed to the immoral teachings of the others, then he believes the one sort will nullify the other sort. But what are you to do, if good maxims are not at hand? Besides have not bad maxims on their side the inclination of our natures to evil, so that they are stronger than the good? And, finally, he comes to the conclusion that he confesses that reading poets is hurtful, unless you are very cautious indeed. If that is so, it seems they ought not to be placed in the hands of boys, for it is the instruction of boys with which Plutarch is dealing, and the study of the poets might be deferred until the boys become grown men of settled convictions. With all these grounds and reasons before us, it seems to me that the following is the course which should be adopted. There are so many things in the poets, which are charming, beautiful, great and worthy of admiration, that poets ought not to be excluded from boys' study, but should be expurgated. The diseased limb should not be cut off, but should be cured by treatment with medicine. Obscene passages should be wholly cut out from the text, as though they were dead, and would infect whatever they touched. Does the human race, forsooth, suffer an irreparable loss, if a man cast the noxious part out of an unclean poet, and if he does to a book, what he would not hesitate to do to his own body, if necessary? The Emperor Justinian mutilated the writings of very many lawyers[1]. Is it then wrong to exclude those verses from Ovid, which would make a young man worse than he is? So many works of so many philosophers and holy writers have been lost, would it then be a crime if Tibullus or the *Ars Amandi* of Ovid perished? Whoever will undertake this expurgation will do a great service not only to his contemporaries and to posterity, but also to poetry itself and to poets. This would be, as in a garden; a gardener only leaves the healthy herbs, and weeds out all the poisonous plants. In this way poetry will be kept from ignominy and the readers from an evil poison. When however poets depict the bad, let those who read know that the poems are only pictures, and impress upon them that they are the pictures very often of the worst men. When they hear about gods, let them think of

**Poets should be purified.**

[1] Prolegomena *de libris Juris*.

them as kings, when of heroes, as noblemen, and when of men, as common people. Sometimes, they must take the god as standing for the quality which is attributed to him, for instance, Jupiter for the majesty of kingship; Minerva for wisdom and counsel; Mars as the impulse to go to war; Mercury as an ambassador; Apollo for the pleasure of knowledge and mental clearness. Reliance on the poets personally must be weakened. They had great natural advantages by their inspiration, but still they were men of ordinary capacity, often with no learning or experience of life, or at any rate very little; besides they were slaves to evil passions and tainted with vice.

**Whence comes the "authority" of poets.**

Perhaps someone will wonder whence comes this great admiration for them not only among the common people but even in the schools of those who follow after wisdom? There are reasons for this. The poets were the first and most ancient writers and so they were called "poets"; and all men have great respect for what is ancient. A pleasant style inspired trust in them, for we easily believe what we like to hear. When men sowed the seeds of all kinds of knowledge which were scattered about in their works, they were thought to be perfect in them all. There is no human mind, however silly and far removed from human instruction, which has not received from nature certain germs of all arts. Whether the germs are really present or only potential, I will not argue. And if this happens to men who are foolish and dull, how much more to those who are endowed with sharpness and keenness of wit? So we find with our own poets, who compose poetry in the vernacular languages, and who, although we know them to be unlearned men, yet they insert into their poems such things as we, who know them, marvel that they should be able to include; and they easily persuade the ignorant and

**Thus:**
**1. Antiquity,**
**2. Eloquence,**
**3. Instruction in all branches of human knowledge.**

**The seeds of arts are found even in our unlearned poets.**

unlearned that they have pursued every branch of knowledge with long and deep study. We have it on record that Aratus, who knew nothing about astrology, and Nicander of Colophon, who had nothing to do with agriculture, wrote most elegant poetry on those subjects. A divine inspiration came upon them, which they believed incited them to write, and so their words were received as if God spoke by them, as it were, through a reed. Philosophers have indeed abused the respect which has been paid them so far as to allow themselves to persuade the people as they wished to be persuaded. And because the minds of the people were stirred up, and through the poetic ardour their nature was raised aloft, they thought that whatever they heard from the poets was as fully established as if it were by the teaching of nature.

But now I will speak of individual writers.

# CHAPTER VI

## LATIN AUTHORS

The whole Course of Latin Instruction. Relation of classical authors to Instruction in History. Reference Books for Latin Teaching.

**Names of authors.**

THE teacher has for guides to the rules of the first rudiments of language, Donatus among the older writers, and Nicolaus Perottus, Sulpitius Verulanus, Antonius Nebrissensis, Aldus Manutius, Philippus Melanchthon among the later writers. Let him take whichever he pleases, they seem to me about equal for teaching purposes. A more exact work is still required for the syntax, and should be written in verse that it may be the better committed to the boy's memory. What books on Syntax we have up to now, are merely collections of examples without rules, or rules with too great a number of exceptions. He who would write such a book of syntax would require much reading and long and careful observation of the Latin authors. I think that Thomas Linacre's six books on right syntax (*de Emendata Structura*) would help a pupil a great deal, also Mancinellus' *Thesaurus* and the books of Lancilotus Passius on Latin Grammar (*de Litteratura non vulgari*). Meanwhile, let the boys use the rules of Antonius Nebrissensis or of Philip Melanchthon, and let them have in addition the little book on the eight parts of speech which passes under Erasmus' name; it was composed by Lily, and revised by Erasmus.

**Grammatical writers and restorers of knowledge.**

The Latin tongue, formerly, as all others also, was learned from popular usage, but after the state became corrupted, it began to be sought in the writers, those, that is, who wrote from the time when Cato was Censor to the time when Hadrian was Emperor. The first of these authors is Cato himself, and the last Suetonius Tranquillus. Here we have, as it were, the progress of its life. Its childhood coincides with the age of Cato, its old age with that of Trajan and Hadrian, and its prime and vigour about the time of M. Tullius Cicero, not but what there were amongst the other authors who followed him many writers who in their writings included brilliant, polished and elegant, passages, valuable, some for grammar, some for figurative and for rhetorical purposes. But for some reason or other the works which were written in the time of Cicero seem more original and natural, for example, his own works, and those of M. Varro, Caesar, Sallust, Livy, Vitruvius. Afterwards the language became extravagant, and changed towards voluptuousness along with the ways of the state, so that the writings are more like counterfeits and semblances than the earlier ones, and the writers seem rather to want to please, than to teach or to express in words the thoughts of their minds. So, as much care must be taken as possible that the words and phrases used belong to that earlier century. We are not, however, in our lack of knowledge and amidst the difficulties of the Latin language to scorn the works of later writers, Seneca, Quintilian, Pliny, Tacitus and their contemporaries; otherwise we should have to remain dumb, and form no opinion of all the numerous and varied subjects, concerning which we have to speak in the arts and sciences and in the affairs of daily life, hour by hour. The good writers of Latin are not always the most suitable for a grammarian because they have to discuss all kinds of knowledge, with which the student of correct grammar does not profess to concern

**Authors in the Latin language.**

**Progress and decline of the Latin language.**

**Latin authors suited for the student of grammar.**

himself, and the man who pursues one art must not be overwhelmed by those who profess many. The grammarians should make notes from those writers who are busied in the observation of other knowledge and take such extracts as suit their special purpose. From all these authors a Latin lexicon can be collected, which can never be too full or accurate. This should be in two parts, the one containing a list of as many words as possible with a short translation of each, the other more comprehensive with quotations bringing in each word. This will not only make the reader more certain in translating, but will also show how the word ought to be used, which he would perhaps never learn without the example.

**Latin dictionary.**

It is well in a Dictionary to give two parts, the one to show the meaning of the Latin word in the vulgar tongue, the other to give the vulgar word in the Latin, as Antonius Nebrissensis did in our language (Spanish), though his work is not sufficiently comprehensive, and is more useful to beginners than to more advanced students. Let the master take from a dictionary, perfect and flawless in all its parts, whatever words are needed for daily use, so that he may collect those suitable expressions which the boys will want to use. At first easy words will be chosen suited to their age and such as are used in games. Gradually the boy will proceed to the more difficult words needed to describe parts of the house and all its furniture, clothes, food, the weather, horsemanship, temples, the heavens, living creatures, plants, the Deity and the republic. The teacher will spice all these with jokes, witty and pleasant stories, lively historical narratives, with proverbs, parables, apophthegms, and with acute short precepts, sometimes lively, sometimes grave. Thus the pupils will drink in willingly, not only the language, but also wisdom and experience for life as well. There are however certain special technical subjects which need not be undertaken by boys such

**Antony Nebrissensis.**

**Method of teaching the vocabulary.**

as metaphysics, medicine, law, jurisprudence and mathematics. Let the boy leave these to their own departmental specialists, and occupy himself with the commoner things of life such as I have enumerated above, which are limited to no age, condition or profession.

**Which authors should be placed before the pupils.**

Meantime, while we have no dictionary of the kind I have described, the teacher must himself make notes from his reading as far as he can, so as to supply to his pupils a vocabulary that will be useful. Then let him choose easy authors for reading, suited to the capacity of his pupils, such as the fables, which delight boys of the earliest age and prepare them for more serious subjects. Modest and simple little verses, such as the Distichs of Cato, which are elegant and very wise, and those of Michael Varinus, or the short sayings of philosophers, which they may learn by heart. Then should follow the letters of Pliny Caecilius, which are written in good style and have little flowers of speech and turns of expression worthy of imitation, and are therefore serviceable for the courteousness of school pupils. They also treat of matters which learned men have been in the habit of discussing and of writing about; for these reasons teachers have learned these letters by heart, and prefer them, because of their sweetness and style, to even the letters of Cicero, a choice almost criminal. Aegidius Calentius has also written some uncommonly entertaining letters, which vastly delight boys.

**How variety of expression can be furnished.**

For variety and copiousness of words the teacher should expound the first part of Erasmus' *de Copia*, and after having given examples of general rules, then his book on correct pronunciation (*de recta Pronuntiatione in genere*). Figures of speech can be taken from Quintilian or Diomedes, or Mancinellus, or John Despauterius. Peter Mosellanus has also prepared for use a table of figures of speech, which can be hung up on the wall so that it will catch the attention of the pupil as he walks past it, and force itself upon his eyes. The boy may now begin to apply his pen (to Latin writing), at first using what others have written in prose, and he should be allowed great freedom in extracting from Latin authors not only single words, but also phrases and whole sentences; care, however, being taken to see that he fits them in properly with his own. Erasmus' second book of the *de Copia Rerum* may follow. Then general views of history may be given, with divisions into some well-known periods and named like well-known roads, for example from Adam to the Flood, from the Flood to Abraham, from Abraham to Moses. Then to the Trojan War, from this war to the founding of Rome, from that event to the expulsion of the Kings, from that time to the capture of Rome by the Gauls. Then to Alexander of Macedonia, so on to the First Punic War, from that to the Second, and from the Second to the Third. Then to Sulla and Marius and afterwards to the Birth of Christ. From the Year of our Lord to Constantine, then to the Goths, then to the Huns, to Charles the Great; then to the election of the Emperors (Otto I), from that to Gottfried of Bouillon, from him to the invasion of Europe by the Turks, from that to the capture of Byzantium, from that event to the re-taking of Granada, and lastly, from that time to Charles V, under whom we live. The teacher must explain in each period what famous wars were waged, what noteworthy towns were built, and what celebrated men lived. Besides supplying these particulars, he should add a short description of the whole world, of the chief divisions and provinces, and of whatever in each of them is worthy of attention. Pomponius Mela is useful for this purpose.

**How "places" and "times" may be taught.**

Now the pupil can proceed to those purer writers who are most worthy of imitation: since for a long time pupils ought to imitate those writers, who never let down their followers, until they become so accustomed to the best style that they can listen to other writers without danger. Caesar is noticeably the most useful author for daily

**The reading of authors.**

conversation; Cicero[1] says that his style is pure and unspoilt, whilst Quintilian[2] calls it elegant, a quality to the cultivation of which Caesar paid special attention. In addition to Caesar, let the pupil read Cicero's letters to his friends. Those letters which he wrote to Atticus are, however, simpler and more useful for a beginner, with the exception of certain passages, which were partly, purposely so written by Cicero on industry, and partly have been so perverted through ignorance of the times that it is now impossible to restore them.

The plays of Terence were thought to have been written by Scipio Æmilianus[3], or by his friend C. Laelius, who was called the Wise, because of the elegance of their style, and Caesar calls Terence a lover of a pure style. The works ot Plautus are much less pure, for he was an antiquarian, and allowed his slave-characters great licence, while he sought to gain the laughter and applause of the theatre by frowardness of speech and by not too much purity in his ideas. I should like to see cut out of both of these writers all those parts which could taint the minds of boys with vices, to which our natures approach by the encouragement, as it were, of a nod.

Poets.

The reading of the poets is more for the strengthening of the mind and raising it to the stars, and for the cultivation of the ornaments of discourse than for supplying subject-matter for conversation. The comic writers are nearer prose than poetry. The tragic writers come midway between the two. They use many lofty phrases, which are too bombastic for ordinary conversation, but also many phrases which can be applied to ordinary use. Seneca is the only Latin tragedian left to us. I think the early ones were not preserved for us because people thought them rough and crude, and did not value at a high price what they had written. Whilst reading poetry the pupil

1. Comedians.
2. Tragedians.

[1] See Cicero, *de clar. ora.*; *de Oratore*, bk II and III.
[2] Bk X, cap. I, a little before the end.
[3] i.e. Scipio Africanus—as Quintilian says: X, I.

must learn the whole scheme of prosody and the exact and minute quantity of each syllable. Let him also read (*audiet*) Virgil's *Bucolica*. In studying this book there is one warning necessary, which applies to all dramatists who introduce speeches by various characters, and that is, that there are certain words and forms of speech which suit the part of the person speaking, rather than that they are correct. These opinions would have been expressed differently by the writers, if they had put the words in the mouths of other people. This occurs chiefly in the practice of the comic writers and those whose aim is more to amuse the reader than to compose seriously. We see this happens daily in compositions in the vernacular languages. Therefore we must not seek for examples from Plautus to verify the soundness of our Latin, nor from Terence, although he is more sparing of licence in this respect, nor from Theocritus for the Dorian dialect, nor from Virgil in his Eclogues, from which book certain people quoted two verses with much ostentation, wishing to make it appear that they were fine Latinists :

> Dic mihi Dameta cuium pecus? an ne Latinum?
> Non, verum Aegonis: nostri sic rure loquuntur[1].

They either did not know or pretended not to know that Virgil was striving to catch the charm of the country dialect, in which kind of effort Theocritus allowed himself considerable indulgence.

**Which poets should be interpreted.**

Next the teacher should explain some of the Odes of Horace. He should add some Christian poets, the ancient Prudentius, and our modern writer Baptista of Mantua, who is more copious and fluent than free from mistakes. Nor is he sufficiently responsive to the loftiness of his themes. Even in the hymns of Prudentius there is much to be desired in the Latinity.

After these should follow Virgil's *Georgica* and the *Rusticus* of Politianus. Then the pupil should begin to compose verses

[1] Virgil, *Eclogues* III, 1, 2.

himself. The teacher should expound the fables of the *Metamorphoses* of Ovid and the six books of his *Fasti* (since no more have come down to us) for the better knowledge of mythology. Some of Martial's *Epigrammata* may be selected. Let Persius be added, because the ancients thought him well worth reading, as Quintilian[1], Martial and St Jerome bear witness. To these authors should follow the *Aeneid*, Virgil's great work, full of serious and lofty matters, which does not even yield in importance to the *Iliad*[2]. The poem of Lucan has great virility and is most warlike, so that he does not seem to sing of battles, but to fight them before us, and to blow the trumpet, and to describe the weapons with as much fervour as Caesar wielded them; so that his sounds are, as it were, too vast and unrestrained for the ears of some people and they cannot bear to read him.

**The poetic mind.**

But we must not ignore the fact, that poetry is to be relegated "to the leisure hours of life." It is not to be consumed as if it were nourishment, but is to be treated as a spice. I consider that man to have a poetical temperament who possesses great passion, which sometimes raises him above the usual and ordinary state of his nature, and in this elation he conceives lofty and almost heavenly inspirations. Then the sharpness of his mind contemplates and concentrates itself on not only great and animated ideas, but also arranges them and thus causes within his body a harmony, derived from the exaltation of his mind.

**Which historians should be read.**

In history let the pupil become acquainted with some books of Livy and in addition let the teacher lecture upon Valerius Maximus, for this author can contribute many ornamental words and phrases for the painting of eloquence, such as he puts, for instance, at the beginning and at the end of each chapter, though they are perhaps more elegant than sometimes befits the heaviness of his subjects.

[1] Bk X, cap. 1.

[2] Quintilian, bk X, cap. 1.

Lastly, Cicero's *Orations* will hold a place in the boy's studies. In them are found grace, insight, and all the qualities of a good style. The master should pick out which he wants to explain to his pupil, for it is not necessary to read through them all.

Cicero.

From all these works that I have suggested let the pupil learn by heart whatever the instructor directs; but whatever authors may be expounded, some writers who discuss morals ought to be heard twice every week, so as to correct the faults of the hearers, and either to drive them away from students, or to prevent them from making inroads on them and growing up in them.

The master will expound these authors but the pupil, after he has mastered the first elements and can discern more clearly the meaning of the books, should study them privately. In the grammatical art let the scholar then read Thomas Linacre, who revealed many mysteries in the Latin language and recorded them without introducing any irreverence. Then the two Antoniuses, Nebrissensis and Mancinellus. Laurentius Valla affords the chief help in the choice of elegant words. It is true that he is somewhat pedantic in some parts, but he is extremely useful for students. Whenever he says that a certain word is not to be found in any writer, we must rely upon his judgment for the time being, and not use the word until we read it in a writer of indisputable correctness. Add to these authors some of those who explain the ancient writers but only the commentators on those classical authors whom the teacher will explain in detail; as for example Servius Honoratus, or others like him. Cardinal Hadrian Castelleschi is of no small value in the collection of instances, although he is of less use for the purposes of teaching than he should be, as he is too sparing in his exposition of rules. He thought he had done enough in collecting the sayings of the authors, and he timidly refrained from

Private reading.

Linacre.

Valla.

explaining difficulties. Guillaume Budé did a great service for Latin in his two books on the *Pandects* and his five books on Coinage (*de Asse*), and he has rendered most important aid in the study of Latin by his careful investigation of both the subject-matter and vocabulary in both of those works.

**Budaeus.**

The writers of Roman discourse must be diligently studied, for if those ancients, who drank in with their mother's milk the language which we have to acquire, said that they ought to be studied, and that by reading them language was refined and width and fluency in Latin acquired, what do you think we ought to do to whom the language is foreign, and seeing that we have to take it in drop by drop? In history let the pupil read the rest of the books of Livy; his Paduan provincialities, which Asinius Pollio noticed, we do not now perceive, for we have not now such a refined or so scrupulous a taste[1] as he had. Then let the boy read Cornelius Tacitus, who has written indeed certain somewhat difficult passages which are not to be imitated without danger, but he is sublime, bold, and possesses much power[2]. Then follows Sallust, who has borrowed much from the ancients, a fact which was expressed in a popular epigram. Atteius Philologus warned Pollio to avoid the obscurity of Sallust. I wonder, therefore, all the more that he should be given to boys to read. Still to those readers who understand him he is a most pleasant writer, and such readers are never weary of reading his books.

For a knowledge of mythological poetry the pupil has Giovanni Boccaccio, who, although he has borrowed very much from Ovid and from those other authors whom I have mentioned, yet he has reduced the genealogy of the gods to one book, more happily than could have been expected in that century, although he is often too discursive and trivial in his mythological accounts.

[1] See Quintilian, bk I, cap. 9 and bk VIII, cap. I.

[2] Quintilian, bk IV, cap. 2.

The pupils should choose Cato, Varro, Columella, Palladius, who wrote on the country, and Vitruvius, who wrote on architecture, for Latin vocabulary, and imitate them as their guides, for in them very great is the abundance of the most classical and most appropriate names for every possible thing. Cato is an antiquarian, but you will find in him words not to be found in any other writer. Varro is rough and suitable for artificers. Columella is more elegant and exact; so is Palladius, with the exception of certain words and idiomatic twists which belong to his own time, for he wrote in the time of Hadrian. Vitruvius often uses Greek terms, and is at first difficult to understand, even with the help of the illustrations of a certain Jucundus of Verona, because that old style of architecture has gone out of use, so that Budaeus says, not without reason, of Vitruvius, "that it is not every man's business to go to Corinth." To these authors one may add Grapaldus on the House (*de Domo*), not because of his style, but because of his explanation of words. He attempted more than he accomplished, and almost everything is taken from the above-mentioned writers and from Pliny. Where he is uncertain himself, he has left the reader uncertain also. Further, let the [advanced] pupil read all the orations of Cicero and all the declamations of Quintilian.

Authors to be followed by pupils for choice of diction.

Which Latin authors are to be followed.

There are some modern writers who can add something to the pupil's style. Longolius apes Cicero, and so does Jovianus Pontanus, but the latter has less of Ciceronian antiquity than Longolius. Angelus Politianus has great brightness. Erasmus has wonderful fluency and lucidity. Since he is yet living he is to be reckoned more among the modern authors, for he thus is more like us than the ancients who are far removed from us in a certain method of thinking and of morals.

Books for consultation.

The following books should be accessible in a library for reference; Varro's three books on the Latin tongue (*de Lingua Latina*) which are very involved and singular in their style and, on that account, have been spoilt and corrupted by the copyists. The abridgement of Festus Pompeius. Nonius Marcellus. Of the more recent writers, the *Cornucopiae* of Nicolaus Perottus, a book which no one will ever repent spending time in studying if he can find leisure. Nestor, who is not very learned. Tortellius, who is careful in his orthography. Ambrosius Calepinus compiled his dictionary from these writers. He was a very good compiler, but was not good at supplying the deficiencies of others.

# CHAPTER VII

## THE STUDY OF GREEK

Teaching of Greek. When to begin. Order of Study of Authors.

WE have now described the course for instruction in Latin. Afterwards, the beginnings of Greek ought to be brought up to the same level so that the two may proceed together side by side.

**The study of Greek; by what authors it is best promoted.**

Certain Greek tables can be used for the first elements, for instance, those of Aleander or someone like him, from which the pupil can gain a knowledge of the sounds and accents of the syllables. Then he should learn the declensions and the conjugations from the first book of Theodore Gaza, which Erasmus has translated. Then the scholar should translate Aesop's Fables, because the words in them are easy and the sense is suited to that stage. A Greek proverb pointed at the ignorant shows that the Greeks themselves used to begin with Aesop. Let the second book of Gaza be added to these. In it he expatiates with lively emphasis on what he only hinted at in the first book and then turned aside from it. He treats the subject quite in accordance with the manner of Aristotle and with its natural requirements. Then some oration of a pure and easy writer, e.g. of Isocrates or Lucian, should be put into the pupil's hand, provided it is not of a corrupting influence; or a discourse even of John Chrysostom, whose Greek is pure and extremely clear. Syntax was not very carefully sketched by the Greeks, because the language was well spoken for a longer time by the people than was the case with Latin, so that there was less need for scrutiny and rules, and also Greek constructions are highly varied and could scarcely be confined to the channel of the current speech. Theodore presents a good deal of material in the fourth book. John Lascaris has sketched out rules in imitation of Latin, but they are very faulty. Gaza's rules are also very unsuitable for teaching. The chief thing is to note in what ways Greek and Latin differ in their constructions. Now let the pupil begin to translate something to us and to gain a knowledge of the propriety in both languages, and to prepare a good vocabulary. Then he should draw out the ornaments and elegance of Greek discourse and turn them to use in his Latin composition. Let him also learn prosody and orthography, in both of which the Greeks are most clear and unhesitating, although in many cases each writer does as he pleases. Gaza discusses these points in the third book. The Greek language remained untouched and pure longer than ours [i.e. Latin] because it was less exposed to the attacks of the barbarians than the language of the West. Its most flourishing time, and the age in which it came to fruition, was when Athens specially prospered and the whole of Greece flourished; that is, from the tyranny of Pisistratus to the death of Demosthenes. Nothing was written worth reading before Pisistratus, or even before Pericles. A great deal was written after Demosthenes, it is true, but it is scarcely to be compared with the purity of the language in that age. Therefore let the teacher expound a few letters of Demosthenes, Plato and Aristotle, some speech of Demosthenes, and something from those ten orators, whom Athens produced in the same age. A Greek dictionary is still a desideratum. It should be copious and full, such as I have described as desirable in a Latin dictionary. Before the pupil passes on to the poets, let him learn something about the dialects,

**Purity of the Greek language.**

concerning which there is a little work by John Philoponus and another by Corinthus. Then let him hear some rhapsodies of the father of all poets, namely Homer. Then one or other comedy of Aristophanes and some tragedies of Euripides, who are very elegant authors amongst the few Attic writers. Aristophanes is gay whilst Euripides, as Quintilian[1] says, is on a level with the greatest philosophers on account of the deep seriousness of his maxims. The Doric Theognis (he was Sicilian) and the Ionian Phocilydes are also to be recommended for the sake of their precepts.

**Which Greek authors are to be read.**

After these writers the remainder of Homer must be studied. First the pupil must carefully listen to his teacher's explanation and then read it over alone. Many passages must also be learned by heart. Many are the qualities of this great man. It would take too much time and trouble to enumerate them all. In the first place he not only seems to mean what he writes, but also to make it stand out before the reader's eyes[2]. He possesses a great and effective power of presenting pictures, in which beyond controversy he surpasses all later poets. He gives fitting expression not only to the movements of the body but also to those hidden actions of the mind, which the senses do not represent. So that in his poems[3] there seems to be nothing else but a continual reflexion of human life. His sense of common human feeling is so strong, and everything that he says is so much in accord with the actuality of life that, after all these centuries, with their altered customs and habits and changes in the whole way of living, his words, precepts, conversations, speeches etc. are still suitable to our age and for every other. And therefore it happens that he

**The merits of Homer.**

[1] Bk X, chap. I.

[2] See Quintilian, bk I, chap. 13 and bk X, chap. I.

[3] Anaxagoras in Laertius, bk II, says Homer's poem is made up of virtue and justice.

has endured for so long a space of time, and through so many centuries has not only attained the authority of antiquity but also remains as a delight to modern readers, since he preserves the charm of novelty in every portion of his works. Still he has his faults, which we will mention in order that they may be avoided, just as we enumerated his good points, which are to be imitated, if only anyone possesses sufficient fluency and force to do so. Jerome Vida accuses Homer of being too superficial and wordy, and of digressing too much and introducing what is superfluous in his stories. He does not hesitate to prefer Virgil and other Latin writers to him, because they are terser and more restrained. The Greeks are liable to this fault, because they have followed Homer too closely, and sometimes even have outdone him and have become tedious. Nor does Vida like the descriptions of the chariots in the midst of the picture of battle and the invective against Thersites, although the latter is intended to let the reader see what sort of a man had dared to revile the king, whilst the heroes kept silence. He also condemns his humble, and sometimes mean, similes, as when he compares the soldiers to flies in a meal-sack, or Ajax to an ass, which will not leave its pasture although beaten with sticks. Virgil speaks more fittingly, for he compares the armies to ants and bees, which are much nobler insects than flies. Besides it is hardly fitting for Diomedes and Glaucus to converse so idly in the midst of the fight. Many repetitions, such as we also see in the Sacred Writings, seem to belong to that period of history.

**The faults of Homer noted by Jerome Vida.**

**The epithets.**

The same epithets ought not to be repeated everywhere, for Paris calls Menelaus *ἀρηΐφιλος* (i.e. beloved of Ares) just as the Greeks do, and the Trojans call the Achaians *εὐκνήμιδες* (i.e. well-greaved), and in the middle of the single combat Menelaus calls Alexander *θεῖος* (i.e. divine) and at the same time upbraids him as an evil-doer and a violator of hospitality, so that the epithets only seem to be added for the sake of the metre of verse and not for the meaning or for gracefulness. The way in which the work was composed may excuse these faults, for Homer did not compose the whole at one time when he could have weighed everything carefully and eliminated the faulty, but he composed it in separate rhapsodies to be sung for the popular pleasure. These rhapsodies were all collected long afterwards, and arranged by the grammarians at the command, and under the supervision, of Pisistratus of Athens. This may also be the reason why no one ever remembered the descent, or even the native land, of Homer. Now indeed there exist two works by Homer, the one is full of passion (*calidus*), the other full of craft (*callidus*). The two works contain many things which do not serve as good examples for imitation, and whatever he says about the nature of things or the morals of men his too zealous admirers twist into any meaning they wish.

**Homer defended.**

**Pisistratus.**

This however is enough about Homer. If the reader likes he may add for reading what is left us of Aristophanes and Euripides, then the ἔργα καὶ ἡμέραι (i.e. *Works and Days*) of Hesiod and a few Greek epigrams which are witty without being immoral. Lastly let the pupil read Pindar, who is hard to understand and uses a great many unknown out-of-the-way words, and the Academician Archesilaus says that Pindar is especially useful for emphatic speech and for the collection of a good and abundant vocabulary. Theocritus' pastorals in the Doric dialect are very charming, but the allegory must be explained in order to make them more intelligible, just as is the case with Virgil's *Bucolica*, otherwise they are mostly uninteresting to the point of chilling the student.

**Which of the other Greek poets should be read.**

In history the pupil should read Herodian aloud in order to compare him with the translation of Angelus Politianus. He is himself a very clear and easy writer but Politianus has translated him with such charm that

**Herodian. Politian.**

the work seems to have been composed by a Latin writer, not by a Greek. Then add Xenophon's *Hellenica*, for you will find nothing purer and more unaffected on the subject. We would also recommend some of Thucydides' books, though he is indeed a difficult and, so to say, an iron writer.

**What Greek grammarians the pupil should read.**

For the student's own reading, I should recommend the following: the *Dragmata* of Oekolampadius for grammar; Adrianus Amerotius for declensions and conjugations; Urbanus for the knowledge as to poets and literatures. The commentators of these poets, whom I have named, explain many obscure expressions, and there is no poet, who has not got something obscure about him. Homer possesses the best-known commentator of all, Eustathius of Constantinople. Add to him Thomas Magister on *Atticisms*. For its political contents the *Commentarii Graecae linguae* is of the first importance, a work which is most carefully composed, like Budé's Latin works. Many parts were abstruse and he has brought light to these dark and obscure matters. For the writers of the language itself let the pupil study Isocrates carefully, for no one could express himself more simply and purely. Then Xenophon and the ten orators. Lucian's words are well chosen and very clear, but being an Asiatic, his language is drawn up, as if in battle-array and is too rhetorical, whilst his subject-matter is woefully scanty. Let the reader add to these authors the Attic Thucydides, and Herodotus, who, though an Ionian, is still easier. For miscellaneous information let him possess Aristotle's work on *Animals* and Theophrastus' work on *Plants*. Both have been so translated into Latin by Gaza that it is most advantageous to compare the Greek and the Latin of the two books as one reads. For the rest, it is well to read those books with more regard to the expression and style than for the way the subject-matter in them is treated. In Demosthenes, who is to be constantly in the hand, the

**Commentaries of Budaeus.**

**Lucian.**

most complete vigour and charm of diction are to be found, just as I have remarked is the case with the Latin language employed in the orations of Cicero.

**Which Greek works are to be consulted.**

The following books should be kept for reference in the library: a twofold dictionary (Greek-Latin and Latin-Greek); Hesychius for an interpretation of the words of poets, particularly Homer. Julius Pollux provides a variety of expressions and a copious vocabulary, but he is of more value to a learned reader, for he is more serviceable in giving hints to the learned than in his guidance to the unlearned.

# CHAPTER VIII

## CLASSICAL PHILOLOGY

### The Study of Classical Philology.

Authors in the "mixed" languages of Latin and Greek.

THERE are certain writers in both Latin and Greek who include in the same volume history and fables, the explanation of words, orations and philosophy. Their true and appropriate name is that of "philologist." Of this kind we have in Greek Suidas and Athenaeus; in both languages Aulus Gellius, a true rhapsodist, a compiler rather than a composer, more pretentious than his knowledge warrants, full of words without wisdom, and affected in his words and precepts. What he says about the meaning of words is silly, and for the most part is wrong, and displays his ignorance. He may be read, but with a consciousness of the slightness of his value. His imitator, Peter Crinitus, has more intelligence. For philology much can be gathered from the study of St Augustine's *de Civitate Dei* and Erasmus' *Adages*. What is gained from these works will prepare the youth, so that he shall not come to the reading of the great writers quite as a stranger and a novice. The annotations of Budaeus in the *Pandects* and *On Coinage* (which I mentioned before) are of the same kind; also the *Lectiones Antiquae* of Caelius (Rhodiginus), which sometimes shock not only by the antiquity of the subject-matter but also by the archaic language used. The *Saturnalia* of Macrobius contain good and useful matter. Peter Textor has woven only a thin piece of cloth, but it is

Aulus Gellius.

Rhodiginus.

Textor's *Officina*.

sometimes well to consult his *Officina*. His work, however, is confused and not always reliable, for he was a writer quite ignorant of Greek, nor did he possess great skill in Latin, but he deserves some praise for his earnestness.

**Volaterranus.**

Raphael of Volterra, a man of far-reaching learning, should be mentioned here among the others. I do not know whether grammarians would suffer Isidore of Seville to slip into this class. He gives us many facts from antiquity which are not to be despised, especially since the sources from which he acquired his knowledge no longer exist. There remain other writers in both languages whom it will be necessary to get to know, partly in connexion with the various branches of knowledge, on account of the subject-matter they contain, and partly, need only be read by those who are specialists in the subjects of these writers, or such as one takes up when one is tired of higher studies, and can make time for mental recreation.

**Isodorus Hispalensis.**

This is the plan of instruction for eight or nine years, from the seventh to the fifteenth or even sixteenth year, according to the capacity and progress of each pupil. I know that I have lingered long on this subject of language teaching. I have done so because many children are badly instructed in childhood, although so much depends on how the foundations are laid from the beginnings. For all later knowledge and learning pour forth their streams in different directions from these springs.

**Which minds are fitted for reading Greek authors.**

Instruction in languages should go thus far, even for those who are prepared and, as it were, are educated for studying other branches of knowledge, or for those who pursue the philological sciences for their own culture and pleasure, and wish to confine themselves simply to the knowledge of these subjects. For those who are slow-minded and foolish, and who apply themselves to higher studies ineffectively, or are wrongly suspicious of them, who only accept what they hear on its worst side, it will be sufficient if they learn Latin and just a very little Greek, and they should be kept off from reading higher authors. Let them however learn enough of the language to converse with men, otherwise they will become wild and senseless, but it is better to keep them away from the language of the learned lest they should not understand more difficult and less obvious points in the languages, and this should lead to the great injury of themselves and others. Those who are sounder in wit and judgment, but do not want to go further, or cannot conveniently ascend to higher studies, let them be content with a knowledge of the languages and the writers. This knowledge will be of use in life, and such youths will become public secretaries of the city or be employed as inferior public officials, or perform duties in an embassy. These will have, like the previously-mentioned youths, a knowledge of languages, which will serve all for the reading of authors sufficiently for the purpose of lightening the tedium of their old age; some, whenever other occupations will leave them at leisure; others, when they have been taught by a richer experience of life, and all that was bitter in them has been softened down.

**The value of language study for life.**

These then are philologists, and that subject to which they devote themselves is philology. From them should be chosen those who instruct others. I do not wish to confine them within the bounds which I have mentioned, but they may investigate and thoroughly study everything which refers to philology, so long as they refrain from the anxious and vain pedantry of the Greek Scholars, which is exhibited in every work they have written on language, whether they were dealing with separate poems or with the whole body of poetry, or in connexion with oratory or with figures of speech. Let the philologist follow the dictum of M. Fabius Quintilian[1], a very great teacher, that *not* to know some things is to be esteemed a virtue in a grammarian.

**Philologists.**

**The erudition of masters.**

[1] Bk I, chap. 13.

The philologist must read those authors whom I have recommended to other students as counsellors, for special studies must of course be pursued by the philologist, so that he as a single scholar must undertake, as a consequence of his line of study, the labour usually divided amongst many men. Thus there remain for him in grammar, Priscian, Diomedes, Asper, Phocas, Caper and Capella. These writers, it is true, are not well suited to give instruction, but they warn us of many points which the master can turn to his own and to his pupil's use. Likewise the book of Terentianus on prosody and poetry. Among those nearer to our own time, we have Perottus, Sulpitius Verulanus, Curius Lancilotus, Aldus, John Despauterius, who are much more satisfactory than those just named. For Greek there is Herodian and Tryphonius, and the two who brought Greek literature into Italy within the memory of our fathers, Chrysoloras and John Lascaris.

**Grammar—authorities.**

If Latin or Greek authors contain discussions on obscure questions of the higher learning, such as "first philosophy," or the investigation of natural causes, medicine, civil law, or theology, they should be left entirely for the experts in those subjects. If they discuss easier subjects, such as astronomy, cosmography, moral philosophy, practical wisdom, description of nature, or subjects formerly named, so long as they treat of them simply and clearly, I see no reason why these matters should not concern a philologist. If anyone comes to a passage of higher study let him be content to take in as much as he is able, and pass on to other matters, discreetly leaving its explanation to those who have a specialised knowledge of that kind of subject. In this way each profession may retain its honour and its dignity, nor are the bounds of each subject confused, and each subject does not boldly invade the rights and province of the others. In this spirit the philologist must study Seneca, from whom much help can be gained, for the use of various words, their copiousness

**Authors whom grammarians need not read.**

**Seneca.**

and variety, their proper use and meanings. He shows how it is possible to repeat the same thing often without monotony and to express it in various ways, and he is also in respect to the other Latin writers the most dexterous in his use of metaphors.

It is superfluous to say how much Marcus Tullius Cicero can help, since Caius Caesar calls him the father of the copiousness of the Latin language. Laurentius Valla adds Quintilian to Cicero, as a companion or more truly an ally, who without injustice may be compared to him, in the correctness of his expressions, his figures of speech, and in the acuteness of his whole phrasing. Quintus Curtius is clear, but some critics accuse him of being monotonous. Justinus is not so brilliant.

Cicero.

Quintilian.

Curtius.

After these writers everything is more or less dangerous to recommend. Gellius strives after elegance, but shows a great hardness in doing so. Apuleius is altogether unpleasant in his *Ass.* In his other writings he appears human, except in the *Florida*, which is stupid, though the title at all events makes some amends. Macrobius is better than these writers, and clearer. He possesses matter which is not so useful for general conversation as for offering explanations of philosophy. Tertullian speaks very confusedly, as an African would. Cyprian and Arnobius, of the same race, are clearer, but they too are sometimes very African. Augustine has much that is African, but rather in the style of his writings than in his words; this is especially so in the books of the *de Civitate Dei*, which, alone of all his works, I consider ought to be read by the philologist; for the greater part of it is concerned with philology, as I remarked above. St Ambrose[1] is not so much a Latin stylist as a pleasant writer. St Jerome writes better Latin, except when he sometimes

Christian authors in the Latin tongue.

[1] Jerome says on the *Commentaries* on Luke, by Ambrosius, that they had gone to sleep in words, plays, and opinions.

remembers that he is a sacred writer. He is then more solicitous about his subject than about his language. Lactantius is the most eloquent of all the Christian writers. He has almost a Ciceronian sound, and is worthy of imitation except in a few passages. Lastly, there is Boethius, who may be compared to any of the above-named. As regards Symmachus, Sidonius Apollinaris, and Paulinus, I will spare the philologist and let him off the labour of reading them.

# CHAPTER IX

## VIVES' CONTEMPORARIES

The writers who flourished not long before the time of Vives.

FROM the times treated above we have to pass over a long period to reach those writers who lived in the age which immediately preceded us.

Francis Petrarch, little more than two hundred years ago, first opened up the closed libraries and shook the dust and dirt from off the works of the greatest writers. In this respect Latin owes him a very great debt of gratitude. He is not altogether impure, but he could not rise above the filth of his time. John Boccaccio, his pupil, is not to be compared to his master in any detail.

Again there is a long silence until we reach the time of our grandfathers. In that age, Leonard Bruni of Arezzo wrote. He is fairly correct, simple, natural, and sometimes in writing history he seems to me to have caught a certain touch of Livy's style. Laurentius Valla displays conspicuous talent. His use of language is correct and characteristic. What he wrote before the *Elegantiae*—for instance *de Voluptate*—is not so good as what he wrote after it, and so the works which he translated from Greek as an old man are of a better order, e.g. his translations of Thucydides and Herodotus. There is almost nothing left to wish for in the power of expression of Franciscus Philelphus, but still he is sometimes tiresome to read because he lacks motion and vivacity, and this is probably the kind of power which Martial looks for of every book that is to be permanent. Theodore Gaza may enrich our language very much by his translations from the Greek. George of Trebizond is less successful, for though more verbose, his choice of words is smaller. Jovianus Pontanus has taken his language entirely from Cicero. Pomponius Laetus is a man of slight learning; all his fame rests on his painstaking collection of words and some histories, and he applied his industry also to ancient inscriptions and ruined monuments. Campanus is merry and easy, but contains little matter. Hermolaus is hard, he affects a peculiar style composed of very ancient and very newly coined words; for example, he seems to mix Ennius and Plautus with Apuleius and Capella. Politian is very careful in working out his books, his words are good and suited for common use, especially for the use of inferior scholars. He has less weight than I could wish, and while he only produces a few well-sounding expressions, as if he desired to show off his jewels, he leads the reader on by a circuitous route and uses too many words and sentences, and overburdens his work more than is necessary. John Pico has more authority, and is sufficiently restrained, except where he is disputing with the theologians. Antonius Sabellicus flows on full, but sometimes in a muddy way; like the writer from whom he gets his facts he seems to take his colour from whatever soil his river is running through, which often happens to those who are more concerned with their subject than with their style. In our own time we have Erasmus, Budaeus, Melanchthon, Sadolet, Bembo, Franciscus Picus, Andreas Alciatus, and many others who are already great or will soon be considered so. I will say nothing about them, as they are still living; let their descendants speak, since they will be less prejudiced.

Mirandola.

Of the Greek writers, the philologist should read almost all the works of Plato, who, as the Greeks say, speaks the language of Jove; the *Ethica* and *Politica* of Aristotle, in which there is an admirable originality of style; the *Morals* and the *Lives of famous Men* of Plutarch; some works of Galen, for example that on the preservation of health (*de tuenda Valetudine*), together with Linacre's translation. Galen is diffuse and rich in words, of course, since he was an Asiatic, but his language is good and elegant. Philostratus has a flowery and picturesque style, Libanius is clearer and simpler.

Among Christian writers, Synesius is laboured in his style, but full of borrowings of passages more than a little obscure. Basil and Gregory are cultured writers. Chrysostom is clearer and has a greater command of words. He is like Isocrates in his prefaces, and like Lucian and Galen in his text.

**Chrysostom.**

These are the prose writers and, if Pliny the Younger be added to the list, it is as if not one writer merely had been added, but a whole and distinctly sufficient library, so great in him is the wealth of facts and vocabulary. Who then could pass him by, and at the same time dare to call himself a philologist?

**Pliny.**

The poets still are left, along with whom one should read as a kind of antidote, Plutarch's work on the reading of the poets (*de Poetarum Lectione*) and also the work of the great Basil[1] on the reading of the heathen writers (*de Legendis Ethnicis*); it is true the latter is somewhat short but it abounds in piety. The *Ars Poetica* of Aristotle contains little good fruit. It is occupied entirely with the consideration of old poems and with those niceties in which the Greeks are so tiresome, but which one may, with their kind permission, call inept. Palaephatus, an ancient writer, has tried to harmonise the tales of the poets with history, and truly he has done it, not altogether badly, though in some places his conjectures are unconvincing, and in others they are mistaken.

**Greek poets.**

[1] In *Homilia ad Nepotes*.

Horace is musical, lively and, as Quintilian[1] says, bold in his metaphors. Ovid says of him that he sang on the Roman lyre polished poems. In heroic verse he is as it were, a pantomime-dancer. He could not rise to its fulness and dignity. Catullus is, as Pliny[2] says, somewhat hard and requires to be well weeded; not less charming are Tibullus and Propertius, and Ovid, who possesses wonderful ease, and of whom Seneca expresses the regret that he did not provide his Age with good precepts instead of the Art of Love (*Ars Amandi*). Manilius' *Astronomicon* is heavy but learned, though without "movement," as Quintilian[3] says of Aratus, although it sometimes breathes forth with a warmer life. Silius Italicus is careful, but he has to thank art more than nature, in the opinion of Pliny[4]. I do not see what is gained by reading Valerius Flaccus and Apollonius of Rhodes, as though there were not authors over whom the time could be better spent. I do not censure so much the poetic form or diction of their works as the frivolousness of their subject-matter. Juvenal is rough and hard in many places, as his material requires. Statius is soft and sweet. From Martial we must remove the immodest passages, for the rest I would trust the judgment on him of Pliny Caelius.

Long after these writers we come to Ausonius of Gaul, keen and exciting everywhere, a writer who does not allow the reader to fall asleep[5]. Claudianus is better, and is clearly poetical in mind and soul. Juvencus, Sedulius, Prosper, and Paulinus are to be compared to muddy and disturbed rivers, whose waters are nevertheless health-giving, as they say of certain streams. Apollinaris is less disagreeable in his style when he writes in verse than in his prose, for the rhythm either hides or checks his hardness. John Hautuillensis, who was nicknamed "Architrenius" on account of a work he wrote,

[1] Bk x, chap. 1.

[2] See Pliny, *Epistolae*, bk IX, or *Epist.* 229.

[3] Bk x, chap. 1.

[4] See Pliny, *Epist.* 3 at end and 57.

[5] See *Epist.* 61.

is not altogether bad, and is decidedly better than his time. After a long interval there follows Francis Petrarch. If he had not combined great genius with as great study, the age in which he lived would have been sufficient to corrupt his style. Franciscus Philelphus composed too many poems, so that they are frequently felt to be immature.

Jovianus Pontanus is more finished and more worthy to be read. The muse of Politian has much sweetness, much wit, liveliness and elegance, but the shameful epigrams must be expunged, for they are unworthy of a heathen, let alone a Christian. Marullus is less known, and not equal to him in the pleasure which he gives. The two Strozzi, father and son, are fairly polished. Jerome Vida and Actius Sannazarius are committed as though by a sacred oath to the imitation of Virgil. Thomas More is full of keen wit. Erasmus is like Horace, as he would wish to be.

There are other Greek poets, besides those whom I have mentioned: e.g. Quintus Calaber, who added *Paralipomena* to the Homeric epos just as Mapheus Vegius wrote a thirteenth book to the *Aeneid*. Hesiod's *Genealogy of the gods* (*Genealogia Deorum*) is very useful for a comprehension of the poets; beyond that it is very useless. Sophocles wrote tragedies, the worth of which was never lightly esteemed, although Euripides is preferred to him. Aratus wrote the *Phaenomena*, which Cicero and the Emperor Germanicus translated into Latin. We possess Latin and Greek plays by John Lascaris which are rather unintelligible on account of their short and as it were point-like subtlety.

**Expositors.**

The principal expositors are Valerius Probus, of whom there still remains a very little of what he wrote on the *Bucolica* and *Georgica* of Virgil. There is Aelius Donatus, who is well-known because of his explanations of Terence and Virgil. In Terence he imagined himself to be the interpreter of Latin expressions, although he was often unhappy in his explanations, especially in his account of the differences of words. In his conclusions he invented a great deal which never occurred to the minds of the writers themselves. Servius Honoratus is, as everyone will easily believe, a painstaking philologist, but he asserts much that is still open to doubt. Philip Beroaldus has also written some notes on Terence, but he is a man not much more exact than Servius himself. There are many things in Servius besides, which one would rather say at once were false than attempt to prove right by clear argument. Acron and Porphyrio, the expositors of Horace, are far below most modern writers. They often sleep and sometimes even snore as well. Beroaldus and Sabellicus are better commentators on Suetonius. Sabellicus is short. Beroaldus is more diffuse, but also more careless, e.g. in the *Asinus* of Apuleius. Mancinellus has furnished a very good grammatical work on the *Bucolica* and *Georgica* of Virgil. Landinus philosophises too much in his commentaries on Virgil's poetry, in the same way that Petrus Marsus' loquacity on the *Officia* of Cicero becomes almost intolerable. Parrhasius has added many good and accurate philological notes to the *Capture of Proserpina* of Claudianus; Nicolaus Beroaldus in the Notes to the *Countryman* (*Rusticus*) of Politian and Franciscus Sylvius in his Notes to the *Gryphus* of Ausonius present many passages carefully taken from the subject of Philology. If Asconius Paedianus had reached us whole and untouched (would that it were so!) he would have afforded much help in comprehending Cicero and his language. For there are in Cicero not a few very obscure passages, and passages so dark that no light can be thrown upon them now, because of the want of knowledge of the history of the time. Hermolaus Barbarus has given a good deal of the kernel of many matters in his annotations on Pliny and Mela; Angelus Politian in his Notes on the *Centuries*, Budaeus, Alciatus, Sabellicus, Beroaldus and Aegnatius in the common work which they wrote under

**Servius.**

**Beroaldus.**

**Sabellicus.**

**Asconius Paedianus.**

the title of "Annotations on Authors," Ludovicus Caelius, Antonius Nebrissensis in the *Quinquageni*, John Pierius Valerianus has corrected the text of Virgil by comparing different manuscripts, a work which is particularly useful to readers of the great poet. I have no desire to speak of Baptista Pius and Cornelius Vitellius. Posterity may judge of our contemporaries.

# BOOK IV

## HIGHER STUDIES

# CHAPTER I

## LOGIC. NATURE-STUDY

The Study of Language as preparative to further studies. Logic. Text-books. Nature-study. Use and abuse of the study.

**Knowledge of languages.**

So far we have dealt with the knowledge of languages, which are the gates of all sciences and arts, at all events, those languages in which the works of great minds are handed down to us. Thus ignorance of any language shuts the gate to the knowledge which is written, signed and sealed in that language. But let those who study remember, that if nothing is added to their knowledge by the study of the language, they have only arrived at the gates of knowledge, or are still hovering in the entrance hall. Let them remember that it is of no more use to know Latin and Greek, than French or Spanish if the value of the knowledge which can be obtained from the learned languages is left out of the account. And that no language is in itself worth the trouble of learning, if nothing is sought beyond the linguistic aspect. Rather let students gain as much of the language as will enable them to penetrate to those facts and ideas, which are contained in these languages, like beautiful and valuable things are locked up in treasuries.

A method of investigation comes next to the study of languages, a means whereby we can test the true and the false by simple and well-arranged rules. This is called logic. A young man, who has advanced thus far in the study of languages, will easily understand what is put before him. Nor need anything prevent him from considering logic before he has finished his language studies, so that he goes on to the completion of the one whilst making progress in the other. In this art, or rather instrument and organ of art, those definitions are first explained, which are peculiar to it. Thence we pass to simple and compound judgments, and lastly to the rules for proof. This is called the critical dialectic, that is, the science of logical proof. For this purpose there are certain little books by recent writers, which are very helpful, such as those by George of Trebizond, George Valla, and Philip Melanchthon; these should be first explained. Then there is the περὶ ἑρμηνείας of Aristotle, omitting the passages which discuss judgments of future possibilities, as they are very complicated and suited for more mature study at a more advanced stage. The books of Aristotle's *Analytica Priora* contain much that is obscure and, in my opinion, unnecessary. The teacher should choose what is suited to the age of his pupils and to the knowledge which he is imparting. Practice in logic should not arouse a desire for competition, for that is the spirit of the art itself, and if strife is added to strife, what else would that be but throwing oil on a fire, as they say? It would be wiser for the teacher to conduct his pupils' studies by means of questions rather than by wordy arguments, for at this stage the pupils have not usually sufficient material of knowledge about which to argue[1].

**Dialectic.**

*Censura veri.*

**Exposition of terms used in logic.**

**Κριτική.**

*Libri Priorum* **and an estimate of them.**

[1] See last chapters of the *Elenchus* of Aristotle and the *Organon passim.*

Next let them prepare for discussions on other sciences by means of set theses, in order that they may learn by orderly observation to include nothing that is inconsistent and to reject nothing that is consistent. Such exercises we call "obligationes." They are not a branch of knowledge nor any part of one, but the pursuance of rules of logic and their application to a particular case[1]. In these exercises there are only two things to be avoided (which have just been mentioned), namely, not to accept what is inconsistent, and not to reject what is consistent, with what is laid down as basis of the discussion. Socratic questioning is very useful not only for induction but also for sharpening the wits and convincing an opponent, as if bringing out the adversary's meaning, and undermining its weakness through a right use of divisions and definitions.

*Obligationes.*

The youth might read quietly to himself Boethius, Capella, Apuleius and Augustine, although to some extent they introduce Graecisms. Politian has put together some flowers of speech for ostentatious display, which is the only thing he strives after, but still he is useful as he supplies certain technical expressions.

The pupil should know thoroughly the Dialectic of Aristotle. The books of Aristotle have been arranged and quoted by the ancient writers, Tullius Cicero, Laertius Diogenes, Servius Honoratus and others, in a way quite different from that in which they have been divided by the more recent writers, but we, to whom those early writings are unknown, may follow the later authorities.

**The books of Aristotle.**

The Greek expositors of Aristotle are Psellus, Mangenetus, and Ammonius, who overwhelm the readers with empty words, as is almost the custom of the commentators of that race. James Faber wrote on Aristotle and then composed a *Dialectica* himself, in which he drew out as it were from the mud many of the opinions current in his time.

**Expositors of Aristotle.**

[1] See *Parva Logicalia.*

**The knowledge of the things of Nature.**

Next should follow a knowledge of nature. The youth will find this much easier than an abstract subject dealing with the experiences of life, for it can be acquired by the sharpness of the natural senses, whereas an abstract intellectual study requires knowledge in many subjects of life, experience, and a good memory. What we know of nature[1] has been gained partly through the senses, partly through the imagination, though reason has been at hand as a guide to the senses; on this account we have gained knowledge in few subjects and in those sparingly, because of those shadows which envelope and oppress the human mind. For the same reason what knowledge we have gained can only be reckoned as probable and not assumed as absolutely true. There are some men so hard and difficult that they demand a reason for everything, either one which can be given through the senses, or which is indisputable to the mind. Such men were Aristotle and Pliny. They become incredible of the discoveries of others, and unbelieving in matters of religion, and although they are so inexorable to others, they nevertheless often accept on very slight and unsubstantial grounds what they have themselves approved, or adopt the opinions of the one man to whose authority they have once submitted themselves.

Therefore, those who are suspicious, or who twist everything into the worst shape, should be kept back from this study. Nor should those who are weak in religious convictions be introduced to this subject, unless the indisputable axioms of the first philosophy, which extend to a knowledge of the divine, are added to their studies at the same time.

The first precept in the contemplation and discussion of nature, is that since we cannot gain any certain knowledge from it, we must not indulge ourselves too much in examining and inquiring into those things which we can never attain, but that all our studies should be applied to the necessities of life,

[1] "We are as birds," as the author says elsewhere.

to some bodily or mental gain, to the cultivation and increase of reverence. Indeed, with all our care and pains we gain nothing but affliction, as King Solomon wisely said. Nor does such excessive application leave time for any thought of God, and even if a man attempts it, his own investigation, in which he is totally wrapped up, presents itself instead before his eyes. Thus the contemplation of nature is unnecessary and even harmful unless it serves the useful arts of life, or raises us from a knowledge of His works to a knowledge, admiration and love of the Author of these works[1]. Hence everything, which merely serves to stir curiosity, must be cast well on one side, lest the mind, distracted by curiosity, should omit to inquire into the understanding of better things, the knowledge of which is of true and real value to a philosopher. Furthermore, whatever is meant for empty show, and contains nothing solid in itself or which will be useful in the future, is to be despised. The *Suicetica*[2] are of this kind, since they prevent one from paying attention to better things, and what is still more serious, they render one unfit to do so. He is not a philosopher, who talks subtly about that which is impending (*de instantibus*), and about regular and irregular motion (*de motu enormi aut conformi*), but he is one, who knows the origin and nature of plants and animals, and the reasons why, as well as the way in which, natural events happen. The unlearned, silly and godless talk of the Arabian should not be seriously studied. It is not necessary to read closely all the opinions and maxims of the ancient Greeks and Romans, although those of really learned men should be studied. For of what use is it to know that there were men who argued that snow is black and that fire can be cold? Perhaps it is not disadvantageous sometimes to know that such

**Contemplation of Nature must be directed towards the Creator.**

**Arabic lore.**

[1] [For Plato rightly says that Nature is what God wills it to be.]

[2] Rugerus Suicetus was an English Scholastic philosopher, whose speculations became a by-word for inanity and fruitlessness.

things have been argued, but it is in truth too great a waste of time to devote oneself to opposing or defending propositions like those. For this reason I consider that in Aristotle those tiresome disputes, or rather invectives, against the ancient philosophers should be omitted. Besides, Aristotle does not always quote correctly, for he twists the sense or the words, and does not give all the counter arguments. He does not offer valid confutations and he replies to them by answering ideas which are invented by himself; so that it is not worth much to have read those passages. In all natural philosophy, the scholar should be told that what he hears is only thought to be true i.e. so far as the intellect, judgment, experience, and careful study of those who have investigated the matter can ascertain, for it is very seldom that we can affirm anything as absolutely true.

**Description of Nature.**

First we must consider the easiest kinds of knowledge, viz., those things that are evident to the senses. For the senses open up the way to all knowledge. There should be, in the first place, a general explanation, an exposition or, as it were, a picture of the whole of nature, of the heavens, the elements, and those things that are in the heavens, and in the elements, in fire, air, water and earth; so that a full representation and description of the whole earth is included as in a picture. With this object, a short book on the world, as a whole[1], was written by Aristotle, as it is said, though it is not known if he was the real author, or not. The style is more pleasant than one would expect from Aristotle, and it is much clearer than Aristotle usually writes on Nature-subjects, but Justin Martyr and John Picus ascribe this little work to him and, certainly, it sprang from the Peripatetic school. Apuleius translated it as Aristotle's, and called it *Cosmographia*. Some topics, however, must be explained more fully and more carefully, for example, by the *Celestial Sphere* of John Sacroboscus, then George Purbach's

[1] Aristotle's book : *de Mundo*.

*Theory of the Planets* and also the second book of Pliny. Pomponius Mela wrote on geography and hydrography, and Pliny should be further read from his fourth to his seventh book. In these studies there is no disputation necessary; there is nothing needed but the silent contemplation of Nature. The scholars sometimes will rather ask questions than contend or dispute. There are some students little suited for the higher investigation of causes, viz., those who are of sluggish wits, who, so to say, let their heads drop down, because they cannot rise to such topics, or cannot bear the bright light, e.g. the blear-eyed. There are also those students who will not, or through their condition of life, cannot, gain this deeper knowledge. Such students must stop at this point.

**The authors to be read in the sciences.**

Outside the school, let the pupil read privately the *Phaenomena* of Aratus and the *Coelestis Historia* of Julius Hyginus. In the *Astronomicon* of Manilius there is interspersed much Chaldaic superstition and vanity. This book should neither be read without a guide (who will give hints as to the parts to be avoided) nor without much discretion.

The pupil should read Strabo, who wrote a description of the world and gave its history at the same time. Let him also consider the maps of Ptolemy, if he can get a corrected edition. Let him add the discoveries of our (i.e. Spanish) countrymen on the borders of the East and the West. Let him also read Aristotle on *Animals*, and his pupil Theophrastus on *Plants*, and Dioscorides on *Herbs*, together with the commentaries of Marcellus Vergilius, who translated it, and the Corollaries of Hermolaus Barbarus. Then on agriculture let him read Marcus Cato, Varro (*de Re Rustica*), Columella and Palladius, having respect to the subject-matter to be discovered in them, not as before for the vocabulary. Peter Criscentianus, who is little polished in style and expression, knows well how fields and farms should be worked and managed. Oppianus, a countryman of Dioscorides, writes on the fishes of every country. In this part of nature-study, we are extremely ignorant, for Nature has been almost incredibly prodigal in the supply of fishes, and in the naming of them there is similar prodigality. In every region of the sea, on every coast, are found varieties differing in shape and form from one another. Not only do national languages vary in naming them, but also there is a difference in the local names given to fishes by the various towns and cities which are quite near each other, and whose inhabitants speak the same language.

**On fishes.**

Concerning gems, metals, pigments, Pliny has written in his *Natural History.* He has indeed embraced all the subject-matter, which I have just described. Julius Solinus has done the same. Solinus is the little ape, or rather the plunderer of Pliny. Of not less helpfulness in this study is Raphael of Volterra in the third part of his Commentaries which he called *Philologia.* This author deserves high praise for his industry.

**Julius Solinus.**

These books must be read by the student who wishes to get a real hold on this part of studies, and they must be thoroughly and industriously studied. He who would advance still further must study outward nature by close observation, and this will be as it were a pleasant recreation. We look for him to be keen in his observation as well as sedulous and diligent, but he must not be obstinate, arrogant, contentious. There is no need of altercations and quarrels. All that is wanted is a certain power of observation. So will he observe the nature of things in the heavens, in cloudy and in clear weather, in the plains, on the mountains, in the woods. Hence he will seek out, and get to know, many things from those who inhabit those spots. Let him have recourse, for instance, to gardeners, husbandmen, shepherds and hunters, for this is what Pliny and other great authors undoubtedly did. For no one man can possibly make all observations without help in such a multitude and variety of directions. But whether

**Contemplation of Nature.**

he observes anything himself, or hears anyone relating his experience, not only let him keep eyes and ears intent, but his whole mind also, for great and exact concentration is necessary in observing every part of nature, in its seasons, and in the essence and strength of each object of Nature. Such students bring great advantage to husbandry, for the culture of palatable fruits, for foods and for drinks, and in remedies and medicines for the recovery of health. For the well-to-do old man, the pursuit of Nature-study will be a great delectation, and it will be a refreshment of the mind to those who have business affairs of their own, or who conduct affairs of state. For not easily will any other pleasure of the senses be found which can compare with this in magnitude or in permanence, since it stimulates the desire of knowledge, which for every human mind is the keenest of all pleasures. Therefore whilst attention is given to observation of nature, no other recreation need be sought. It is a sauce to appetite. It is in itself a walking-exercise (*deambulatio ipsa*) and a study at one's ease. It is at once school and schoolmaster, for it instantly presents objects which one can look at with admiration, and at the same time a man's culture is advanced by the observation.

**Every blade of grass announces the living God.**

Let us return to the school and teacher.

# CHAPTER II

## DISPUTATIONS AND THE "FIRST PHILOSOPHY"

The "First Philosophy." The Teachers and Scholars suited for the study of this subject. Text-books for class and for private reading.

**The "first" philosophy is that which leads us to God.**

AFTER this short and simple description of facts the hidden workings of nature should be set before those who wish to learn further. This is the "first philosophy," an examination of the connexions of things, and of all the functions which arise naturally from the very essence of any thing. Thence we pass to external causes, as though to the workings of the most secret powers, and from the external causes we rise, provided of course that we keep the right path, to God, the Father and Author of the whole world. For the invisible things of God offer themselves to the eyes of the mind through the things that are made, even His eternal power and Godhead[1]. If we once step aside from the right way we shall continue to err more and more. Accordingly this philosophy is not to be treated rashly or in any way you like, since there is such great danger of making mistakes. We must not examine nature by the poor and bad light of heathen knowledge but by the brilliant torch, which Christ brought into the darkness of the world. With this end in view I have striven to write a work so that we may not have to follow the heathen, to so great an

[1] Romans i. 20.

injury of our religion, or certainly at the risk of inflicting an injury on it. Besides, I thus treat everything more plainly, even if not more accurately.

**Aristotle's books:**
1. *Physica.*
2. *Metaphysica.*

At this point the Aristotelian *Metaphysica* and the eight books *de Auditu Physico*, which belong to the same subject, ought to be studied. They contain much learning and ability as all his works do, but also much that is obscure. His subtleties which are often drawn out to fine distinctions, render blunt and dull the keenest intellect. He has shown an inclination in some matters to ask questions where there was never any occasion to do so, and through his excessive care and attention he has believed himself to have discovered something, and has fancied he has seen something which he never saw, and which never even existed, just like a man who looks for stars on a bright clear day and is then deluded into thinking that he has seen some.

**Aristotle's** *Libri Physicorum.*

The eight books on *Physics* should be read with the pupil very carefully, whether one thinks that they were written by Aristotle himself or whether, as some think, they were collected and published at his suggestion by his son Nicomachus after he had heard Theophrastus, on which account they are called φυσικῆς ἀκροάσεως.

**His** *Metaphysica.*

No less carefully should the first six books of the "first Philosophy" be treated; for the pupil may read to himself the other twelve (or as some people think fourteen) books, and select sentences and precepts which he thinks worthy of remembrance. The rest are very difficult and long, but also very unfruitful, and should only be read carefully and thoroughly by the teacher in order to pick out for himself and his pupil whatever is at all useful. In the fifth book the categories are explained. Here Porphyrius' work on the five categories which sprang from Aristotle should be added, then Boethius' *Method of Definition and Division*, which contains an explanation of essences. Speusippus' little book on the *Definitions of Plato* is well known. From it you can seek examples for every possible kind of definition.

**The kind of teacher needed.**

For all this important investigation we require a careful, temperate teacher, one who is not too presumptuous or hasty in his statements. Nor should he advance otherwise than cautiously, knowing that he is walking in darkness and over slippery ground. This kind of mental discipline calls for the pupil to be one who is progressing and rising above the senses, to causes and first principles, to a generalisation towards the universal from the particular. Knowledge arises out of the general whilst the particular affords us pleasure; the former is of the intellect, the latter of the senses. For this reason Pliny gives most pleasure and Aristotle most instruction. A foolish, trifling mind, is not capable of receiving this instruction, nor is the student who is weak in making right inferences, or one who is quarrelsome and demands a plain and irrefutable reason for everything. This is not always possible in every case, since everyone must be content with that degree of probable truth, which will easily satisfy a sound mind, which is possessed neither by prejudice nor strife, but is eager for the truth. The teacher should connect this and all contemplation of nature with the cultivation of moral character, that he may lead his pupils' minds to virtue, and instil into them a reverence and respect for piety; for which the contemplation of nature offers a most abundant supply of opportunities. Seneca and Plutarch seem to have wished to teach with this aim. Sometimes the same aim also animates Pliny.

**Knowledge of 1. Universals, 2. Particulars.**

**Precepts of first philosophy.**

Certain roundabout ways have to be taken in the introduction to the "first Philosophy." One has constantly to proceed, and then to return whence one started, from *a* to *b* and back from *b* to *a*, because in investigating these matters we do not lead our minds by the things themselves but by our senses, which have many windings. Therefore we must always work to simplify matters to their utmost, so that they may be perceived and known by the senses. Afterwards we can guadually proceed further and bring criticism to bear, after, as far as possible, we have made use of our senses. Names in themselves of natural objects are not adequate for giving knowledge, since the people from whom the ordinary speech emanates, do not grasp the essence, nature, or force of things, and yet it is only from a knowledge of these that right signification of names could be derived. Nevertheless it is not fitting that we should wholly withdraw ourselves from the custom of the mass of the people, and certainly if we attempt to speak with some degree of exactness, the common usage must be made clear that we may not mislead others.

**Names in "first Philosophy."**

Here disputations and a quiet comparison of studies rather than altercation should be directed no longer to victory and self-glory, which used to be permitted to boys, but instead they should be brought to the search for truth. This is the most ample reward of toil. The struggle for truth may be likened to a battle which takes place for the deliverance of truth. But when truth has been released, forthwith arms must be laid down and, as the spears formerly showed their glitter in the contest, they must be lowered before their Empress. Do not be ingenious or count yourself learned against the truth[1]. You will not by your brilliancy overshadow truth itself, but often you may mislead by it the dim-sighted and infirm human intellect of someone else, and even your own intellect. This will not be to the damage of Truth, but it will be to your own hurt and that of others. Therefore keep always the straight road in these matters, and as far as it is possible, let each one follow Truth with his soundest judgment. Put on one side whatever presents itself so as to lead you astray as you thus advance, that is to say, in those doubtful points which will arise from the matter itself.

**Disputations.**

**We cannot do anything against truth, we can only avail in working for it.**

[1] S. Paul in II Corinthians xiii. 8.

Do not, however, desert the broad and royal way, and thus seek the hindrances and stumbling-blocks which lie in the midst of devious by-paths ready to obstruct the passer-by; that is, do not let the keen edge of the mind wander as a stranger through the whole of nature, that it may sweep up gatherings from any part soever, for by this means you may obscure the light of truth both for yourself and for others. Now and again let the philosopher separate himself from conferences with his pupils, so that alone and undisturbed, he may call to remembrance and think over the things he has heard and read. , He will then see more clearly the details and judge them more exactly. This stimulates in no small measure his understanding and his power of judgment. Chrysippus the Stoic used to say, "if I were to exercise my art in the midst of a great number of people I should never be a philosopher."

**Physical Exercises.**

For students at this stage, bodily exercises of a somewhat more strenuous nature should be allowed, i.e. "more strenuous" for the stronger and more fully developed. They need longer and more eager walks, running, leaping, throwing, wrestling. These exercises should be adapted to the school age, and not be of a military nature. The aim should be the renewal of strength in order that the health may be more firmly established in the youthful frame, and that youth may have more bodily alacrity, lest the intellect be weighed down by ill-health. Nay further, these studies require frequent mental recreation, for by their very subtlety and difficulty they greatly tire the intellect. Mental recreations over and above those which serve as physical relaxation will be sought from subjects of the higher studies, e.g. from the reading of poets, of cosmographers, of historians, of both those who deal with natural, and those who treat of civil, history. After showing the picture of nature and an exposition of the inner

**Method of collecting evidence.**

system of nature and the essences of things, there should follow the study of the standards of demonstration, and immediately afterwards the study of the art of collecting arguments and, in the next place, the art of presentation of subject-matter should be studied. For in this way pupils will understand everything in the best order. If these subjects were introduced earlier, the understanding of them would be hindered by ignorance of those things which it is necessary to make use of in observations of this kind, because these materials are taken, partly from the other branches of knowledge, and partly from the current of the experiences of life. But these studies ought not to be postponed longer, since other very great and thorough studies are assisted through their instrumentality. The method of searching out of evidence is one of the two parts of dialectics, the other is the one I have mentioned above, viz. the theory of judgment or the test of truth. Nevertheless I have separated them in treating of instruction, since this course is beneficial to the pupils. Both the arts of Dialectic and Rhetoric are contentious from their very nature, being provocative of strife and obstinacy. On this account, these subjects must be denied to a youth of quarrelsome and contentious disposition, one who is suspiciously inclined towards evil; for such a youth will twist everything to that end. Nay, both of these arts breed very much malice, and for this reason it is not fitting that a malicious mind, and one with any tendency towards acting deceitfully, should be instructed in them. They must not be taught to a bad man, nor to one who is seditious, venal, given to anger, greedy of vengeance; to such an one they would be as "a sword in the hand of a madman" as saith the proverb. Nay, even if they are entrusted, in a moderate manner and for a short time, to anyone, he should sip at them rather than quaff them; for they render students thorny, quarrelsome, deceitful. If it is said that this comes to pass from the fault of those who make bad use of them, that undoubtedly is so. But many others also fall into this fault when the occasion presents itself.

**Parts of Dialectic.**

**Who are not suited for the study of Logic and Rhetoric.**

Here we have need of a most eloquent tutor, and what is still more important, one with a sharp intellect, a sound and unbiassed judgment, versed in all kinds of learning and erudition; one who as a corrector of faults will be exact and keen. Cicero earnestly testified in his *Brutus* that such a teacher is of the greatest good. He tells us that he had such an one in Milo of Rhodes, a man as prudent in marking and censuring mistakes, as in the teaching of Rhetoric. Nothing is of course so difficult as to correct mistakes in speech. It requires observation, first of all, of the mistakes; then to point them out as it were with the finger; then to give the ground of their wrongness; and lastly to correct them. We see often there is something short of the mark without immediately being able to say clearly what it is; as Cicero writes of L. Gellius, and certain other orators.

**The sort of teacher required.**

For study in forming judgments the master will expound at length the *Topica* of Cicero, and will add the commentaries of Boethius, or, as I prefer, the *Dialectica* of Rudolph Agricola, most eloquently and ingeniously expounded in three sections. Let the pupil read several times for himself Cicero and Boethius, for to M. Tullius we owe almost the whole of this art, which was discovered indeed by Aristotle, though what he wrote was only expounded in a slight manner, not nearly enough for those who wish to know the subject thoroughly. Let the pupil also read privately the fifth book of Quintilian and two books *de Inventione* of Cicero, which work he says he completed when a youth. In addition the commentaries of Victorinus should be read. Again and again he will carefully study the eight books of the *Topica* of Aristotle (as indeed all the works of this great philosopher), not so much with a view to refining and adapting this instrument for judging what is credible, but much rather so as to observe the maxims and the precepts upon all matters which are gathered together in that work, and to have them at hand when the subject under consideration

**Cicero's and Aristotle's *Topica*.**

requires it. The master, like a diligent bee, must fly round through all the garden plots of knowledge, and, particularly for his pupils' sake, gather and collect examples which he has observed. However, for the affairs of human life the orators supply abundant material, and the tragic poets abound in illustrations of every kind. The method of treatment in the first place will be as follows: The teacher will ask for, and the scholars will render, an account of what they have had taught them by the teacher. They will add the examples which have been given them or sometimes such as they have found for themselves. Then should follow an examination as to the manner in which great and eminent men discovered their proofs and cases, and what use they made of them in these various passages, and how suitable they are. Then let simple subjects be suggested, and let the pupils consider what subject-matter there is for illustrations in every part, and put them together in a composition in accordance with the rules of the art; as, should a particular man be suggested, or a philosopher, or a chief, or a state, it will be necessary to take a second idea (or if necessary, more) so as to make a comparison. One might for instance make a comparison in the case of the philosopher by adding the idea of his wife[1]. When all these parts are carefully threshed out and the method known thoroughly, a special and (as it were) regular theme (i.e. according to logical rules) may be taken in hand. For this, the arguments for both sides must be thought out, the weight of each should be considered, both separately and also by the method of comparison.

**Like bees on flower-growing mountains, so we extract everything which serves our purpose, etc.**

**Practice and examination.**

[1] *Uxorem*. Some editions read *sutorem*, i.e. a shoemaker.

# CHAPTER III

## THE STUDY OF RHETORIC

On Rhetoric. The opinion is refuted of those who consider this art of eloquent speaking to be as it were perilous and absolutely demanding rejection. What is to be taught in the subject. A description of the writers on Rhetoric, their subject-matter and suggested improvements in them.

**The art of speech must not be despised.**

HEREUPON follows the Art of Rhetoric which, least of all, it becomes good and wise men to abandon or neglect[1]: since it is of the greatest influence and weight. It is necessary for all positions in life. For in man the highest law and government are at the disposal of will. To the will, reason and judgment are assigned as counsellors, and the emotions are its torches. Moreover, the emotions of the mind are enflamed by the sparks of speech. So, too, the reason is impelled and moved by speech. Hence it comes to pass that, in the whole kingdom of the activities of man, speech holds in its possession a mighty strength which it continually manifests. Not undeservingly does Euripides call eloquence τυραννικόν τι. And it is well known that by means of speech some men have won for themselves the most ample resources, power and royal authority, e.g. Pisistratus and Pericles. But it is said on the other hand, that morals

**The power in speech.**

[1] See Aristotle, *Politics*, I, 2.

have deteriorated. Therefore men must not be entrusted with knowledge of a subject like Eloquence which might be used for the injury of others. I have shown above, to what minds I considered that this power should be entrusted and how far it seemed to me the power should be cultivated.

Certainly, the more corrupt men generally are, so much the more ought the good and intelligent men to cultivate carefully the art of Rhetoric, which holds such sway over the mind, so that they may lead others from misdeeds and crimes to, at least, some care for virtue. Its very necessity is manifested from this fact, that no course of life whatever, and no human activity can continue without speech, whether the activity pertain to the state, or to the individual; whether it be at home or abroad; whether amongst friends or enemies; amongst superiors, inferiors, or equals. This is the cause of the greatest of the goods and evils of life. How highly important therefore is it to use becoming and agreeable speech with regard to persons, things, places and times, that nothing may be spoken perversely, childishly or unbecomingly[1]. For the whole treatment of Rhetoric must devote itself to this very purpose. The aim of Rhetoric is not directed to any empty use of words; that they be accounted beautiful and splendid kinds of speech; that they may be elegant and connected by a pleasant style of composition: but that we should not speak impurely and inaccurately and, to put the whole matter shortly, we should speak so that it may be made clear that this most powerful of arts is a part of practical wisdom.

**Its necessity.**

Wherefore indeed in my opinion it will be best if first of all we examine what is the end of Rhetoric, and then proceed to the means and way of teaching. The end of Rhetoric is, for example, to teach, to convince, to rouse. The means are words, simple and compound, and the conceptions in them, which must be

**How Rhetoric should be taught.**

[1] See Epistle of S. James, chap. iii.

disclosed and examined through their qualities considered one by one. Then we shall see in what manner the expressions must be applied to the subject in hand: that is, we ask who or what the subject is, for what purpose and how? Then especially we inquire into the method of teaching, and the parts thereof, viz. convincing, rousing, and their rhetorical forms. We have to consider what is the personality of the speaker and of the listener, and the nature of the particular business in hand, to decide what are the means suitable to produce a particular effect in relation to a particular place and time, having regard to the particular speaker and listener. With regard to these matters, unless I am greatly mistaken, confused and unordered directions, ill-suited for use, were formerly drawn up by our ancestors. Nevertheless much material may be gathered from them by a careful tutor, namely, from the rhetorical books of Cicero, from the *Institutions of Oratory* of Quintilian, from Hermogenes (*de Dictionum Formis*), especially from his fifth book, which deals with forms of oratory, and from George of Trebizond, for the most part the expositor of Hermogenes. Demetrius Phaleraeus also teaches much "concerning the forms of speech" in his book περὶ ἑρμηνείας and Aelius Aristides in his περὶ τοῦ πολιτικοῦ λόγου. For the latter deals with the simple speech as does that of Apsines of Gadara. Dionysius Halicarnasseus undertook the task of handing down certain precepts concerning the kinds of speeches, or of their arguments, according as they concerned panegyrics, epithalamiums, epitaphs and such like. Then (the pupil) will take into his hands, from the Latin writers, the fifth book of Martianus Capella, Rutilius Lupus on the *Figures of Speech*, which work, they say, was translated from Gorgias, not Gorgias Leontinus, but another Gorgias. Julius Ruffinianus and Romanus Aquila have bequeathed to posterity books on the same subject. Sulpitius Victor has written certain precepts

**The end of oration.**

**Instruments.**

**Rhetoricians.**

on the rhetorical art. From all these the teacher himself will pluck, as it were, the blossoms, and arrange a posy to present to his scholars, or he will quote to them extracts from these works when he gives them an account of the old teachers of the art. Should he need at first any easy and short compendium of the art, let him use such as that of Martianus Capella or that of Philip Melanchthon; or the four books of Rhetoric to Herennius[1], ascribed by some writers to Cicero, though I do not understand the grounds of their opinion. It seems more likely that they were taken from the works of Quintilian and put together by Cornificius. Then should be read the five books of Quintilian, namely, the third, fourth, eighth, ninth and tenth, the *Orator* of Cicero, and the *Rhetoric to Theodectes* of Aristotle, a work of great ability and art as is always the case with this author, and one of great utility for aiding sound perception, and wisdom in matters of ordinary life. The youth himself will read for his private study the rest of Quintilian, the *Partitiones* of Cicero addressed to his son, the *de Oratore* and the *Brutus*, the *Rhetorica* (addressed to Alexander) of Aristotle (or whoever may have been the author), and the treatise of George of Trebizond. Since we no longer have a race of people speaking Latin or Greek, it would be very difficult to think out new rules for expressions in those old languages. We must content ourselves with the old ones and with such others as are quite universal, and from their very nature are the same in all languages.

**A theory of linguistics.**

A general account of philology (*ratio linguarum*) should be added; in what manner languages arose, developed and decayed; how the power, nature, riches, elegance, dignity, beauty and other special virtues for discourse of each language should be estimated. Cicero thinks that the precepts of rhetoric should not be too strictly followed, if for no other reason than because, as he says, scarcely any teacher himself has ever been eloquent in the art of rhetoric.

[1] *Rhetorica ad Herennium.*

It seems to me that the same must be said of every instrument of knowledge. Grace of style is not required predominantly for adornment and the achievement of elaborate composition, but that the art should aptly serve for practical use in life.

**Practical exercises in the art of speech.**

I should not wish the "exercises" in the art of speaking to be too laborious and frequent, lest when occasion presents itself, the dangerous instrument should arouse a readiness to wound the feelings of others, and call forth an inclination towards deceit and malice: however, I would have practical exercises more numerous in the beginning than when pupils come to varied and multiform arguments in the form of a theme. At first they will deal with certain somewhat easy and simple subjects which do not greatly require δείνωσις (exuberance) nor much formal arrangement, e.g. fables and short stories, or the expansion of a shortly expressed idea, or the compression of something expressed at length, cases of which will be found very frequently in the reading of authors. Then the teacher can turn to other instructive and, at the same time, pleasing methods. Next the pupil should proceed to matters which involve an opponent in controversy, or which raise a question. Lastly, let the pupils be occupied with subjects stirring the feelings and passions of the mind.

**Common-places.**

In rhetorical subjects of debate (*quaestiones*), in the first place, those themes should be chosen which concern no particular cases, but which are commonplaces and traditionally accepted maxims (*sententiae translatitiae*), as Seneca says, which in and for themselves have nothing to do with a controversy, but which easily lend themselves to application and transference to definite circumstances. Thus, e.g., expressions concerning the chances of fortune, cruelty, and maxims on the passage of time. Portius Latro used to call such expressions the "furniture" (*supellectilem*) of rhetorical exercises. In former times, some writers brought together commonplaces for this very purpose, e.g.

Quintus Hortensius, Protagoras, Prodicus, Thrasymachus of Chalcedon. Youths must have many examples for practice on this point so that they may express their own thoughts and understand those of others. Then follow subjects (*quaestiones*) which include determining "circumstances." These are called *quaestiones definitae.*

**Never to argue against the truth, nor to add to the subject-matter of what is disgraceful.**

Scholars must make it a practice never to speak against the truth, nor on behalf of a topic which rhetoricians call *infamis* (i.e. disreputable), as e.g. against Socrates, or on behalf of Busiris, or on behalf of pleasure as against what is just and honourable, lest they should afterwards do in earnest what previously they expressed as a joke, urged on by some depraved desire of the mind. Let all eloquence stand in full battle array for goodness and piety, against crime and wickedness. Words behind which there is no intention, forthwith fall down broken, and are mere bombast. We deride and scorn what is unfelt and unfitted for the practice of life. Prudence without uprightness is wickedness, and dangerous deceitfulness. Therefore true and genuine rhetoric is the expression of wisdom, which cannot in any way be separated from righteousness and piety. Neither must we imitate those practices which have been in vogue among the heathen, viz. slander, tauntings, the insinuation of the basest suspicions, inversions of what is true, and the attempt to do evil from a good purpose, and to do good from an evil motive. It is better to suffer the loss of the cause for which we fight than to lose our own integrity. We must not imitate whatever is in its essence bad, in wicked people, nor even if we find it in any man, however holy and unblameable he may otherwise be.

**Those things which are bad of themselves cannot by any circumstances become good.**

We need in no wise to cultivate the *Judiciale genus*, i.e. the rhetoric of the judicial Courts, in which, as Aristotle says, there is much wickedness. The nature of this kind of

Rhetoric sufficiently testifies to this. To go to law does not well become a Christian, how much less those evasions, by impostures, snares, deceit, which creep into those unwise legal processes almost, as we might say, against one's will.

Quintilian[1] says "what if a man cannot gain his end and obtain a just request by any other means? What if one cannot recover his toga except by the sword or by poison, is it better to be without the toga, or to recover it by such a means?" I answer: It would be better to lose one's life, not to mention a toga, than so to preserve it.

**Declamation.**

Let young men declaim, before their teachers, on those matters which may afterwards be useful in life: and not as was the habit of the ancients in the philosophical schools, on matters which never occurred in real life. Of this point of practice Quintilian[2] justly complained. Let scholars withdraw into a quiet nook to meditate and write orations; in a spot where no voice, no clattering can be heard; even let it be somewhat dark, lest anything striking their eyes or ears should cut short the reflexions of the mind. It is said that this was the custom of Demosthenes[3]. Scholars themselves will read the "declamations" and "persuasives" which Seneca has gathered from the orators of his day, even those which are distorted and mutilated, for not a few of the Greek passages are wanting, and the Latin ones are most corrupt. Nevertheless they will be of use to the orator; for in them very many arguments are keenly and shrewdly invented, and gracefully and charmingly expressed; and there are many figures of speech and, as it were, "lights" of style in the modes of expression in both vocabulary and precepts. There are extant very prolix διαιρέσεις ζητημάτων (Treatment of Contentious Questions) by the Sophist Sopater, which the

[1] *Institutiones*, bk III.

[2] Bk II, chap. 11; bk III, chap. 10.

[3] See Cicero, *de Finibus* 5; Valerius, bk VIII, chap. 7; Plutarch, *in Demosthenem*; Quint. bk X, chap. 3 etc.

teacher himself should closely examine and, as far as seems good, bring material from the book into the school.

**Pronunciation.** The method of pronunciation must be considered, and that too as not of slight significance, for Demosthenes felt this to be of the greatest importance in oratory. For this reason youths intending to declaim will preserve their voice in pure condition by diet and exercise, but let it be their natural voice, not one simulated and feigned as if the pupil was being trained by a teacher of singing. Each week the tutor will correct one declamation before a gathered assembly. In connexion with it, he will consider first the matter which is spoken of; then who speaks, at what time, to whom he is pretending to speak; then he will examine the words, simple and compound, the sentences, the arguments, the order, and the quality of each one of these by itself. Then he will criticise how far the matter is suited to the subject, to the time, to the place, to the hearer, and the speaker who is being considered. The teacher will not expect that all will be perfectly exact, that the arguments will be thoroughly strong and incontrovertible. He will rather look that there may be no inanities: since in this art nothing is more objectionable than what is unfitting, and the main principle may not unsoundly be said to be "always do what is exactly suitable." You will see what ability, what experience, how much practical wisdom and concentration, are required for the work of correction: wherefore this is the most difficult task of the master. Though so arduous for himself, it is by far the most profitable part of his work for his school. For the hearer gains more insight into learning and power of judgment from a single criticism than from many lectures and expositions. For this purpose scholars should attend in great numbers and with intent minds, and bring with them their writing tablets to take down the headings and most

**Correction of declamations.**

**Fitness must be observed.**

**The usefulness of correction.**

important points. Presently in their own rooms they should write out these notes exactly, and at greater length, and imprint and engrave them upon the tablets of their memory, so that now a particular danger has once been pointed out, it may be for ever avoided. Let the young men know that, on account of the quantity and variety of the bad, by which we are continually assailed on all sides, it is a task of greater judgment and toil to avoid the bad, than to preserve the good.

# CHAPTER IV

## IMITATION

Imitation. What it is, and of what great power imitation is. Who and what are to be imitated. Various indications how each of the ancient writers exercised this power.

ALTHOUGH it is natural to talk, yet all discourse whatsoever belongs to an "art" which was not bestowed upon us at birth, since nature has fashioned man, for the most part, strangely hostile to "art." Since she lets us be born ignorant and absolutely skilless of all arts, we require imitation. Imitation, furthermore, is the fashioning of a certain thing in accordance with a proposed model. Hence models which aid expression must be set forth, the best obtainable, not the best absolutely, but those which are best suited to the present state of progress of the pupil. It is a wise precept of M. Fabius Quintilian that boys should not at first attempt to rise to emulation of their master, lest their strength fail them. An easier and quicker method will be to let them imitate someone more learned than themselves among their fellows, and contending with him let them gradually rise to copying their master himself. We see this plan followed by husbandmen in binding their vines to trees. And just as in man there is seen a certain similarity in body and mind, so is imitation in an oration[1]. In oration, words

Imitation.

[1] See Pliny bk XVII, chap. 23. The similitude is taken from Quint. bk I, chap. 2.

and composition take the place of the body, whilst ideas, arguments, arrangement and economy of matter are, as it were, the mind and spirit of the oration. A son is said to be like his father, not so much in that he recalls his features, his face and form, but because he shows to us his father's manners, his disposition, his talk, his gait, his movements, and as it were his very life, which issues forth in his actions as he goes abroad, from the inner seat of the spirit, and shows his real self to us. If someone could be found who in himself alone combined all excellences most like and most approaching God, or much more if He were God Himself, He would alone be the One who clearly must be imitated; but no man is so excellent in every direction. Wherefore Seneca rightly says "We must not imitate any one man however excellent he may be," because an imitator is never equal to the author imitated. This is in the nature of things: what is imitated always remains behind the original. The more models we have and the less likeness there is between them, the greater is the progress of eloquence. The same opinion is expressed in Quintilian who does not think that "that which is the most worthy of imitation is alone to be imitated."

**No one worthy of all imitation.**

There are those who, out of all authors, select only Cicero[1], whom alone they imitate. Cicero indeed is the best, though he does not contain every merit. Nor is he the only author with good style. When he delights and teaches us he is admirable beyond the rest; shrewd in collecting his arguments, he is not equally dexterous and strong in tracing their connexion and in their arrangement. He is sometimes wanting in power on account of that luxuriant and Asiatic kind of speaking which was noticed in him by certain men of great ability, e.g. by Caelius, Brutus, Atticus, Tacitus and Quintilian. The last-named says that he fought with heavy weights whilst Demosthenes

**The imitation of Cicero.**

[1] See dialogue *de Oratoribus*, ascribed to C. Tacitus.

employed driving force. But these modern imitators regard not so much the mind of the orator in his expression, as the outward appearance of his words and the external form of his style. But everyone is not framed so as to imitate well. For nothing is more chilling than the effort of a man to imitate Cicero, when he is without sufficient heat of feeling and strength of judgment. The whole oration falls flat, and is without motion and life. Such an orator is Jovianus Pontanus. Imitation of Cicero's words is useful and safe; but not of his style; for if anyone cannot achieve success in the attempt he will degenerate into a redundant, nerveless, vulgar and plebeian kind of writer. He may be a very near neighbour of Cicero, but Cicero keeps himself clear from this cheapness of effect and speaks with admirable dignity of speech, with matter drawn from science and from the knowledge of many of the greatest subjects of thought. He has also graceful and charming rhythm with very apt and natural metaphors, antitheses and periods with an inexplicable grace; he is truly inimitable.

But certainly if Cicero is the best and most eminent stylist, others are not, on that account, bad or contemptible. "The countenance of eloquence is not always one and the same," says Tacitus, "nor is that which is different necessarily worse." Cicero himself, in his *Brutus*, places many orators of most diverse kinds in the highest rank. In this respect Cicero and Demosthenes (not to mention others) may be cited as examples.

**The mind follows what is suited to itself, and those authors fitted to its genius.**

For this reason there must be exact observation as to the kind of oratory to which the disposition of the youth is suited (for wise men consider this is to be noted in all the instruction of life), in order that each may apply himself to that to which he is inclined by his natural impulse, provided only he is not disposed to step towards the vicious, but is attached to the virtuous[1]. Thus if he likes copiousness

[1] See bk IV, chap. 2, p. 177 *supra*.

of words let him go to Cicero; if compression of speech, to Demosthenes and the Athenians; if restricted brevity even to the verge of the laconic, to Sallust; for Quintilian testifies that nothing can be more perfect to attentive and cultured minds than this brevity of Sallust. So it will come about that the scholar will reach in this matter of oratory if not the highest pitch, yet a position by no means to be despised: for all, or at any rate the majority, desire rather than expect to gain the highest success, or even the nearest approach to it. Furthermore the subjects to which each is inclined will be recognised by the delight which arises from the harmony between the subject and the power to deal with it. The scholar may make an attempt on his own account, but in his earlier years he should write under the supervision of his teacher; later, as he has made further progress, by himself alone. But if his disposition should lead him into faults, e.g. copiousness of words, to the point of exuberant redundancy; or parsimony of words, to the extent of becoming arid and devoid of force, then the scholar should be led back into a right and sound course by imitation of a different style. Quintilian wisely wishes the gift of the teacher to be this: to assist the good qualities which he may have found in each of his pupils, and, as far as possible, to add those that are lacking, and to help him to amend and change what is inadequate[1].

**The chief authors in every kind of writing worthy of imitation.**

The master will also point out which authors are conspicuous in each kind of style: thus Caesar and the *Epistles* of Cicero will come into the first rank for conversational style; not however, as if Cicero did not equal any author in his selection of words (not to mention any other point), but his diffuse style of writing in his other works is not quite fitting for everyday conversation. The commentaries added to Caesar's work by Hirtius or by Oppius are quite different from Caesar's, and have less purity

[1] See bk I, chap. 2 and bk II, chap. 2.

and majesty in their composition. The books written by Caesar give the impression of being written by a General, whilst the added books show the characteristics we should expect from a civilian. For a bright style we have Plinius Caecilius and Politian. For a diffuse historical style there is Livy. For the unfolding of counsels Tacitus is an example. For commentaries of history, Suetonius and Florus must be named. For precepts of the arts, for scientific expositions, Aristotle. In questions of language or style, Quintilian and Rudolphus Agricola. For paraphrases, Themistius and Erasmus. For epic poetry, Homer and Virgil. For lyric poetry, Pindar and Horace. For tragedy, Euripides and Seneca. For comedy, Aristophanes and Terence. For accurate translation, Theodore Gaza[1]. Politian does his work well, and Erasmus is not without elegance, even to the translation of a single word. But a model of translation to be studied is the book of Cicero, *de Universitate*, which consists of a rendering of a part of the *Timaeus* of Plato. For graceful form in dialogues we have Plato and Cicero. For an astute method of catching one's adversary in the wrong the Socratic inductions should be studied, if they were only more concise than they are as handed down to us by Plato. For effective methods of argument we turn to Aristotle; for such as meet the wants of the ordinary citizen, the dialogues of Cicero and Lactantius are particularly fitted. To encourage to right manners and morals, Cicero is good; to ward off from what is morally bad, read Seneca. Seneca has elegant, sharp and brief sentences which he hurls like thonged darts. For short observations on moral philosophy after the manner of a Commentary, take Plutarch. For harangues to people not thoroughly learned, read Cicero. For school teaching, use the *Declamations* of Quintilian[2] (or whoever else was their author); they are certainly of his period. For an intellectual

[1] See L. Humphrey, *de ratione interpretandi.*

[2] Quintilian's *Declamationes* were imitated by Vives, 1520.

and learned circle, the speeches of Demosthenes are suited. So, too, are those to be found in Livy, in whose histories orations are interwoven. For sweetness and rhythm we have Isocrates. Plato has a still higher flight. Plato, indeed, to quote Aristotle, flows on between prose and verse. But Dicaearchus, the Peripatetic, blames the whole method of Plato's writing as though it were harsh and irksome.

From all these authors, the scholar will choose what is useful to the aims of his work, and he will follow the method of painters, who, from the aspect of fields and plains, transfer all the most pleasing sights on to their own canvas. Not undeservedly is Zeuxis of Heraclea praised by Cicero[1] himself, because in painting Helen, he chose from many very beautiful women of Crotona[2] whatever he saw most charming in each. To attain good imitation there is need of a quick and keen judgment, as well as a certain natural and hidden dexterity. Therefore a true imitation of what is admirable is a proof of the goodness of the natural disposition. For there are some people who, either by the slowness of their judgment, or by the lack of harmony of their nature with the affairs of life, in matters of composition, think that every style is to be referred back to the same model of speech, as if with some one gesture they could imitate every other gesture, or as if, with one movement of the fingers, they could run through the whole oratorical gamut. There are others who, to quote the opinion of Seneca, both understand their own faults and delight in them. Such an error is very great in all studies, but especially in eloquence, the rules of which are not exactly defined for every case. The teacher should observe if the young man imitates a model in a stupid manner. If he does so, he will persuade him from such imitation, and induce him to follow his own bent, so that he may be true to himself

[1] Bk II, *de Inventione*.

[2] Pliny has it that the town was Agrigentum, *Nat. Hist.* bk XXXV, chap. 9.

when another's example will not suit his purpose. In the beginning indeed, as I have suggested before, let the scholar only write on the most easy subjects. For this reason I will permit him to transfer from the model itself into his own work what he cannot render into his own form of expression, only let him not deceive himself. This is not imitation, but pilfering; and in this error, very many are versed. Gradually, however, he will imitate truly, that is to say, he will fashion what he wishes to express according to his model, and yet will not take stealthily patchwork (*centones*) from his model and stitch it into his own work.

How imitation is to be effected.

Still the zealous imitator will study, with the greatest attention, the model he has set up for himself, and will consider by what art, by what method, such and such was achieved by the author, in order that he himself with a similar artifice may accomplish his own intention in his own work. For the art and workmanship, as far as possible, must stand out as they do in the model; in a manner, they will be stolen, but the scholar will not use the same material, nor write so as to steal the author's workmanship. For example, supposing someone intending to thank a certain person were to repeat the same speech as Cicero made to the Senate, or to the Roman people; or such as Ausonius made to Gratianus Augustus, he would indeed be stealing; but it would be imitation, if he were to consider what effect the author aimed at producing in the opening (*exordium*) of his speech, what in the second part, what in the third, and so on in succession: what he says in furtherance of this aim in the first place and what in the following, what opinions he makes use of in each place, what arguments, from what sources they were sought, how collected and connected, what comparisons he introduces, what examples he takes, to what emotions of the mind he appeals, where, how

How imitation may become theft.

What must be closely observed in a model which we have undertaken to follow.

and with what and by whose authority he maintains his arguments. After a study of these points, we do not make use of the same material, but adapt those which stand in the same position to us, as they did to our author. Let the scholar study how the author joined together the more excellent things intended to be committed to posterity, what words bound together single parts, what was the structure of the words.

Then indeed let him copy the same workmanship, but not the same words or conceptions. Let us suggest a short example for illustration. In his *Orator* Cicero states that Carbo, the tribune of the plebs, said these words in a certain speech, when Cicero himself was present: "'O Marcus Drusus, I mean the father; thou wast accustomed to say that the republic was sacred; and whoever should violate it, he should be punished by all. The saying of the father was wise, the rashness of the son has confirmed it': and when this was said a loud shout and applause of the whole assembly followed."

**Example of imitation.**

If someone should imitate that passage thus—"O holy Paul, I mean the native of Tarsus: thou wast accustomed to say that charity was sacred and whoever should violate it, he should be punished by all. The saying of the Apostle was wise, the rashness of the wicked has confirmed it"—this will not be imitation such as if one said "O holy Paul, I mean, Paul of Tarsus, thou wast in the habit of preaching that great was the strength of charity, and that whosoever did not live in accordance with it was no member of Christ's kingdom. The familiarity men have had with what is wicked has disowned this gracious precept of the Apostle."

**1. What cannot be imitated.**

In this imitation there is everything which was felicitously expressed in the previous passage, the same incisive clauses, and the same rhythmical conclusion of the double-trochee (*dichoreus*)[1]. Some

[1] See p. 200 *infra*, the above passages in the Latin.

parts of those passages which are proposed as models can never be completely imitated, owing to the natural genius of the original writer. Such must always be followed, since they cannot be rivalled. None but a madman would attempt it.

**2. What can be imitated.** Others can be attempted on almost all the events which happen to men, and can be rendered again on the same model either in *species* or *genus*, e.g. by imitating copiousness of speech, brevity, splendour, dignity, grace, arguments, order of procedure and the like. Nevertheless there are some human inventions, of which either the art or the practice has altogether perished; with these you will have but poor success. Of this kind are the writings of those authors who lived when the art or practice was flourishing. So it is in the Latin and Greek tongues, since the people who spoke those languages are no longer in existence, we have to ring the changes on the words they left behind; we cannot make new terms or, at any rate, new terms must be very few[1].

**Mode of imitation.** Style is not equally borrowed from them; for when the material has been gathered from any source whatsoever, the scholar should treat it in accordance with his own judgment. Nevertheless the attempt to excel or at least to equal the ancients in adornment and elegance, is not so much bad and blameworthy as dangerous, for fear lest we depart from our own strength and fall into absurdities. Certainly it is difficult for ears now to become accustomed to the judging of the sound of the ancient languages. For this reason, it would be better to write in the vernacular languages, in which the great mass of the people are themselves authorities, teachers, and judges.

**We ought to exercise imitation.** That a boy should imitate is honourable and praiseworthy; that an old man should do so, is servile and disgraceful. It is meet that a boy should have a master and guide, whom he should follow;

[1] Concerning Imitation, see Quintilian.

but not so, an old man. For this reason when you have had sufficient exercise on the racecourse (so to speak) of this imitation, begin to emulate, and to compare yourself with your guide, to see where you can approach nearer to him, and how far you are left in his rear[1]. As a fair and diligent critic, examine his virtues and defects, what is becoming in him, and what is to be accounted faulty, which virtue is easy of reproduction, which is his own particular grace, and if it is incapable of reproduction by others. You will compare these passages with your own, either what is said in them with adequate expression, or otherwise. You will yourself correct your own work, whilst avoiding the mistakes of the model and at the same time you will give your attention to his beauties. Try to attain to his great beauties, and afterwards even to excel them. Certainly this is an absorbing and arduous task, and in it there is need of great industry. But excellence in everything is placed high in front of us, and as the old proverb hath it "the beautiful is difficult of attainment." And not only will you meditate upon your own works in comparison exactly with those of your leader, but you will also compare your own earlier, with your later compositions, so that you may estimate progress from the comparison. The kind of writing, whatever it may be, which you are accustomed to imitate for a long time, however exact and elaborate it may have become, will be regarded by others as your own natural style; as Aristotle tells us was the case with Euripides. For fixed habit in any direction passes over into a state of one's own nature. Wherefore it is sheer foolishness to accustom oneself to vile monstrosities, extravagances of expression, or a roughness of style in oration rather than to an easy, clear, pure, and elegant style, since the labour is equal or even less in the case of what is good.

The subjects of instruction discussed hitherto are the instruments of knowledge, and do not offer the material of

[1] Quintilian, bk I, chap. 2.

knowledge. They have to be applied to other branches of knowledge, by which they form and prepare the minds of those learning them[1]. If such instruments are applied to the needs of the practical life, both public and private, then the scholars so equipped become the governors of states, nay their founders even, and the princes, the judges, and learned in the law. If such studies are directed to theology, the scholars serve as preachers, and as such help to build men up in right practices, and make them morally better. Indeed it becomes a wise man not only to be wise himself, but to fashion others to virtue; and for this reason it is not sufficient that his life be pure, his oratory must also be persuasive. Powerful indeed is the word of truth, most powerful of all, as Paul says, is the word of God[2]. This was sufficient for the apostles, and more than sufficient. For the wonders and the other miraculous acts, which they performed, stood in the place of the strongest arguments, and evinced a strength beyond mere natural strength. They also lived a guileless life, in which even a calumniator could find no grounds for accusation, a life without injury, which it is well said carries the strongest persuasion. And whenever there was need God gave His special help, that help which He giveth to His beloved.

**The whole power of the instruments of knowledge is placed in practice and action.**

But as the manners and morals of speakers and the hearers now are, it is a signal service to truth, if drawn up in battle array, and sustained by the strength of eloquence she may be able to win men's faith. Not but what I should greatly prefer facts of experience which should lead to faith without speech rather than speech deprived and destitute of facts. But undoubtedly facts themselves, clothed and decked with speech, with sober and modest elegance, sink deeper into the minds of the hearers, and do not stumble, as it were, upon the very threshold

**Where eloquence is necessary.**

[1] Aristotle, *de Anima*, 18.

[2] Hebrews iv. 12.

of the ear. And for this reason saintly men have never scorned chaste and pure eloquence, unless indeed those who could not attain to it. Lactantius wished for himself eloquence like that of Cicero, in order to fight more keenly for truth, and to persuade men more readily to it. Eloquence pedantically exact and laboured, remarkable for its picturesqueness, illustrious and glittering with splendour, and fully equipped, perhaps has been far from befitting the presentment of sacred subjects; but on the other hand, language which is base and polluted with errors is much less suitable. It is seemly that sacred matters should be clothed in white and clean linen, not in fine velvet or silk; certainly not in hairy cloth or spotted flax. So much for rhetorical speech.

**Eloquence in divine subjects.**

NOTE. Passage from Cicero: see p. 196 *supra*.

*O M. Druse, patrem appello: tu dicere solebas sacram esse rempublicam: quicunque eam violavissent, poenas esse ei ab omnibus persolutas: patris dictum sapiens, temeritas filii comprobavit.*

The suggested Imitation:

*O dive Paule, Tharsensem appello: tu semper praedicare consuevisti magnas esse vires charitatis, quicunque secundum eum non viverent, nec pertinere ad regnum Christi. Apostoli sententiam piam consuetudo scelerum abdicavit.*

# CHAPTER V

## THE MATHEMATICAL SCIENCES

How many they are, and what is the subject-matter of each. Who are fitted to their study, by what method and through what authors instruction in those subjects should take place.

**The Mathematical Sciences.**

NEXT the young man should be led to the study of the mathematical arts, in order that muteness may succeed talk, and silence may be imposed on a tongue previously busy; wherefore work will be transferred from the ears to the eyes. Mathematics concern themselves with quantity and number. One part is called arithmetic, another geometry, and these are the earliest and simplest mathematics. Geometry raised aloft to the heavens becomes astronomy, or if applied to visible things is called Optics or Perspective. Arithmetic applied to sounds, gave Music. And each of these has two aspects; the one which consists of the contemplative attitude is called theoretical (*speculativus*); the other issues in work and is called practical (*actuosus* or *effectrix*)[1]. From the former the latter takes its source, which is common to all those things connected with practice and exercise in life. For the reflexion of the mind precedes all human actions and handiwork, in the relationship of sire and son. There are some students who give themselves up entirely to the contemplative studies, others

**Geometry.**

[1] As to this division of Arts see Quintilian bk II, chap. 19.

more to the practical. But we, as we have done hitherto, prefer rather to treat concerning the contemplative arts. Yet we shall refer sometimes to their practical aspects.

**The kind of minds fit for these studies.**

The mathematical sciences are particularly disciplinary to flighty and restless intellects which are inclined to slackness, and shrink from or will not support the toil of a continued effort. For they engage these minds and compel them to action, and do not suffer them to wander. Forgetful minds are not suitable for these studies, since the hundreds cannot be known and held if the prime numbers have slipped from memory. In this subject, there is the necessity in what is taught of the idea of series and a perpetual string of proofs. We can thus easily let them slip, unless they are frequently made use of and thoroughly impressed on the mind. Often those students who have no bent for the more agreeable branches of knowledge, are most apt in these severe and crabbed mathematical studies.

Besides, if anyone allows himself to follow up deeply these reflexions and observations, he will be led by them into the infinite: and anxious inquiry into such mathematical problems leads away from the things of life, and estranges men from a perception of what conduces to the common weal. Socrates was so great a mathematician as to be able to shape the work of Euclid of Megara (who was ridiculed by Aristophanes because he gave his attention too little to the practical affairs of life). Yet Socrates[1], wisely, was of opinion that attention ought to be bestowed upon geometry, only so far as will enable everyone to give and receive land according to a just measurement. By this limitation he meant that everything should be referred to its practical use in life and to its effect on the character, and that studies should not draw a man to vain and profitless speculation, and that of a most irksome kind, such as unduly prolonged attention to the subject of mathematics necessarily tends to produce. Let scholars study the elements of mathematics

[1] See Diogenes Laertius, bk II, *in Socratem*.

indeed and even some more advanced work, greater for some, less for others, according to the ability of each pupil, to lead up to their application in the affairs of life and to the better understanding of philosophical subjects. Plato[1] was in the habit of expelling those students who had come to his class-room without any mathematical preparation or who were weak in them. For in his own case and in that of Aristotle, and the rest of the early philosophers, very many of their examples were taken from mathematics, not only because they were most suited, and offered the most certain proof, but also because in their day they were by far the best known.

**Arithmetic.**

Arithmetic should be learned in the first place, since indeed it is the simplest; and for this reason, to be studied first. Practice in this subject and in the treatment of numbers not only tests the understanding, but also sharpens it and makes it keener[2]. No part of life can be devoid of the use of numbers. Writers of sacred and profane history teach many mysteries of Nature and of things divine, to be understood and noted by means of numbers. Certain crass noblemen think it a beautiful and 'if God pleases' a high-born characteristic, not to know how to reckon. The consequence is that to be a man is not considered as high-born, as it is to be a lion, or a bear, or a boar, acording to their own coats of arms[3]. For the whole brute creation is ignorant of calculation; man alone counts. Not that I shall make scorn of [the counting of] money a matter of reproach to our chief men, nor shall I frighten the wealthy from their munificence, but I want all virtues to spring from a knowledge of good, not from an ignorance of evil.

[1] See Plato, *de Republica*, bk VII.

[2] See p. 81 *supra*.

[3] Cf. Erasmus, *de Civilitate Morum Puerilium* (1530) end of Preface: "Let others paint on their escutcheons, lions, eagles, bulls, leopards. Those are the possessors of true nobility who can use on their coats of arms ideas which they have thoroughly learned from the liberal arts."

**Ground and method of learning Arithmetic.**

Let young men know the elements of numbers and their names and shapes. Hence they will become accustomed to add them together, to obtain their sum, then to separate those joined together, to subtract, and to show what the remainder is. But since there are many methods of numbering, e.g. by letters of the alphabet, or by Latin figures, that seems to be the most expedient which, from the name of the inventor (as some suppose) is called Algorismus. I believe that it was an Arabian invention. Then the names of the terms which indicate the quality and the nature of numbers should be added; as e.g. the relations of equal and unequal, prime and composite numbers, and the relations of the numbers amongst themselves, and Arithmetic in its whole inner structure.

**Algorismus.**

**Geometry and the ground for teaching it.**

In Geometry there will be set forth the explanations of all the terms used in the subject. Then those principles which seem to be most in agreement with the constitution of our minds, and which we possess as though they were impressed upon our mind as anticipations (i.e. axioms). Then come theorems and their proofs which (in accordance with what is granted) not merely satisfy us, but also compel us, and take by force our assent. From Geometry are developed optics or perspective, and architecture, and the art of measurement, all of which have great usefulness in ordinary life for protecting our bodies; for from geometry we proceed to all measurement, proportion, movement and position of heavy weights, whether regarded as movable or fixed at the moment, or as immovable. Then follows the study how to measure fields, mountains, towers and buildings. How great comfort does architecture bring to us in our dwellings! How greatly Perspective assists in the observation of pictures! Optics further gives the theory of the mirror: would that a theory of hearing (*auditiva*) had been discovered.

**Acoustics.**

In music we have deteriorated much from the older masters, on account of the dullness of the ear which has utterly lost all discrimination of subtle sounds, so that now we no longer distinguish even the long and short sounds in common speech; and for this reason we have lost some kinds of metres, and that primitive harmony of tones, the effects of which the ancient writers testify were vast and marvellous. Young men should receive theoretical instruction in music, and should also have some practical ability. Only let the pupil practise pure and good music which, after the Pythagorean mode, soothes, recreates, and restores to itself the wearied mind of the student; then let it lead back to tranquillity and tractability all the wild and fierce parts of the student's nature, as it is related in the ancient world, under the guise of stories, that rocks were moved and wild beasts allured by it. So at least we are told in the stories of Orpheus and Amphion.

**Music and what is born from it.**

Astronomy concerns itself with the number, magnitude and motion of the heavens and constellations, in all their aspects, single and in combination. The study of astronomy should not be applied to the divination of the future or to that of hidden things. For this kind of application draws human minds with consummate vanity, and gradually lures them on to impiety. But, instead, Astronomy should be applied to descriptions and determinations of time and seasons, without which rustic toil, on which all life is dependent, could not be carried on; then to the positions of places, showing what is the longitude and latitude of each, and to questions of distance. All this is very useful to cosmography and is absolutely necessary to the general theory of navigation; without this knowledge the sailor would wander in uncertainty amidst the greatest and most grievous dangers. For the determination of the height and declension of the constellations, their nearness to and distance from one another, an astrolabe has to be employed, either a quadrant, as in the

**Astronomy.**

13—2

time of Ptolemy or an *orbiculare* (i.e. a whole circle) as is our own custom.

Mathematical writers, and translators of mathematical works.

James Faber writes suitably enough on both the theory and practice of Arithmetic, in a book adapted for school use, partly drawn up by himself, and partly founded on the works of Jordanus Nemorarius and Boethius Severinus. Similarly, he has made a compendium of Music founded on the last-named author. Nor has he done less for geometry. Further he has written on the sphere, in addition to which book, we have the work of John of Sacroboscus, which is also suitable to be used in class work unless anyone prefers that by Proclus Diadochus. The same Faber composed also *Theorica Planetarum* ("the theory of planets") which his pupil Jodocus Clichtoveus elucidated by commentaries. The outline and foundation of the whole work was taken from Georgius Purbachius. Concerning the use of the astrolabe, Proclus has left some very short writings, but my countryman, Juan Poblacion, is better suited in his exercises for scholars, to which the master will add information gleaned from John Stoflerinus of Justingen and from Ptolemy. For the sound grounding in these subjects, what is said on Mathematics in the *Margarita Philosophica* should at least be consulted in the rudiments of the subject. If the teacher should regard it as too burdensome to lecture on this book himself, then he might at least advise his scholars to peruse it for themselves. Carolus Bovillus has prepared an introduction to geometry and optics, and there is a book on optics by a certain John of Canterbury.

Euclid.

After all these have been mastered, we come to Euclid. I wish him to be very carefully explained. For in his work we find a far more exact treatment of great mathematical questions than in the work of anyone else. In his writings, geometry, arithmetic, mirrors, optics, phenomena of the atmosphere are discussed with great acuteness.

The student will read for himself Martianus Capella, on Mathematics, as well as the Introduction to geography of Raphael of Volterra and the twenty-fifth volume on Philology. Censorinus has much to say on Musical subjects. Petrus Cirvelus has left commentaries on "the Sphere" of John of Sacroboscus. Also Francis of Capua has written upon the same subject, and upon Purbach's *Theory of Planets*.

For these studies in the master and pupil there must be a calm intellect, and to a certain degree they must be steadfast, careful, attentive, intent, and keen upon the work. There is no need of disputations. Short questions and short replies will suffice, or demonstrations and illustrations by drawing. A radius, sand, the abacus—these are sufficient apparatus. This sort of knowledge will easily be forgotten, and he who wishes to retain it, must go over it again, from time to time. He who, for lack of ability or lack of means, cannot further pursue the subject, may here make a halt. He will have procured such help as will be useful in his life, as I have stated above, if he has brought from his study the theory to put into practice and work. He can even then teach others. He will know those authors, whom it is not necessary for those students to study, whose mathematics are only pursued as preparatory to entering on other branches of knowledge. For example, in arithmetic, Cuthbert Tunstall, John Siliceus; in geometry, Thomas Bradwardine; in astronomy, Ptolemy; and in general mathematics, Georgius Valla. There is no doubt that the works of Archimedes are the most accomplished in this kind, works which I myself have not seen. My pupil Juan Vergara directed my attention to them. He read them in Spain, with the greatest possible care, and wrote them out in the night-watches from a secret manuscript. This is the curriculum for a youth up to the twenty-fifth year or thereabouts.

**Mathematical authors.**

**Archimedes.**

# CHAPTER VI

## AUXILIARY, PRACTICAL ARTS AND SCIENCES. KNOWLEDGE OF PRIESTS. MEDICINE

On arts and inventions prepared both as subsidiaries for use and for pleasure in life. Also on the knowledge of priests where especially the investigation *de Anima* is commended. Lastly on the medical art, how it behoves physicians to be instructed in many arts, and which accomplishments they ought to have as adornments if they wish adequately to follow medicine.

**The consideration of inferior arts.**

By this time a man, of age, ability, learning, has become riper in knowledge and experience of things. He should now begin to consider more closely human life and to take an interest in the arts and inventions of men: e.g. in those arts which pertain to eating, clothing, dwelling. In these subjects he will be assisted by the writers on husbandry. Then he should pass on to those subjects which treat of the nature and strength of herbs, and of living animals. Then let him turn to those writers who have treated of architecture, e.g. Vitruvius and Leo Albertus. Next let him consider those arts which belong to travel and conveyance, in which subject the horse, the mule, the ox and all kinds of animal that draw vehicles are to be considered. Next, navigation is to be studied, for that art deals with conveyance. He will study all these subjects; wherefore and how they were invented, pursued, developed, preserved, and how they can be applied to our use and profit.

Already those things have been studied which, through all the senses, conduce to the comforts of life, either in connexion with the private society at home of the husband, the wife, the children, kinsfolk, relatives, attendants, slaves; or those materials which in the affairs of the commonwealth are thought out and discovered for it, by the genius of man, or through folly are given a name, and come into reputation without any real usefulness. All these topics must be included in an encyclopaedic course of knowledge, and in a summarised form. In parts they have been treated by such writers as Plinius, Athenaeus, Aelianus, Macrobius. Cicero says that on these matters old men speak better in their social circles and clubs than the most erudite men in their schools. Pliny makes the same plea in his preface.

**By whom they should be learned.**

Thus, there is no need of the school to teach these subjects, but there is need that the pupil should cultivate a keenness for hearing and knowing about these matters. He should not be ashamed to enter into shops and factories, and to ask questions from craftsmen, and get to know about the details of their work. Formerly, learned men disdained to inquire into those things which it is of such great import to life to know and remember, and many matters were despised and so were left almost unknown to them. This ignorance grew in succeeding centuries up to the present, and in a long succession of years nothing was disclosed concerning the morals and the art of life. So that we know far more of the age of Cicero or Pliny than of that of our grandfathers, in respect of their food, attire, worship and dwellings. I could wish that certain learned men would delight in that custom, as to which I was lately told, of a certain Charles Virulus of Louvain, a man not as learned as he was good; but that was neither for the lack of ability or diligence, but merely of opportunity and time. He was the head of the Lilian Gymnasium at Louvain. And because he had many

**The custom of Carolus Virulus praised.**

boys entrusted to his care, men of different callings in life came to see their sons or their relatives in his school. As it was necessary that the visitors should talk with him, and even, according to the custom of that district, dine with him, he made a point of inquiring, some hours before the time fixed for dining, in what topics any coming guest was best versed. One was perhaps a sailor, another a soldier, another a farmer, another a smith, another a shoemaker, another a baker. In the meantime before their arrival, he would read and meditate upon his visitor's particular kind of work. Then he would come to the table prepared to delight his guest by conversing on matters familiar to him, and he would induce him to talk on his own affairs, and give him information about the most minute and secret mysteries of his art. He would thus hear in the briefest time details which he himself could scarcely have gleaned from the study of many years. So they would leave the table, the guest made quite happy, and the host wiser and better informed. How much wealth of human wisdom is brought to mankind by those who commit to writing what they have gathered on the subjects of each art from the most experienced therein! This will be a pleasant change and recreation of the mind from their studies for the more advanced students, and a relief from the cares of set work; for it is a most honourable occupation and one clearly worthy of a good citizen. By such observation in every walk of life, practical wisdom is increased to an almost incredible degree; those who make such observations should hand them down and let them serve posterity, for whom we ought to care as we do for our own sons. They will add their own judgments in the approbation of virtue and right conduct, manners, and morals, and by briefly and keenly condemning the vices, they will more easily pierce the readers' minds as though they were stings. Let us now return to the school and its classes.

**Reason for learning arts.**

On spiritual matters much that is false amongst ancient writers.

Much that is false has been written by the ancients on spiritual matters, as e.g. by Apuleius and Plutarch in their writings on the *daimon* of Socrates; by Porphyrius, Jamblichus and Michael Psellus; especially since *daimones* have greatly lied as to themselves and as to the angels, partly as the prompting of their own pride, partly from the desire to deceive men, for the devil, as saith the Holy Scripture, is "a liar and the father of lying[1]." When he says the truth, then he speaks from another's perception, but when he speaks lies, it is from his own impulse. So both with reference to angels and demons only few things should be gathered, and those from our own faith and in sober fashion. For an elaborate knowledge of these matters is not necessary to us (nay frequently it is harmful); and therefore on this account, uncertain.

Man's soul.

On the other hand the study (*speculatio*) of man's soul exercises a most helpful influence on all kinds of knowledge, because our knowledge is determined by the intelligence and grasp of our minds, not by the things themselves.

Treatment of the subject of the soul.

This treatment of the development of knowledge within our souls will proceed parallel with the order of nature itself, first the discussion should be of life itself, in general, then of vegetation, sensation, the feelings and the intellect, which may be said to consist of diverse functions, e.g. intelligence, memory, reason and judgment. The teacher will get subject-matter on all these things, best of all from the sacred authors, then from Aristotle, Alexander, Aphrodisaeus, Themistius, Plato, Timaeus and Plotinus. If he wishes to expound Aristotle, as is the custom, he has the three books *de Anima*. He may omit Book I, but let him expound the others: which deal with the senses and the sensations, the memory, sleep and waking, youth and age, sleeplessness and divination through dreams. Let the teacher draw attention to the fact that Aristotle was a

[1] S. John viii. 44.

heathen, point out the dangers of heathendom, and how these may be avoided, and apply immediately the antidotes to these poisons. The students will read for themselves Alexander, Themistius, and Plato's *Timaeus*, and also Timaeus of Locris himself; Proclus, Chalcidius and Marsilius Ficinus will explain the Platonic numbers. The same Marsilius will elucidate Plotinus in his obscure and intricate passages. He divides the study as it were into two parts, so that those go one way who as doctors intend to pursue the health of the body, and they take the other path who wish to heal the mind.

For those who take the former path, let natural history be taught in outlines at this point, without dwelling upon subtle points of the inquiry into the causes of things. At the beginning, however, this aspect should be described to a slight extent until the pupils have grasped with some interest the idea of causation in nature: I mean those changes which are more clearly visible to the senses. No one has written a work on this subject taking in the whole of things, and giving a suitable order for teaching them, but there are scattered passages, e.g. in Aristotle's eight books of Physics which I have mentioned before, four concerning the heavens, two about generation, four of meteors, with passages in the *Problems*; from Alexander's book on *Problems*; from Plato and from Timaeus whom I have mentioned just above: from Apuleius *on the Doctrine* of Plato: from Alcinöus on the same subject *de doctrina Platonis*; from the works of M. Cicero: *de Natura Deorum*, *de Divinatione*, *de Quaestionibus Academicis*. A part of Cicero's *de Universitate* was translated from the *Timaeus* of Plato. Usually Cicero reviews the opinions of others rather than states his own.

The *Quaestiones Naturales* of Seneca are drawn from Peripatetic and Stoic teachings. Plutarch has many such topics of nature knowledge in his *Convivia* in the *Quaestiones Platonici* and others of his shorter works. His four books *de Placitis Philosophorum* as well as Diogenes Laertius in his *Lives of the*

*Philosophers* will serve to show the intelligent student how many kinds of absurd opinions well-known philosophers have held on nature-knowledge. Students will see that they, too, were men, and often held mistaken opinions on matters which are most self-evident. So the studious will become accustomed to give their assent to reason, rather than to human authority. They will not marvel that in the deeper subjects, e.g. in disquisitions on God and religion, there are also errors of the same kind which the wise philosophers with their eyes open used to commit, even in matters of a very simple nature. Such stumbling would not even have happened to the blind, if they were not of the same weak intellect as the philosophers, or unless they were driven out of the right way by the impotence of their minds. Censorinus has left a booklet *de Die Natali*, in which there is some treatment of facts of nature: there are more still in Macrobius, and most of all in Galen. Of more recent authors, not a few facts are to be found in Albertus Magnus (i.e. Grotus), although he ventures to assert some very dangerous views.

The teacher will read thoughtfully all these authors unfolding the secrets of Nature, and by selecting from them, he will put together for his pupils a work supplying the foundations of Nature-study, with such clearness and brevity of method as to enable them to clearly comprehend and grasp the subject. First he will speak of the four material elements, then teach all those topics which come under the heading of perception. Then he will deal with the elements, first in their simple form, then with what is mixed and incomplete. Next come the phenomena engendered in the air, which the Greeks term μετέωρα; then stones; then on all which has life, on life itself, on metals and all mineral bodies; on herbs, fruits, trees, quadrupeds, birds, fish, insects and on man's body. The teacher will not expound by means of narrative, since that task would be unlimited, but rather seek to investigate causes, whence things are derived, how they exist, develop, continue, act, and discharge their own functions; which of them increase and which decrease, fall, perish, dissolve.

It will be in no wise necessary to bring forward the varying opinions of writers; neither will he burden the minds of his pupils with his own weight of learning. He will be content to bring before them what seems to him to be most certainly and strongly established by reason. If he lacks leisure to put together such an account, or if he fails to have the self-confidence to think he is able to do it, let him explain simply the principles of Aristotle, for no other writer is equally useful for pupils.

In Plato there is much learning, but of a recondite kind, with the consequence that, since art is concealed in his works, his writings are not sufficiently obvious to the learners. He is more excellent for learned men, for although in the observation of nature he cannot bear comparison with Aristotle, yet he is superior to that writer in the precepts of morals. Other writers on Nature the pupil will peruse in his private study. In this subject they especially need an instructor with keen insight, but one who will be very cautious, in making definitions, and in forming judgments. The youths will exercise themselves in frequent disputations, but they must not be allowed to dissipate their strength on trifling and petty cavilling. Let them become mellowed with self-control, without arrogance and hatred. Let them not forget that we very rarely attain actual knowledge; or rather we get none, as long as so-called knowledge consists in people's views of it. So there is no reason why anyone should pride himself on his knowledge, or should scorn others for thinking differently, or holding other views than his own.

**Method required in these studies.**

He who is about to pass on, with his gathered knowledge, to the medical art must learn with exactitude the powers and essences of all mineral substances, which are of manifold kinds, viz. pigments, stones, gems, plants, animals, the human body. From this

**Medicine.**

nature-knowledge arise two subjects founded on observation, Dietetics and Medicine proper. Hippocrates, the prince of physicians, did not wish them to be treated as two separate subjects, but as I remarked before[1], as one body of knowledge developed out of two members. When we have acquired a knowledge of the powers and natures of things, and compared together other living beings, especially with the nature and constitution of the human body, we see what is stronger than the interior of the human body could bear, as well as what is too small and weak to strengthen the body, and to sustain it; what substance brings to the body that tone or quality which is alien or inimical to it, and, if it is taken into the body, leads to its great affliction, or pains and sufferings of the most grievous kind. We see, on the other hand, what is congruent and friendly to the life of the body, to its senses, mind, intellect, i.e. what will preserve it, invigour and confirm it in strength, so that there will result a certain joyous sense of health. In this treatment in the first place, what is suitable to the whole race of man, in common, must be considered. Then, the individual man must be studied in particular aspects and relations, e.g. as to age, place, time, activity, manners and habits. Similar observation is necessary with regard to the foods which satisfy his needs.

**Dietetics.**

**Dietetics: its discovery.**

So far the subject of Dietetics holds sway, without which, as Hippocrates teaches, life would be boorish and beast-like, and suffering would assert itself almost every moment. Ignorance on these matters would produce all kinds of violent suffering, nay even the sudden unexpected deaths of many. Perception would be dulled, the life of the mind would be stupefied. Moreover, men would fall miserably into raving madness and insanity. Most people think that this kind of knowledge must have been more difficult to discover than medicine; they are even surprised that it ever was discovered.

[1] See bk I, p. 42 *supra*.

Undoubtedly the first discoveries in it must have been due to divine help, not less in man, than in the mute animals. Else would the greatest part of the races of man have perished, had they been obliged to attain to the "exploration" of Dietetics by their own search.

**Indeed, of divine origin.**

When something has happened to the body, which brings its original and ordinary constitution into disorder, and gives rise to affliction and pain, the hindrance of the normal functions in a particular place, time, age, or in habits of life, health (*valetudo*) is said to be affected and the body is said to be sick. From a due observation the means are discovered to hinder the "sick" state from spreading or gathering strength. Other precautions are taken to drive the sickness away and to sustain the body and thus life may be prolonged. These subjects belong to medicine. Those two arts of Dietetics and Medicine are so much alike, are bound up so closely with one another, that sometimes medicine is thought to be dietetics and *vice versa*. But Dietetics is more simple and universal in its functions, since it only contains general precepts and formulae, whilst the physician goes into details over a case, and proceeds not by precept, but by action. For no art concerns itself as to particular details which are innumerable. Moreover, medicine is peculiar to the particular time of sickness, and to particular people (viz. the sick); whilst Dietetics has reference to all men, and at all times.

**Weak health.**

**Union of medicine and dietetics.**

Let us now treat of medicine. This art has power of life and death over the bodies of men. To it a power is entrusted greater than any King or Emperor has ever possessed. Wherefore God and man demand that the physician himself should perform diligent work; they assert and require that he shall treat as wisely and affectionately as possible, those matters which are assigned to his good faith and authority[1]. How great and disastrous

**Qualifications of the physician.**

[1] See Hippocrates, *de Medici Officio*.

a plague follows, if ignorance is the ally of this authority! What if (as is frequently the case) arrogance is united to this ignorance, and from this conjunction arises frenzy, and the obstinacy of not yielding?

Therefore taking into consideration the discernment necessary in the very important men, who practise this art, it is certain that he is unworthy of the title and profession of doctor, who does not possess all these qualifications: natural qualities, a long period of daily instruction; uprightness of character, devotion, experience. There is need of a diligent disposition and keen attention, of being excellent in diagnosis; prudent, moderate, neither ambitious nor ostentatious. The doctor must not be self-opinionated, but one who is willing to adopt whatever is best in the opinion of another. He will be this sort of man if he has convinced himself that nothing should be first, or dearer, than the life and well-being of a man, so that he may esteem neither his own opinion of himself nor filthy lucre more highly than the man who has committed himself to him for a refuge, as it were, from some deadly evil. This truly is the duty of a good man and a Christian. For if he kills a man through ignorance or invincible obstinacy, how will he later on atone for this injury? How will he render to God an exact counter-balance? If a mistake is made by one theologian it is corrected by another, if a mistake is made by a jurisconsult it is ameliorated through the fairmindedness of the judge, by restitution of the exact amount, or, finally, by a money fine. But who indeed can repair the error of a doctor? When a man has breathed his last, who can supply a remedy? So great is the responsibility, that I wonder that so many are found who do not hesitate to undertake and to enter a profession, perilous to the last degree: but, to be sure, for the most part, they enter upon the profession before they understand how great is the responsibility they are undertaking. This indeed is so great, that many doctors are of the opinion that good fortune

**Good fortune necessary to the physician.**

should be added to the other qualifications of the good doctor, and they think too that prayers ought to be made in order that, after the physician has duly discharged the requirements of the precepts of his art, the undertaking may have a successful issue. We have in our nature great infirmity; in diseases, there is great violence and persistency; in remedies, a weak and slow aid; in the intellects of men, lack of knowledge. Against these foes, always armed and always lying in wait to bring destruction on our head, with what strength must we fight, if we are to prevent them from overwhelming us!

# CHAPTER VII

## THE TRAINING OF THE PHYSICIAN

On the function of physicians: how great it is and how multitudinous a knowledge it demands. It should not be undertaken by every one —even from amongst the learned, and why. In the contemplation of his great art, the doctor surveys the whole outlook of things, so that others seek precepts from him as if from an oracle.

**The order of teaching medicine, and which authors are to be read.**

THE master will start with easy and simple precepts, say, the *Aphorisms* of Hippocrates or with the "*Art*" of Galen, which his pupils will learn thoroughly. Hippocrates is, as it were, the source and father of all: then comes his expounder Galen. These may be followed by Paulus of Aegina, Largus Scribonianus, Celsus, Serenus, Psellus, Nicander, as well as the Arabians; Avicenna, Rasis, Averroes, Mesues. From the early writers Johannes Ruellius has put together quite recently in Latin a book from ancient writers on the *Veterinary Art.* I will say nothing about the order of these writers, since I have not read them with due care and attention, neither have I, so to speak, penetrated into the inner shrines of physicians so as to be able to express a judgment on them. Let this be undertaken by those who happily are well versed in this particular branch of knowledge.

The method of instruction in the medical art, as far as I have pursued it, is this, in the first place, to set forth and examine all parts of the human body, to tell what force each one possesses, what natural disposition, and what proportion and, as it were, harmony exists between them. Thus (we study) those diseases which beset all mankind: those which have not one fixed seat; those which have. What is the origin, seat, growth, progress, effect, result, the marks and traces left, of each one of these. Of what quality and strength is the substance which is beneficial to the body against the disease which afflicts it. Whether the effect is to restrain the body from growing weaker, or to drive the disease from within outward. Then an inquiry must be made as to what this remedy is in its nature. If exactly what is needed cannot be discovered, the next best remedy must be searched for, and what is wanting in it must be made good by another, possessing power which the former does not possess. Amongst these are considered the operations of every kind of natural product; then whatever efficacy is added or removed by the places or times of using them, e.g. as in Italy or in Flanders, in summer or in spring, in inland districts or on the sea-shore, in dry or moist climate. Also directions must be given how it is to be applied in cases of necessity. If the remedy is composed, as is often the case, from many and different things, then the property of each must be indicated and the reason why one is to be added to and mixed with the other; why it assists and supplements, or makes null, or checks, or sharpens the other.

**Disputations.**

Disputations will take place as to the universal rules which are deduced from the various experiments on each substance; nor do I make it my concern to carefully examine those things as to which there is even now a doubt whether they exist. Let rather those substances be regarded which it is quite ascertained are in existence, which are numerous and which will occupy a sufficiently long period, lest students be perplexed by silly investigations pertaining to trifles and the cavils of quarrelling people. With such people a great loss of time ensues, time which ought to be spent on the best and most necessary things.

Threefold exercises in medical training.

The exercises of this art are threefold. First of all, study must be made with regard to the identification of all those things which are usually termed remedies, e.g. minerals, pigments, stones, gems, stocks, animals, and of whatever is found associated with them. And in particular because healing properties useful for all medicines are to be found in plants, these must be constantly observed not once for all, but also at various times and places, in spring, summer, autumn, winter; at sunrise, sunset, and at noonday; under a sky cloudy, rough, wet, dry and calm; in fields, gardens, woods, mountains, and inland places and on sea-coast districts, in hot and in moist climates; for plants receive a great many modifications from all these conditions, in root, leaves, flowers, whether contracted or expanded, whether tinged now with one colour, now with another, so that you would not pronounce them to be the same in autumn, as they were in winter, and not the same in a dry and serene, as in a damp, climate. And not only will these changes modify their appearance but also their properties and strength, nay even it is good to consider the same plant as it appears in its early growth, as it sprouts out, and as it increases, as it approaches full growth and also as it decays: and also as it is found at the apothecary's.

Anatomy.

Students should follow, frequently and assiduously, the dissection of the body (which the Greeks call ἀνατομία), to study whence the veins, the nerves, the bones originate, whither they proceed and whence, what is the size of them, what is their purpose in a living body and what relation there is between them. In the second place, there will be practical training of such a kind that students may visit with some experienced physician, and diligently observe, sick folk, and note how the physician applies the precepts of his art to his practice.

In the third place, when they themselves, alone, put their hand to the work they must note when they succeed, and just as in the case of fruit, we reserve certain specimens for seed, even so in the case of doctors there will be very many, almost all, whom it will be convenient to place, for the period of life that is left to them, in the execution of their profession and in caring for human bodies. On the other hand, there will be others who will abandon medical practice to others, whilst they will engage in the work of medical observation, and lead their life as it were in the very mysteries of the profession. These will be men who, either by reason of their own disposition shrink from the intercourse with their fellow-men, or who have been unable to endure the loathing of the diseases, or who will be unequal to the toil of rushing hither and thither, or who are of too tender a constitution to be able to endure such numerous things as a doctor must experience either by sight or hearing. Lastly there will be those in whom the nature of the art of medicine will be lacking, the art which, in the case of a doctor above all, is to be desired and manifested by the practitioner. But there will be those in whom, besides this endowment of nature, there is also allied keenness of intelligence and strength of discernment, and learning also of a diffuse and wide kind, from which arises indeed a strong love for study, so that not easily even for profit do they permit themselves to be called away from professional investigation. These men, like masters of a craft, will be continually versed in its hidden mysteries: they will instruct others, will write, will be consulted, and besides, they will give some attention to languages, and philosophy, and freely read every class of authors. But I should be unwilling that those who apply the art to the service of the human race, as soon as ever they have dedicated and consecrated themselves, so to speak, to the public service, should transfer their attention more fully to other branches of knowledge or to practise other arts: for there is in this one employment alone, enough and more than enough for them, to occupy their whole life, though it be a protracted and long

**Difference in physicians.**

**Physicians of the first rank.**

one. Therefore let not teachers train one destined to afford practical assistance to health, to read Cicero or Demosthenes, Virgil or Homer: still less to study authors of the art of grammar, neither to study the historians nor even the philosophers: unless it be such as can bring some assistance in the treatment of those who have committed their health to their doctor's care. These subjects must be learned before, and not studied concurrently with, their professional work. To all practices and studies of the literary art he will say "farewell"; his attention will be bent and strained forward to this one art alone. I should be more ready to allow the professor of any other art whatsoever than this, to dabble in other occupations: for this art is so lengthy, wide-reaching and obscure, that scarcely any intellect however well-endowed is sufficient for its full perception, and equal to practising it duly: and how much less then some fraction of an intellect?

**Authors not to be read by the medical man.**

Nevertheless these men will consign their own experiences to literature for the use of posterity. Let the physician clearly recognise, that whatever time he withholds from the study of his art, just so much does he steal and pilfer from the health of his patients. If he has entered on his practice under good auspices, he will esteem nothing more precious than the human body. Wherefore all first experiments, which are full of danger, he will not try upon the human body; it does not promise well to begin his potter's trade on a jar, as the proverb says, but rather set to work on a less valuable material, that is to say, in the physician's case on dumb animals. If it must of necessity be done on a man, let the human bodies at least not be tender and delicate ones which cannot stand the hurt of the surgeon's knife, but those which the strength of the fomentation stirs perchance and shakes, but not such as may prove fatal; so that it may be what the ancients used to call the "Danger of the Carians" (i.e. an apparent danger).

**Medical experimentalists.**

**On what bodies experiments should be made.**

**A proverb of Cicero.**

For the stage when the physician has commenced to visit the sick, copious directions have been given by other doctors what his dress is to be, what his refinement, what care he is to observe and what speech he is to use. In particular Hippocrates of Cos has written short and wise directions. However I will set forth a few instructions somewhat fully according to my custom. First of all, let the doctor take good care of himself and not be in infirm health, and not pallid in countenance, proclaiming by his own face, his own indisposition to the eyes of those whom he meets. And moreover let him not hear quoted with regard to himself that saying from the sacred Gospel, "Physician heal thyself." For what hope will be inspired in a patient by that doctor whose art, it is perceived, is productive of so little good for his own health. Then on account of the fastidious taste of sick people let the doctor be clothed neatly rather than sumptuously. At the first sight of his patient, he will immediately take in his appearance and his constitution, age, and vitality. He will make inquiries concerning former illnesses, his manner of life and usual habits: all this information he will gather in an urbane and affable fashion. Then he will listen with patience and not pant after the glory of long-windedness, and not prophesying as to the course of the case, whilst seeking to find out what is amiss with his patient. Those who in this way attempt to seek this empty whiff of fame, bring serious trouble to, and affect the health of their patients, indeed, even on occasion, cause their death; for, not satisfied with the art of healing they also strive to reveal in themselves a power of divination.

**Essentials in the physician.**

**Physicians should not give themselves too much to divination.**

The good physician in truth will not accept as ascertained beyond doubt whatsoever he hears from the women in attendance (on the patient). He will himself form his own judgment on what they say, even as a man sprinkles his own sauce. The physician will gladly learn from others, nay he will be grateful for advice. Let him gain justness of mind in forming his judgments, lest he allow himself to be overcome by any feelings. He will perceive that he has acted distinctly in accordance with his position if he accomplishes his aims by his own moderation, and not by the mere formal discharge of his necessary duties in an agitated and distraught fashion. Let the doctor who is good and wise believe himself to be as it were an angel, busying himself upon the earth as a giver of health, so that he may copy the gods in the uprightness of his character, and in his disdain of wealth. Let him preserve his hands clean, and his eyes unstained by any impurity. Let him not consider in an inquiring manner, what return for his labour he will obtain from the rich[1]. I, for my part, am often lost in wonderment to see many doctors intent on filthy lucre, since none more clearly understand, and experience, every day how short is life, how fleeting, unstable, and how light, are the causes that snatch away the strongest of men; and accordingly, of how little account is wealth, since the time in which it can be enjoyed is so short and its use so limited. What therefore shall I say of those who prolong sickness from greed of gain? It is impossible to conceive of anything more inhuman. Such ought not merely to be rebuked privately, but rather should be punished by public severity, not less severely indeed than those who are convicted of capital crimes. Why should he who kills a free man be punished, and those be left unpunished who protract illnesses with a sure ruin to their patients' health. But if the kind of illness of body or weakness of mind disinclines the patient to conversation, the physician will transact his inquiries with few and specially prudent words. If the patient can endure talk, he will narrate some anecdote, wittily, pleasantly, suited to the mood of his patient, and to enliven those present without lapsing into any buffoonery. In the beginning he will make attempts to see whether he can heal his patient by a rational mode of living,

**How a physician ought to adapt himself to the sick man.**

[1] See Jerome Cardan, *de Libris Propriis*, pp. 97, 98, 99.

that is by dieting, but if the case demands it, he will use in addition, medicine, yet of a simple sort: but if the force of the malady be rather severe and widespread, he will have recourse to mixtures of medicines. If the case demands that a consultation be held, other medical men must be summoned: he will place before himself not his own reputation, or payment (for what are both of these considerations in comparison with the health of a human life?), but that which is of advantage to the health of the man who has placed his trust in him. He must have a fatherly feeling towards his patient if he wishes to perform his function as a good man. Is there anything which inclines us more to good-will and good action, than the fact that we are trusted? Wherefore let the physician enter into a consultation with the readiness to yield gladly to the opinion of anyone who advises better than he himself. Physicians will not discuss in the presence of patients, and will neither exchange nor discuss views whilst others than themselves are present, for in the conflict of opinions on matters as to which lay-people cannot judge, they know not which side to take. Thence arises easily, a certain despair of themselves, and a hatred against knowledge, which comes to be regarded as a matter of uncertainty.

**Conduct of the physician.**

# BOOK V

## STUDIES AND LIFE

# CHAPTER I

## PRACTICAL WISDOM

On the Practical Wisdom of Life. Its aim and Use. On History and its subject-matter.

We have now traversed the road which leads to a knowledge of the nature of things—and to the knowledge of bodily nurture, and of the antidotes for the diseases which menace men, and the remedies for those illnesses which have actually befallen them. Now we approach that other question: How the soul is to be trained and made sound, so that there may be enlightenment for preventing diseases entering the mind, or if they should enter it, or should have attacked it already, how they may be expelled from it, and a restitution of its soundness be effected by the sovereignty of reason.

**Practical wisdom and its efficacy.**

In the affairs of life, practical wisdom stands at our side, ready to be an ally; in matters of religion, we have piety to teach us who God is, and how it behoves us to act towards Him. This latter kind of knowledge stands alone and has a special claim to the name of Wisdom, but this is not the place to treat of it in detail. So great a subject demands a painstaking treatment, to be solely devoted to it.

Practical wisdom, however, is the skill of accommodating all things of which we make use in life, to their proper places, times, persons, and functions. It is the moderator and rudder in the tempest of the feelings, so that they shall not by their violence run the ship of the whole man on the shallows, or on the rocks, or let it be overwhelmed in the magnitude of the waves. Practical wisdom is born from its parents, judgment and experience. Judgment must be sound and solid, and at times, quick and clear-sighted. Experience is either personal knowledge gained by our own action, or the knowledge acquired by what we have seen, read, heard of, in others. Where either of these sources is lacking a man cannot be practically wise. For in matters which are connected with any practical experience, unless at some time or other you have yourself gone through the experience, however much precepts may be expounded to you, if you never duly seek it yourself, of a surety, when you apply your hand to the work, there will not be much difference between your coming to it quite as a novice, and never having heard of it before. So we find it in arts, such as painting, weaving, sewing. However equipped with theoretical precepts a man may be, if he applies himself to a piece of work without having had the slightest practice, his task will be performed crudely. Similarly practice and experience of themselves, unless guided by judgment, will not profit a man much, for practical wisdom will be lacking, and very often a man will be infirm and useless just at the moment of critical action. For there are many who have experience in variety of affairs, and who have known the manners of numerous nations and races, and yet because they were of sluggish and confused judgment, or rather of a judgment but little in accordance with wisdom and sometimes of none at all, they have gained little by their experiences. On that account wisdom is not to be looked for in youth, nor in young men whilst they lack experience, nor in

It consists in judgment and experience.

Practice and experience;

must be confirmed by judgment.

old men, who are slow, dull, or depraved in judgment. Wherefore we have postponed the treatment of this great theme of the grounds of the development of this power of using experience till after the methods of gaining knowledge in all the arts have been discussed.

**Practical wisdom has a twofold aim.**

The aim, and as it were, the target of practical wisdom is a double one. One part has regard to that "prudence" which brings everything into the service of the lust of the body and its affections, whatsoever either the judgment or experience of affairs has contrived for ingeniously converting into pleasures, honours, wealth, power. This employment of "prudence" is craftiness and astuteness. It is called by our sacred scriptures carnal wisdom, because it is bent on what the flesh lusts after[1]. The second aim is with regard to those things which belong to the improvement of the mind, and the helping of all the actions and thoughts of others, i.e. the consideration how to better our own minds as well as those of others. And, since the former, i.e. carnal wisdom, as the apostle Paul says, is foolishness, we will speak of the latter. Those who are stupid by nature, stolid, inept, and puerile diviners, all these are unfitted for wisdom, because the best part of wisdom consists in the conjectures which we form of future things from the combinations of past events. Practical wisdom is thus a certain kind of divination, as that old maxim declares: Account as best prophet him who has made the best inferences.

**Practical wisdom has something of divination in it.**

*Bene qui coniecerit hunc vatem perhibeto optimum.* But these will not be frivolous wits, such as are indulgent to themselves, for the wisest men are not those who flitter over the superficialities of things, but those who go the deepest into things by a diligence and assiduity such as pleasure-seeking minds cannot enjoin upon themselves. Much less suited still are buffoons, impostors, garrulous and facetious people who make light of

[1] Romans viii.; S. James iii. 15, 17; I Corinthians i. 26, iii. 3.

matters of the highest importance with their festive chatter. They frustrate the great hope of those consulting them on the weightiest affairs with jocular licence, and show themselves inept triflers on grave issues, as was wisely observed by the men of old, "It is easier for a buffoon to be rich than to be a good pater-familias." Also stubborn and contentious men cannot possess much wisdom, as I shall soon show. Men of this kind, since they have no capacity for practical wisdom, i.e. the art of ruling, should rule over none, but should rather be directed by those whom nature has fashioned with a greater capacity for government.

Judgment is cultivated;

1. by reading,

2. by dialectic,

3. by rhetoric,

4. by experience.

Judgment such as is inherent in wisdom, cannot be taught. It can be driven out, or it can be cultivated. Steps can be taken for its cultivation by the reading of those authors who have been most strongly distinguished by this good quality,—Plato, Aristotle, Demosthenes, Cicero, Seneca, Quintilian, Plutarch. Of our Church writers; Origen, Chrysostom, Jerome, Lactantius. So, too, is helpful the study of the instrument of inquiry into truth (logic) by which will be shown what is true in anything, or what is like the truth (i.e. the probable). From this study comes the greatest light into the mind. For the art of right speaking being understood, a great help may be afforded to the judgment, since experience, which is the second part of practical wisdom, brings a very great mass of detail to the power of thinking, as one hand helps the other.

Experience.

We gain our experiences by course of time in the pursuit of practical affairs. What has happened to others, we get to know from the memory of past ages, which is called history. This brings about the state in which we seem to be not less interested in past ages than in our own, and we can continually make use of their experience as well as that of our own times. That Egyptian priest deservedly gave to Solon and the Greeks, who retained no memorials of earlier ages, the name of mere children. Where there is history, children have transferred to them the advantages of old men; where history is absent, old men are as children, since history is, following the definition of that wisest of men, the "spectator of time" and the "light of truth[1]." But apart from this consideration, it is incredible how highly pleasant the study of history is for right living. Its usefulness is also great for all the arts of life. How greatly it delights and refreshes the human soul we see in the old women's fables, to which we listen with close attention and high pleasure, for the sole reason that they bear upon them some appearance of history. Who indeed does not prick up his ears and arouse his mind, if he hears anything told which is unusual, great, admirable, beautiful, strong; a noble deed or saying from those stories, of which histories are so full. There are those to be seen who, on reading or listening to some narration of events, although only fiction, almost die for desire to know all about it. They forget food, drink, and sleep, and overcome their natural desires for these necessaries, so as to reach the conclusion of the history they are reading.

History.

The delight of the study of history.

The usefulness, nay also the necessity, of history is realised in daily life. No one would know anything about his father, or ancestors; no one could know his own rights or those of another or how to maintain them; no one would know how his ancestors came to the country he inhabits; no one's possessions would be certain and valid, were it not for the help of history. What am I to say of the great importance of history for the government of the commonwealth, and the administration of public business? Cicero writes, with respect to L. Lucullus, that he set out from Rome, almost crude in his knowledge of military affairs, and

The vast utility of the study of history.

Cicero *in Lucullo*.

[1] Cicero, *de Oratore*.

that when he had accomplished his whole journey by land and sea, having exercised himself partly in making inquiries from men of experience, partly in the reading of great achievements, he came into Asia so far transformed into a general, that Mithridates, the greatest king after Alexander, recognised him as a greater leader than himself, and than any of whom he had read or seen. Alexander Severus, as we read in Lampridius, was accustomed, in doubtful circumstances, to consult those acquainted with history. Queen Zenobia, through her knowledge of history (indeed she is said to have been a writer of histories) was endowed with more than the ordinary practical wisdom of women. How do we account for the fact that our philosophers have not been suited for ruling cities and peoples, except on the ground of their deficiency in historical knowledge, which is the nurse of practical wisdom? It is true there are those men who persuade themselves that a knowledge of antiquity is useless, because the method of living all over the world is changed, as e.g. in the erection of elegant dwellings, the manner of waging war, of governing people and states. Since this opinion is opposed to the judgment of wise men, it is a strong indication that it is against reason. To be sure, no one can deny that everything has changed, and continues to change, every day, because these changes spring from our volition and industry. But similar changes do not ever take place in the essential nature of human beings, i.e. in the foundations of the affections of the human mind, and the results which they produce on actions and volitions[1]. This fact has far more significance than the raising of such questions as to how the ancients built their houses or how they clothed themselves. For what greater practical wisdom is there than to know how and what the human passions are: how they are roused, how quelled? Further, what influence they have on the commonwealth, what is their power, how they can be restrained, healed, put aside, or on the contrary, aroused and fomented, either in

[1] Aristotle, *Ethics*, II, I.

others or in ourselves? What knowledge can be preferable for the ruler of a state, or more expedient for any of his subjects to know? and what so delightful, in the highest degree! and what more conducive to the happiest kind of practical wisdom! For how much better is it that a man should be warned by the evils which have befallen others, than await the experience of them in his own person? So history serves as the example of what we should follow, and what we should avoid[1]. Even a knowledge of that which has been changed is useful; whether you recall something of the past to guide you in what would be useful in your own case, or whether you apply something, which formerly was managed in such and such a way, and so adapt the same or a similar method, to your own actions, as the case may fit. Indeed, there is nothing of the ancients so worn out by age and so decayed, that it may not in some measure be accommodated to our modes of life. For although now we may employ a different form, the usefulness yet remains. This could easily be shown by discussing customs, one by one. Now the study of those very arts could not even persist if the study of history ceased.

**History is useful to all the arts.**

How often are Hippocrates, Galen and other physicians, historians, when, for instance, they relate the succession of their experiences[2]. So the Medical Art is collected from history, as Pliny, following Varro, asserts. How many kinds of diseases (how and whence derived, augmented, checked, assuaged, removed) are made known by an ancient account? Without knowledge of these, the art of medicine would be defective and would be bereft of a most powerful factor. For out of how many practical experiences on all sides has the art of medicine to be built up, like rain-water composed of drops! In Moral Philosophy, examples are of more avail than precepts; for everyone more willingly and more promptly imitates what he admires. Who

[1] See the *Proem* to Livy's Decades.

[2] See *de Trad. Disc.* bk IV chap. 7 *infra*, and *de Causis Corrupt. Art.* bk II.

is not more quickly drawn to keeping his word by the loyal and magnanimous example of M. Attilius, even in the midst of the most pressing danger, than by twenty treatises on the subject[1]? So, too, we are inflamed with the desire of enduring bravely all things for the glory of Christ rather by the example of martyrs, than by the admonitions of theologians, and we are deterred from crimes rather by the terrible end of malefactors than by the detestation of vice proclaimed by philosophers. I pass by the great number of maxims, proverbs, apophthegms, by means of which the formation of character is so greatly helped—they are all taken, by the way, from history.

**The origin of law is to be found in history.**

The whole of law flows out of history as is shown in the chapter of the jurisconsult Gaius: "On the Origin of Law." In that chapter the position of law is described as being just what the Romans wrote, determined, performed, what the Senate decreed, what the magistrates, according to their power, ordained, what the leaders ordered. But whence do we find out all these things, if not by history? So that Law, whether the Roman or any other Law, is nothing else than that part of history which investigates the customs of any people. In customs is included the intercourse which they have amongst themselves as a people, and their intercourse with other nations.

**History an indispensable advantage in theology.**

And again. How great a part of Theology is a narration of the deeds of the Hebrew people, of Christ, of the Apostles, of martyrs, and lastly, of all the Saints, and of the whole Church? And these both teach, and most strongly incite us to act worthily. I should not like to seem impudent in thus mentioning such highly serious subjects in this connexion, but I know not how otherwise history could be proved to appear more excellent than all studies, since it is the one study which either gives birth to, or nourishes, develops, cultivates all arts.

[1] i.e. Marcus Attilius Regulus. See Cicero, *de Officiis*, bk III.

It does this, not through bitter and troublesome precepts and exercises, but by delectation of the mind, so that you obtain from its study at the same time the most glorious and fruitful knowledge, and a real recreation and refreshment of the mind. In the instruction of children, we have already said, historical instruction should be given, but for this purpose, only what is necessary for a knowledge of an outline of Epochs and the names of distinguished men. But at the stage we are now considering, History must be more closely and more fully studied, because it is better understood by those of riper age, and by those somewhat experienced in the affairs of life. It may then be turned to profit in practical living, by the application of a trained judgment, just as moisture is diffused through the body by natural heat, whence the man is nourished and the whole organism stimulated. But it profits us but little in History, to linger over frivolous and offensive details, the study of which involves great pains and labour, with absolutely no fruit, especially since so great a store of useful knowledge is within our reach. We must listen to the wise teacher, M. Fabius Quintilianus, who speaks in his *Oratorical Institutions*[1] concerning the future orator, thus (we will borrow the words of this wise author which exactly bear upon our present subject):

"The exposition of historical events should be added. This must be done with great care, and not be undertaken as a superfluous labour. It is sufficient that what has been generally accepted, or clearly related, by renowned orators should be expounded; to study whatsoever any contemptible man has once said involves too much fatigue and idle ostentation. It holds back and overwhelms the mind which should be kept open for more valuable knowledge. For he who, in his reading, searches out everything, even unworthy writings, may as well devote himself also to the study of old women's fables."

So says Quintilian. So, for the study of the subject-matter of History, must be prepared a plan of the Epochs. Then

[1] Bk I, chap. 13, bk II, chap. 5 and bk X, chap. 1.

come events and sayings, which may afford some good model, or make us shun an evil example. Wars and battles need not be studied closely, for they merely equip the mind with examples for the performance of evil, and show the ways in which we may inflict injuries, one on another. Yet we cannot help noticing briefly, who took up arms, who were the leaders on either side, where the conflict took place, who were beaten, and what happened to them. But whatever is said or read in history, wars should be regarded not otherwise than as cases of theft, as indeed they usually were, excepting perhaps when undertaken against thieves. But even amongst Christians other causes less justifiable, are only too often the grounds of war. Let the student then give his attention to peaceful affairs, a far more satisfactory and fruitful study, so that he may realise the glory and wisdom which have been gathered from virtuous acts, and the disgrace which has followed on horrid crimes; how joyful have been the deaths of benefactors, how mournful and miserable the deaths of evildoers. Then should be read the sayings and answers of men who have been gifted with wit, wisdom, experience of affairs, especially those sayings known by the Greek word *ἀποφθέγματα*. Attention should also be given to the counsels, which led to actions being undertaken, accomplished, or recorded, of those men especially who have excelled in honesty, wisdom, and the other studies of good arts, such as are the philosophers and, most excellent of all, the saints of our faith, so that we may know not only the results of the temporary excitement of the mind, but also what has been said with the full force of weighty intellect and judgment. It is unworthy to hand over to our memories the historical actions due to our passions, and not also to study what took place as the outcome of the rational judgment.

**What should be noted in the study of history.**

In the first place for History there is necessary a knowledge of places, without which it cannot be understood. But this has already been shown by us elsewhere.

# CHAPTER II

## HISTORICAL STUDIES

What order should be preserved in the study of history and which historical authors have obtained the highest praise, some from some critics, others from others.

**The writers of history.**

THE oldest writers of History were honoured differently by different nations. The Egyptians press on our notice their priests; the Greeks, Cadmus the son of Agenor. But it is much more certain that Abraham of Ur left behind him a history, written earlier than all those writers, and from his account Moses obtained the description of the creation of Heaven and Earth. This history was received by Abraham from the sons of Seth, who, as Josephus observes, recorded with letters on two pillars of brick and stone the beginning of the world as well as the first elements of the chief arts[1]. Hence it appears that History took its rise at once with that of men, because it was thus expedient for the human race. It is well to learn the course of history from the beginning of the world or of a people continuously right through their course to the latest time for, then, all is more rightly understood and more firmly retained than if we read it in disconnected parts, in the same way that in a description of the whole world, land and sea are placed before the eyes at a glance[2]. For thus it is easier to see the face of the world and the arrangement of its parts one by one, and to understand how each is placed.

[1] *Antiquitates Judaicae*, bk 1, chap. 3.

[2] See Polybius, *Histories*, bk 1.

Polybius of Megalopolis likens the history of the whole human race to a complete living being, but separate histories of races he considers are like that living being, torn to pieces, limb by limb, so that looking at its mutilated parts, no one can distinguish its form, beauty, and strength. Therefore we will so join together the limbs of history as to regard them as a connected whole, if not as a single animal, at any rate as a single building, adapted in all its parts to the whole design. Thus we should do as far as the diversity in writers will permit us, by employing the method of chronology, than which nothing is more apt and suitable in the study of history.

**Times are to be distinguished in history.**

At first, an author should be read who weaves together history from the earliest times up to within our own memory, or approximately so, in a connected whole, so that a full historical outline is provided in the form of a summary. Such a writer is Nauclerus, or more copious, pure and laborious than he, and moreover more learned, is Antonius Sabellicus. Paulus Orosius describes the course of history from the foundation of Rome to his own times, giving a suitable summary of historical events. Then the parts of history treated by whole works of authors must be summarised and be put together so as to make a connected whole, which will be a more convenient course than taking them as detached pieces. Moses treats of the Creation of the World in the book which, on this account, is entitled Genesis. On the same subject a book is published under the name of Berosus the Babylonian[1], but it is a fabrication, wonderfully pleasing to unlearned and lazy men. In the same class of books are the *Aequivoca* of Xenophon and the fragments of Archilochus, Cato, Sempronius, and Fabius Pictor, which are gathered together in the same book by Annius of Viterbo. This material he rendered more ridiculous by his own inventions; not but what there is some truth in them, for otherwise the narrative would not have such a face to it, but the body itself

[1] See last [in 1612] edition 1552.

of the history is built up on lies, nor is it the work of the man whose name it falsely bears on the title. The Egyptian Manethon and the Persian Metasthenes are taken out of Eusebius. Next to be studied are Exodus, Numbers, Joshua, and the Judges of Israel. Philo the Alexandrine traced, in outline, history from Adam to the death of Saul. Diodorus Siculus wrote on the period between the Flood which occurred under Ogyges, a King of Boeotia, to his own times, i.e. up to C. Caesar the Dictator, of whom Pliny[1] says (I do not know on what ground) that he was the first amongst the Greeks to degenerate into trickery in historical writing, though, as a matter of fact, there is no greater inventor of tales than himself, only he has given to his work no seductive or high-sounding title but merely calls it *βιβλιοθήκη*.

Greek History up to the beginning of the Olympiads is very fabulous, nor can anyone distinguish between what is true and false[2]. But even the history of the following ages is not free from falsities, although it contains a slightly larger amount of facts. For its study Homer supplies some help in both of his poems, although almost all of him is wrapt round with the fabulous. Dares Phrygius and Dictys Cretensis are the inventions of those who wished to romance about that most renowned war. Dion Prusiensis prattles of the fable that Troy was, after all, not taken. Philostratus in his history corrects the great lies of Homer, by lies still more pronounced. Quintus Calaber added a completion to the Iliad of Homer.

**Books of the canon of the Apocrypha.**

Then the student should proceed to the books of the Kings and the Paralipomena [i.e. the Chronicles], Esther, Tobias, Judith, the Apocrypha. Esdras is divided into four books, the first two of which are recognised as canonical by the Jews, but the latter two are apocryphal.

[1] Pliny in the Preface to divine Vespasianus. Vives, *de Corrupt. Art.* bk II.

[2] Juvenal, *Satires* X, 174; Vives, *de Corrupt. Art.* bk II.

The beginnings of the history of the Romans are obscure, and have reached their posterity in attenuated accounts, because, as Livy says, before the city of Rome was conquered by the Gauls, there was but little experience in writing. There is a work of Josephus directed against Apion, in which he speaks of antiquity in a way that aroused the admiration of St Jerome, who was astounded that a Jew should show such knowledge of Greek culture. Herodotus is called the Father of History, because he was the first to unite elegance and grace of style with power of narration of events[1]. He includes very many fabulous matters, but he is excused by the title of his work. For he calls it *The Muses*, by which he indicated that some of the topics were treated somewhat freely. For this freedom is permissible to the Muses, so that the attention of readers may be enchained the more pleasantly. The severity of dry facts, which must occasionally happen in historical accounts, would not secure this result. With more conscientiousness, Thucydides of Athens gives his record of the Peloponnesian War. Then follow: History of Xenophon, the Paralipomena, the Laws of Lycurgus, the *Anabasis* of the younger Cyrus. For the παιδία of the elder Cyrus is an account of the education of that prince, not his history. Aemilius Probus has written on foreign generals up to Atticus; he has not dealt with any Roman leader. The events connected with Alexander of Macedon have been described in Greek by Arrian; in Latin by Curtius. That sea (of biography) of Plutarch lies open most widely on the *Lives of the Greeks*, from Theseus to Philopoemenes. That author is full of events; full of admonitions to virtue. Trogus has written forty books of history of almost the whole earth. We now possess a compendium which Justinus has made of that work. Pausanias, in treating of the Greek people, brings together much of the knowledge of antiquity concerning that nation. The same Plutarch writes the lives

**Xenophon.**

**Plutarch.**

[1] See Vives, *de Ratione Dicendi*, bk II, § Color.

of ten rhetoricians, and gives many details of Athenian life, since most of the men of whom he writes were public administrators.

**Diogenes Laertius.**

Diogenes Laertius composed the lives of the philosophers, for some woman. There is, in that work, a great knowledge of affairs, and it is extremely well worth reading. It has not been my good fortune to see Ælian's history, but he is cited by recent writers. The affairs of the Roman people, as Julius Florus well said, do not merely include the history of a race, but also of the whole world, and of all humanity. It will greatly lead to its due comprehension, to learn about the functions of the magistrates and priests of that city.

**Fenestella.**

On these points there is a little book called the *Annals* of Fenestella (this may be the name of the author or it may be the work of some unnamed author). There is also another book, that of Pomponius Laetus, taken from Fenestella. Then as to the divisions of the city, Faustus Victor has written, at brief length, but he only gives a list of bare names. Livy began the history of the deeds of the Romans from the beginning of the city. He wove together these threads up to his own times, i.e. up to the reign of Augustus, but by far the greatest part has perished. For a long time past there have been only three decades extant, out of fourteen.

**History of Livy.**

Lately two books have been added. And, as we are writing, five further books out of the fifth decade have been just discovered in an old library. Livy is a very painstaking author, of the highest service, as an eloquent historian, and one writing thoughtfully on affairs of state. There are some people who are not inclined to divide his work into decades, but the Prefaces to every tenth book are conclusive evidence that this division was made by the author himself.

**History of Florus.**

There is an *Epitome* of Livy, drawn up by Julius Florus. Florus has also composed a small work himself on Roman History. It would be impossible to imagine anything of that kind of writing more clear-sighted or more charming. Dionysius Halicarnasseus has handed down in Greek what was narrated to him by M. Varro, his master, with regard to the beginnings of the Romans and the earliest times of the city. We have to note, in the case of Polybius, as well as in that of Livy, a loss of a great portion of his writings; out of forty books of his histories merely five books remain to us.

**Polybius.**

There are three books of Maccabees, two of them are translated in Holy Writ, the third is only accessible in Greek. It is uncertain who was the author of these books. Some scholars ascribe them to Josephus, and think that he wrote them in Greek, since that language seems to permeate the idioms. Sallust has written on the Jugurthine War, as well as on the *Conspiracy of Catiline*. Then come the *Commentaries* of Caesar. Lucan has sung the Civil War of Pompey, but it appeals more to historians than to poets[1]. Then there is Cornelius Nepos, of whom Catullus says that he disclosed the Roman History in three sheets. Julius Obsequens on Prodigies is important for information on his times. Appianus Alexandrinus, a Greek author, handed down to memory the wars, civil and foreign, of the Romans. Then follows Velleius Paterculus. For the later stages, we have the *Lives of the Romans* by Plutarch, from Romulus to Otho, and his *Parallels*. Valerius Maximus, in a superficial manner, touches on the histories of many peoples, since he was only collecting anecdotes in general.

**Books of the Maccabees.**

The Holy Gospel was expounded by four writers. It is the Book of Life, and the adorable history of the human race restored. The great happiness of the collection of these books belonged to the age of Augustus and Tiberius. St Luke, who wrote the Gospel, also consigned to memory the Acts of the Apostles. Suetonius Tranquillus, the most painstaking and most uncorrupted of the Greek and Latin writers, seems to me to have written most justly on the history of the twelve Emperors. For he is silent neither as to the vices of the

[1] See Vives, Epistle 2, *de Ratione Studii Puerilis*.

best princes, nor even as to the suspicion of a vice; whilst in the case of the worst Emperors, he does not omit to show any tincture of virtue. With like trustworthiness and painstaking Laertius Diogenes has composed the *Lives of the Philosophers*. There is extant also a small work of Suetonius on the Grammarians. Cornelius Tacitus is weighty in judgments and thus directs the reader to practical wisdom. He is the more valuable because he is concerned with domestic politics rather than with warfare. There is also the book of Tacitus on the customs of the Germans. We have also the *Antiquities* of Flavius Josephus and the *War against the Jews* which the Vespasians had waged. On these books Ægesippus wrote shortly afterwards, and his book was turned into Latin by Ambrose, Bishop of Milan. Dion Cassius Coccejanus wrote in Greek a history of the Romans in eighty books, also an account of the deeds of Trajan, and the life of Arrian, as Suidas bears witness. His complete history is not now extant to us. Julius Frontinus has written on aqueducts, and is of importance for the knowledge of places in Rome, as well as for the knowledge of the festival-calendar, and he describes the times of many of the consuls.

Tacitus.

Ægesippus.

Philostratus gives an account of the Sophists, amongst whom are some philosophers. Orators are described by Eudoxus of Cnidos (who accompanied Plato to Egypt) up to the time of Aspasius, who lived at Rome under the Antonines. The life of Apollonius, by the same Philostratus, is almost entirely a rabid and blasphemous fabrication by a man not unpractised in romancing, who made up histories of people, whom nobody had ever seen or heard of. Herodian has written of the Emperors, from Commodus to Gordianus. Aelius Spartianus, Capitolinus, Lampridius, Volcatius Gallicanus, Trebellius Pollio, Flavius Vopiscus, have written on the Emperors from Hadrian to Carinus. The portion which remains of the work of Ammianus

Philostratus.

Marcellinus is neither the work of an orator nor of a historian. Pomponius Laetus deals with the period from Balbinus and Pupienus to Heraclius. If anyone has not yet read Paulus Orosius, then at this point he should be consulted. So, too, with Eutropius who composed an *Epitome* of Roman history from Janus up to the time of the Emperor Jovianus. Likewise let the student of history read Sextus Aurelius, who wrote a history of the Emperors from Augustus to Theodosius. Flavius Blondus (Biondo) has depicted, in ten books, *Rome in its Triumphs* (*Roma Triumphans*), and, in another work, *The Restoration of Italy* (*Italia Instaurata*)[1]. Peter Crinitus has produced a work in five books on the Roman poets from Livius Andronicus the freed slave of Salinator, up to the time of Sidonius Apollinaris. Paul Warnefried, the Longobard, also surnamed Diaconus has written on the Emperors from Valentinian to Leo. Procopius and Agathias have transmitted to posterity the deeds of Justinian. From these authors, Leonardo Bruni, of Arezzo, has put together his *War against the Goths*. From these wars, up to his time, i.e. up to the Pope Pius II, Flavius Blondus has written three decades of Roman history which he has entitled: "From the Fall of the Roman Empire, to the year 1440."

**Whom Blondus epitomised.**

Church History from the time of Our Lord Jesus Christ up to the reign of Constantine has been unfolded by Eusebius in nine books, which are called the *Ecclesiastical History*. The tenth and eleventh volumes, which carry the history to the reign of Arcadius and Honorius, were added by Rufinus, the commentator on the original work. We have also read another Church History written by three writers. The book is therefore called the Threefold Work (*Tripartita*). It was brought into an abridgment by Cassiodorus, and extends from the time of the

**Ecclesiastical history.**

[1] Apparently Vives has made a mistake in the title. Biondo's work was *Roma Instaurata* 1471. Biondo lived from 1388 to 1463.

consuls and Emperors Crispus and Constantine up to the 17th year of the Emperor Theodosius Augustus. Saint Jerome has surveyed the ecclesiastical writers from Peter up to his own time, under the Emperor Theodosius. Gennadius, at the same time, added his books from James, Bishop of Nisibe in Persia, who was a martyr under the Emperor Maximinus, up to Honoratus, Bishop of Marseilles. Bede, the English priest, committed to writing his account of his Church. We have also the *Acts of the Councils* which, according to the view of John Gerson, were collected by Isidore of Seville. First the decisions of one Council, then those of another, were added, as e.g. the decisions of the Council of Basle by Pius II, who was himself present at the Council.

**The catalogue of Jerome.**

When the Roman Empire was cut up and dismembered, each separate people, relying on its own strength, carried on its own domestic and foreign affairs. Then arose separate histories of different countries. Eginhardus the secretary of Charles the Great, committed his master's life and acts to posterity. Turpinus and lately Donatus Acciajolus (Acciolaus) (briefly yet pleasantly) have also written on Charles the Great. Gaguinus traced the history of France up to his own time, i.e. up to Louis XI, and it is said wrote it with a good deal of feeling. With more trustworthiness, Paulus Aemilius wrote an old French History, i.e. from the first Kings of the Franks, after the downfall of the Roman power, up to the time of the brothers Philip and Charles, sons of Louis. Jordan, at the suggestion of Castalius, handed to posterity the history of the Goths. Roderick, Bishop of Toledo, wrote on Spanish history; Albert Crantzius (i.e. Krantzius) on Saxon history; Sabellicus on Venetian history; Maria Siculus on the history of Aragon; Hector Boethius on Scottish history; Pope Pius on Bohemian history. Beatus Rhenanus dealt with the origins, position and manners of Germany, and the customs of its inhabitants. Saxo

**Gaguinus.**

Grammaticus wrote in a manner bordering on the fabulous, with regard to the Danes, so that one might think he wished to arouse the astonishment of other races, though you will also wonder at the words and elegance of his diction, writing as he did, in that age and in such a country. Yet more fabulous are the stories, which are stated concerning the origins of Britain, tracing them from Brutus the Trojan, who never existed. Agython, a Praemonstratensian monk, left a book on the peoples of the East and especially the Tartars[1]. This author lived in those regions for some time, two hundred years ago. We read the lives of the Roman pontiffs in Platina's book, which ranges from the time of Peter up to Sixtus IV (d. 1484). Trithemius, Abbot of Spanheim, collected the biographies of ecclesiastical writers, starting with Clement, Bishop of the Romans and proceeded up to the present time, for he records the names of many who are still living. Leonardo Bruni wrote a history of his own times. Pontanus is the historian of the Neapolitan War of Alphonsus. Michael Ritius (Ricci) has gathered together accounts of several Christian kings, but in his book there are many corrupt names of places, men and families, to be ascribed, in my opinion, to the fault of the authorities from whom he has quoted. Baptista Aegnatius has written a very brief treatise on the Emperors up to Maximilian. Peter Martyr of Milan has compiled monumental books in his records of the navigations of the ocean, and the Discovery of the New World, which took place in his time. But since then, yet vaster events have followed. These cannot but seem fabulous to our posterity, though they are absolutely true.

**Recent historians.**

Various men have prepared lives of separate individuals, e.g. Tacitus, the life of his father-in-law, Agricola; Severus of St Martin; Paulinus of St Ambrose; Pontius of St Cyprian; St Jerome, of Paula, of Hilarion, and of Malchus the Sophist. In recent years, Laurentius Valla wrote the life of Ferdinand,

[1] See George Lilius' *Chronicon Anglorum Regum*, at the beginning.

King of Aragon. Antony Panormita wrote an account of the deeds and sayings of Alphonsus, son of the above Ferdinand. Campanus wrote the life of Braccio of Perugia; Raphael of Volterra brings together in his *Anthropologia* and his *Geographia* much historical matter. His works have benefited history greatly. There are many others who may help historical study, even when they are not professed historians, e.g. Cicero, Seneca, Gellius, Macrobius and, still more, Polydore Vergil in his book, *De rerum inventoribus*, and St Augustine in his *Civitas Dei*; also Pliny and the plunderer of Pliny, Solinus. There are the geographers also, Strabo and Pius Secundus. Of the Greeks, Plato and Plutarch (i.e. in their smaller ethical works) should be mentioned. Suidas, Athenaeus, and the commentators on the poets, when they do not confuse everything, may be added.

**Solinus, the ape of Pliny.**

When all these have been studied, we shall still have to mention some auxiliary works of reference in the library, not that they should be completely expounded, but that they should be pointed to, as if with the finger, and be brought back to memory. Amongst these will be a manual of chronology such as the *Supplementum Chronicorum* of the Bishop of Bergamo, though it is often lacking in accuracy. Otto of Freisingen and Rhegino are better. Eusebius of Caesarea would be of the highest service in this respect, were it not that he has come down to posterity so faulty, through the negligence and idleness of copyists. Jerome continues the chronology of Eusebius for a further fifty years. Prosper of Aquitaine takes us another sixty years onward. Then follows the Florentine Matthew Palmerius (Palmieri) up to the year of Our Lord 1449. Then, through another thirty years, chronology is supplied by Matthias Palmerius of Pisa. In addition, some further chronological material is furnished by Sigibert, a monk of Gemblours. The work of Bede, the priest, is like that of Eusebius, but somewhat more clearly written.

**Ecclesiastical historians.**

Herman Contractus followed him, up to the year 1066. If a man has leisure to read more on Imperial and Pontifical history, let him add the work of Archbishop Antonius of Florence.

Such are the chief Greek and Latin historical writers, who have reached our times. The historians, especially those who wrote in Greek, who are now unknown, are almost innumerable. Even the names of those authors to whom Plutarch is the only writer to allude, cannot be recalled. Plutarch, for instance, says that three hundred writers had written on the Marathonian War. I have not mentioned those, who have written on some small race or state, such as Flanders, Liège, Utrecht. Nor have I included those writers who used the vernacular language such as the Spanish Valera, Froissart, Monstrelet, Philip Cominius (de Comines), of whom there are many not less worthy of being known and read than the majority of Greek and Latin historians.

**Complaint as to the history of the Church.**

But this mention of the deeds achieved by those great men arouses in my soul a great grief which I frequently feel when I ponder within myself with what diligence and care the deeds of Alexander, Hannibal, Scipio, Pompey, Caesar, and other generals; of Socrates, Plato, and other philosophers, have been closely detailed and fixed on the memory for ever, so that there is no danger of their escaping recall, but the deeds of the Apostles, Martyrs, and lastly the Saints of our religion, both in the early Church, and in the later ages of the Church, are almost unknown, and involved in the greatest darkness[1]. Yet they would be so much more fruitful both for knowledge, and for imitation, than the deeds of generals and the sayings of philosophers. For what has been written on the lives of the Saints, with few exceptions, has been polluted with many fabrications. The writer followed his own inclination, and has told us, not what the saint actually did, but what the writer would have wished him to have done,

[1] Melchor Canus, *de Locis Theologicis*, bk XI.

so that the writing of the *Lives of Saints* has been directed by the caprices of the writers, not by the truth of the facts. There have been those who, instead of using great scrupulousness, shaped together small falsehoods, on behalf of religion[1]. This is dangerous, since it may take away confidence in what is true, on account of the falsity found in it; and in religion no sort of necessity can be pleaded for such a procedure. There are so many true things to produce as evidence on behalf of our religion that any falsities, like cowardly and useless soldiers, are more of a burden than a help.

The knowledge of fables must be added to that of history. But they must be of that erudite kind which is adapted to usefulness in living, that they may be applied to a practical purpose. To this class belong poetical fables, and the apologues of Aesop, and books of proverbs and maxims by which general sentiment is assimilated.

Someone may here exclaim: When is all this to be read? The answer is; when men are of ripe age, even when they are advanced in years, at such times as would otherwise be spent in play and trifling[2]. For if anyone were to consider how much time he spends in playing, how much in empty, often even, in harmful, conversation, how much in slothful ease, he would find there was plenty of time to pursue his course through all the subjects I have mentioned, and sufficient time to spare for many other things. We have an overflow of time, if we only use it wisely. It is when we dispose of it badly that it becomes so very limited. But if anyone cannot read everything for himself, let him employ a reader, after the custom of the Romans, and give heed to a clear, instructed, and fluent recital of the authors[3].

[1] So Varro thought falsehood concerning the very gods to be of use to citizens as Augustine says in the *Civitas Dei* III, 4.

[2] Seneca rightly remarks in his Epistle to Lucilius that a great part of life slips away from those acting badly whilst to those acting otherwise none is lost.

[3] See Epistle of Pliny to Marcellinus.

# CHAPTER III

## MORAL PHILOSOPHY, ETHICS, ECONOMICS, POLITICS, JURISPRUDENCE

**The philosophy of morals.**

INTERWOVEN and bound up with History, will be taught the precepts of training for both public and private life. The whole education must tend to the preservation of the right order of studies, and to the due and constant performance of everyone's duties, so that what Nature and right reason ordain to be done on a lower stage do not get left for a higher grade; and that which should present itself authoritatively (as a duty) becomes stale, and its mandates ineffective, and that which should be prepared for with all wisdom, be not allowed to be overruled by foolishness. When the nature of the body and the soul has been explained, no one is so bereft of all sense and judgment as not to see plainly and certainly, that the body ought to obey the mind, and the unreasoning impulses of the mind must be subjected to reason as mistress and empress. In other words, it is this that makes us men; and from all the things amongst which we move, by the possession of reason we become most like to, and most united with, that divine Nature, which rules everything. It cannot be doubted that this state was ordained by the Creator for men, when man first came from the hands of his Creator and was left to himself, since every work is the fullest and most perfect in proportion as the shaper of it is the wisest and best. But through sin all things were inverted so that man's lower nature desires the higher

**The fight between the passions and reason.**

position for itself; the passions contend for attention in place of the reason; reason, conquered and overwhelmed is put to silence, and is made the slave to the temerity of the passions.

**The necessary utility of moral philosophy.**

Thus there is an eternal military service or rather actual battle, in man, in which he has a perpetual toil and struggle not to let the maid get the upper hand of the mistress. For if this should happen, there would be a most bitter tyranny exercised, and the man would be driven from his manhood into becoming a beast. All the precepts of Moral Philosophy have been prepared, like an army, to bring support to the Reason. Wherefore the whole man must be understood, from within and without. Within the mind are the intellect and the emotions. We must know by what things the emotions are aroused and developed; by what things on the other hand they are restrained, calmed, removed. This enables a man "to know himself" which we are ordered to do by an injunction of ancient wisdom[1]. But this would have to be demonstrated in a treatment *de Anima*. It is now our task to show how the passions of the mind should be subordinated to the authority and judgment of Reason.

Our intellect is enveloped by too dense a darkness for it to see through, for the passions, aroused through sin, have spread a great and most obscuring mist before the eyes of reason. Reason has need of being clear, and of being as little perturbed as possible. But this state necessarily belongs to the divine reason and to that only. There are many and the most convincing reasons for this. Either because God's reason is the wisest of all, or because He is the Creator of our reason, and therefore is the Canon and Rule of our reason, so that it can direct itself to none more rightly; partly, because reason shows the way by which we may come to God, which is the end for

[1] It is ordered that we know ourselves, not our bones, flesh, nerves, blood, but the nature of the mind, its quality, wit, strength, feelings, says Vives in the Preface to *de Anima*.

which man is created. Who could point this out better or more certainly than God Himself? Therefore we must obtain the precepts from God's own teaching. No one has seen God at any time[1]. We have as the interpreter of God and as mediator, Jesus Christ, who was not of the same condition as the rest of mankind, but His only Son, who was ever in the bosom of his Father. The interpreters of the Son are his Disciples, then the hearers of the Disciples, and afterwards the other holy men, though the river is the purer the nearer we get to its source. From the teaching and words of these men should be gathered, as it were, remedies for the diseases of the mind, so that the passions may be subjugated to the hand and power of reason. When this precedence is established, and as far as is permitted, is firmly grounded, man then bears himself rightly towards himself and towards God, and towards those higher, lower, and equal to himself in station, whether we speak of private individuals, of families, or the commonwealth; whether we speak of public life at home or abroad. With regard to this instruction, a short, clear book, in accordance with the Christian religion in all things, should be written, which the teacher will expound.

**The divisions of moral philosophy.**

The writers on human wisdom have divided this subject of Morals into four parts. In the first place, is Ethics, which concerns itself with the mind and the formation of individual Morals. Secondly, Economics, which deals with the concerns of family-life. Thirdly, Politics, which states the principles of groups and gatherings of the peoples. The fourth division concerns the treatment of those intermediate duties of life which would not be found in the training of nature so much as they would be posited in the custom or education of each region and people. What has been written on these subjects by writers in the monuments of literature still extant may be studied privately by each for himself. Let the student only realise that he has

[1] S. John vi. 46.

entered on a dark road beset with thorns, and let him proceed with wary feet, nor let him even set down his foot light-heartedly, except where he has before him the light of our religion, and except it shows him that he can safely tread there. For however great and clear-sighted human intellects may be, they cannot attain to more than just what is consistent with Christianity, i.e. as man with his God. There are extant ten books on Ethics by Aristotle to his son Nicomachus (which some critics maintain were not written for, but by, his son Nicomachus. Cicero suggests this in Book v of his *de Finibus*). Laertius tells us in his life of Eudoxus, that Nicomachus, the son of Aristotle[1], said to Eudoxus that pleasure was the highest good, a maxim which is maintained in the *Ethics*[2]. Suidas says that Aristotle left behind him six books of Ethics, only the doubt remains whether he means those ten mentioned above, or the two books *Magnorum Moralium* or the eight books to Eudemus. But whoever may be the author, we certainly possess altogether twenty books with the name of Aristotle attached, on Morals, all of which tend to the knowledge of, and discussion of, Morals, more than they impel the readers to want to live the moral life. Similar in scope is the second part of the *Summa* of St Thomas Aquinas, which is divided into two volumes. St Thomas is the soundest and least inept of all the scholastic writers. These volumes are partly collected from the sacred, partly from profane, writers, the common opinions of the time being accepted by him. In many places you easily perceive that he has followed someone else's judgment, that he has not given his own, a course which was common amongst the scholastics. The Platonic writings on the subject of Ethics produce a greater effect. So, too, do Xenophon's *Memorabilia*, Plutarch (*on Morals*), Cicero *de Finibus*, the *Tusculan Questions*, Laelius

[1] Augustine, bk VIII, chap. 3, and Quintilian, bk XII, and S. Eucherius of Lyons in his letter to Valerian, attribute it to Aristippus.

[2] Arist. *Ethics*, I, 4.

and Cato Major, Seneca, *de Beneficiis*, *de Clementia*, *de Consolatione* (to Martia), *de Vita beata* (to his mother Helvia), *de Tranquillitate animi*, *de Brevitate vitae*, *de Ira*, *Epistolae ad Lucilium*, which were not letters written to be actually sent so much as a literary method, whereby a question of right living and the formation of character could be treated in each one of the letters. Other books on Ethics are Boethius, *de Consolatione Philosophiae*, and Petrarch, *de utraque Fortuna* (i.e. Happiness and Misery). The teacher of Moral Philosophy must be a holy, pure man, with no ostentation about him, a man of practical wisdom not only with many kinds of knowledge, but he must also possess experience in ordinary life. Let him thus teach the precepts of right living that his pupils not only may know, but may also be incited and wish, to act well. Let him therefore be a man of erudite and effective conversation, abounding in weighty maxims, strong and ready in his equipment of histories of good deeds. It will not be sufficient for him to point out that this mode of action is good; that, bad. But he must give the reasons for his judgment, why it is so; why this course should be shunned and why that should be pursued.

There is no necessity to make a carefully close and intimate investigation into vice. Would that we did not even know evil in any way! But since in the state, and in the assemblies of men, there are instructors, some of whom draw people to one kind of disgraceful acts, others to others, and however much evil be kept concealed by teachers, yet it cannot be that anyone remains in ignorance of it since everywhere it meets the eyes and ears—therefore I would wish that it should be recognized that there are two kinds of vices. In the one kind are those which are contained within the mind without affording any use or bodily pleasure. In the second kind certain vices spread themselves through the body and are accompanied by some delectation of the senses. The vices

Two kinds of vices. 1. of the mind, 2. of the body.

of the mind of the first kind should be explained and disclosed fully, so that their foulness may be placed the more openly before the eyes, as, in pride, anger, hate, envy, which torment and torture men's minds; nor is there any advantage to be got from them, so that not unjustly they are called "furies." But the other vices in which men delight, and in the opinion of men at any rate serve some use, although they are thoroughly disgusting, and only bring with them the appearance of pleasure, whilst they are really an alluring destruction and the hollow pretence of being a natural need, all these vices I would have described in a guarded and veiled manner, but at the same time they should be attacked energetically by the teacher, who should point out the deep-dyed disgrace, at the time of indulgence in them, and the bitter remorse which they bring in their train. In connexion with this subject, examples are never lacking us, not only derived from antiquity but also such as everyone has seen for himself, although he be quite a young man. I would not wish that a knowledge of vice should be learned at the risk of personal experience, for often vices rend asunder the victim who once has tasted them for himself, and in them, the sovereignty of habit is most tyrannical[1]. Those who have never indulged themselves at all will find it easier to abstain. Like as formerly the Spartans showed their children drunken slaves, so that they should be horrified with drunkenness, even at the very sight, by the vileness of the drunken countenance, by the incongruity of the words and deeds, so now it would well repay the pains taken, to show to the youth the frightful consequences which lustful pleasures have brought on the mass of men. Similarly I ought to speak of those vices which are bound up with some advantageous usefulness in the opinion of the great mass of people. Of these, are: avarice, craft, deceit, revenge, all of which attract not a

**Hence Melanchthon wishes that tragedies should be frequently read.**

[1] See Plutarch, *Demetrius*.

few people by their baneful appearance of usefulness. For these are the most pernicious of all, since it is to them that praise and approbation are so freely awarded. For when that which is the appropriate reward of virtue is transferred to vice, what hope remains to the wretched race of men, particularly prone to commit disgraceful acts. For if the shame by which the youth has hitherto been frightened, be taken away from vice, then will not all men rush headlong into transgressing, and openly, before all, boast of their evil, as if it were virtue? Crimes of this kind are the murder of men, the horrors of war, and with some, the violation of most honourable matrons. We must show that the nature of man revolts against such crimes, and such misguided judgments must be determinedly combatted.

**Disputations.**

Disputations on these questions of vices and virtues must be earnestly conducted. There may be permitted somewhat more discussion on these points than in Economics or Politics, but for the most part rather on the definitions, and as to the knowledge of the nature of the emotions, than on the application of this knowledge to the practical problems of how a man should live rightly.

**Duties of life.**

The practical duties of life are best learned from men of practical wisdom, and from those citizens who have been well brought up. For every nation has its own special practices. But in every State, care should be taken by wise citizens to choose from other countries, which they have themselves visited, whatsoever they may adapt for use in their own State, in so far as it is consistent with right judgment, and may serve to correct perverse manners in their own country and provided that the new introduction is not in opposition to the genius of the people. For some customs are highly suitable to the Germans, which would be but little fitting to the Spaniards. In these distinctions of places, times, and men, practical wisdom must be the guide, and this ought everywhere to be present. Of ancient Greeks, Panaetius and

Hecaton wrote on duties. Now we only possess the treatise of Marcus Tullius Cicero, which St Ambrose adapted for Christians. Jovianus Pontanus wrote some tracts on magnificence, forbearance, and other similar subjects, but they were not so full of matter as I should expect on such great themes.

Economics.

Care for household affairs must not be treated as consisting in the search for the preservation of wealth, as heathen people supposed, but in the enjoyment of peace and tranquillity of family life, so that we spend our lives in a fitting manner, and each man's home may be to him, as it were, a haven from the worries and anxieties of life. Therefore there must be appointed for each inmate of it, a special appropriate office, so that no one may be lazy, nor must anyone intrude on the duty of another, or consult the interest of his own convenience only. And care must also be taken that the members of the family are fed healthily, clothed suitably and live satisfactorily, and love one another and their home not less than their native country, and look on it as their nurse, or more truly as their mother. The master of the house should be the director, and the governor of all, whom all should love as a father, and revere as a master. In him should be vested the supreme authority over all household affairs. This is the plan (*institutio*) of a family. The precepts with regard to it are to be found in that part of Moral Philosophy which is called by the Greeks οἰκονομική.

Writers on Economics.

Amongst writers on the subject are Xenophon of Athens, who is generally considered to be the foremost writer of those whose writings remain to us. Then there is Aristotle, whose work has not come down to us as a complete whole. Many references on this subject are scattered through the works of Plato and Plutarch, who also composed precepts on subjects connected with marriage. Similarly, Erasmus wrote a book *de Matrimonio*, and Franciscus Barbarus also wrote *de re Uxoria*, but in many places it is stupid. For the study of Economics, there is no need of classroom, master, or disputations, but of conversations with wise fathers of families, as e.g. the converse of Socrates with Isomachus in the *Memorabilia* of Xenophon.

**The State.**

**Love and justice.**

The State has for its scope the preparation of quiet, peaceful, living, so that its citizens may help one another to live in a generous and benevolent manner. Love is increased by the communication of mutual usefulness. Peace is preserved by this same love. But where love is absent, the function of legal justice takes its place, and this should be neither complacent nor without the force of weapons behind it. Justice should have such armed power and strength that it may put the curbs on the insurgent spirits. And since often one administrator of justice cannot himself carry out all the duties which call for performance in a State, others are chosen, equal or unequal to him in power, who are called magistrates and judges. This has then the form of a State. It then becomes the study and concern of the political philosopher, to declare what dispositions the citizens ought to have towards one another, what relations there should be between subjects and princes, and magistrates, what relations there should be between the magistrates amongst themselves, and towards subordinates, what actions and works arise from these relations. When the question is raised: What justice there is for each person with regard to other persons and to property; then laws are made. Political philosophy only has to consider the disposition of the minds of the people and morals of the State. Often, it is true, political philosophy and laws have a mutual bearing towards each other, since many laws arise from political considerations and *vice versa.* In this subject we require no master, and no disputations, but as we said at the beginning, reflexion on the passions and habits of the mind. Hence the value of the experience of business in the forum and in the Senate-house. Sometimes old men converse with one another in an experienced way,

**Political learning.**

and allow youth to listen, so that they may receive from them the wisdom to be gained from experience and a sense of the worth of moral character. As to the latter subject, Cicero[1] has made the noteworthy remark, that it is a subject on which we ought to secure that there are no contentions. For this reason, cavillers and obstinate men are by no means suited for public counsels, since there is nothing in the life and morals of men which may not be distorted and bent from its right sense, by a process of cavilling. For a man to be more anxious about achieving a victory, than discovering the truth, leads to the ruin of practical wisdom, as indeed Cicero said.

**The qualifications for administration in the State.**

For administering the affairs of the State, judgment is necessary, which must be sound, whole, rather solid than subtle or acute. A man should be of a cold rather than fervid disposition, and somewhat slow rather than hasty, ready to accept single-mindedly what is said in council, and reflect over it a great deal, before he offers a judgment. But he should assent to the judgment of anyone speaking what is right, readily, without contention and thorny subtleties, anxious rather for the common good than for his own reputation. And thus for ruling over subject-peoples, a Roman is better than a Greek, and the people of the North better than those of the South. For the people, for the most part, are to be weighed in an ordinary weighing-machine like that for weighing coals, not in the balance manufactured for the goldsmiths. The

**The leader of a city.**

leader of an assembly of men cannot be ignorant that he is, as it were, the architect of the whole building, as Aristotle wisely teaches, that he must order both what ought to be done, and likewise what ought not to be done, in the State. Wherefore it is fitting that if he be not closely acquainted with details, one by one, yet that he should have a general acquaintance with the contents and aims of the sciences and arts, both those which are practised by use of the hands,

[1] *de Officiis*, bk I.

and those which solely occupy the mind, so that he should know, to what extent, and in what way, every innovation should be admitted to the State or be expelled from it.

Writers on Politics.

Plato was the first of the ancients to write on the State. According to his teaching, men will live rightly when the State shall be entirely composed of wise men. The same idea occurs in the *Utopia* of Thomas More. Both the *Republic* and the *Laws* of Plato should be read, as well as the above-mentioned *Utopia*, for from them may be gathered many suggestions very useful for the rule of States. The eight books of the *Politics* of Aristotle contain still more of what is serviceable for instructing the minds of men, and for the confirmation of morals by practical experience, since the author was a man of the highest practical wisdom, and most skilled in judging of public opinion. The three books of Cicero in the *Laws* are most delightful reading and have considerable usefulness. But his *de Republica* is lost. Isocrates gives precepts to the King Nicocles and to his subjects in his *Symmachikus*, all that remains of which, as is usual, is of the nature of commonplaces. The *Cyropaedia* of Xenophon appears to me, although it has received the highest praise of Cicero[1], and others of the ancients, to have too much of military matters in it. Agapetus composed for the Emperor Justinian some documents *de Rege*. Erasmus wrote *Christiani Principis Institutio* (1515). We can read the two works of Franciscus Patritius *de Republica et de Regno*[2], books of great comprehensiveness. In these books he has brought together the words and deeds of many peoples. He scarcely added anything of his own. He is lazy and sluggish in many places. He has collected without exercising any wise choice and judgment. Yet these two books are especially useful in their profusion of anecdotes. This subject (Politics) is the science of princes, councillors, judges, and finally, of those who rule over states and peoples.

Franciscus Patrizi.

[1] *Epistolae*, I, I, to his brother Quintus.

[2] First printed 1518.

Laws.

Justice, the soul of human society.

Laws are closely united with the idea of a State. Their origin and development are substantially as follows. The States and assemblies of men are all bound together by justice as if by glue. For justice is the preserver, and, as it were, the soul of all human society. Reason discovers what true justice is, for it is not the capricious pleasure of each, but it is that which is prompted by the pure and great force of nature, or that which is thoroughly disclosed by the admonitions of wisdom. For, those who are confused by their passions, or who have sluggish judgments, or who are not stirred by any of the teachings of philosophy, only attain to any intuition of justice with the greatest difficulty. Those who are of higher grade, who are held in rare estimation amongst the people, turn the fountain, as it were, of justice into the right channels (suited to the places, times, and the minds of men) so that the present state of society may derive the greatest good from their actions. This is the significance of what is called legislation. The magistrate, who has authority to compel others to obey the law, is called a judge or *lex loquens*. Hence it is manifest that it is a part of the philosopher's task to treat of law, and to place law on a philosophical basis. Nor can this be accomplished by any other subject of study. It is agreed, indeed, by all who have written on the origin of states and peoples, that those who decreed the ancient popular laws were philosophers, e.g. Draco, Solon, Lycurgus; as well as those who handed down writings on the ruling of a State.

# CHAPTER IV

## THE STUDY OF LAW

The office of a jurisconsult. There ought to be a new branch of study which should be called by the name of Justice—dealing with the essential quality of laws, which will serve as their interpreter, and in what manner it ought to be taught.

**The office of a jurisconsult.**

THOSE who defend and interpret the laws, which have already been ordained and accepted, are called jurisconsults. We ask them what is the law which has been established with regard to this and that matter. If anyone thought that it would be sufficient merely to learn what legislation had taken place, so that he, as it were, carried about with him a Register of laws, and that he would thus attain the function of a lawyer, without the need of other qualifications—such a man would have neither understanding nor judgment. But, on the other hand, if it is the function and office of a true and thorough jurisconsult to explain the sense and spirit of laws, so as to discover the justice that is present in each law, i.e. what its life-giving force is, what its preservative force to the community is, what laws are usefully maintained at each period of time, what are of old-standing, all this surely demands philosophical knowledge in a man; a considerable amount of natural philosophy, and also a full and complete equipment in moral philosophy. Then he will not be a priest (*sacerdos*) and interpreter of Roman and Spanish law, but as Celsus and Ulpian wished, the interpreter of *the good* and *the right* in laws. I should greatly like this knowledge

**The art of teaching what is just and good.**

to be thought out by some powerful minds, and put in a form for future jurists to learn. It might be called the *Ars Justitiae*. It would then be no longer necessary that countless laws in every state should be heaped together one on the other, without aim and without effect. Cicero[1] in the person of Lucius Crassus says that he had at one time thought of writing such a book so as to reduce the whole civil law into a system, first dividing all the different kinds into classes, then into formularies, into which the classes would fall. But he sketches his plan too briefly and shows it as if through a lattice (i.e. whilst passing) as others have done in writing on this point. Aristotle[2] has noted some beginnings, but as is usual with him, in an intricate manner, through geometrical and arithmetical analogies.

This might yet more fittingly be done by first stating the principles of natural law, i.e. what is agreed upon by the unanimous sense and judgment of all men. Then would come those subjects on which a variety of opinions are held, on a part of which again unanimity would be found for the most part amongst those of right-minded judgment, but another part would only be determinable by morality and custom, and would be changeable according to times, places, persons. Yet amongst all these systems which differ from one another, each has a reason of varying degrees of logical value for its own view. These last points therefore must be brought before the judgment of men of practical wisdom, in each state. In two other points it must be considered and decided how far it may be permitted for the control of the magistrate to be extended towards a private person, what commands are right, and what authority is permitted to each of them. It must be decided what obedience, what honour, what dignity, what outward respect must be required from the private person to the magistrate. Then, too, which of the magistrates are to be more powerful than the others, which

**The relation and subordination amongst subjects and between magistrate and subject.**

[1] *Epistolae Familiares*, bk VII.

[2] Aristotle, *Ethica*, bk V.

parts of the State are more necessary than others or which are entitled to higher honour than others. Further it must be decided in what manner private persons must deal with one another in their buying, selling, hiring, letting, exchanging, giving, receiving, promising, in the acquisition and preservation of what is useful; in the repulse of what is harmful; what rewards and honours should fall to the lot of those who do good to the community; what punishments and humiliations should await those who injure the common weal; what are to be the legal processes, or what can be done when you wish to avenge an injury, or to recover your own again; what is to be done to protect, to except, or to refuse others. As to the adaptation of each single circumstance to the settled *norm*, nature and right reason will teach us, whether they belong to the general order, or must be decided according to the dispositions of men at particular times or in particular places.

**Conditions of good legislation.**

**1. Laws must be known by all.**

**2. And be written in few and appropriate words.**

Before everything, it is necessary that the laws be known by all. For who will willingly entrust himself to be led or to be guarded by an unknown person? What an injustice it is that a breach of the law should not be pardoned by ignorance of the law, if the law itself is absolutely unknown to exist. Hence to lay down laws which remain unknown is said to be, as it were, to set snares, not to state rules by which we can mould our life. For there is less opportunity for cavilling and deceit, where a requirement is made clear to all. It is in obscure and hidden spots that traps are placed, not in the light, or before the eyes of the crowd, where there are witnesses and judges of what is going on. The laws will be easily known if they are short and written in the clearest language. For the best laws are short, and that is the case with the wisest of all laws, viz. those of the Divine Law-giver and His followers. If any matter is expounded in few, and those the most appropriate words, so much of equity will have been brought within general knowledge as shall be sufficient for all. The rest will be left to right-minded interpretation so that everywhere the highest consideration may be given to *the right* and *the good.* But if anything is declared in long and laborious phrases, we seem to want everything explained, and to have nothing left over to a sound interpretation. So the law will then only have validity so far as the draughtsman of it has been able to write eloquently, though there is no eloquence so great that it can possibly enclose the vast ocean of justice. Thus it will, in fact, happen, instead of deciding what is just and good, cavilling, deceit, pit-falls will take its place. This we see every day in the laws and legal documents which attempt to determine everything in the minutest detail. But this is doing nothing else than opening the windows[1] as widely as possible, to deceit.

**3. And in the vernacular.**

Laws should be written in the vernacular, and in intelligible and clear language. If in the course of time, the original method of expression, as happens sometimes, becomes somewhat obscure, it should be made clear, or altered into words current at the present time. This was understood by the foresight and singleminded sense of justice of the men of old, who required the laws of the Twelve Tables to be learned by boys, whilst playing, even up to the time of Cicero, i.e. for about 400 years. By this means they saw whether the language of the laws was easily understood, and further, they wished thus that every single individual should be made acquainted with the right way of controlling his life.

**4. And should be accommodated to different men.**

Towards the weak, the laws must be mild; towards the strong, severe; to the obstinate they must be determined. For it is part of the genius of a good governor, as the wise poet expresses it in his elegant verse:

> Parcere subjectis, et debellare superbos.
> (Virgil, *Aeneid*, Book VI, l. 853.)

[1] Or, as we say, the door.

The laws should feed and nourish the maintenance of peace, and treat sternly those who disturb it, such e.g. as informers, calumniators, and those who undertake far too readily lawsuits on small matters, so that, as Isocrates advises, men must be brought to think it hateful to go to law, whilst to abstain from litigation ought to be regarded as distinctly fruitful. But the laws should not only take precautions to preserve the harmony of the citizens amongst themselves, but of the whole race of mankind, whose religious condition of regeneration should be regarded by citizens as sacredly as the family concord within the threshold. Nor would anything more conduce to this end than the practical application of that one Christian precept common to all men: "Love one another." For this reason, no laws should be ordained which should bring advantage to citizens of a country, at the expense of foreigners. Since with good customs, few or almost no laws are necessary, so, on the other hand, with bad customs, no number however great can suffice. Therefore, in the constitution of the State, and also by the command of the laws, to which men ascribe the highest authority, care must be taken, that the education of youth be pure and uncorrupted. Rewards and punishments may be ordained, so that the morals of men and the whole state may become honourable, stable, and reverent. Xenophon says wisely, in speaking of the Education of Cyrus: "Most States do not concern themselves in the least as to how the youth of their citizens should be educated, and give no prescriptions as to the moral training of their young men; but simply order them not to steal or rob, not to violently attack anybody's house, not to kill anyone unjustly, not to commit adultery, not to bear themselves insolently to their magistrates, and give other similar orders. If anyone acts contrary to these injunctions, then he is punished. But the Persians first endeavour beforehand

**5. And in accordance with love and harmony.**

**6. And should be in accordance with the education of children.**

**7. And be approved by the great mass of the people.**

through their laws, to prevent evil deeds being done by their citizens. These laws provide that from the very first, care be taken that no one grows up desirous of committing a wicked or foul deed." Thus says Xenophon. Also that philosopher answered not less wisely, who, when he was asked: How might one have one's children good, answered that it was only necessary that they should be placed in a well-directed State.

Before laws are fixed and decreed, they must be proposed, i.e. it is right that the people should deliberate over them and say if they approve them. In such a consultation, the time must first be considered within which the law then prevailing shall cease. It must be understood whether the new laws are appointed for an indefinite time, or for a definite time, and for a definite place, or if for a definite individual, or for a definite town. In the latter case they are called privileges. If the law is approved, then it has to be placed a certain length of time in a public place (in Rome the time was seventeen days), so that if it should seem to anyone an unjust measure, he might protest to the magistrates against it[1]. After that time the law was established and made valid. It had then to be written out carefully and clearly, and to be placed in the State archives which must be kept in a safe place, unexposed to risk of destruction, or the ravages of fire. Two copies of the law had to be made; one for reading and transcription (if they wished) by the people. In that copy were contained the bare words of the law. In the other the law was given with grounds and reasons, so that sensible men might perceive its value, and so that no one in the State should attempt to upset the law, or to make innovations in it. For reason is the leader (*dux*) of law. Take reason away, and it is tantamount to doing away with law, which has been accepted, because it is founded on reason. Add to this, that it is through reason, that law can be the better understood. But in our minds there is such stupidity

[1] Cicero calls it 'trinundino' in his *Orat. pro Domo sua ad Pontifices*. See Fenestella, *de Magistratibus Romanis*, cap. 14.

and rawness, and in our words such childishness that we can get nothing so clearly stated that it may not possibly, by some people, be regarded as confused and obscure. Therefore, interpreters are necessary.

**8. And should have wise interpreters.**

And because the Civil Law ought to have regard to the harmony of citizens, the interpreters of it must have a similar aim, and out of the same oracles (so to say) learn how that same harmony is preserved and restored. They must be acquainted with the common nature of mankind, the point of view and customs of many kinds of people, but especially of their own country. This is brought about by wide experience in seeing, hearing, observing things; through reading of the deeds of ancestors and varieties of changes which, from time to time, have befallen the State. Such men need alert minds and keen judgments, so as to observe and to estimate circumstances one by one. The special name of *Prudentia* (practical wisdom) was formerly given to the class of men, who possess the qualities which have just been described, and the subject itself is called Jurisprudence. Many should know this art; but only few should pursue it as their profession, viz. those to whom it is permitted by the Senate or the Prince, as was the case at Rome under the Emperors. These men were asked in writing by the Judge to interpret the laws, and, personally, the litigants sought their counsel. They might, if they wished, write out their interpretations, but in language somewhat recondite and known only to the learned, and certainly not according to their own or other people's ideas and sentiments, but by the application of reasoning alone to the question in hand, so that their interpretation should not possess more emphasis than reason itself demanded. Nothing other than what was dictated by reason was written down, nor did they think out hypothetical cases. For this is an endless business, which often merely perplexes, and moreover is, for practical purposes, useless.

**Those learned in the law.**

The method for teaching and learning law is as follows: Those books of laws (about which I have just spoken) with their underlying principles and reasons, should be accessible to all the most thoughtful men. On appointed days of the year, as may be most convenient to them, they should assemble together in a peaceful and modest manner, and consult together on those laws. Let them compare reasons, as to what laws by experience of their working should continue as they have been, and which laws it would be well to alter and recast, through their having become obsolete, and then let them apprise the Prince, or Magistrates or Senate, of their conclusions. At Athens, the Thesmothetae were men of this type, so long as that city flourished. Students of law should follow the example of Quintus Scaevola, when it is permitted, and listen to the discussions of old men such as these, as they give their answers to those consulting them on law. Let the teacher expound to students the grounds one by one and, as it were, the sources of law, partly those laid down by the law-givers themselves, or those which have been suggested by former experts in jurisprudence. Let them dispute amongst themselves in conversations of a modest and serious kind, with a view to realising how consonant to reason law is, and to the determination of the fact that reason is, as it were, the life of justice, except as modified by special causes and the date of the introduction of the law. Such expositions should not take place in a public assembly before a circle of listeners of the type that invite ostentation of arguments for their amusement. For such exhibitions are dangerous both to those pronouncing a judgment, who may be rendered conceited by it, and to the listeners, because their minds become less respectful to a law, which they perceive to have a strong reason against it, for it is reason alone which the human spirit obeys of its own free will. In the course of quarrels and disputations, the laws provide plenty of handles

**9. How laws should be taught.**

**How legal disputations should be conducted.**

for exercises in twisting arguments, and thus strife is aroused, nourished and cultivated. Hence, if disputations are encouraged, harmony, the chief blessing of society, receives a serious injury.

Roman Law and its excellence.

Of all written laws, now known to us, the most excellent seems to be the old Roman Law. This system is the most fitted for the life of men, as lived in common. For it draws men together. It tends to promote peace, so that men are deterred from evil deeds, and no one dares to be the cause of an injury to another. Roman laws were devised with learning and due gravity, and thenceforth were to be found excellently expressed in appropriate, clear words. They were brought by their collectors into an order best suited for being studied, only that sometimes the alteration of the earlier, in the later versions, produced some uncertainty of meaning, and the lack of knowledge of the earlier ages perverted many points which were not properly understood. But these details it was found possible to correct in accordance with a manuscript, which is said to have been brought to Florence by the Pisans, and some scholars conjectured that it was the original. Anyway, it is a very old MS., and freer from mistakes than others. Short and clear explanations should be given in exposition of the text, although, in some places, this is wellnigh impossible, partly on account of the confusion in the text, partly on account of the significations of some of the words, which are completely obsolete.

Exposition of laws.

Legal exercises.

The practical side of the study of laws consists in the rationalising of the *good* and the *just* in these laws[1]. It is necessary to investigate the origin and the aim of each law considered, and this is the work of great intellects. So as to attain to the highest practical wisdom it is especially useful, as in other things, to let reason be our guide, with whose help we may come to the knowledge of

[1] Aristotle, *Politics*, bk III, chaps. II, 12.

perfect justice. In the study of each of the arts, reading should not be confined to those authors whose works we have prescribed. For we do not doubt that some writers, most worthy to be known, have escaped our notice, and that also, after our time, others will arise who will be equal to, and even greater than, those who have preceded our age. But teachers should take care that they themselves taste all kinds of writings, and show to their scholars what should be learnt thoroughly, what should be read, and what they should have at hand in the library, when any matter calls for reference, and also point out to them which volumes serve rather as an ornament and for the filling up of the book-cases.

**Which legal authors are to be read.**

He who is endowed by God with a greater power of intellect, and does not let himself be kept back by worldly cares, but is stirred to concern himself in intercourse with heavenly subjects, happy and dear is that man to the powers above! Such an one will soar up to the study of Theosophy and Theology. Concerning this blessed and wonderful subject we must not speak whilst treating of other topics, especially as we are now fatigued at the end of so long a course. These subjects demand a special treatment to themselves. Sometime we will speak on them[1], if God will, at leisure, with fresh spirit, and stirred by the Muses to a greater ardour. For this theme is more comprehensive and more noble than men ordinarily think.

[1] This task Vives accomplished in his *de Veritate Fidei Christianae*, published posthumously in 1543 at Basle.

# APPENDIX

## THE SCHOLAR'S LIFE AND CHARACTER

# CHAPTER I

## THE AIM OF STUDIES

How many considerations restrain a really learned man from being ashamed of learning from others. The four elements of which all learning consists, natural capacity, judgment, memory, application, but no development of these qualities is of such moment as to justify the learned man in boasting of them. Each man must study so as to be of benefit to others through his study. Especially must the student flee from that noxious evil, flattery, as well as human glory, as assuredly worthless and empty.

Now that we have finished the consideration of the humanistic arts, let us state what the man thus cultured should do, how he should spend the rest of his life, whether separately by himself or with others, in the employment and practice of the knowledge he has acquired, and in its dissemination; how he should bear himself towards his colleagues who are similarly equipped with knowledge and training; how he should receive their opinions and judgments concerning himself; and how he should consign his contributions to literature, so as to transmit them to posterity.

He will not necessarily follow the details one by one, in the order in which we have dealt with them. He will not think it wrong to glance back again at what has been discussed earlier, even when he has reached a later stage. He will mix his studies and consult again the first part when he has reached the third, and the third when he is studying, say, the sixth[1]. For all studies have a connexion with one another, and a certain affinity. One may be taken in hand because it is necessary for present usefulness; another because it is an alleviation from present labour. The student will be always desirous of learning, and will never suppose that he has already reached the highest point of learning. Seneca[2] has said very incisively: That many men would attain to true learning, if they did not believe that they had already attained to it. So Lucilius said: A man must go on learning, as long as he is ignorant of anything, and if we credit the proverb, "as long as he lives," since there is no subject in the whole of nature so manifest and easy, which might not occupy the whole age of man's life. The man really desirous of learning will not blush to learn from any man whatsoever, who can teach him anything. Why should one man be ashamed to learn from another man, when the whole human race is not ashamed to learn many things from beasts. But a man must so study as not to shatter his mind by overwork. Especially one must have due regard to sound health, and the health of those committed to our care.

**The connexion between studies.**

**Against the arrogance of teachers.**

When learned men realise that they excel the rest of mankind in mind, judgment, knowledge of things, or that at least others regard them as if they did so excel, they then entertain haughty spirits, as if the men amongst whom they lived, were cattle—whence is developed an incredibly great arrogance. That is a holy saying of the Apostle Paul[3]: That men are puffed up by knowledge whilst they are edified by love. The follower of wisdom may turn his eyes on himself, nor does he need any other testimony than that in which his own conscience reposes. He

**The greatest part of what we know is the least part compared with what we do not know.**

[1] See Cicero, *pro Archia*.
[2] In his *Epistolae*.
[3] I Corinthians viii. 1.

will weigh in his mind how many things there are which he is conscious that he does not know, yet which others never doubt he does know; how often he wanders in mind, how often he slips, how often he is deceived, and how far he departs from the truth, so that not without the greatest reason and cause, Socrates, who was called by the consent of Greece, the wisest of men, confessed that "neither he nor any other man knew anything." This great saying has constantly possessed the minds of the philosophers. And certainly if anyone rightly weighs the matter, and counts it out, he will find that "there is nothing we know more certainly than the duties of religion." But rightly the opinion of Theophrastus is praised, "that even the knowledge possessed by all men, is a very small portion compared with the amount of that, of which all men are ignorant." To follow this aspect at further length is apart from our purpose. What if anyone would examine things one by one, and bring them to a close testing, would not those magnificent titles to knowledge begin to appear paltry? What are languages other than words? Or what importance is it to know Latin, Greek, Spanish and French, if the knowledge contained in those languages were taken away from them? Dialectic and Rhetoric are the means of knowledge, not knowledge itself, and are better taught us by Nature, than by a master.

All philosophy has depended upon opinions and conclusions from probability. But this is not the place for expounding this question in detail. Well, then, we will grant that you know something sure and ascertained. Do you not recognise that you have had that benefit of knowledge conferred on you by another? Why should another's garment fitted on you make your mind arrogant? If you have got something good, it is another's; if it is bad, it is your own alone. For if you learn well, then it is God's gift, and you will displease Him, if you do not ascribe to Him all the glory which

**What knowledge have you, which has not been received from others?**

accrues to you through your learning. I have nothing to say against a learned man perceiving that he is learned and esteeming himself as wiser than other men, for he would neither be learned nor wise, unless he saw this clearly. But I wish him to remember from Whom he received that wisdom, and having received it, to ascribe it to Him alone, from Whom he possesses it, even as if it were a mortgage. If he sees that he is admired by men, let him not be self-satisfied, which is a dangerous thing, nor let his eyes settle on the ground, so that honour should be offered him by men, and applaud himself as if he had performed his work by his own merit. This, as Job says, is to kiss one's own hand, the greatest of iniquities, and the greatest denial of God.

**Of what elements learning consists.**

Erudition involves four factors: natural capacity, judgment, memory, application. Pray tell me, whence the first three of these come: whence except from God? If praise is to be given to a learned man, it must be sought in the last-named element. And this element is the lowest and least of all, and even for that how greatly is a man helped by having a bodily frame, not heavy, nor stupefied, but of sound health. And are not these states of the body the gift of God? What then remains in himself for the learned man to boast about? Well, do you say; He has willed to work? But how many others would will, if it were, through the goodness of God, permitted to them to do what it is permitted to you? Amid the praises given to himself, the wise man directs himself to the contemplation of that holy and divine wisdom, in comparison with the lowest part of which, as Paul says[1], all human wisdom is mere foolishness. Let it come into a man's mind, that, if men are stirred so greatly by the sight of a single little drop, how would they bear themselves, if there were vouchsafed to them the sight of that full and eternal spring, whence the whole current of wisdom flows? Then will he adore, with humble

[1] I Corinthians i. 19 etc. and iii. 19.

mind, the Giver of all good gifts, and return thanks that He has held him worthy of gifts in richer proportion than He has imparted to others; and that He has willed him to be the instrument of any part of His counsel and His work. For all of us are the instruments of His will. Therefore no man has so great an erudition, or is so endowed with so much practical wisdom, that he should suppose that God has need of him for the working out of His plans. For firstly it is a most thorough piece of presumption to suppose that you can excel in something, in which no other could excel if he applied his mind to it. For God needs no human instruments for carrying out His plans. With clay he can open the eyes of the blind. "From stones he can raise up sons to Abraham, and he has chosen the weaklings of the world to confound the strong." If you then have become so wise and distinguished a man, by the goodness of God, then also those others to whom He has vouchsafed a similar blessing will also be as wise and distinguished as you.

We must therefore pray to Him, Who gives us everything, and Who works through us, what seems good to Him, that our learning be turned to our good, lest He make us an instrument to the good of others, whilst it becomes an injury to ourselves; so that it may not happen to us, as is the case sometimes with bad doctors, who cure others, but cannot heal themselves; or as with the trumpeters who incite others on to battle, whilst they themselves take no part in the fight; or as with candles, which afford light to others, whilst they themselves are burnt out. And so, as often as we proceed to study, let us begin by prayer, as is recorded of Thomas Aquinas and many other holy men. Certainly we ought to pray that our studies may be sound, of no harm to anybody, and that we may be sources of sound health to ourselves and the community at large.

**Pray before beginning to study.**

If now we must propose some end to each of the actions of our life, so much the more must this be the case with studies, so that it may be settled whither our labour tends. We must not always be studying so that we do nothing but study, nor must the mind, bound by no law and with no useful aim, delight itself in any inane sort of contemplation and knowledge of things. Socrates said that he had no time to busy himself with poetic fables, since he did not as yet know himself, and that it was ridiculous that he who did not know himself should closely investigate other people's concerns. Much less is the fruit of studies to be estimated by their return in money. Such an opinion has only been held by debased natures, who are far removed from any true idea of studies. For nothing is so distant from literature as either the desire or the anxiety for money; so that wherever this desire settles in a man of studies, forthwith it drives away the zeal for intellectual research, because study does not commit itself with full confidence to any souls, except those free and loosed from that disease. People say: "First get rich; then become philosophical." Nay, rather it should be said: "We must first philosophise, and afterwards get rich." For if we first get rich we shall soon no longer wish to busy ourselves with philosophy, and, made anxious by the possession of wealth, snatched away to a thousand vices, ignorant of philosophy, we shall be ignorant of the true use of riches. But if once we become philosophers, then it will be easy, afterwards, to get as rich as it is at all necessary to be. One can suggest no case in which anyone applying industry to the study of philosophy would not be impelled to the pursuit of practical wisdom. A poor man must study philosophy, because he has nothing, so that the sense of his poverty may be alleviated. The rich man must study philosophy, because he has possessions, so that he may use them more wisely. The happy man will be a philosopher so that he may turn his happiness into a rightful

**The end of studies is not mere reverie.**

**The student should not put remuneration before himself as an end.**

**Who especially should become students of philosophy.**

channel. The unhappy man will be a philosopher, so that he may bear his misfortunes the more lightly. To be sure, every kind of knowledge is sold, but with the greater proportion of men, only to their injury; but at any rate the professions should not be practised merely for gain, e.g. law, medicine, theology. The learned man should not press forward to the undertaking of state affairs, although he ought to desire to be of use to as wide a circle as possible. He should not think that he is born for himself alone, as the old philosopher admonished Plato[1]. On this point we have that saying of the Apostle: He who seeks a bishopric seeks a good work[2]. Further, let a good man take possession of the place which previously was held by a bad man. But he who has pressed himself forward has not so much charm and strength as he who is chosen by others. If he be invited, let him first observe diligently the minds of his fellow citizens whether they are sound or curable, so that if by any means he may be able to be of use, he must not refuse to undertake the labour, but if it would only be to take up a useless and irritating work, let him altogether decline. This, Plato is said to have done, because he despaired that he could ever bring the minds of the people into any soundness of health. Princes are, for the most part, of hearts so corrupt, and so intoxicated by the magnitude of their good fortune, that by no art can they be reformed for the better, since they show themselves harsh and insensate to those who would heal them. Those blind men and leaders of the blind, as the Lord calls them[3], must be left alone. We must transfer our solicitude to the people, who are more tractable, for they offer themselves more easily to be dealt with and are more responsive to one caring for them. This also did Christ, with Whom a Prince is not valued more highly than anyone of the people.

Nothing has so sullied the glory of all kinds of knowledge and of all learning, and debased it, as the frivolity of some

[1] See Cicero, *de Officiis.* [2] I Timothy iii. 1.
[3] S. Matthew xv. 14.

smatterers who constantly flatter any people whatsoever especially princes, being particularly drawn to some new rather than some longer-known person. But this is precisely what truly learned men will not do. The mass of the people, it is true, do not understand the difference. They suppose that every one is a learned man, who writes or speaks the Latin tongue in some form or other. Yet those who thus act defend themselves by the specious argument that they did not praise the pseudo-learned men for such, as they really were, but for the qualities which they ought to have shown. This gives but a very slight "colour" to their praise, and one which others do not recognise. Hence they accuse the learned man of sycophancy, and attach the stigma to the profession of literature itself and detest it, as if it commended a wicked Prince, and made him out to be a very good Prince. Nay even the Prince himself, imbued with the depraved opinion, believes that he is estimated as his flatterers describe him. Hence he becomes from day to day more and more arrogant and intolerable. When he has begun this kind of life he gets confirmed in it, since he finds he obtains so much praise from it, and seeing that it has all been handed down to posterity in the works of the learned, he thinks it must therefore be fixed for certain. If the learned men had not been accustomed to flatter princes, then the latter would, on the one hand, have esteemed learning higher, and, on the other, they would rejoice immeasurably to be praised by them, i.e. according to the saying of the ancient poet *a laudatis viris*. Then, too, the learned man's upbraiding would have had great weight. Nor, then, would the approval of a learned man be otherwise than the weightiest testimony of a most conscientious authority. So, too, a prince not less than any others would regard it as the amplest reward of his virtue in this life, to receive the approval of the learned man. But now princes do not value it at a hair, since they see they can buy it for a farthing or two, nay even for a

**Learned men do not flatter ignorant princes.**

**Inconveniences from flattery.**

bit of bread. When circumstances justify the praise of princes, let the praise be somewhat sparing, and in such a manner, that they feel that they would rather be admonished and stimulated in their actions than have their praises sung, as if their course of life were already ended. If you may hope for any good from it, vices ought to be freely condemned, only let there be no bitterness nor rage. But if you are only causing hatred, and you can do no good, then it is better to abstain from the useless task. Nor ought the faults of the powerful, nor indeed of any man, to be covered over, on the ground of expectation of a reward, or for the sake of any gain, for this is particularly shameful. For it has the effect that the bad go on the more boldly in their wickedness, and moreover, with the consent of learned men, others are encouraged to follow their example.

**How princes 1. should be praised.**

**2. should be reproved.**

There are others who do not seek from their studies to obtain money, but glory. This is a little better I confess, but only if in youth and in the young man, it may supply very great goads to noble actions. But when this motive appears later in life, it is the ground and source of many evils, as I have elsewhere shown, because we set all our store on being seen by those looking on, nothing on our conscience, which will judge us, in our actions, more justly than any fellow-man possibly can. And thus we often fall by the hope of glory which we have seized, because he who gave us false credit afterwards perceives his error, or he who judged rightly begins himself to be deceived, although it happens more frequently that mistaken estimates are turned to what is sounder, since time confirms what is true and solid, but shatters and removes false and empty judgments. Therefore let no one have confidence that he will secure glory with posterity through the empty favour of the living and by pretence of noble work. For so soon as the passions which have been stirred up have

**The empty glory of the studious.**

subsided, judgment enters in their place, and this puts things in more exact proportions. Thus, there are many who were honoured in their lifetime, who, after their death, have been accounted ignoble and contemptible. Hence it happens, as I have already said, that time destroys the falsity of opinions, whilst it strengthens right judgments. How uncertain is fame! how slippery! Many have promised immortality to themselves, and have not been able to retain fame for their lifetime, as e.g. Apion, the grammarian, who, as we read in Pliny[1], said, That he had endowed with immortality those to whom he had addressed some of his works, yet of his own books, not even a single letter is extant. Nay, also, how unfortunate is the fame of those who have done deserving work! The works of Ovid remain, but not those of Chrysippus or Crantor. The works of Vincent of Beauvais have come to us complete; but not so those of Titus Livius, not those of Polybius, not those of Marcus Varro, not even those of Marcus Tullius Cicero! As Martial not inaptly said, "If a book is going to have a long life, it must have a (protecting) genius." We must add, how changeful a book's fame is! The same book seems beautiful at one time and in certain places, and at another time and in other places, detestable. Many splendid discoveries become obscure by the natural powers and diligence of posterity, so that the later books block up by their size many of the earlier books, just as lights are darkened by the heights of surrounding buildings.

**The vanity of glory and an immortal name.**

But, put the case that you have obtained renown, praise, glory; what good will it be to you when you come to die? For then you will perceive none of these things, which are happening here, no more than the horse, when he is proclaimed victor in the Olympian games, or the picture of Apelles, which we study closely with admiration. What is all the renown of his name, to Cicero? or to Aristotle? So with others, how does their glory

[1] In the Preface to *Naturalis Historia*, addressed to Vespasianus.

now affect them though they were once illustrious in arms or in letters? Or in life itself, if out of public view, what glory does a man feel? What glory affects him when he is asleep? If you are present when you are praised then it necessarily follows that those who praise you to your face, are vain; or else that you willingly listen to words of praise said in your presence. What can in that case be said with propriety? O learned, O eloquent man (nay, rather, O light and empty-minded man!),—not even if you consider a slight meed of praise the due reward of your literary labour. But if you take no note of the praise of men, and desire to obey faithfully your own conscience, and through it, to serve God, how much more lasting and solid glory will be yours, if the living God praises you in your life, if the Ever-Present praises the man before Him; the Immortal God, the mortal man. He who ever looks on thee, He who will pronounce no false judgment, but who will judge you from your own evidence! "Not he that commendeth himself is approved," says Paul[1], "but whom the Lord commendeth."

The student often thinks of the eternal life. It has been noted that the blessed Jerome said: Whether I am eating, etc. always that word sounds in my ears: *Rise, ye mortals, come to judgment.*

A learned man must often reflect on the migration of our temporal life, and on the eternal life, and by meditating often and deeply, make the thought of death familiar, so as not to be terrified by the mention of it. Then will come into his mind, that Judge, the Rewarder of his actions, one by one, before Whom, in a short time, he must appear, when he has left the stage and the hypocrisy of life. To be approved of God will then become the sole aim of his life. For to whom else would the accused person or the patron desire to vindicate himself, if he were wise, but to his Judge? To whom else, the athlete, to whom the pugilist, to whom, everyone who does anything which has to receive a judgment upon it? When that old Greek poet had recited his poem, and all men had abandoned him, Plato was

[1] II Corinthians x. 18 and I Corinthians iv. 5.

worth the whole of the people of Athens to him. Will not Christ be the same to us, by the wisdom of God? "It is a great thing," says an old proverb, "for an athlete to have pleased Hercules." How much more then for us to have pleased God? by Whom we are praised so often as we have done anything pleasing to Him. Certainly there can be nothing more pleasant to Him, than that we offer our erudition and whatsoever of His gifts we possess to the use of our fellow men, i.e. of His children, for whom God has imparted those great goods that to whomsoever they are allotted, they should be of use to the community at large. God wishes us to give freely of that which we have freely received—although for giving up those things which He has so richly bestowed on us, He most abundantly recompenses us. O wonderful kindness of God! For what He gives us freely, He most amply rewards us, if we bestow it on others.

**The fruit of studies consists in the application of them to public good.**

This then is the fruit of all studies; this is the goal. Having acquired our knowledge, we must turn it to usefulness, and employ it for the common good. Whence follows immortal reward not in money, not in present favour, or pleasures, which are fleeting and momentary. Do we then live rightly and teach rightly, if we do it for the sake of money? Would we exchange the rich gift of God for so vile and contemptible a reward? Would we exchange it for glory? Wretch that I should be, if I were to chase so eagerly after that which, in spite of such labours and pains, cannot be preserved, and which is so uncertain and fleeting, that no servitude can be compared with it; more wretched still, if I were to buy people's good word in exchange for such an excellent and holy reward, and prefer to be praised by mortal men rather than by the immortal God; by fools, rather than by Wisdom Itself. O how we fish with a golden hook, for merely foul eels!

With bold confidence, therefore, we must study all

branches of knowledge for that use, for which they were appointed by God. We ought therefore, not always to be studying, but our study must be attuned to practical usefulness in life. Every study is unlimited in itself, but at some stage we ought to begin to turn it to the use and advantage of other people. For this purpose, practical wisdom is necessary, because practice leads us to the consideration of subjects separate from one another, and practical wisdom rules as the valuer and judge of the circumstances considered as a whole.

# CHAPTER II

## THE SCHOLAR AND THE WORLD

The learned man always will reflect that others may look upon him and imitate him, to their harm, and that therefore he must bear himself as becomes a wise man, i.e. as an imitator of Christ. He will wish to do good to others, not to secure a large school of pupils. He will wish to be of such affability and ease of conduct that others will desire to be associated with him and to preserve friendship with him when once begun. Criticism, and the method to be adopted in giving it.

**How the learned man is to occupy himself among men.**

If the learned man intends to go into the sight and haunts of men, then should he have thought over his preparation for this purpose, as if he were in training for a fight, so that he should not be taken possession of by any of those debased passions which attack and beset us on every side. For he who is often listened to by others will sometimes listen to himself. Let him strengthen his mind at home, with great and strong thoughts, tending to the disdain of honours and dignities. Let him think of those words which he has heard from God: That they are the salt of the earth, the light of the world[1]. It is little fitting that the salt become savourless, or the light become darkness. For then what are we to think will happen to those things which are salted with such salt, or lighted by such light? Let him then go forth furnished and armed with reasons by which he may successfully resist any attack of his enemy. Let him, in very deed,

[1] S. Matthew v. 13, 14.

preserve that 'salt' and 'light' in the whole framing of his mind, and in the restraint of all emotions; let him use the wisest and most opportune words—so that he be not importunate even in his wisdom, for in that case he will make his wisdom offensive and hateful. But as often as opportunity serves, and wherever he betakes himself, let him show himself to those in his presence, as if he brought health to the assembly. Let him adorn his own bodily bearing with modesty and self-control. In all his words and deeds let there be gravity and consistency, so that he may be an example to others for a like rationality of life. He will indeed convince greatly by his rhetoric, but most of all by his blamelessness of life. So that all which proceeds from him may be the more exact and pure, let him constantly take thought that he says and does nothing which has not got good ground for it, and which may not be followed as an example by right-minded men. For they should be able to think that what he does is a law for their life. But to the evil-minded and envious he should serve as a suggestion to inquiry and an example against false judgments. He must therefore be somewhat cautious in action, slow in judgment, and particularly circumspect in his speech. Through him literature and knowledge will gain a respectful hearing, and many men through their desire for such excellence which they observe in him, will give themselves up to the study of knowledge, because they see such delightful and splendid results in him.

**The learned man should afford an example to others.**

How ashamed must learned men be, that often uneducated men have better control of their passions than they themselves, steeped as they are in the precepts of wisdom. It is for this reason there is often a great outcry by many against the pursuit of learning, and it becomes hated by many, who think they will have more practical wisdom if they have nothing whatever to do with it. For those advantages which learned men bring to the sight of men should in truth excel in their inner worth, not in mere display. A hypocritical mind betrays itself at length, and is so much the more hateful and detestable, the longer and the more prominently it has maintained its false position. Moreover, the roots of truth are great and solid. However much it may be hidden, light will send forth its splendour eventually. Wisely says Epictetus: "The sheep boast not in the presence of the shepherd how much they have eaten on any day, but they show it through its effects, by their milk, wool, and offspring." The mass of studious people call that age happy, in which there is a great amount of learning. But much more is that period of time fortunate in which the learned men show themselves so in very deed, because they have read what will be of advantage to know, and have suggested it to others, who when they hear and see it, are compelled to cry out: Here are those who speak as they live, and live as they speak. This is what the philosopher Adamantius is said to have pronounced on Origen as Eusebius tells us[1]. Do not blush if you do not achieve success in something which you have done as well as you possibly could. Blush to do badly what you could do well. Learned men should show themselves gentle, affable, self-controlled, unvanquished by depraved desires, and should demonstrate how much wisdom can accomplish in the human mind, when it has the sovereignty; and what a great distance there is between the wise man and the fool. It will be sufficient for them if they can be strong and efficacious in the really great and noble matters; not to desire to be esteemed highly in all sorts of occupations, in war, in horsemanship, hunting, fishing, dancing, games, in impudent trifling and raillery. All this is the part of busy-bodies, not of wise men, and learned men become ridiculous who are as zealous in such pursuits, as in that of forming wise judgments. For in the same manner as we perceive nothing clearly if we come out of the light into

**The learned man knows exactly what he can do effectively.**

[1] See *Ecclesiastica Historia*, bk VI.

darkness, nor in going from the dark into the light, so it is not surprising that the learned man talks idly when he is brought in to the discussion of foolish matters, in the same way that triflers are blind in questions of practical wisdom.

It is the work of a learned man to pass on that same learning to others; and, as it were, from his own light to kindle light in the minds of others; like as it is said in the vision of Daniel[1]: That those who have brought many to righteousness "shall shine as the stars for ever and ever," and our Lord said that that man would be called great in the Kingdom of Heaven who himself had fulfilled the precepts of righteousness and taught them to others. And in teaching, what master shall we rather imitate than Christ Himself Whom the Father sent from Heaven to teach the human race. After Him, though at a great distance, come those who have been His followers. He indeed, since He was the Divine Wisdom, only put forward those teachings which would be of service to his listeners, not those which would show how great He Himself was. For if he had sought to declare His glory, or to disclose Himself, what was there He could not do, and what marvels could He not have disclosed! Yet He would have gone beyond all power of comprehension, even of angels. Yet all that He said was for our service, not for His own ostentation. We must seek neither luxuriousness nor delight. Pliny is of opinion that there is an especial ground for studies in the case of those who, unconquered by difficulties, have undertaken, as their own pleasure, to be helpful to others. The Lord was content to have only a few disciples to whom He showed the wisdom of God and the way of eternal salvation. Who can now bewail the fewness of his scholars, when the Creator of the human race was satisfied with a school of twelve men? A large class-room rather serves the object of

**On teaching.**

**Ambitious teachers.**

**The oracles of the ancients as to the school.**

[1] Daniel xii. 3.

ambition than that of serious education. Moreover, we ought to take to heart those sayings of the ancients concerning the school: That we must teach without envy, learn without shame, always acknowledging our thanks to the teacher, and not ascribe to ourselves the credit of what has really been discovered by others.

**It does not matter who says a thing, but that the thing said is good.**

The wise man will reflect that this world is, as it were, a certain State, of which he is a citizen, or as a certain great house, of which he is one of the family, and that it is not matter of consequence by whom anything good is said, as long as it is said truly; that further, here in this State those treasures which are collected together are to be applied to public use; it is of no consequence by whom they were collected, the main point is, they are provided and they should be distributed. Therefore each man, for his part, to the utmost of his strength, will himself contribute, and will freely help others to contribute. Since he is conscious of and alive to his weakness (otherwise he cannot be called a wise or a learned man), let him call to mind how much injury he would inflict on the human race, if he should wish that nobody should be either better or more learned than himself[1]. Moreover, as to the course of instruction, Cicero quotes a passage from Plato, expressing the opinion of Socrates. He writes that the latter was accustomed to state, that his work would be completed, if everyone was sufficiently aroused by his exhortation, to work zealously to see and know the truth. But we will use a better known analogy; a student needs a leader just so long as he does not know the road; but when he is able to proceed along the road alone, he has more need of courage than of a master.

**The harmony of teachers.**

Learned men should live in unity with one another and deal with everyone courteously. For it is very disgraceful in us, that robbers and lions[2] live

[1] See Seneca, *Epist. ad Lucilium*, bk I.

[2] Leones, some editions have *lenones* (panders).

in greater harmony amongst themselves than do the learned. Neither unanimity nor benevolence will be lacking in the learned, if they have pursued their studies whole-heartedly and religiously; not for glory or reward, for where the desire of these things prevails it is difficult to preserve the sanctity of society. When a comparison of studies is made, then the name of "vanquished" should not be given to the man, who allows that another has argued better than he. For that word "vanquished" signifies something very different from the fact to which it is in this case applied. For in this sort of battle, those who differ are not enemies. This is a very bitter and inimical word applied to what is a very pleasant contest, one in its nature full of good-will between the opponents. For what greater or closer union can we find than that of the mind of one man who is helped by another man's mind towards practical wisdom or virtue. It is a similar relation to that of the husbandman to his field, so that not undeservedly those who train the minds of others may be termed their parents. As is sight to the eyes, so is insight to the mind. Those who cannot see sufficiently clearly through their eyes, yield their judgment to those who have more distinct vision, and do so ungrudgingly. That man possesses sharper and sounder eyes; this man has a mind of clearer insight by nature, or is better trained by experience, age, and industry. Though, of course, sight-observation receives greater praise than mental vision, according to circumstances, as e.g. when a coin is lost, plenty are to be found able to join in the search.

**The union of minds amongst students.**

When a man has come to a mature age, we may describe his speeches by such terms as contests, struggles, fights, victories. Let everyone, I beg, consider how great a benefit it is to be freed from the tyranny of ignorance, which is the heaviest and most shameful of all servitudes. Plato says wisely: That it is as much preferable to be beaten in a disputation than to beat, as it is better to be freed from a great evil than to be the one who liberates. For what more deadly thing can happen to men than to form a false opinion? Though in some cases it may be more glorious to be a liberator, it is certainly more useful to be made free. But we should all gladly be delivered from this great evil of ignorance, if disputations were less theatrical, and there were not so much deference shown to the listeners who surround the disputants. The disputation ought to be rather a friendly discussion than a hostile fight for victory. This should be the case in all kinds of discussions, but particularly in theology, in which subject, impious attacks are made on holy truth, and doubts are started in the minds of listeners, about things which ought to be held as certain, fixed and unshakable. The Demon-Enemy then stirs up these scattered doubts and increases them. Men set their hands to the same work, whilst each one exerts himself for the glory of his intellect, rather than for the assertion of truth. We ought to yield to every truth, not only that which concerns pious and sacred matters, but also in secular affairs, and we ought to obey the precept of the wise man: "In no circumstances, to contradict the word of truth."

**Scholastic theologians.**

Clear and wise judgments are of the greatest use in all studies, when, as Tacitus says, "critics have pronounced their judgments without inflicting injury." For there is nothing more harmful than to confuse the standard of judgments, as in the course of volitions, that a man should not clearly know what sort of actions he approves and what he disapproves. This is an especial danger of our times, when it is most dangerous to speak on almost any subject. So stirred are all men's minds to contentions, and prepared for wordy fighting, that it is not safe to offer observations on any matters even if one is looking at them from another standpoint than that in debate. The tender and weak self-consciousness believes itself to be attacked, as horses afflicted with ulcers instantly are aroused in action, when they hear the

**Criticism.**

scraper or *strigilis*. Nevertheless, very many have offered incitement to the increase of this vice (whilst they bitterly blamed others), not so as to advance the truth, but only for insulting and bringing shame on another's name, either drawn on by hatred or allured by the hope of a false glory, under the impression that by this means they would be regarded as splendid and excellent, just so far as they should manage to show others to be disgraceful. It has happened to them quite otherwise than they expected. For whilst all men praise the intellect of the learned man, when it is pure there is sure blame for the malice of even the most erudite scholar. But, further consider how great a blow all this hatred brings on knowledge. The influence of those men thus hatefully wrangling and, as it were, at enmity to the death, steadily is lost; men of distinguished ability lose courage, and after being made disgusted with all this bitterness, and these perpetual gladiatorial displays, they recoil and shrink from studies. All progress in studies is ruined, and truth is obscured whilst some scholars prefer that letters should remain corrupt rather than be restored to soundness by those men to whom they are unfriendly. How great a crime it is when eloquence, wit and other marvellous gifts of God, given to men by God, for the good of mankind, are converted to its injury, by wrong employment of what is good. Such courses of conduct are not fit for beasts, let alone men. Quintilian, though a heathen, had more religion in him than we Christians. For he said: "It would have been better for us to have been born mutes and to lack all reason, than to convert the gifts of Providence into the injury of men to one another." Of what consequence is it how one person attacks another, whether it is with the sword or with the pen, when the intention is just the same? For the most part, you injure more keenly with speech or with the pen, than with the sword; for you only severely wound the body with the

**Malignant judgment.**

**The harmfulness of enmities of students.**

sword, but with language you pierce even the soul. The branches of learning are called humanistic, since they make us human. They have their source in God, to make us good men. He who looks in jealousy on another, in regard to anything with which God has endowed him, does he not impugn the sacred judgment of God and condemn the distribution of His gifts? And yet what ground is there for complaining of God? Has He not dealt profusely in His gifts to you? You see some placed above you, but how many more are there placed less favourably than you? The scholar should be slow in imposing limits, and be far from making rash assertions. When he is going to reprehend anything in others, let him read it over and over again, turn it over in his mind, closely examine it, lest in his condemnation, he affirm anything rashly. If he is commending anything, I would be willing for him to be less circumspect. Let him take care lest he does not sufficiently reflect on what he condemns, so that it shall not happen that the man, to whom he attributes a fault, has greater reason for his view, than he, as a critic, has against him. It would be better to say nothing than that the condemnation should recoil on the judge. But if I expect this practical wisdom, or courtesy, in the learned man, how can I adequately express my feelings with regard to those who twist and distort what has been rightly said, so that they may be thought to be clever controversialists. For if to alter any statement to make it better for some pious and very useful purpose is unlawful in the eyes of many people, it is certainly a great crime to twist it into something worse.

**No one can boast that he has received every gift of the mind; no one can complain that he has received none.**

When the Florentine Hadrian (who afterwards was Pope) was yet dean at Louvain, he was often present at the public disputations. If any expressions were brought forward which had been borrowed from authors, he would explain them sympathetically, but never would he speak

**The custom of Pope Hadrian.**

deprecatingly of any of them, even if some of those quoted were still living, e.g. James Faber and Erasmus of Rotterdam. We ought to speak guardedly of the living, of the dead reverently; for the latter are now exempt from envy and have returned to their Judge, and have undergone that judgment which remains for all, particularly with regard to their life and moral conduct. It is indeed permissible to speak with somewhat more freedom of their learning. Those authors by whose writings a scholar has made progress should be quoted with gratitude. "Nor should he wish," says Pliny, "rather to be caught in a theft than in paying back a loan, especially when personal advantage has accrued from the borrowing." Formerly men were so just and generous in rendering everyone his own that not a single word would they snatch from another author. This is evident in Plato, Aristotle, Cicero, Seneca, Plutarch and others. Now, words, meanings, and even whole arguments, sometimes discoveries, and works, are appropriated stealthily. This is absolutely a slavish practice and is the source of many animosities in the learned world. For to whom would it not be a serious matter to have his slaves, not to say his sons, led away from him? Would that against this sort of kidnapping there might be the protection of a *lex Fannia*. Nor is it pleasant to find disputes as to the fatherland of a writer, the school of thought, or the date to which he belongs, like that foolish person, whom Horace so wisely censures:

**The judgment of authors.**

**Wherefore did Pliny not apply the dictum, Physician, heal thyself!**

qui redit in fastos et virtutem aestimat annis[1].

Not that it is a matter of indifference, for books deserve more respect, when they have satisfied thinkers for many ages, and the consensus of so many minds for so long a period has confirmed the judgment so that there is only substantially one

[1] Horace, *Epistles* II, I. 48. "He calculates the date and estimates its value according to the number of years it has been written."

opinion offered concerning the writers. Here, every new opinion only is a hindrance, because it has not yet been thoroughly known and tested. If anyone has corrected another writer in a word or two, or in many words, he should not demand to be constantly considered more learned on that account, or to have it thought that he has therefore rendered greater service to that particular subject. Many men foolishly make this claim for themselves. If they make an emendation in any great author, they think that they must immediately be held superior to that author, as e.g. if a great man makes a slip through lapse of memory or through thoughtlessness (for Horace[1] declares that Homer sometimes is caught napping). Then, too, sometimes knowledge of the (learned) language falls short, and then those semi-learned men seize hold of any mistake in Latin or Greek, as if it were a very great iniquity. They demand from us a knowledge of Latin and Greek speech, i.e. of foreign and unknown languages, such as scarcely is shown in Cicero or Demosthenes, or in any of those writers, who sucked in their language with their mother's milk, and who had the whole of the people as it were for their schoolmaster, and in those points of usage in their language as to which they were in any doubt, they could consult a neighbouring cobbler or a smith. But if those same keen critics were to offer themselves and their works for judgment, they would, I believe, soon become more gentle in their charges against others. We have not a few examples of this most ungracious severity of judgment, not only in ancient times, but in this latest age, e.g. in Laurentius Valla, Politian, Beroaldus, Mancinellus. Nor has our own time produced a smaller number, even if I now pass by the calumnies of this nature, in those writers of whom I have spoken when I was dealing with the corruptions of grammar[2]. I should not, indeed, deny that it is in the interest of knowledge that great writers should

[1] Horace, *Epistolae*, bk II, 2, to Augustus.

[2] *De Causis Corruptarum Artium*, bk II.

be criticised adversely, if necessary. But the critic does not instantly contribute more or even as much to the subject by his notes as he who composed the work itself[1]. In the writer on any one branch of learning, you should interpret favourably his mistakes in speaking of another branch, e.g. the mistakes made in theology by the writer of history; the mistakes made in history by the metaphysician; as long as he is satisfactory in his own subject. You should still more leniently excuse any errors of language. We ought to welcome a good sentence expressed in French or Spanish, whilst we should not countenance corrupt Latin. I maintain with Marcus Tullius Cicero himself, that I should prefer the words of wisdom, inelegantly expressed, rather than foolish fluency. Augustine[2] rightly observes, that men are injured by solecisms and barbarisms in proportion to their own weakness of knowledge. The weaker they are, the keener their wish to seem more learned, not in the knowledge of the things which build up their wisdom, but through the signs of outward knowledge, which make it easy to become inflated with arrogance, since even material knowledge often raises a man's neck, if it is not bowed under the yoke of the Lord.

But I would not have the inexperienced and base writers boast as if they had the knowledge of things, because they lack power of expression. On the contrary, such writers deserve double condemnation, first because they are lacking in real knowledge and secondly because they have abandoned all grace and eloquence of words. If indeed the investigation into the subject-matter of knowledge were in their hands, it would be an ignorant and unsuitable demand to begin a controversy with them concerning the words they used, and to start a quarrel with them on that point. For example, it is clear that many words were poured forth, to no purpose, by John Pico in his well-known letter to Hermolaus. For the

[1] Aristotle: last chapter of the *Elenchi*.

[2] *De Doctrina Christiana*, bk II, chap. 13.

subject-matter complained of is not to be found in Averroes and Scotus, as he assumes it is, and these writers are not so much to be blamed by us as being base, as for their emptiness.

In the schools and in all life wherever anyone receives praise for his native ability, judgment, study, manifold learning, and knowledge widely spread over various subjects, a man ought certainly never to be extolled in his presence for his virtue and piety, lest he become puffed up by this breeze of praise, and lose the very good itself for which we are praising him, by the fact of his being praised. Nor should he receive other than well-weighed praise, in his absence, and that only for works which we have read. Paul does not wish any man to be the judge of what he has done, or to notice what other men see in him, or what he hears of himself. And the wise man says: A man does not know if he is worthy of hatred or of love[1], i.e. we must wait for the end of every man, for man is an animal exceedingly susceptible to change. Learned men

**Rash judgment of others.**

should so treat one another that, according to the doctrine of Paul, they should neither judge one another, nor hear unwillingly a judgment passed on themselves, but await patiently that tribunal, and holy and just Court, of God. He judges dementedly and acts shamelessly, who anticipates the judgment of his own fellow servants, which is in the hands of our common Lord. He who has fallen under the judgment of men, let him bear in mind what Paul counselled[2]: "I esteem it as nothing that I am condemned by you or by any human court. The Lord lives. He will truly and justly pass His sentence on me. His examination of me I fear. For that I will prepare myself as far as I am able."

[1] Ecclesiastes ix. 1.

[2] I Corinthians iv. 3.

# CHAPTER III

## THE SCHOLAR'S DIFFICULTIES

Learned men are admonished to be prepared against the unavoidable darts of envy. Suggestions are offered to those who are fitted to become authors as to the considerations to be borne in mind, before they bring their work to the light of day by publication.

**How envy should be borne.**

MEN of great learning will not escape the attacks of the envious, who seek to get their teeth into even the highest and noblest, whilst they pass by without injury what is foul and hateful. Themistocles[1], an Athenian of keen insight, as is proved by his deeds, was asked by someone: "Whether he seemed to himself to act excellently?" He answered, "Yes, at those times when I find no one envying me." If, then, this is the law which human badness has imposed upon itself, let the wise man bear the common lot, nor let him be indignant that it happens to him as to all men. Let him not seek to obtain from God what His only and dearest Son could not obtain—viz. that in His own world, He should be without detractors and enemies, who put the most evil interpretation on His divine works. Will not, by this showing, the slave be recompensed in the house of another after the same fashion that the Son was entertained in His own house? Nevertheless we must not cease from well-doing on account of the envious and wicked. Listen to the words of Socrates, written by Plato in his *Apologia*: "Men of Athens, if you were now to grant me my life, on the

**Go forward against it boldly.**

[1] See Plutarch, *Themistocles*.

condition that hereafter I should no further devote myself to the search for wisdom, I esteem you highly, but I am resolved to obey God rather than you, and as long as I live, and have strength to do it, I shall not cease from pursuing philosophy, and from exhorting everyone of you to follow the path of virtue."

**On writing books.**

And since he who has acquired learning not only wishes to be of use to those who come into his company and to those with whom he lives, but also to those who are distant from him, and to posterity, he will write down the thoughts of his mind in monumental literature to last for a long time to come. First he will know himself, and measure out his strength, in those things in which he is strong, on which he is fitted to write[1]. The most suited of all the products of his thought for transmission to posterity are those which are endowed with sturdy and strong judgment, and those which are best calculated to give inspiration. But those people who are at their best in what they do with great labour, rather than by native ability, let them take up subjects, in which there is need of diligence and not sheer mental power. Let them abstain from eloquent orations, history (in which speeches are mixed), from metaphysics, from moral philosophy. They will deal with observations, the bare collection of annals, the emendations of authors, the comparison of manuscripts such, e.g., as Valerius Probus has done, without adding his own conjectures, for this is a task requiring a special exercise of judgment. It is not the business of the same man to collect a mass of material and then to be also responsible for a critical judgment on all matters contained in the collection. Therefore students who read many authors without any intermission, listen to all subjects, write and collect in many directions, almost deprive themselves of a well-balanced judgment, the most excellent of all good things in life. Relaxation from studies must be

**Mode of studying.**

[1] Horace, *de Arte Poetica*, ll. 38–41.

provided for, since the judgment is far more vivid, if the mind is absolutely fresh. Running, leaping, and in a word all physical exercises should be pursued steadfastly and vigorously at intervals. One who intends to become an author must read much, reflect much, write much, correct much, publish very little. The proportion in these activities, unless I am mistaken, expressed numerically, is as follows: Reading = 5; reflection = 4; writing = 3. Emendation brings the last named number to 2, and from these two, actual publication of a scholar should be counted as 1.

This work of writing for publication, which is of great importance, should be approached by a man with his mind pure and restful from all passion, even more so than in anything else you could name, after having first prayed for the peace and grace of God. Let the author remember that the right word is quickly lost, that what he says is only closely listened to by a few, and that what he is about to write may be known to all, and in all ages, and therefore anything which is bad in it will not be innocuous. Let not, therefore, writers take their pen in hand, whilst they are swayed by anger, hatred, fear, or ambition, or any other base emotion. If they cannot suppress their feeling, let them quickly lay down the pen, lest they transfuse into their writing any poison from their mind, i.e. the real source of their work.

**Corrections of works written by ourselves.**

After you have written, show the work to those friends, from whom you think that you will receive sound counsel, listen to their opinion with close and patient attention[1]. Think it over again, with balanced mind, so that you may correct those points which seem to need it.

How much better it is to be admonished by a friend privately, than to be blamed publicly by an enemy. Yet there are some discoveries which the author himself could better decide upon and judge than any other man. When first he

[1] See Epistle of Quintilian to Tryphon the bookseller.

brings to birth a discovery, let him not be so affected by love of the offspring (of his mind), as yet unseen by others, which may seriously weaken his power of judgment, since we sometimes are strongly drawn to a matter before we have thoroughly investigated it. This is what parents do with their sons, who already love them before they are born. Thus it happens, that later on they cannot form a right judgment on them when they are born. Hence it would be well, as Quintilian advises, that a work be put on one side for a while, so that the author may let the ardour of his new ideas get cooled; and return to his work, as if he were an ordinary reader of someone else's work. Much power of judgment will be added by making such a delay, and he will be better able to make comparisons between his own work and that of others. If all of this suggestion be thoroughly carried out, and still the work continues to seem satisfactory, the author may let good hope arise within him that his work will give satisfaction to others. Concerning publication of one's writings, there is the verse of Horace,

**Publication.**

> Ne praecipitetur editio,
> ...nonum prematur in annum[1].

Do not hurry forward the publication of what has been written; let it be delayed till the ninth year.

As to the two parts of this opinion, I agree with the first, but not with the second part. For it does not seem to me to be expedient, in so short a space of time of one's life, that we should wait till the ninth year for our offspring to appear. But no universal rule can be given with certitude in the matter, on account of the variety of men's abilities and works. It would be sufficient that authors should be advised to apply practical wisdom to the question, and recognise that it behoves them not to effect an immature birth of their writings. For when anyone has proposed to himself any subject for writing, it is necessary to give an all-round consideration attentively

[1] Horace in *de Arte Poetica*, l. 388.

and minutely to all things which have any connexion with it before he passes judgment on it, because over-hasty thoughts do not permit him to concentrate the mind on any one point, and completely divert it from the contemplation of the whole. The writer himself is thus deceived, and he deceives others who have placed their trust in him, and drags them into the same error with himself. Then if anything wrong has been stated, when it is pointed out by any critic, the author stoutly defends himself, lest he should be thought to have made a slip. Hence arise sects, the most fruitful seminary of quarrels. But even if the author spontaneously acknowledges his error, he does not correct it in a straightforward way, but in an ambiguous, confused manner, having regard rather to his good name than to the interests of truth. Hence appears edition after edition, composed and revised over and over again, so that some time afterwards, it is not known which was first, second or third, and which is the real opinion of an author; or what is to stand. And the confusion becomes all the greater whenever the second, third, or the following emendations have not been effected.

**Sects.**

**Editions of authors.**

Nor does it escape me that there are some works which must be published as early as possible, such as narratives of events which are of importance to many of us living now, as well as those books which are composed by us for the purpose of repressing a noxious crime committed against the community or for rebutting an aspersion. It will be sufficient if these works are carefully thought out and written down by us at once for such matters cannot bear delay. They are not of such a nature that they can be prepared for beforehand, but they must be despatched at the time. There are some books which are made worse, not improved by excessive care; for some minds are of so sudden and lively an impetuosity that their works are all the better as they are just thrown off by the author, rather than if they had been over-elaborated by him.

The improvement of what has been published.

After his book has been published, whatever points appear to him on reflexion to require correction, let him alter clearly, openly, simply, with an anxiety rather for making the truth clear, than for his own glory. By doing this he will not suffer in estimation. For who is there, so ignorant and inexperienced in human affairs as not to know that the very best and wisest men, with time and study, make better and better progress. Am I not then justified in believing that a man with excellent natural ability to begin with, will have more understanding when he becomes older than when he was young? Certainly that man's mind is slack and wretched, if the next day does not bring him something more than the preceding day. If books are of a dogmatic kind, and have already reached a wide circulation, it is most wise that a book of corrections be added, after the example of St Augustine. Or if additions are made to the text then it is well to arrange a separate edition as we have seen in the case of Boethius Severinus. But if the work contains nothing didactic, and also is not very diffuse, then it will be permissible, as the poet says, "to forge anew the badly constructed verse[1]," to thoroughly revise the work and, if it is necessary, to begin it afresh. But if the work is corrected by some other writer, let the author recognise it as a kindness and publicly thank him for it. The truth, for which it behoves us all to stand in battle-array, is not private property, but is common to all. If, therefore, anyone has found any truth, you ought not to be angry, but rather to congratulate him on the happiness of his discovery—a happiness which you can share with him. Without doubt, the state of the matter is this: Those who make a struggle to obtain truth have minds ready for understanding what is discovered by anybody else; but those who struggle for their own discoveries, i.e. for their own name and glory, as if for hearth and home, protect whatsoever

Revision of an author's work by himself.

[1] Et male tornatos incudi reddere versus. Horace, *de Arte Poetica*, l. 441.

is produced by them as their own property. There are always plenty of this kind of people in all branches of knowledge, but especially in those arts which occupy themselves in subjects of discourse, e.g. grammar, poetry, rhetoric, and closely allied subjects in philology. For, firstly the knowledge of words, as Augustine[1] rightly observes, greatly puffs up the writer; and next the works of these writers seem to be more particularly their actual offspring than is the case with the writings of the philosopher or theologian. For the orator, as it were, gives birth to his speech, the poet to his song; whereas it is not the philosopher or theologian but Nature which gives birth to truth. So the true philosopher interprets a contrary opinion to his own, as an injury to Nature, rather than to himself. But he who invents what is false is more annoyed if he is rebutted, than he who asserts the truth. For no man is the father of truth whilst the false is born from the liar himself. So, too, he who affirms what is true, commits his cause to Nature, Time, God. He who asserts the false, takes upon himself the defence of himself. Add to this, words, like the face and bodily form, are external, whilst thought, like health and understanding, is concerned with the internal. But men who are handsome show considerable indignation when their skin and features are mentioned slightingly, more so than good men show when their goodness is belittled. More easily will the good man think it right and just that he should be called bad, than the good-looking man would allow anyone to consider him plain-looking. In all that is connected with morality, it is a serious mistake to form our taste and judgment to suit outside opinion. But in those matters in which men may become either better or worse by reading books, it is expedient that there should be certain public magistrates for the examination of books. These must be men conspicuous and well-tried amongst the whole people, for their judgment, learning and integrity.

**Censors of books.**

[1] *De Doctrina Christiana*, bk II, chap. 13, and bk IV, chap. 11.

# INDEX